# India Studies in Business and Economics

The Indian economy is one of the fastest growing economies of the world with India being an important G-20 member. Ever since the Indian economy made its presence felt on the global platform, the research community is now even more interested in studying and analyzing what India has to offer. This series aims to bring forth the latest studies and research about India from the areas of economics, business, and management science, with strong social science linkages. The titles featured in this series present rigorous empirical research, often accompanied by policy recommendations, evoke and evaluate various aspects of the economy and the business and management landscape in India, with a special focus on India's relationship with the world in terms of business and trade. The series also tracks research on India's position on social issues, on health, on politics, on agriculture, on rights, and many such topics which directly or indirectly affect sustainable growth of the country.

**Review Process**
The proposal for each volume undergoes at least two double blind peer review where a detailed concept note along with extended chapter abstracts and a sample chapter is peer reviewed by experienced academics. The reviews can be more detailed if recommended by reviewers.

**Ethical Compliance**
The series follows the Ethics Statement found in the Springer standard guidelines here. https://www.springer.com/us/authors-editors/journal-author/journal-author-helpdesk/before-you-start/before-you-start/1330#c14214

Ajitava Raychaudhuri · Arpita Ghose
Editors

# Managing Pandemic and Correcting Development Fundamentals

## India's Great Challenge

Springer

*Editors*
Ajitava Raychaudhuri
Department of Economics
Jadavpur University
Kolkata, India

Arpita Ghose
Department of Economics
Jadavpur University
Kolkata, India

ISSN 2198-0012 ISSN 2198-0020 (electronic)
India Studies in Business and Economics
ISBN 978-981-19-8679-6 ISBN 978-981-19-8680-2 (eBook)
https://doi.org/10.1007/978-981-19-8680-2



This Springer imprint is published by the registered company Springer Nature Singapore Pte Ltd.
The registered company address is: 152 Beach Road, #21-01/04 Gateway East, Singapore 189721, Singapore

# Preface

This volume is a collection of chapters comprising (i) the invited papers presented by four very eminent economists Professors Kaushik Basu, Dipankar Dasgupta, Abhirup Sarkar and Sugata Marjit at the Webinar on COVID-19 pandemic held on 5–6 March 2021, organised by Planning and Development Unit (NITI Aayog), Jadavpur University (PDU); (ii) some invited papers presented at the other seminar/conferences organised by PDU; and (iii) the outcome of different projects sanctioned by PDU and completed by different faculty members of the Department of Economics, Jadavpur University.

It is well understood that the COVID-19 pandemic disrupted the normal functioning of the Indian economy and regarded as sudden negative external shock operating in the economy since early 2020. It is also true that there are some fundamental weaknesses in the Indian economy inhibiting its development. The pandemic aggravated these weaknesses and widened income disparities. In order to assess the extent of favourable impacts of the policies, it is thus important also to have a glimpse of some basic lacunas prevailing in the economy.

The present volume, titled *Managing Pandemic and Correcting Development Fundamentals: India's Great Challenge*, is a balance of the two aforesaid aspects. An effort has been made in this book to put these two aspects together so that the policies adopted to counter downswing of the COVID-19 pandemic help to mitigate the adverse impact of some of these fundamental shortfalls. The book is divided into two segments—one is directly related to policy dilemmas stemming out of the COVID-19 pandemic and the second one handling the state of development fundamentals which exist in the economy independent of any unforeseen shocks. So a thorough reading of these two parts will enable the reader to put the policy responses in connection with the COVID-19 in the backdrop of certain inherent historical deficiencies of the Indian economy and accordingly will give an opportunity to judge the success stories of the policies undertaken.

In the first part on COVID pandemic and its management, there are six papers. In the first chapter written by Alka Basu, Kaushik Basu and Jose Tapia highlight that the COVID-19 pandemic has exposed the inadequacy of public health systems worldwide, casting a shadow that we could not have imagined. Moreover, a parallel problem may well exceed the direct death toll from the virus. This is the growing economic crisis globally and the prospect that these may hit emerging economies especially hard. This essay takes stock of the policies adopted by governments in emerging economies, and what effect these governance strategies may have had, and then speculates about what the future is likely to look like and what we may do here on.

The next chapter written by Dipankar Dasgupta and Meenakshi Rajeev brings to the focus that the COVID-19 pandemic, and the associated lockdowns have given rise to certain singular macroeconomic conditions in India. One observes both demand deficiency and supply constraints operating simultaneously with high inflation of essential commodities and large-scale underemployment. Most of the studies on these issues are empirical in nature, and theoretical modelling of the situation is lacking. This paper fills this research gap by unfolding the scenario using both empirics and theory. It develops a simple macroeconomic model of Keynesian type but brings the concept of transaction costs which occurred due to the fear of the disease and the lockdown to show how it affects both demand and supply, to give rise to a unique situation which is termed as a supply-constrained Keynesian equilibrium. The paper then looks at the medium-term effects by considering the subsequent invention of vaccines and other geopolitical developments.

In an interesting chapter, Sugata Marjit and Gouranga Das explored the short-run, medium-run, and long-run impact of pandemic on the contact-intensive entertainment industry in terms of a simple general equilibrium model that can accommodate unemployment and underemployment. Finite change as a response to large shocks may lead to vanishing occupations in this industry, even when pandemic is over and leads to underemployment. Pandemic tends to eliminate fixed wage contracts in this sector for its survival, but over the longer run affects fundamental occupational choice in a society.

The chapter by Abhirup Sarkar and Agnirup Sarkar has touched upon the financing issues of recovery packages for COVID pandemic, which is always a headache for any such policy measures but is much less discussed. The paper looks at the various alternatives of financing economic recovery in India in an environment where output and employment have taken unprecedented hits due to the COVID-19 pandemic. It examines three alternatives: increasing money supply (by lowering interest rates and expanding bank credit), a surge in public borrowing, and monetisation of public assets. It is concluded that under the present conditions, the only feasible alternative before the government is to adopt an expansionary fiscal policy by increasing public debt.

In his chapter, Saumen Chattopadhyay seeks to understand and anticipate the future of the Indian higher education in the post-COVID era in the wake of the implementation of the NEP 2020. The chapter begins with the conceptualisation of the debatable issue of whether higher education is a public good or common good. This is followed by a brief discussion of the challenges facing the Indian higher education system and how are they being addressed in the proposed NEP. This is followed by a discussion on the possible implications for the two major functions of the universities such as teaching and doing research with the academic profession being at the centre of discussion. The context of the discussion is extended by incorporating a major force which is gaining momentum, i.e. internationalisation. This chapter also brings the discussion on the major issues and objectives, access and equity, conceptualisation of quality, autonomy and accountability, and the nature of public good character of higher education. The chapter concludes with observations for the evolving market for higher education and the nature of public character of higher education focusing on inclusive expansion and attainment of quality education.

In the last chapter in this part, Sushil Haldar studied trends, patterns, and regional variations of COVID-19 pandemic in India at sub-national level. The study considers 27 states in India that covers 99.7% of India's population. Using spatial econometrics techniques, the study concludes that the space and neighbouring effect does matter towards rapid spreading of the virus; therefore, COVID-19 protocol should be implemented among the economically well off states. Strict lockdown for longer period of time is unhealthy for an economy like ours where more than 90% labour force are engaged in informal sector; therefore, vaccine with free of cost may be suggested to further contamination of the virus.

The first part on COVID pandemic, its spread and measurement, brings forth the important gaps in India's infrastructure and policies to overcome the disastrous effects of such an unforeseen pandemic. The papers also highlight some of the structural changes which come aftermath such worldwide pandemics. But at the same time, one needs to be reminded of the fact that India suffers from some ingrained deficiency in development fundamentals in terms of education, health, public expenditure on infrastructure, taxation system as well as state-level disparity in external trade. This creates unavoidable inequality among socio-economic groups and may also slow down poverty reduction efforts. So these fundamentals have to be kept in mind while facing random negative shocks like COVID-19 for the simple reason that these developmental gaps inevitably widen aftermath such shocks.

So the next set of chapters have all focused on such development fundamentals. The first paper by Siddhartha Mitra and Paramita Bhattacharya argues that food security is important because it is a basic human right and also because it possibly has important positive implications for cognition, the basis for human capital formation. Thus, it is possible that income poverty by resulting in food insecurity generates conditions that result in poor human capital formation which in turn keeps the next generation trapped in poverty, with the cycle repeating itself over and over. A food insecurity mediated poverty trap is thus generated. The paper suggests the importance of conducting RCTs on population to estimate and analyse such type of poverty traps which escape the standard argument of poverty trap as discussed in standard literature.

In their chapter on state-level export performance, Simontini Das and Saikat Sinha Roy raise the important issue that methodology to estimate state-level performance has important gaps. Thus, the true picture of involvement of a state in taking advantage of liberal trade regimes worldwide is not revealed leading to possible misalignment of export promotion policies across the states in India. Thus, the gains from trade are arguably sub-optimally distributed across the states, which needs proper attention (perhaps assumes more importance in the light of dwindling world trade after COVID pandemic).

In their chapter, Bidisha Chakraborty and Dedipyo Basak have taken up another less discussed but very important topic on subaltern culture and the concept of happiness. These points to the neglect we have shown towards the marginalised communities in the society need to be part of the development fundamentals in a diverse society like India. This project attempts to find out how different aspects of traditional cultural practices vis-a-vis modern outlook of three major tribal communities of South West Bengal—Shabar, Bhumij, and Santhal—impact the self-reported indicators of happiness comprising the aspects personal happiness, worth of life, safety for future, personal relationships with spouse and other family members, loneliness, and Anger. Based on their results, policies for enhancing the happiness of tribal communities of West Bengal are prescribed.

Poulomi Roy has taken up another important dimension of development in terms of pro-poor aspect of GST reform in India. In the short run, economic policy change in the economy affects the income levels of different income/social groups mainly through prices of commodities they consume or income transfers. However, in many developing countries, income transfer schemes for the poor are usually constrained by the lack of information that government agencies have on the distribution of well-being. This makes indirect taxation a predominant tool for social welfare policy in these countries. In this paper, the author uses Engel curve techniques to judge whether GST tax reforms have helped the poor by lessening their tax burden on commodities they predominantly consume.

Next, Vikas Dixit has taken up an equally important topic about the quality of public expenditure in the states in India. This perhaps assumes greater importance after COVID pandemic. The analysis of this paper reveals that the majority of states have generally performed better in terms of their public expenditure effectiveness and efficiency indices as compared to adequacy index, though most of the states depicted an increase in their public expenditure adequacy indices from pre-rationalisation period to post-rationalisation period. The trend analysis and the regression estimation results seem to suggest a positive impact of compositional shift in intergovernmental fiscal transfers in favour of untied grants on states' public expenditure adequacy. This, however, has to be complemented by good governance at the state level in order to realise the full impact of central transfers to states.

Education is really the backbone of human capital formation, and Arpita Ghose and Sangita Chowdhury have analysed the technical efficiency (TE) of the government and government-aided schools in Kolkata, the state of West Bengal. In fact, investing in terms of only funds may not produce the desired result and is another development fundamental. The results suggest that amount of TE which is not explained by the percentage number of students taking private tuition is very low and will range from 1.5% to 23.8%. This is a finding which is very worrisome since private tuition happens to be the driving force of increased efficiency in education for the public schools in Kolkata, which is another very fundamental problem. The paper also finds the other determinants of TE. TE is also negatively and significantly related to service experience of headmaster/mistress (HM) and full-time teachers, meaning that schools with relatively junior HM and junior teachers will have higher TE. TE is positively related to (a) the role of the HM in school management, i.e. while taking any policy decision whether HM interacts with students and teachers, and also the interaction between these variables with the variable specifying the frequency of interaction of HM with state education department; the existence of interaction term implies, given the value of one variable, TE will in turn depend on the value of the other, showing the importance of the both, (b) school infrastructure variables, i.e. whether Librarian of the school is on duty, and the number of smart classrooms in the schools (however, the level of significance is low), (c) policy variable like (i) percentage number of students getting Kanyashree (an initiative taken by the government of West Bengal to improve the life and status of girls by helping economically backward families with cash transfer so that they do not arrange for the marriage of the girls before eighteen years), where nonlinear inverted U-shaped relationship between Kanyashree and TE is obtained, with positive marginal effect for the present sample, implying that an increase in percentage number of students getting Kanyashree will boost up TE, and (d) the school characteristics, student composition, and students characteristics-related variables like the class size as represented by the number of sections in the class, the proportion of reserved category students, and the proportion of students having textbook at their home. Some policy measures are suggested to boost up TE.

The last paper by Achin Chakraborty raises the issue, while concerns for inequality in the specific dimensions of human functioning such as health and education are now common, along with the income dimension of inequality, and attempts to measure such inequalities have not been matched by thorough discussions of the ethical underpinnings of such measures. The paper concludes that a comparison between intergroup inequalities in income and various non-income dimensions reveals interesting observations on ‘unequal inequalities’ in India. The paper highlights that making a substantive statement on changes in economic inequality in India necessitates the use of multiple sources of data and careful consideration of multiple methods in order to check robustness of the statement.

Thus, the edited volume will be a valuable contribution to understand the extent of COVID pandemic and its management in India and is strengthened by an analysis of the state of development fundamentals which determines the boundary of success of COVID management strategies.

The chapters in the volume will satisfy the needs of various strata of the readers like graduate students, researchers, business practitioners, and policy planners with some recent developments of thoughts in the respective fields.

It is expected that the purpose of publishing the volume will be highly fulfilled, and the readers will have increasing returns to knowledge after reading of the volume.

Kolkata, India

Ajitava Raychaudhuri
Arpita Ghose

# Contents

# Editors and Contributors

## About the Editors

**Ajitava Raychaudhuri** is currently Professor Emeritus and Head, Economics Department, Adamas Univeristy. Earlier, he retired as Professor and former Head and Coordinator of Centre for Advanced Studies, Department of Economics as well as former Dean, Faculty of Arts of Jadavpur University, Kolkata, India. A Ph.D. from American University, USA, he was Senior Fulbright Scholar at Economic Growth Center, Yale University, USA, and Reid Hall Scholar in Residence of Columbia University, Paris Campus, France. He has undertaken several important projects from UNESCAP, ADB, World Bank, UNDP, PEP, etc. He has also written and edited several books and contributed numerous papers in international and national journals as well as in edited books.

**Arpita Ghose** is a Professor, Department of Economics, Chair-Professor (honorary), Panning and Development Unit (PDU), NITI Aayog, Government of India (GOI), Jadavpur University (JU), Kolkata, India, former Dean, Faculty of Arts and Head, Department of Economics, JU. A Ph.D. from Indian Statistical Institute, Kolkata, she worked on disequilibrium economics; has written and edited books; contributed numerous papers in international and national journals, edited books from reputed publisher on computable-general-equilibrium-models/productivity/efficiency analysis using data-envelopment-approach and stochastic-frontier-models/applied time-series econometrics. She has presented various invited lectures/research papers and chaired sessions at different international conferences/symposium, completed several important major projects funded by DFID-UNCTAD-GOI—JU—Trade Research Capacity-Building-Program/Shastri—Indo-Canadian Institute, Calgary, Canada/Department of Health and Family-Welfare, Government of West-Bengal/UGC-UPE(University-as-Potential-for Excellence), JU/ICSSR/PDU, JU among others and is the joint PI of a collaborative research project of PDU, JU with NITI Aayog. She has supervised Ph.D. students; her major research interests are Econometrics/Macroeconomics/empirical models including International Trade/economics of social-sector and regional-development.

## Contributors

**Dedipya Basak** Department of Economics, Jadavpur University, Kolkata, India

**Alaka M. Basu** Department of Sociology, Cornell University, Ithaca, USA;
United Nations Foundation, Washington D.C, USA;
Department of Global Development, Cornell University, Ithaca, USA

**Kaushik Basu** Global Economy and Development, Brookings Institution, Cornell University, Ithaca, USA

**Paramita Bhattacharya** Department of Economics, Jadavpur University, Kolkata, India

**Achin Chakraborty** Institute of Development Studies Kolkata, Kolkata, India

**Bidisha Chakraborty** Department of Economics, Jadavpur University, Kolkata, India

**Saumen Chattopadhyay** Zakir Husain Centre for Educational Studies, SSS, JNU, New Delhi, India

**Sangita Choudhury** Department of Applied Economics, Maulana Abul Kalam Azad University of Technology, Haringhata, West Bengal, India

**Gouranga Das** Department of Economics, Hanyang University, Sangrok-gu, Gyeonggi-Do, South Korea

**Simontini Das** Department of Economics, Jadavpur University, Kolkata, India

**Dipankar Dasgupta** Indian Statistical Institute, New Delhi, Kolkata, India

**Vikas Dixit** Department of Economics, Jadavpur University, Kolkata, West Bengal, India

**Arpita Ghose** Department of Economics, Jadavpur University, Kolkata, India

**Sushil Kr. Haldar** Department of Economics, Jadavpur University, Kolkata, India

**Sugata Marjit** Indian Institute of Foreign Trade, Kolkata, India;
CesIfo, Munich, Germany

**Siddhartha Mitra** Department of Economics, Jadavpur University, Kolkata, India

**Meenakshi Rajeev** Institute for Social and Economic Change, Bangalore, India

**Poulomi Roy** Department of Economics, Jadavpur University, Kolkata, India

**Abhirup Sarkar** Indian Statistical Institute Kolkata, Kolkata, India

**Agnirup Sarkar** Indian Institute of Technology Guwahati, Guwahati, India

**Saikat Sinha Roy** Department of Economics, Jadavpur University, Kolkata, India

**Jose Maria U. Tapia** Cornell University, Ithaca, USA

# The Dark Shadows of Pandemic and Its Management

# The Complexity of Managing COVID-19: How Important Is Good Governance?

**Alaka M. Basu, Kaushik Basu, and Jose Maria U. Tapia**

## 1 The Issue

The COVID-19 pandemic has exposed the inadequacy of public health systems worldwide, casting a shadow that we could not have imagined even a year ago. As the fog of confusion lifts and we begin to understand the rudiments of how the virus behaves, the end of the pandemic is nowhere in sight. The number of cases and the deaths continue to rise. The latter breached the 1 million mark a few weeks ago, and it looks likely now that, in terms of severity, this pandemic will surpass the Asian Flu of 1957–58 and the Hong Kong Flu of 1968–69.

Moreover, a parallel problem may well exceed the direct death toll from the virus. We are referring to the growing economic crises globally and the prospect that these may hit emerging economies especially hard.

The economic fallout is not entirely the direct outcome of the COVID-19 pandemic but a result of how we have responded to it—what measures governments took

This paper was originally published *online* in *Reimagining the Global Economy: Building Back Better in a Post-COVID-19 World*, Global Economy and Development, Brookings Institution, Washington, D.C., November, 2020

A. M. Basu
Department of Sociology, Cornell University, Ithaca, USA
e-mail: ab54@cornell.edu

United Nations Foundation, Washington D.C, USA

Department of Global Development, Cornell University, Ithaca, USA

K. Basu (✉)
Global Economy and Development, Brookings Institution, Cornell University, Ithaca, USA
e-mail: kb40@cornell.edu

J. M. U. Tapia
Class of '21, Cornell University, Ithaca, USA
e-mail: jut3@cornell.edu



A. Raychaudhuri and A. Ghose (eds.), *Managing Pandemic and Correcting Development Fundamentals*, India Studies in Business and Economics,
https://doi.org/10.1007/978-981-19-8680-2_1

and how ordinary people, workers, and firms reacted to the crisis. The government activism to contain the virus that we saw this time exceeds that in previous such crises, which may have dampened the spread of the COVID-19 but has extracted a toll from the economy.

This essay takes stock of the policies adopted by governments in emerging economies, and what effect these governance strategies may have had, and then speculates about what the future is likely to look like and what we may do here on.

*Nations that build walls to keep out goods, people, and talent will get out-competed by other nations in the product market.*

## 2 The Ideas

It is becoming clear that the scramble among several emerging economies to imitate and outdo European and North American countries was a mistake. We get a glimpse of this by considering two nations continents apart, the economies of which have been among the hardest hit in the world, namely Peru and India. During the second quarter of 2020, Peru saw an annual growth of − 30.2% and India − 23.9%. From the global Q2 data that have emerged thus far, Peru and India are among the four slowest-growing economies in the world. Along with UK and Tunisia, these are the only nations that lost more than 20% of their GDP.[1]

COVID-19-related mortality statistics, and, in particular, the crude mortality rate (CMR), however imperfect, are the most telling indicator of the comparative scale of the pandemic in different countries. At first glance, from the end of October 2020, Peru, with 1039 COVID-19 deaths per million population looks bad by any standard and much worse than India with 88. Peru's CMR is currently among the highest reported globally.

However, both Peru and India need to be placed in regional perspective. For reasons that are likely to do with the history of past diseases, there are striking regional differences in the lethality of the virus (Fig. 1). South America is worse hit than any other world region, and Asia and Africa seem to have got it relatively lightly, in contrast to Europe and America.

The stark regional difference cries out for more epidemiological analysis. But even as we await that, these are differences that cannot be ignored.

To understand the effect of policy interventions, it is therefore important to look at how these countries fare *within* their own regions, which have had similar histories of illnesses and viruses (Fig. 2). Both Peru and India do much worse than the neighbors with whom they largely share their social, economic, ecological, and demographic features. Peru's COVID-19 mortality rate per million population, or CMR, of 1039

[1] "GDP Annual Growth Rate—Forecast 2020–2022," Trading Economics, https://tradingeconomics.com/forecast/gdp-annual-growth-rate.

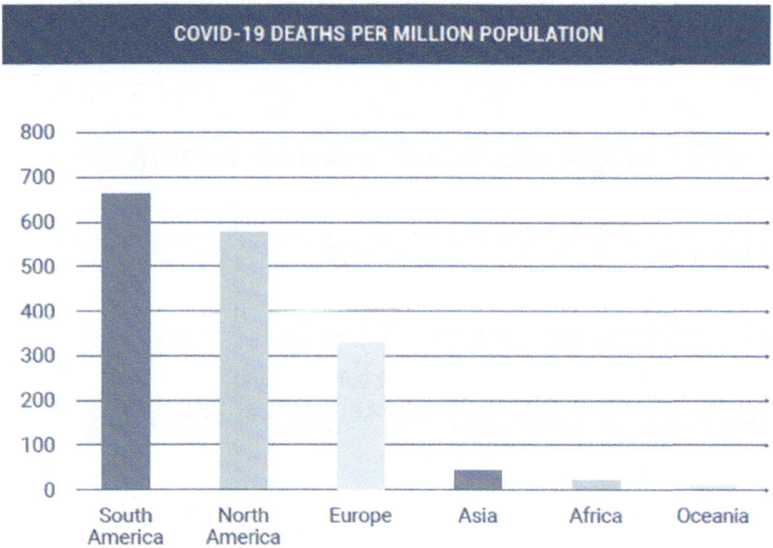


**Fig. 1** COVID-19 deaths by region. *Source* Coronavirus Worldometer. Data accessed October 27, 2020

is ahead of the second highest, Brazil at 749, and almost twice that of Argentina at 679.

Similarly, India at 88 compares well with Europe and the USA, as does virtually all of Asia and Africa, but is doing much worse than its neighbors, with the second worst country in the region, Afghanistan, experiencing less than half the death rate of India.

The official Indian statement that up to 78,000 deaths[2] were averted by the lockdown has been criticized (Raju, 2020) for its assumptions. A more reasonable exercise is to estimate the excess deaths experienced by a country that breaks away from the pattern of its regional neighbors. So, for example, if India had experienced Afghanistan's COVID-19 mortality rate, it would by now have had 54,112 deaths. And if it had the rate reported by Bangladesh, it would have had 49,950 deaths from COVID-19 today. In other words, more than half its current toll of some 122,099 COVID-19 deaths would have been avoided if it had experienced the same virus hit as its neighbors.

What might explain this outlier experience of COVID-19 CMRs and economic downslide in India and Peru? If the regional background conditions are broadly similar, one is left to ask if it is in fact the policy response that differed markedly and might account for these relatively poor outcomes.

---

[2] "Government Cites Various Statistical Models, Says Averted Between 1.4 Million-2.9 Million Cases Due To Lockdown," Business World, May 23, 2020, https://www.businessworld.in/article/Government-Cites-Various-Statistical-Models-Says-Averted-Between-1-4-million-2-9-million-Cases-Due-To-Lockdown/23-05-2020-193002/.

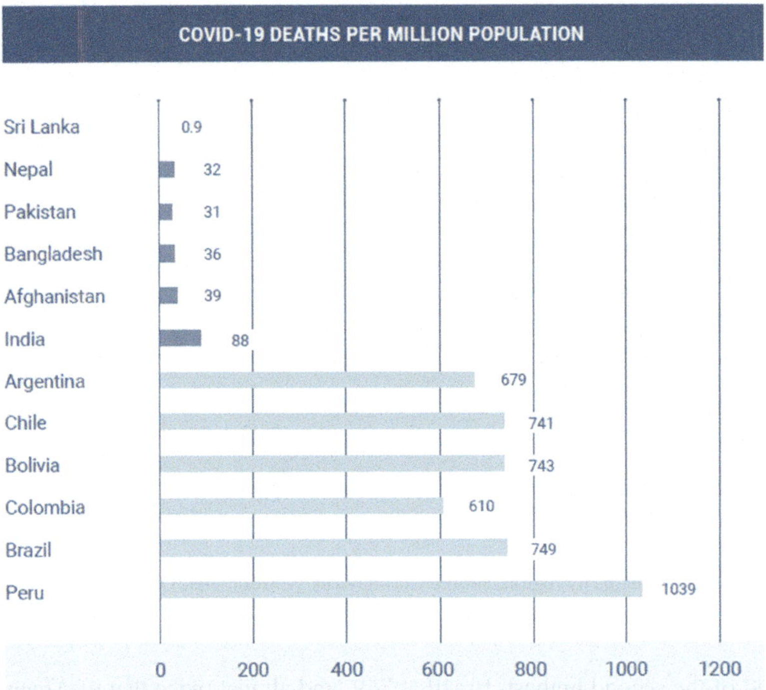


**Fig. 2** COVID-19 deaths in South America and South Asia. *Source* Coronavirus Worldometer. Data accessed October 30, 2020

Peru and India have performed poorly in terms of GDP growth rate in Q2 2020 among the countries displayed in Fig. 2, and given that both these countries are often treated as case studies of strong governance, this draws attention to the fact that there may be a dissonance between strong governance and good governance.

The turnaround for India has been especially surprising, given that until a few years ago it was among the three fastest-growing economies in the world. The slowdown began in 2016, though the sharp downturn, sharper than virtually all other countries, occurred after the lockdown.

On the COVID-19 policy front, both India and Peru have become known for what the Oxford University's COVID Policy Tracker[3] calls the "stringency" of the government's response to the epidemic. At 8 pm on March 24, 2020, the Indian government announced, with four hours' notice, a complete nationwide shutdown. Virtually all movement outside the perimeter of one's home was officially sought to be brought to a standstill. Naturally, as described in several papers, such as that of Ray and Subramanian (Ray & Subramanian, 2020), this meant that most economic life also came to a sudden standstill, which in turn meant that hundreds of millions

[3] "COVID Policy Tracker," Oxford University, https://github.com/OxCGRT/covid-policy-trackert.

of workers in the informal, as well as more marginally formal sectors, lost their livelihoods.

In addition, tens of millions of these workers, being migrant workers in places far-flung from their original homes, also lost their temporary homes and their savings with these lost livelihoods, so that the only safe space that beckoned them was their place of origin in small towns and villages often hundreds of miles away from their places of work.

After a few weeks of precarious living in their migrant destinations, they set off, on foot since trains and buses had been stopped, for these towns and villages, creating a "lockdown and scatter" that spread the virus from the city to the town and the town to the village. Indeed, "lockdown" is a bit of a misnomer for what happened in India, since over 20 million people did exactly the opposite of what one does in a lockdown. Thus, India had a strange combination of lockdown some and scatter the rest, like in no other country. They spilled out and scattered in ways they would otherwise not do. It is not surprising that the infection, which was marginally present in rural areas (23% in April), now makes up some 54% of all cases in India (Gopakumar & Ghosh, 2020).

In Peru too, the lockdown was sudden, nationwide, long drawn out, and stringent (Pighi Bel & Horton, 2020). Jobs were lost, financial aid was difficult to disburse, migrant workers were forced to return home, and the virus has now spread to all parts of the country with death rates from it surpassing almost every other part of the world.

As an aside, to think about ways of implementing lockdowns that are less stringent and geographically as well as functionally less total, an example from yet another continent is instructive. Ethiopia with a COVID-19 death rate of 13 per million population seems to have bettered the already relatively low African rate of 31 in Fig. 1.[4]

*We hope that human beings will emerge from this crisis more aware of the problems of sustainability.*

## 3 The Way Forward

We next move from the immediate crisis to the medium term. Where is the world headed and how should we deal with the new world? Arguably, that two sectors that will emerge larger and stronger in the post-pandemic world are: digital technology and outsourcing, and healthcare and pharmaceuticals.

The last 9 months of the pandemic have been a huge training ground for people in the use of digital technology—Zoom, WebEx, digital finance, and many others. This learning-by-doing exercise is likely to give a big boost to outsourcing, which has the potential to help countries like India, the Philippines, and South Africa.

[4] "No lockdown, few ventilators, but Ethiopia is beating Covid-19," Financial Times, May 27, 2020, https://www.ft.com/content/7c6327ca-a00b-11ea-b65d-489c67b0d85d.

Globalization may see a short-run retreat, but, we believe, it will come back with a vengeance. Nations that build walls to keep out goods, people, and talent will get out-competed by other nations in the product market. This realization will make most countries reverse their knee-jerk anti-globalization, and the ones that do not will cease to be important global players. Either way, globalization will be back on track and with a much greater amount of outsourcing.

To return, more critically this time, to our earlier aside on Ethiopia, its historical and contemporary record on tampering with internet connectivity (Anna, 2020) in an attempt to muzzle inter-ethnic tensions and political dissent will not serve it well in such a post-pandemic scenario. This is a useful reminder for all emerging market economies.

We hope that human beings will emerge from this crisis more aware of the problems of sustainability. This could divert some demand from luxury goods to better health, and what is best described as "creative consumption": art, music, and culture (Kabanda, 2018). The former will mean much larger healthcare and pharmaceutical sectors.

But to take advantage of these new opportunities, nations will need to navigate the current predicament so that they have a viable economy once the pandemic passes. Thus, it is important to be able to control the pandemic while keeping the economy open. There is some emerging literature (Li et al., 2020) on this, but much more is needed. This is a governance challenge of a kind rarely faced, because the pandemic has disrupted normal markets and there is a need, at least in the short run, for governments to step in to fill the caveat.

Emerging economies will have to devise novel governance strategies for doing this double duty of tamping down on new infections without strident controls on economic behavior and without blindly imitating Europe and America.

Here is an example. One interesting opportunity amidst this chaos is to tap into the "resource" of those who have already had COVID-19 and are immune, even if only in the short term—we still have no definitive evidence on the length of acquired immunity.

These people can be offered a high salary to work in sectors that require physical interaction with others. This will help keep supply chains unbroken. Normally, the market would have on its own caused such a salary increase, but in this case, the main benefit of marshaling this labor force is on the aggregate economy and GDP and therefore is a classic case of positive externality, which the free market does not adequately reward. It is more a challenge of governance. As with most economic policy, this will need careful research and design before being implemented. We have to be aware that a policy like this will come with its risk of bribery and corruption. There is also the moral hazard challenge of poor people choosing to get COVID-19 in order to qualify for these special jobs. Safeguards will be needed against these risks.

But we believe that any government that succeeds in implementing an intelligently designed intervention to draw on this huge, underutilized resource can have a big, positive impact on the economy.[5]

This is just one idea. We must innovate in different ways to survive the crisis and then have the ability to navigate the new world that will emerge, hopefully in the not too distant future.

**Acknowledgements** We are grateful for financial support from Cornell University's Hatfield Fund for the research associated with this paper. We also wish to express our gratitude to Homi Kharas for many suggestions and David Batcheck for generous editorial help.

## References

Anna, C. (2020). Ethiopia enters 3rd week of internet shutdown after unrest. Washington Post, July 14, 2020. https://www.washingtonpost.com/world/africa/ethiopia-enters-3rd-week-of-internet-shutdown-after-unrest/2020/07/14/4699c400-c5d6-11ea-a825-8722004e4150_story.html

Gopakumar, G., & Ghosh, S. (2020). Rural recovery could slow down as cases rise, says Ghosh. Mint, August 19, 2020. https://www.livemint.com/news/india/rural-recovery-could-slow-down-as-cases-rise-says-ghosh-11597801644015.html

Kabanda, P. (2018). The creative wealth of Nations: Can the arts advance development? Cambridge University Press.

Li, G., et al. (2020). Disease-dependent interaction policies to support health and economic outcomes during the COVID-19 epidemic. medRxiv, August 2020. https://www.medrxiv.org/content/10.1101/2020.08.24.20180752v3

Pighi Bel, P., & Horton, J. (2020). Coronavirus: What's happening in Peru? BBC, July 9, 2020. https://www.bbc.com/news/world-latin-america-53150808

Raju, S. (2020). Did the Indian lockdown avert deaths? medRxiv, July 5, 2020. https://europepmc.org/article/ppr/ppr183813#A1

Ray, D., & Subramanian, S. (2020). India's Lockdown: An Interim Report. NBER Working Paper, May 2020. https://www.nber.org/papers/w27282

---

[5] For helpful discussion concerning this idea, we are grateful to Turab Hussain, Daksh Walia and Mehr-un-Nisa, during a seminar of South Asian Economics Students' Meet (SAESM).

# Covidonomics or the Curious Case of a Supply Constrained Keynesian Equilibrium

**Dipankar Dasgupta and Meenakshi Rajeev**

## 1 Introduction

The well-known COVID-19 pandemic continues to exert a marked influence on economic affairs more than two years after its first appearance. In a departure from economic shocks of the past, this pandemic has a multitude of simultaneous effects that require an innovative and holistic policy approach, especially when considering measures to alleviate the ills of the crisis.

Data on the actual macroeconomic impacts of the pandemic have been filtering in overtime, comprised of sharp declines in output and national income in the developed and the developing world, coupled with rampant inflation.[1] However, much of the major impact could be considered to be confined to the first year of the pandemic, 2020, as a result of widespread lockdowns to control the spread of the virus, coupled with increased transactions costs arising from public fear of the virus and bottle-necked supply chains (Dasgupta & Rajeev, 2020). Following the introduction of vaccines in several countries and gradual inoculation of the population, alongside markedly reduced reliance on blanket lockdowns to combat virus clusters, the supply and demand constraints of that time have eased somewhat.

[1] https://www.imf.org/en/Publications/WEO/Issues/2022/04/19/world-economic-outlook-april-2022.

This paper is a modified and enlarged version of a commentary that appeared in EPW in May, 2020; For details see Dasgupta and Rajeev (2020).

D. Dasgupta
Indian Statistical Institute, New Delhi, Kolkata, India

M. Rajeev (✉)
Institute for Social and Economic Change, Bangalore, India
e-mail: meenakshi@isec.ac.in



A. Raychaudhuri and A. Ghose (eds.), *Managing Pandemic and Correcting Development Fundamentals*, India Studies in Business and Economics,
https://doi.org/10.1007/978-981-19-8680-2_2

With the reduced transaction costs resulting from decreased fear of infection, coupled with the removal of supply constraints that earlier arose from labour unavailability and non-functional factories due to lockdowns, the situation would be markedly different from what was experienced in 2020 and the first half of 2021. This prompts an analysis that takes these developments into account starting from the initial situation that we observed during 2020, to better explain and chart the trajectory of economies such as India in the presence of what is now approaching an endemic health issue rather than a pandemic one.

While issues of lockdowns and public fear have reduced considerably, newer challenges to economic stability and growth have risen in the meanwhile. Production bottlenecks and disruptions have led to markedly high levels of inflation. India's 2021–22 consumer priceinflation, for example, was estimated at 5.3%,[2] with this figure reaching 5.7% in Q4 of that year. By February 2022, retail inflation was estimated to have reached a staggering 6.07%, which was outside the RBI's target band of 2–6%.[3]

This runaway inflation has recently prompted the RBI to increase the repo rate for the first time since the pandemic started, and that too by a severe 40 basis points in May 2022.[4] Needless to say, all of this will have a corresponding effect on demand and supply conditions within the economy.

Although inflation, monetary policy stances, and their corresponding impacts have been extensively studied for the Indian economy, this is not the only set of issues that India faces today. In February 2022, The Russian Federation undertook a special military operation in neighbouring Ukraine.[5] This has resulted in protracted military hostilities between the two countries. While this region is geographically separated considerably from India, the economic ties are much closer. Ukraine is the world's largest exporter of sunflower oil, and Russia is the world's second-largest.[6] Given that this is a widely used cooking oil in India, reduced supply has expectedly led to an increase in prices and contributed to the already alarming inflation. Moreover, Russia is a large producer of crude oil, and the ensuing war and sanctions imposed on the country have created instabilities in crude supply across the globe, especially as European buyers turn to alternative suppliers. Following Russia's attack on Ukraine, petroleum prices have skyrocketed in India. While Indian oil processors can procure crude oil from Russia currently, such arrangements are bound to be unstable owing to political subtleties and financial sanctions on Russia creating issues in payments for imports, particularly since Russia has been partially disallowed from accessing or using the SWIFT interbank communications system.[7] Once more, these concomitant

---

[2] https://www.rbi.org.in/Scripts/BS_PressReleaseDisplay.aspx?prid=53249.

[3] https://economictimes.indiatimes.com/news/economy/policy/rbi-seen-holding-rates-even-as-retail-prices-top-inflation-target/articleshow/90237527.cms.

[4] https://www.rbi.org.in/Scripts/BS_PressReleaseDisplay.aspx?prid=53728.

[5] https://www.hindustantimes.com/world-news/a-timeline-of-war-as-russia-S-invasion-of-ukraine-enters-third-month-101650699536819.html.

[6] https://oec.world/en/profile/hs/sunflower-seed-or-safflower-oil-crude.

[7] https://www.bbc.com/news/business-60521822.

shocks are guaranteed to result in a multitude of effects, both on supply as well as demand.

While these geopolitical developments have been widely studied in both academic as well as journalistic spheres, much of this body of work to date focuses on empirical analyses and does not develop a theoretical foundation or framework for explaining the changes observed in different economies. Such a framework would allow better classification and understanding of the current status and future effects of pandemic-related shocks, and thus, the present research attempts to address this lacuna by analysing these shocks theoretically within a Keynesian framework.

Given that there existed demand deficiencies in the economy even prior to the appearance of the pandemic, the Keynesian model is the natural choice in such a scenario. While the pandemic undoubtedly exacerbated these demand-side ailments, there were also additional issues in supply chains owing to lockdowns. These bottlenecks imposed constraints on production systems, and moreover, the constraints on supply have been severe enough to sufficiently meet even the lowered demand. We term this situation a supply-constrained Keynesian equilibrium. We then move from a simple Keynesian model to a complete Keynesian framework to investigate and glean insights into the possible effects of the subsequent developments and derive possible policy responses to the situation.

The next section provides a brief review of relevant literature investigating the pandemic's effects in a Keynesian framework, and Sect. 3 supplies some background statistics for the foregoing analysis. The Keynesian framework is then used to trace the evolution path of key macroeconomic variables during the pandemic in Sect. 4, followed by a discussion of the new shocks and forces on the Indian economy within this framework in Sect. 5. A concluding section follows at the end.

## 2 Review of Literature

The coronavirus pandemic has exerted a multitude of influences over a number of spheres of public life, including physiological and psychological health, livelihood, and movement of people. The economic effects of this crisis are widespread and variegated, with marked changes in both the demand and supply sides of the global economy. Owing to the unprecedented scale presented by this crisis, coupled with the uncertainty that it introduces, it is of interest to many scholars to better understand the path of development of this pandemic. Some of these studies are cross-country exercises, while others are country-specific. Macroeconomic consequences of the pandemic had been examined through an economy-wide model which observes a loss of around 6.5% (of median income) in 2020, but the gap was expected to narrow down subsequently (Rungcharoenkitkul, 2021). The study, however, observed a high dispersion of economic losses across economies depending on the spread of the pandemic. Beirne et al. (2021), too, consider a number of countries (a total of 38 countries) to evaluate the response of global financial markets due to the pandemic.

The study in particular considers emerging markets and capital flows to them, together with an evaluation of the impacts of fiscal and monetary policies.

Amongst the country-specific studies, a household-level survey conducted in Thailand and Vietnam on the effect of state support provided under various welfare programmes during the pandemic observed that such initiatives helped improve consumer sentiment and thereby demand. Consequently, trust in the Government was created that aided to produce an optimistic macroeconomic outlook (Bui et al., 2022). Impacts of the pandemic on Japan's economy especially due to the soft lockdown policies adopted in the country were discussed in Kubota (2021), while Conefrey et al. (2021) examine the impacts of fiscal and monetary policies on Ireland's economy. Concentrating on Sub-Saharan Africa, the study by Agyei et al. (2021) analyses the ramifications of the pandemic on food prices. Sector-specific influences of COVID-19 have also been studied by a number of authors; for example, Bazzana et al. (2022) take up different COVID-19 scenarios to evaluate the impact of the pandemic prevalence on the energy sector focussing particularly on transport and industry. Several papers have been written on the pandemic and its impact on the Indian economy (see Barbate et al., 2021). The impacts of the Government stimulus package have also been evaluated for India (Chakrabarty et al., 2021).

Given the differential effects on different sectors wrought by the virus and corresponding policy responses, economic modelling of the ensuing effects has often taken a computable general equilibrium approach, where a matrix of sectoral elasticities and other data inputs are used to compute the effects of shocks to different sectors and chart a future development path (see, for example, Dixon et al., 2021 for the US, Keogh-Brown et al., 2020 for the UK, and McKibbin & Fernando, 2020 for a global computation). While research into the pandemic has been undertaken in the Indian context, much of this is focussed on sector-specific effects and has often not addressed the issue from a holistic perspective.

For gaining an understanding of the possible effects of the pandemic on a developing country such as India, the Keynesian framework provides a useful base for understanding the broad direction of the effects of an economic shock. This framework has been applied in different countries to model the pandemic's supply and demand effects. From a purely theoretical perspective, Eichenbaum et al. (2022) show that there is a simultaneous decline in consumption, investment, and output as a result of the pandemic, which acts as a negative shock both to consumption demand as well as labour supply. For the US economy, Baqaee and Farhi (2022) use a disaggregated model to show that negative sectoral shocks had a stagflationary effect while negative demand shocks had an inflationary one. Similar analyses have been undertaken for Pakistan by Abbas et al., (2022) and Bangladesh by Onik et al. (2021), though these are largely empirical in nature. Supply shocks arising out of lockdowns and layoffs are postulated to be especially dangerous as they are found to be capable of triggering larger and proportional reductions in aggregate demand, and fiscal stimuli are found to be relatively ineffective compared to monetary policy measures in this regard (Guerrieri et al., 2022).

Some of the pandemic response policies are evaluated through a Keynesian framework by Leonel and Young (2021). Padilla (2020) suggests that severe supply shocks can lead to a vicious cycle of falling supply and demand, which can be mitigated through reduced interest rates for improving aggregate demand. Moving away from strictly Keynesian confines, Romana (2020) discusses the applicability of Tobin's (1975) Keynesian framework to model depression and supply shocks arising out of the pandemic. A post-Keynesian involuntary unemployment model is suggested as apt for modelling by Pollitt et al. (2021).

For the Indian context, in particular, several papers have been written on the pandemic and its impact on the Indian economy (see Barbate et al., 2021). The impacts of the Government stimulus package have also been evaluated for India (Chakrabarty, et al, 2021). Dasgupta and Rajeev (2020) utilize a Keynesian framework to demonstrate the concomitant supply and demand shocks that arise out of transaction costs associated with the pandemic—owing to public health fears and concerns on the demand side and the costs of bringing workers to workplaces during lockdowns on the supply side. A longer scale study from 1980–81 through 2020–21 has been carried out by Yoshino et al. (2022), which finds that capital formation through fiscal policy is an effective means of combatting covid-related economic slumps when compared to fiscal consumption or accommodative monetary policies.

Barring a few, most of these studies, however, are empirical in nature, and a review of the empirical literature on the subject is presented in (Frederic & Rungcharoenkitkul, 2020) which talks about the economic costs of epidemics. The paper provides a comparative picture of the current pandemic vis-à-vis some of the noteworthy past epidemics. There is however only a limited number of studies that provide theoretical modelling of the pandemic situation, and this paper is a modest attempt to fill this research gap. Further, newer developments have arisen in the intervening years, namely the introduction of inoculating vaccines that would reduce public health fears and thus prop up demand and increase government confidence in lifting lockdown measures without exacerbating the health crisis, which would improve supply conditions and bolster supply chains. Added to this, however, is the introduction of political instability in Eastern Europe, which threatens key input supplies for India's economy, which is set on a fragile recovery path. It is of importance to look at the combined effects of these new developments and better understand how they would impact an already weak economy. Thus, we outline the short-and medium-term effects of the pandemic on a Keynesian framework in the next section and extend the analysis by introducing the supply and demand effects of the new shocks. The next section provides a background of important macroeconomic variables to ground the analysis.

## 3 Key Macroeconomic Indicators

We start by looking at the figures for inflation and GDP growth during the pandemic, which are presented in Fig. 1.

**Fig. 1** GDP growth and inflation in pre-pandemic and pandemic periods. *Source* Author's compilation using data from the RBI and MOSPI

It is evident that while the economy was showing signs of a slowdown (GDP is measured along the left vertical axis and depicted by the vertical bars) even as early as 2019, inflation (depicted by the solid line and measured along the right vertical axis) was kept largely in check, remaining below 4%, which is well within the central bank's tolerance band. However, by the middle of 2020, during which the pandemic and lockdowns were severest, it is readily discernible that inflation was almost double of what was seen a year before, and GDP growth had turned negative for the second and third quarters of the year, which is a situation of stagflation. As lockdowns were lifted and the vaccine was introduced, and subsequently rolled out to the population in early 2021, GDP growth had recovered considerably, inflation had fallen, as well as producers were able to restart operations and match demand. Although GDP growth continues to be significantly higher than what was seen both during the pandemic and immediately before its appearance, inflation has been climbing to higher levels in late 2021 and early 2022, which can be a worrying issue.

Alongside dampening growth and exacerbating inflation, another important effect of the pandemic was on creating large-scale unemployment, as seen in Fig. 2.

Corresponding directly to the lockdowns imposed in April, May, and June of 2020, it can be readily observed that unemployment spiked considerably so that almost a quarter of the workforce was unable to work. However, this was quickly assuaged by July of 2020, corresponding directly to the lifting of the first national lockdown, where the unemployment rate of 7.4% was fairly close to the pre-pandemic figures. Another small spike can be seen in early to mid-2021, corresponding to the second wave and the lockdowns imposed then. Overall, however, unemployment appears to have returned to levels comparable to what was observed before the onset of the pandemic. Therefore, while there continues to remain an excess supply of labour in the economy, its share in the total labour force is largely unchanged from the pre-pandemic era. Thus, economic expansion and growth would require investments in new capital, since it is likely that the current capital stock is fully utilized by

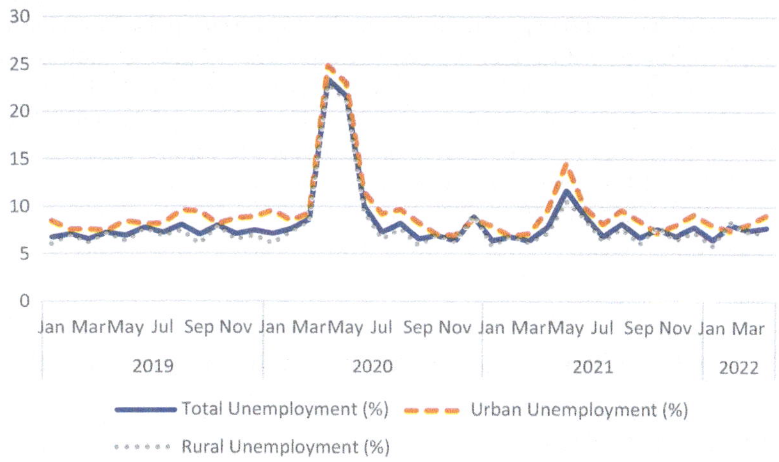


**Fig. 2** Unemployment (%) in India 2019–2022. *Source* Authors' compilation using data from unemploymentindia.cmie.com

the available labour supply given the unemployment levels seen above. Increasing capital is linked to credit, and we consequently discuss credit offtake below (Fig. 3).

The pandemic clearly deepened a continued deceleration in credit offtake, but this situation has slowly started to reverse with acceleration in credit growth towards the latter half of 2021 and the beginning of 2022. Disaggregated sectoral figures show that even though credits to agriculture improved quickly following the lockdown restrictions, and even outstripped pre-pandemic growth rates, industrial credit offtake has mainly remained sluggish and has only started to reach former rates of growth.

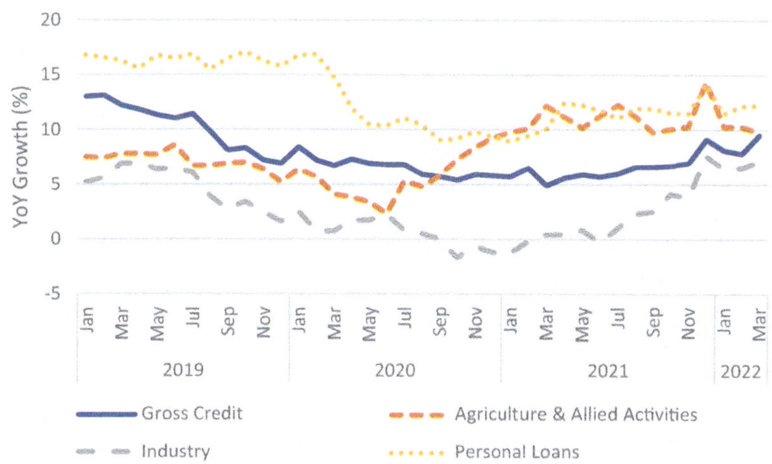


**Fig. 3** Sectoral and gross bank credit growth. *Source* Authors' compilation using data from the Reserve Bank of India

Consumer confidence and expectations of purchasing power in the future, however, have remained muted with credit off take growth rates remaining markedly lower than what was seen before the pandemic began, indicating possible deficiencies in aggregate demand that would create issues in the effective operation of fiscal stimuli.

Given this macroeconomic background, we proceed to explain the developments using a theoretical framework. The next section provides a theoretical explanation for the evolution of some of these variables during the pandemic era using a short-run simple Keynesian model.

# 4 Transaction Cost-Constrained Simple Keynesian Model

## *4.1 Pre-covid Situation*

Beginning with a simple Keynesian model, we observe the operation of effective demand and a short-run fixed supply, which presents a capacity constraint to the economy. In the simple Keynesian model, income ($Y$), or aggregate demand (AD) is given by the following expression:

$$Y = \mathrm{AD}^1(Y; \bar{i}) = \overline{A}^1 + C(Y) + I(\bar{i}) + G + NX \tag{1}$$

where $AD^1(Y; \bar{i})$ is aggregate demand[8] as a function of aggregate income $Y$ and an interest rate $\bar{i}$ that is considered to be fixed; $C$ is private/personal consumption demand, which depends on aggregate income $Y$; and $I$ is investment demand which varies according to the rate of interest $i$ (fixed at $\bar{i}$ here). The autonomous portion of income, labelled $\overline{A}^1$, is the sum of the autonomous portions of consumption and investment. Government expenditure and net export are presented by $G$ and $NX$. We further assume that $P$ is fixed in the model. Some of these parameters will be allowed to vary in the presentation of the complete model.

Equation (1) is graphically presented in Fig. 4. It is evident here that there is excess capacity in the economy, and consequently, equilibrium output is determined by aggregate demand, which is lower than the maximum possible level of output $Y_{max}$ for the capital available. This capacity constraint is represented in the diagram by the horizontal line through the point $Y_{max}$ on the vertical axis and (using the 45° line) the vertical line through $Y_{max}$ on the horizontal axis. Three possible Keynesian equilibria are captured by the points $E_1^1$, $E_2^1$ and $E_3^1$ on the 45° line. Increasing output in this setup requires greater demand creation and policies or measures that increase either government spending G or disposable income ($Y$–$T$) are effective in this regard. Such measures were adopted in the form of the fiscal stimuli, tax cuts, etc., to address the slowdown of the economy prior to the arrival of the pandemic.

[8] For a discussion on CoronaVirus and a somewhat different $AD$ curve linking productivity growth and employment, see Fornaro and Wolf (2020).

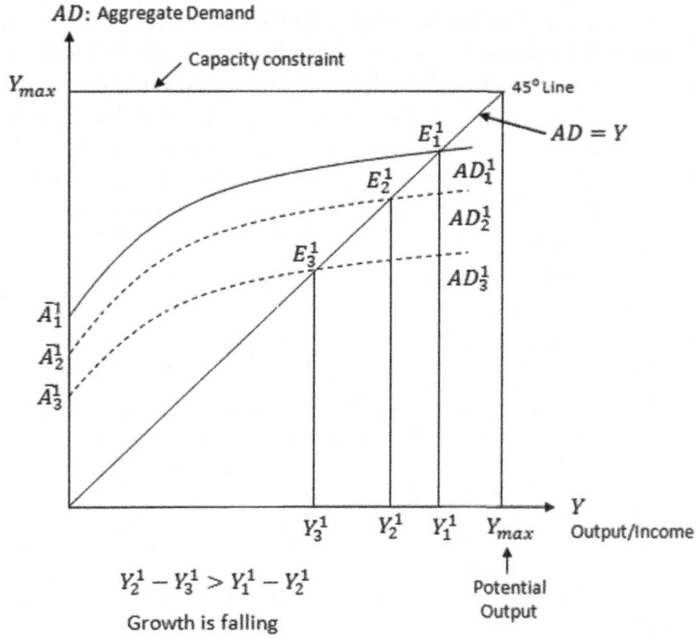


**Fig. 4** The pre-covid equilibrium. *Source* Authors' construction; see also Dasgupta and Rajeev (2020)

The equilibria at $E_1^1$, $E_2^1$ and $E_3^1$ represent equilibrium incomes/outputs $Y_1^1$, $Y_2^1$ and $Y_3^1$ respectively. Here, $Y_2^1$ denotes output in the period immediately preceding the period for which the output is $Y_1^1$. Similarly, $Y_3^1$ precedes $Y_2^1 . Y_2^1 Y_1^1$ the relationship $Y_2^1 - Y_3^1 > Y_1^1 - Y_2^1$ has been chosen deliberately to capture declining growth rates. Although the differences are not growth rates, this is irrelevant for the foregoing analysis.[9] This is a situation of demand deficiency (as capacity was not fully utilized), and a majority of discussions centred around the role monetary and fiscal policy could play in alleviating this. That is, economic improvements could be effected through manipulations of the *AD* (.;.) curve.

## 4.2 *The Covid-19 Case: Transaction Cost-Constrained Simple Keynesian Model*

Most economic shocks result in shifts in the AD curve to lower consumption levels, and production capacity is not often discussed in such situations. The pandemic, however, resulted in transaction costs on both the demand as well as supply sides.

[9] Strictly speaking, the differences would have represented growth rates if the variables were measured in natural logarithmic scale.

The former were the costs associated with the risk of contacting the disease if one visits retail outlets for transactions of goods and services one demands, which has a component of fear resulting from high healthcare costs, lingering medical issues after treatment, and lost productivity. These fears compelled many to avoid physical markets. In addition to the transaction costs, lockdowns introduced uncertainty in income flows and reduced income for many. These uncertainties about the future in Keynesian literature refer to as the state of confidence, and affect both autonomous and induced consumption.

Transactions costs can also be modelled as acting on supply. Lockdowns prevented workers from accessing workplaces, which can be viewed as unboundedly high transaction costs for firms in bringing workers to workplaces. Similar transaction costs will be present in getting raw materials from the source. These acted as constraints, which effectively lowered potential output below *Ymax*.

The aggregate demand function in the presence of transaction cost (*TC*) can be written as:

$$AD^2(Y, \bar{i}, TC) = \bar{A}^2(TC) + C(Y, TC) + I(\bar{i}, TC) + G + NX(TC) \quad (2)$$

where $AD^2$ is the transaction cost-constrained aggregate demand. Figure 5 represents the new scenario.

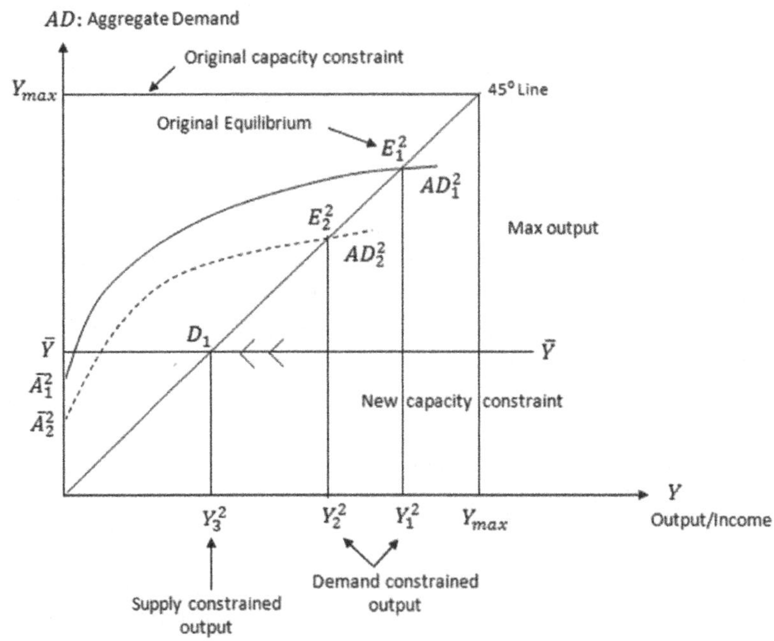


**Fig. 5** Covid equilibrium (first wave). *Source* Authors' construction; see also Dasgupta and Rajeev (2020)

Further, weakened economic confidence reduces autonomous investment demand, and together, these forces result in aggregate demand shifting downwards from $AD_1^2$ to $AD_2^2$, and the equilibrium to $E_2^2$ from $E_1^2$, with the corresponding new output being $Y_2^2$. This is a traditional demand shock in a simple Keynesian framework.

While from the perspective of capital availability, an excess capacity may continue to have been present in the Indian economy, the supply side transaction cost renders this capacity constraint ($Y_{\max}$) irrelevant. As most workers are not able to reach workplaces, a new effective supply constraint emerges at, say, $\overline{Y}$ (Dasgupta & Rajeev, 2020). It is important to note that such an output level is even below the new reduced demand equilibrium $E_2^2$, and thus increasing AD will have no effect on the ultimate solution of the model. Thus, from the point of view of the simple Keynesian model, the economy gets stuck at a disequilibrium point. The point $D_1$ (or $Y_3^2$) captures this changed new level of output. This can be viewed as the situation prevailing during the large-scale lockdowns in the year 2020.[10] The disequilibrium output $Y_3^2$ has two important features. First, it is the result of labour shortages leading to underutilization of capital, which results in reduced incomes for both entrepreneurs as well as workers. The constrained output, further, isn't a scalar reduction of maximum but has a markedly different composition-being comprised mainly of essential goods. Since these do not include exports, there would also be a reduction in income from lower trade revenues.

Therefore, the means of addressing the economic difficulties arising out of the pandemic depend on where the constrained disequilibrium output lies with respect to the non-constrained equilibrium. Indeed, it appears to ~~the~~ be the case that $\overline{Y}$ was lower than $Y_2^2$, and this resulted in output jumping vertically down from $Y_1^2$ to the horizontal line $\overline{YY}$ and then shifting leftwards along $\overline{YY}$. This would have been accompanied by rapid reductions in wholesaler and retailer stocks, as these could have been consumed without replenishment from suppliers, which had the potential to create more supply shortage. Since demand exceeds supply here, there should be an impact on prices to bring the economy back to equilibrium. To appreciate this more clearly, we move on now to the complete Keynesian model.

## 5 Transactions Cost Constrained Complete Keynesian Model

To understand how the short-run disequilibrium is balanced, we need to turn to the complete Keynesian model. In this model, both supply and demand functions interact to determine equilibrium price and output levels. The assumption of capacity constraints reflects in a supply curve that has a steep portion at higher levels of output. This interaction is depicted in Fig. 3, where aggregate demand (AD) and aggregate supply (AS) are functions relating output to price levels. The aggregate demand curve

[10] Alternatively, as we shall point out in the Complete Keynesian model, the demand itself may fall towards $Y_3^2$.

is the locus of points for which the commodity (IS) and money markets (LM) are in equilibrium and are downward sloping because an increase in price levels requires a reduction in income to keep money demand equal to the money supply. This takes the form of a leftward shift of the LM curve against the downward sloping IS curve. The aggregate supply curve, on the other hand, shows the equilibrium outputs that correspond to different price levels and as usual is upward sloping.

The AD curve is likely to be steep owing to a slowing pre-covid economy. The initial equilibrium point is at the intersection between $AD_1^3$ and $AS_1$ at $E_1^3$ in Fig. 6.[11] High transactions costs would have led to an impact on the IS curve which results in the AD curve shifting backward to an even more steep $AD_2^3$ curve. The supply constraints would be captured through the aggregate supply curve $AS_1$, which also shifts backward to $AS_2$ and becomes highly inelastic beyond a point. The new equilibrium is at $E_2^3$, with a corresponding output of $Y_2^3$. Had the supply curve shifted even more, (to $AS$, say) the equilibrium might have occurred at $E_3^3$. The corresponding *equilibrium* prices are $P_1$, $P_2$, *and* $P_3$. As already pointed out earlier, the market equilibrium is brought about through successive rises in the price level. This is seen in the discussion of macroeconomic variables in Sect. 3, where it was observed that there were concomitant falls in output (also observed in sharply increased unemployment) and increases in price levels during the complete and partial lockdowns.

While price adjustments are often considered a natural part of disequilibrium conditions, this successive series of price increases owing to concomitant shifts in both the AD and the AS curves have the potential to make even essential commodities unaffordable to some of the poor, which constitute a large portion of the population in India. This is exacerbated since these workers would be those unable to work remotely, and so would have to contend with reduced incomes.

In the period following this, however, certain developments have occurred which would have resulted in further movement of equilibria. These are the introduction of the vaccine and the military conflicts in Eastern Europe, which are analysed below.

## *5.1 Vaccination Effect*

The introduction of the vaccination program would have resulted in reductions in transaction costs, which act on the aggregate demand function and easing rules for workers accessing workplaces, which would have the effect of easing supply constraints. These changes are shown in Fig. 7.

As seen in the preceding analyses, lockdown capacity constraints had reduced supply, so that the supply curve would have been located at $AS_1^4$, and aggregate

[11] Although we are calling this the complete Keynesian model, it should be emphasized that the *AS* curve is a straightforward aggregate supply curve (to which students are introduced in microeconomics courses)and not the typical *AS* curve one comes across in macro textbooks. The reason why we avoid the macro *AS* construction is that it is usually constructed to capture features linked to wage bargaining *vis-à-vis* the state of unemployment. In our simple minded framework, such details have no role to play.

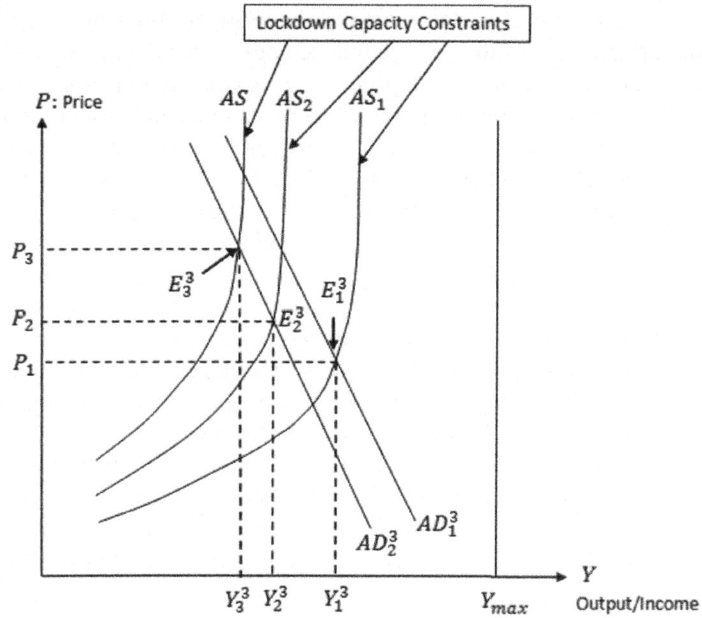


**Fig. 6** The complete Keynesian equilibrium—pre-Covid and Covid periods. *Source* Authors' construction; see also Dasgupta and Rajeev (2020)

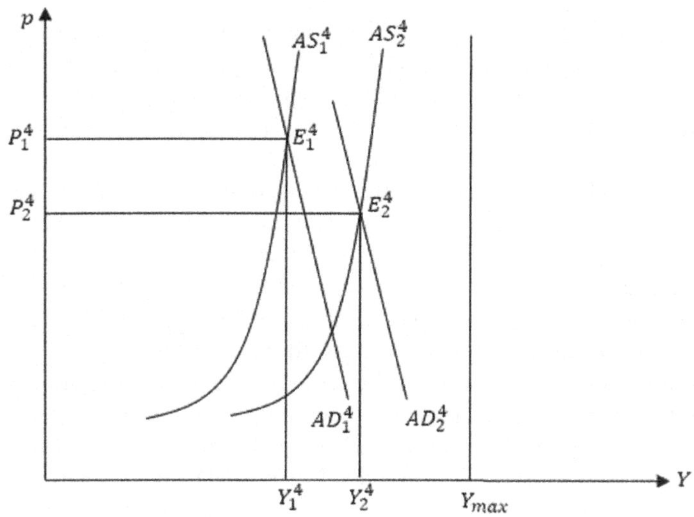


**Fig. 7** Vaccination effect. *Source* Authors' construction

demand would have fallen to $AD_1^4$, leading to a relatively high price level of $P_1^4$. However, the introduction of the vaccine reduced public health fears to some extent, and people would have been more willing to access marketplaces for purchasing goods, and attending in-person services such as restaurants and movie theatres, thus increasing overall demand in the economy. This can be represented by an outward shift of the aggregate demand curve to $AD_2^4$. Concomitantly, the vaccination would have reduced the transmission and spread of the virus, thus prompting the government to allow better movement of people, especially workers. Thus, factories would have been able to reopen with at least some capacity (if not full), and production would have resumed. The supply curve would, therefore, have shifted outwards as well to $AS_2^4$, and this would have allowed the economy to settle at the new equilibrium $E_2^4$, which corresponds to a higher output level $Y_2^4$ and a lower price level $P_2^4$. However, despite vaccination drives, there remained some risk of virus spread. Thus, the improvement in demand may not have been pronounced enough to bring it back to pre-covid levels. Furthermore, although industries were allowed to function, there were limits in place allowing only 50% of the overall workforce to operate at a given time, so even though supply improved, it would still fall short of the potential output level $Y_{\max}$, but the situation is nevertheless an improvement over the one prevailing during lockdowns.

## 5.2 Geopolitical Developments and Possible Impacts

Prevailing geopolitical effects include the ongoing unrest and armed conflict in Eastern Europe, between Russia and Ukraine and subsequent sanctions against Russia. This has inflated Indian demand for crude oil from other suppliers, including Iraq and the United States. As a result of these developments, crude oil price has increased. Since this is a vital input in transport and logistics, it can increase other input prices for producers. Concomitantly, producers are also faced with supply chain bottlenecks, especially for imported inputs. The situation is exacerbated by increases in the price of cooking oil, which is an input for the restaurants and packaged foods industries, thus creating additional downward forces on aggregate supply. If all other things remain the same, the aggregate supply curve must shift to the left, as shown in Fig. 8, where the supply curve shifts leftward from $AS_0^5$ to $AS_1^5$.

On the demand side, the Ukraine conflict may dampen the investment demand, and the tightening of the monetary policy to combat price rise may shrink aggregate demand further. If these effects exert only a small effect on demand, other things remaining the same, the AD curve could shift from $AD_0^5$ to $AD_1^5$ and there will be continued increase in price levels owing to contractions in supply. The associated equilibrium output might fall from $Y_0^5$ to $Y_1^5$, and the realized price would be $P_1^5$, which is higher than the old equilibrium price $P_0^5$. If, on the other hand, these two forces exert a moderate effect on demand, then the new demand schedule may be represented by $AD_2^5$, and output $Y_2^5 < Y_1^5$, but the price levels would stay constant at $P_0^5$, or only vary slightly about this level. Thus, the new geopolitical shocks create some degree of uncertainty regarding the effects of monetary policy, and more observation

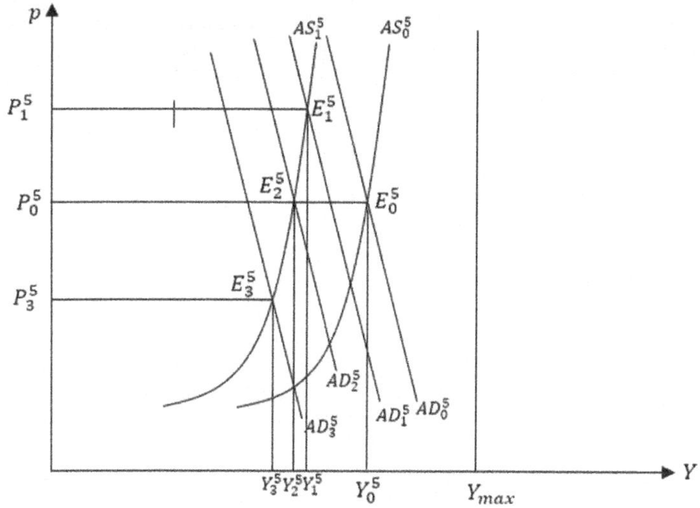


**Fig. 8** Geopolitical Effects on AD-AS equilibrium. *Source* Authors' construction

is required to correctly guide the economy. Looking at the macroeconomic data from Sect. 3, it is evident that price levels are, in fact, increasing as per the most recent statistics of 2022. Thus, monetary policy tightening may not succeed in countering price increasing shocks in supply chains.

In reality, however, output was observed to have increased during this period. This implies the existence of forces exerting a positive impact on demand. This may be explained theoretically as follows. With the effects of the pandemic receding with fewer and fewer new cases emerging daily, as well as selective lockdowns targeting only outbreak clusters, consumer confidence is observed to be improving. This is evidenced by RBI's consumer confidence index survey.[12] The survey data showed that consumer confidence continued to improve as of March 2022, although it remained at a negative value. Future expectations, too, (no commas) displayed an upward trend. Taken together, these would imply bolstered demand, which could cause an increase in consumption despite other economic setbacks. This alternative scenario is represented in Fig. 9, where we see the AD curve shifting to the right from $AD_0^6$ to $AD_1^6$, while the global supply chain bottlenecks induce a reduction in supply from $AS_0^6$ to $AS_1^6$. As a result of these shifts, the equilibrium changes from $E_0^6$ with a price level $P_0^6$ and output $Y_0^6$ to $E_1^6$, which is associated with a higher output level $Y_1^6$, but also a higher price $P_1^6$.

[12] https://rbidocs.rbi.org.in/rdocs/Publications/PDFs/CCSMAR202201E27E8B5D854001BD5652427502C461.PDF.

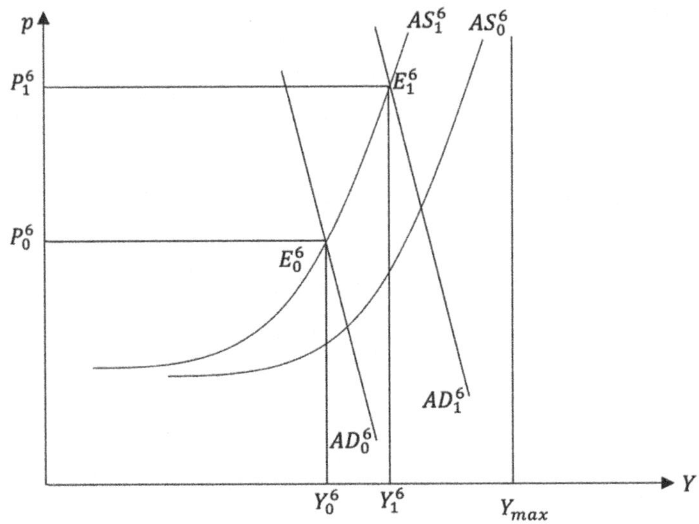


**Fig. 9** Increasing output over time. *Source* Authors' construction

## 6 Conclusions

Unprecedented disruptions created by covid-19 and their socioeconomic impacts have been analysed by a number of scholars across the globe. In the Indian context, too, a large number of papers have been published on several possible topics, varying from the vagaries of migrant labourers to supply chain bottlenecks affecting large entrepreneurs. Most of these papers, however, are empirical or descriptive in nature and theoretical works are few and far between. Against this backdrop, the current paper develops a simple theoretical model to understand the different prevailing situations over the past few years, starting from the economic slowdown that prevailed prior to the arrival of the pandemic. The paper highlights a theoretical paradox that emerged during the first wave of the pandemic and the consequent total lockdown of economic activities. By bringing the concept of transaction costs it demonstrated how supply restrictions became binding, giving rise to what we call a supply-constrained Keynesian equilibrium. The paper then presented the subsequent emerging scenarios using a complete Keynesian model, discussing the improvement in output levels and increase in inflation in the post lockdown period, when the vaccination drive was introduced. The paper ends by discussing some of the possible impacts of the recent geopolitical developments such as the Russia-Ukraine conflict.

We observe that though the situation has improved since 2020, uncertainty surrounding the emergence of a new strain of the virus still looms large. Thus ~~the~~ business confidence is not encouraging and credit off take growth remains low as well, as can be seen from Fig. 3, where growth rate is much below that of the pre-covid period which itself was a period of slowdown. Producers continue to experience problems arising out of supply chain bottlenecks as well as high input costs. This is coupled with issues of pessimistic consumer confidence and, as already noted, the March 2022 survey data indicates that consumer confidence continues to be negative even if improving.

Thus the road ahead for India continues to present several challenges to adequate recovery. Global uncertainties will dominate local economic performance and inflation continues to spiral upwards. Although the central bank (RBI) adopted an accommodative stance to support fiscal stimulus measures, this is no longer feasible as inflation has breached the target band. In response, the Reserve bank of India, in its May 2022 Monetary Policy meet, raised the repo rate by 40 basis points to 4.4%. Since this may imply a reduction in private investment, fiscal policy is more relevant than ever as it needs to address this shortfall to support continued economic growth. An increase in public expenditure on capital (as discussed in the 2022–23 Union Budget[13]) can be of marked importance in this context. The effectiveness with which the government can balance macroeconomic fundamentals and simultaneously affect growth with fiscal stimuli will only be assessed over time. Several infrastructure projects have been announced in the latest budget 2022–23, and speedy implementation of these projects is necessary to foster employment, demand, and consumer confidence, which are crucial at this time. This will encourage the private sector to re-enter with new investments in areas where we are facing supply bottlenecks and perhaps help to ensure sustained growth that is also inclusive.

**Acknowledgements** Dipankar Dasgupta wishes to thank Pradip Maiti and Pulapre Balakrishnan for helpful discussions. Meenakshi Rajeev is thankful to the RBI and ICSSR for their support to ISEC, Bangalore and thanks Pranav Nagendran for his valuable support without which this paper would not have been complete. The usual disclaimers apply.

## References

Abbass, K., Begum, H., Alam, A. S. A., Awang, A. H., Abdelsalam, M. K., Egdair, I. M. M., & Wahid, R. (2022). Fresh insight through a Keynesian theory approach to investigate the economic impact of the COVID-19 pandemic in Pakistan. *Sustainability, 14*(3), 1054.

Agyei, S. K., Isshaq, Z., Frimpong, S., Adam, A. M., Bossman, A., & Asiamah, O. (2021). COVID-19 and food prices in sub-saharan africa. *African Development Review, 33*(S1), S102–S113. https://doi.org/10.1111/1467-8268.12525

Baqaee, D., & Farhi, E. (2022). Supply and demand in disaggregated keynesian economies with an application to the covid-19 crisis. *American Economic Review, 112*(5), 1397–1436.

Barbate, V., Gade, R. N., & Raibagkar, S. S. (2021). COVID-19 and its impact on the Indian economy. *Vision, 25*(1), 23–35. https://doi.org/10.1177/0972262921989126

Bazzana, D., Cohen, J., Golinucci, N., Hafner, M., Noussan, M., Reichl, J., Vincenzo Rocco, M. Sciullo, A., & Vergalli, S. (2022). A multi-disciplinary approach to estimate the medium-term impact of COVID-19 on transport and energy: A case study for Italy. *Energy, 238*(Part C), 122015. ISSN 0360-5442.https://doi.org/10.1016/j.energy.2021.122015

Beirne, J., Renzhi, N., Sugandi, E., & Volz, U. (2021). COVID-19, asset markets and capital flows. *Pacific Economic Review, 26*(4), 498–538. https://doi.org/10.1111/1468-0106.12368

[13] https://www.indiabudget.gov.in/doc/budget_speech.pdf

Bui, D., Dräger, L., Hayo, B., & Nghiem, G. (2022). The effects of fiscal policy on households during the COVID-19 pandemic: Evidence from Thailand and Vietnam. *World Development, 153*, 105828–105828. https://doi.org/10.1016/j.worlddev.2022.105828

Chakrabarty, H., Ray, P., & Pal, P. (2021). The Covid-19 pandemic and economic stimulus in India: Has it been a hostage of macroeconomic complications? *International Review of Applied Economics, 35*(6), 796–812. https://doi.org/10.1080/02692171.2021.1905786

Conefrey, T., McInerney, N., O'reilly, G., & Walsh, G. (2021). Easing the pain? estimating the economic impact of domestic and global policy responses to the covid-19 pandemic. *Economic and Social Review, 52*(2), 161–191. Retrieved from www.scopus.com

Dasgupta, D., & Rajeev, M. (2020). Paradox of a supply constrained keynesian equilibrium the COVID-19 case. *Economic and Political Weekly*, 22–27.

Dixon, P. B., & Rimmer, M. T. (2021). Coping with seasonality in a quarterly CGE model: COVID-19 and US agriculture. *Australian Journal of Agricultural and Resource Economics, 65*(4), 802-821.

Eichenbaum, M. S., Rebelo, S., & Trabandt, M. (2022). Epidemics in the New Keynesian model. *Journal of Economic Dynamics and Control*, 104334.

Fornaro, L., & Wolf, M. (2020). Covid-19 coronavirus and macroeconomic policy.

Frederic, B., & Rungcharoenkitkul, P. (2020). *Macroeconomic effects of Covid-19: an early review, BIS Bulletins 7*. Bank for International Settlements. https://www.bis.org/publ/bisbull07.pdf

Guerrieri, V., Lorenzoni, G., Straub, L., & Werning, I. (2022). Macroeconomic implications of COVID-19: Can negative supply shocks cause demand shortages? *American Economic Review, 112*(5), 1437–1474.

Keogh-Brown, M. R., Jensen, H. T., Edmunds, W. J., & Smith, R. D. (2020). The impact of Covid-19, associated behaviours and policies on the UK economy: A computable general equilibrium model. *SSM-population health, 12*, 100651.

Kubota, S (2021). The macroeconomics of COVID-19 exit strategy: the case of Japan. *The Japanese Economic Review, 72*, 651–682. https://doi.org/10.1007/s42973-021-00091-x

Lenoël, C., & Young, G. (2021). *Modelling the impact of Covid-19 on the UK economy: an application of a disaggregated New-Keynesian model* (No. 531). National Institute of Economic and Social Research.

McKibbin, W., & Fernando, R. (2021). The global macroeconomic impacts of COVID-19: Seven scenarios. *Asian Economic Papers, 20*(2), 1-30.

Onik, M. M. H., Islam, M. S., Hasan, M. M., Uddin, A. (2021). Survival of Bangladesh economy during covid-19 recession with the use of technology: An application of Keynesian Approach. *American International Journal of Supply Chain Management, 2*(1), 1–22.

Padilla, J. (2020). A Keynesian antitrust response to the COVID-19 crisis. *Journal of Antitrust Enforcement*.

Pollitt, H., Lewney, R., Kiss-Dobronyi, B., & Lin, X. (2021). Modelling the economic effects of COVID-19 and possible green recovery plans: A post-Keynesian approach. *Climate Policy, 21*(10), 1257–1271.

Romana, I. E. (2020). Keynesian models of depression. Supply shocks and the COVID-19 Crisis. *arXiv preprint* arXiv:2007.07353.

Rungcharoenkitkul, P. (2021). Macroeconomic effects of COVID-19: A mid-term review. *Pacific Economic Review Wiley., 26*, 439–458. https://doi.org/10.1111/1468-0106.12372

Tobin, J. (1975). Keynesian models of recession and depression. *The American Economic Review, 65*(2), 195-202.

Yoshino, N., Gopakumar, K. U., Paramanik, R. N., Taghizadeh-Hesary, F., Revilla, M., & Ram, K. E. (2022). A New Keynesian AD-AS Model for India, Incorporating the Effect of Covid-19 Pandemic. In *Studies in International Economics and Finance* (pp. 21–41). Springer

# Contact Intensity, Unemployment, and Finite Change—The Case of Entertainment Sector Under Pandemic: A General Equilibrium Approach

**Sugata Marjit and Gouranga Das**

## 1 Introduction and Motivation

The pandemic has jolted the world economy severely, with disruptions on both the demand and the supply side. The trade-offs triggered by the pandemic—health versus wealth, labor-elimination versus labor-saving technology, online (virtual) vis-à-vis offline activities, etc.—are harsh. It has affected trade, employment, human capital, and overall economic performance across nations. For obvious reasons, nothing has attracted more attention than COVID-19 and its ripple effects since 2020 till now. However, within a nation across different sub-sectors, the impacts are diverse. The specific aspect of the pandemic that is relevant for sectoral performance is the riskiness or uncertainty of contagion with apprehension of spread of disease due to possibilities of close contact among the customers (demanders/buyers), firms, or service providers (organizing production combining labor, technology, and machines) and between different groups of people.

As for organizing production, economic activities involve employment of labors of different types in different sectors, and their interaction, 'contact intensity (CI)' of sectors is a crucial factor for differences in impacts across sectors. Sectors requiring 'teamwork' or 'customer-proximity' suffer most (Koren & Peto, 2020). Some sectors contract more than the others, while switching to automation to reduce human interaction or replacing unskilled can displace workers. All these depend on the nature of the

S. Marjit
Indian Institute of Foreign Trade, 1583, Chowbaga Canal Side Rd, Madurdaha, Chowbaga, Kolkata, West Bengal 700100, India
e-mail: sugata@iift.edu

CesIfo, Munich, Germany

G. Das (✉)
Department of Economics, Hanyang University, ERICA campus. 55 Hanyang-Daehak-ro, Sangrok-gu, Gyeonggi-Do 15588, South Korea
e-mail: ggd@hanyang.ac.kr

 
A. Raychaudhuri and A. Ghose (eds.), *Managing Pandemic and Correcting Development Fundamentals*, India Studies in Business and Economics,
https://doi.org/10.1007/978-981-19-8680-2_3

industries, for example, broadly speaking, whether it is agriculture, manufacturing and services, as well as sub-sectors under these broad classifications.

However, thanks to digitization led by ICT and sprawling of virtual or online trade (see Marjit et al., 2020, 2022); intensity of contact is much less for organizing production remotely. As sectoral adjustments take different length of run depending on the scope of exposure due to physical proximity and contact-intensive nature of the occupations, we will consider a core model and then, outline possible extensions to capture medium and long run impact evaluation of pandemic shocks. Typically, we start with a relatively short or medium run where specificity of factors matter significantly before showing the case of long run where skill switching could occur.[1] Our focus is on the cultural or entertainment sector as this sector suffered from major setback due to Coronavirus abatement strategy emphasizing on social distancing.

In this paper, by employing 3-sectors, 4-factors general equilibrium model (Jones, 1965, 1971, Marjit & Jones, 1990, Samuelson 1971-to name some of them), we highlight on how CI could affect employment, output, and wage-differentials across skill types of workers. As background and motivation, Sect. 2 offers some empirical studies across developed and developing world as a background literature. Section 3 develops a core model serving as benchmark. Section 4 offers analysis of pandemic-induced shocks and consequent final changes in the entertainment sector, affecting employment of workers engaged in that sector. Section 5 concludes.

## 2 Pandemic-Led Impact on Creative Sectors: Current Literature and Empirical Facts

COVID-19 has opened Pandora's Box by exposing us with numerous trade-offs affecting socio-economic and political landscapes. Earle (2020a, 2020b) has been an exhaustive study that came out readily covering issues such as effects of Coronavirus on financial markets, mortality and inequality, human development, medical care, trade war, limits of monetary and fiscal policy, etc., as well as paths to economic recovery. McCann and Vorley (2021) are another important volume exploring the

[1] It is quite realistic that a doctor or surgeon or a professor (in any discipline) with musical talent or artistic acumen could choose the medical profession or the role of an educator as primary source of earning (occupation), while the other extra-mural talent provides mental solace to supplement the first activity as returns to skill. Role of the creative or cultural sector for advancing development and generating cultural wealth for human development is discussed recently by Kabanda (2018). However, investing time for her/his to switch will take some time—not substantial though—to make the first profession secondary, while s/he makes transition between two different sorts of skills. On the other hand, for a musician or theatrical personality with no formal training in say, profession like surgery or computer programming, s/he cannot do so easily. However, s/he can switch to different occupation—as and when the crisis hits her/his profession devastatingly—that is, imperfect but closely substitutable profession such as, learning some 'mechanical' skills to run on a virtual or online platform. Such an *inter-occupational switching* takes much longer time and eventually could emerge under dire necessity for survival. For extension, we could outline such case later in extension where same skill could 'work' in both the sectors such as, online or performing arts.

impact of uncertainty related to COVID-19 and its impact on firms' productivity, skill development, shift to online consumption via behavioral changes, etc.

As a result, with the spread of the contagion after the initial outbreak of the contagion, several measures were adopted as part of containment strategy. Lockdowns (total or partial), social distancing, and adopting hygiene and health standards are imperative adopted all over the world with more or less similar policy regulation in practice. This has caused repercussions across different sectors. Most contact-intensive sectors are agriculture (10%), construction (87%), services (80%), manufacturing (63%), electricity (47%), and mining (46%) (Deodhar, 2020).Recent Economic times report surveys that without vaccine, suboptimal levels of operation of some sectors are due to 'consumer wariness' (due to risk of infection and voluntary spatial/social distancing), where contact intensity (CI) of final demand is high like in airports, cinema, opera, entertainment, and shopping malls. CI of services differs across groups with high CI of final demand in trade, tourism, etc. For manufacturing, on the contrary, has low CI of final demand (6%), but CI of supply chain is high for labor-intensive production process such as textile manufacturing and food. As per the recent Economic Survey, contact-intensive service sub-sectors—tourism, aviation, hospitality, trade, hotels, transport, communication, and services—contracted by 31.5% in 2020–21, with overall contraction by 16% only in the first-half of 2020–21. It is projected that gross value-added (GVA) of service sector will contract by 8.8% in 2020–21 (Press Trust of India, 2021). Nam and Lee (2021) in the South Korean context that compared to the financial crisis in 2008, COVID-19 decreased employment rate by 0.82 percentage point and increased unemployment rate by 0.29 percentage point.

Whether be it developed or developing country, developing countries suffer more from lockdowns than the developed countries and with shares of 'informal sector' and SMES being 70% of total employment and 30% of GDP (Fairlie, 2020; Peterson, 2021). By constructing 'physical proximity intensity index' and 'occupational CI index', (Famiglietti et al. 2020; Leibovici et al. 2020) have shown in the context of USA that non-essential CI-industries have suffered most from job losses. Opera and entertainment is one such non-essential CI sector, and hence is expected to suffer from decline in activities or jobs, while supply chain related health care, utilities, and food are CI, but essential, and going online or virtual trade does help these to flourish. Glocker and Piribauer (2021) have estimated output losses in a cross-country study of 130 nations due to contact intensity of services and spatial distancing. Several studies have empirically documented heterogeneous effects of COVID-19 on the labor market—employment, sectoral differences, and output. For example, Kugler et al. (IZA, June 2021), Koren and Peto (2020). has shown that even with digitization or spread of ICT, some industries are totally paralyzed with non-pharmaceutical interventions. To quote them: '*employment losses have been largest in sectors that rely heavily on consumer contact and where the contacts dropped the most: retails, hotels, and restaurants, arts and entertainment and schools. Our results can help quantify the economic costs of social distancing.* (pg. 1)'. Barrero et al. (2021a, 2021b) find that due to multiple waves, 20% of work will be work-from-home (WFH) after the pandemic compared with 5 percent in the pre-pandemic period due mainly to 'lingering concerns about crowds and contagion risks and a pandemic-driven surge in technological innovations that support WFH'. Consequences of such WFH by the privileged, professional high-skilled class as opposed to the underprivileged or informal, unskilled workers struggling for survival due to lack of work opportunities could lead to a different mode of inter-class dependence thanks to herd-immunity by the latter (Marjit & Das, 2022). As more WFH will stay, and as more automation is adopted apprehension of rise in inequality with displacement of low-skilled workers without alternative formal employment is a major concern (Sedik & Yoo, 2021, Maarjit & Das, 2021).

Hu and Zhang (2021) used financial data to show in a cross-country study that firm performance suffered during 2020—2021 especially in countries with worse healthcare systems, and less sophisticated financial systems, and low quality institutions. In addition, high degree of uncertainty has stronger adverse effects on firms. Most importantly, the study finds that 'devastating effects' on business performance originates from both supply and demand sides. Due to the fear of the customers about the spread of the disease, the demand side impacts are more felt in the services and cultural sectors, while bankruptcy and distress in organizing production affect SMES and corporate performance supply shocks come into force, thus, reinstating the role of 'general equilibrium' adjustments via COVID-19. Further, the role of 'demand-deficient recession' where overreaction of demand to supply shock is emphasized. In the context of Japan, Joji (2021) has also explored the role of preventive measured imposing constraints on social and economic activities causing 'demand slump' as well as drop in exports and production thanks to 'precipitous' decline of economic activities, contraction of the world economy and trade. Das et al. (2021) have analyzed the impact of pandemic on inequality in general for 1995–2017 for 70 countries to highlight how COVID-19 could trigger such impacts. Court et al. (2021) have also analyzed the case of 'dampened economic activity' due to preventive measures and consumer wariness on 'non-essential' sectors as well as 'decreased production' affecting other industries. In fact, they show that '*for each 1% decline in the demand for non-essential products, the GINI index across nations is expected to rise by 0.3%. That is, global inequality is likely to rise, contradicting some earlier findings. Finally, we show that economies with less-diverse sets of industries are more vulnerable to such global shocks*'. Other studies that discuss this kind of adverse effects on sectors and their adjustability for survival are Sheridan et al. (2020), Hou et al. (2021), Bartik et al. (2020), Hardin (2021). Adbi et al. (2022) have shown how an unanticipated global shock like pandemic can change the business environment faced by the foreign multinational firms as well as the domestic rival firms based on inadequate industry or health infrastructure, heterogeneity in economic resources, and political alignment. Joyce and Xu (2020) in another study highlighted the exposure of workers and COVID-19-led lockdowns. Jayaram et al. (2020) present the cases in the African context showing the lives versus livelihood trade-offs. In an important study, Buers et al. (2020) considered a model with labor market and financial market frictions to show that non-essential firms suffer most without government subsidies and/or frictions in the labor market to revert to previous job. With permanent sectoral reallocation, the severity of recession is obvious (Baqaee and Emmanuel (2021)).

From all these studies, it is clear that contact intensity—either from final demand side or from supply chains to organize production—is less where labor intensity is less in production, and where remotely performable operation or activities have higher share in final output. In that sense, entertainment sector has high CI, while manufacturing has much less CI, and online sector has least CI. A general equilibrium framework is necessary to capture such aspects. With the onset of COVID-19 crisis, voluminous literatures have emerged dealing with many aspects. As per Conley and Johnson (2021), the dimension of such research is enormous with 142,000 articles over a year and one article per 4 min. Most of these deal with causal relationships among factors with 'big data' and/or econometric exercises. This empiricism is useful exercises exploring the interrelationships among economic variables as well as health-related factors providing rich arrays of information. Conley and Johnson (2021) urge for research going beyond the 'causal revolution' to comprehend 'generalizability' based on the findings in order to address 'longstanding questions in the social sciences'. Ours is an attempt to fill this gap so that any exogenous shock alike pandemic or unanticipated adversity can affect an endogenous system encompassing various economic activities.

However, to the best of our knowledge, providing a framework to theoretically analyze such evidences have not been attempted so far, and that could throw light on the ensuing impacts of COVID-19-led recessionary disruptions. Although Camera and Gioffre (2021) offered an analytical framework based on 'random matching', they explored the impact of lockdowns on contagion prevention and healthcare costs and social welfare via income generation. Our value addition lies in offering an economy-wide repercussion via interlinked endogenous system, and in what follows, we model such ripple effects of the pandemic.

## 3 Modeling Frameworks for Short and Long Run Impact Evaluation

A benchmark model is laid out in this section. This is the core of our analytical framework. Subsequently, by amending some assumptions, we suggest in a more realistic fashion some closely related variant structures to capture some episodes of the pandemic-related adjustments. As the nature of production entails specific factor where different sectors employ workers with diverse skill sets, Heckscher-Ohlin-Samuelson (HOS, henceforth) production structure is inadequate to capture it. For example, the entertainment or the culture sector needs specific skills (opera singer, ballet dancer, or a theater personality needs skills which is not necessary to run an online or virtual trade requiring expertise in software or programming like engineers do). However, to handle multiple level of skills across laborers and multiple outputs, we go beyond the standard HOS types to propose a mixed specific factor hybrid model a la Marjit (1990, 2009), Jones and Marjit (1992, 2009), Marjit and

Das (2021), Marjit and Acharyya (2003), Jones (2019), Das et al. (2020), to name a few.

Typically, from the facts summarized in Sects. 1 and 2, we could envisage the followings:

(i) *contact-intensive industries shrink due to restrictions on physical mobility and hence, contact intensity of production/supply chain disrupts activities*;
(ii) *contact intensity of final demand causes entertainment industry to contract or vanish*;
(iii) *no adverse substantial changes (such as lack of demand) of activities in the sectors where e-commerce/e-business or online services expansion occurs, thanks to digitization, will flourish.*

All these will have repercussions in the labor market creating unemployment and/or underemployment, which is the focus of the present analysis.

## 3.1 Core Model

Consider three sectors, viz. virtual or online sector ($X$), entertainment sector ($Y$), and a manufacturing sector ($Z$). $X$ uses specific types of software experts or those with competence in programming ($S_x$) along with capital ($K$), while cultural sector $Y$ needs experts with skills in performing arts or creativity of different sorts ($S_y$) along with capital. For $Z$-sector, we consider unskilled or semi-skilled workers ($L$) who are engaged in producing machine tools in the MSME sectors characterized by medium or low-tech sophistication along with capital. However, this sector—under the current scenario—might face the threat of automation displacing the low skilled. Capital ($K$) is mobile across $X$, $Y$, and $Z$, while $S_x$, $S_y$, and L are specific factors, without intersectoral mobility in the medium or short run.[2] Thus, the production setup is:

$$X = X(S_X, K)$$
$$Y = Y(S_Y, K)$$
$$Z = Z(L, K)$$

Assume a small open economy (SOE)—a price-taker in the world market—with perfectly competitive markets. Technology is neo-classical with CRS and diminishing marginal productivity (DMR) to factor inputs. Given $Z$, $X$, and $Y$ are readily identified as 2-sector-3-factor textbook style specific factor model (Jones, 1971,

[2] Assumption of malleability of '$K$' across $X$, $Y$, and $Z$ is driven by simplicity because our primary objective is to model the impact on the labor markets. Not only that, '$K$' can also be considered as 'financial capital' providing funds to run these sectors (see Marjit & Das, 2021). Of course, realistically nature of physical capital used in different sectors can be different. Also, we can think of '$K$' as ICT capital or digital capital enabling all kinds of activities.

Caves et al., 2002). One pertinent feature of this type of structure is that each pair of sectors represents a 2-sectors × 3-sectors specific factor (SF) subsystem (SFS). Following notations are used to describe model:

$X$: Skilled online sector
$Y$: Skilled entertainment sector
$Z$: Manufacturing or MSME sector
$P_j$: Exogenously given prices for $j$th final good, $\forall j \in \{X, Y, Z\}$
$W$: Unskilled labor's wage in the host country
$W_X, W_Y$: Skilled labor's wage in the host in $X$- and $Y$-sectors. Assume originally, $W_x > W$, $W_Y > W$.[3]
$r$: Return to homogeneous capital.
$a_i^j$ = $i$th input required to produce 1 unit of $j$th good, $i = L, S_X, S_Y, K$; and $j \in \{X, Y, Z\}$.
$\Theta_{lj} = w_1 a_i^j / P_j$ is the distributive share of $l$th labor types in the production of $j$, $\forall l \in \{S_X, S_Y, L\}$;
$\theta_{kj} = r_k a_k^j / P_j$ is the distributive share of owner of capital $K$;
$\lambda_{ij} = \frac{a_i^j N_j}{f_i}$ = $j$th commodity's input share in $i$th factor's endowment, where $N$ is generic output and f is generic endowment.
$\overline{K}$, $\overline{S_x}$, $\overline{L}$, and $\overline{S_y}$ are given factor endowments of respective primary inputs.
'∧' = proportional changes for variable, say $V$, such that generically.
$\hat{V} = \frac{dV}{V}$. Full employment ensures:

$$a_{SX} X = \overline{S_X} \tag{1}$$

$$a_{SY} Y = \overline{S_Y} \tag{2}$$

$$a_{LZ} Z = \overline{L} \tag{3}$$

$$a_{KX}.X + a_{KY}.Y + a_{KZ}.Z = \overline{K} \tag{4}$$

From (4), rewrite: $K_X + K_Y + K_Z = \overline{K}$ and hence, we write:

$$K_X + K_Y = \overline{K} - K_Z \tag{4a}$$

Competitive equilibrium with zero pure profit condition implies that price equations are:

---

[3] Skilled labor attracts considerable higher wage than their unskilled counterpart, although levels are *lower than* the rich nations. Skill-biased trade or technical change are several reasons that explain wage gaps. Here, nature of skills differs across sectors and with social distancing or different types of physical proximity, skilled occupations also face imminent c dangers in sectors like opera, group theater, etc., where chances of spread loom are large. In case of manufacturing, such barriers exist too.

$$W_X a_{SX} + r a_{KX} = P_X \tag{5}$$

$$W_Y a_{SY} + r a_{KY} = P_Y \tag{6}$$

$$W a_{LZ} + r a_{KZ} = P_Z \tag{7}$$

## 3.2 Equilibrium and Comparative Statics

From Eq. 4, given $S_x$ and $S_y$ for the specific factor subsystem (i.e., $X$ and $Y$), if $K_z$ rises (or falls), $K_x + K_Y$ falls (or, rises) from the supply side and vice versa. Correspondingly, '$r$' rises (or, falls). Thus, in the $r$-$K_z$ space, we trace a positively sloped curve (*AA*) (see Fig. 1). However, in Z, given $L$, $K_z$ rises/falls, means $r$ falls/rises. So, in the $r$-$K_z$ space, we get 'BB' with downward slope. Figure 1 determines $K_z$ and '$r$'. Also, 7 equations determine 7 variables, viz., $W_X$, $W_y$, $W$, $r$; and outputs ($X$, $Y$, and $Z$). $a_{ij}$ ($W_X$, $W_y$, $W$, $r$)'s are determined endogenously via CRS that describes the general equilibrium (GE) system.

Consider ex post changes due to social distancing and lockdown scenarios, and their GE effects. The online sector ($X$) is the *numeraire* sector. We consider proportional changes for the equation system (1)–(7), and employing envelope condition (Jones, 1965, 1971), to derive:

$$\theta_{SX}\widehat{W}_X + \theta_{KX}\hat{r} = \widehat{P}_X = 0 \tag{8}$$

$$\theta_{SY}\widehat{W}_Y + \theta_{KY}\hat{r} = \widehat{P}_Y \tag{9}$$

$$\theta_{LZ}\widehat{W} + \theta_{KZ}\hat{r} = \widehat{P}_Z \tag{10}$$

where

$$\theta_{SX} + \theta_{KX} = 1, \theta_{SY} + \theta_{KY} = 1, \theta_{LZ} + \theta_{KZ} = 1 \tag{11}$$

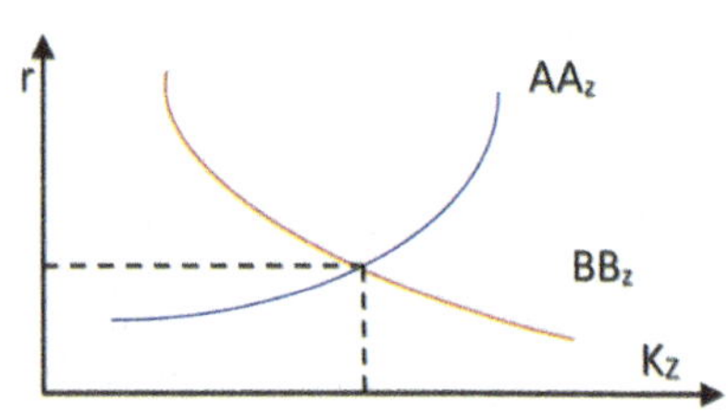


**Fig. 1** Determination of r-Kz

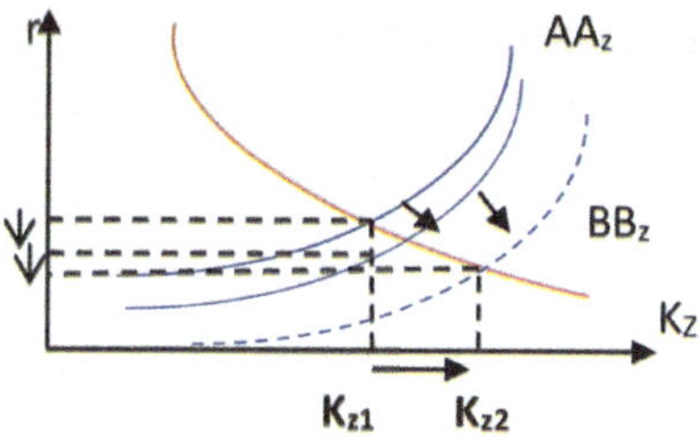


**Fig. 2** Shift of *AA* curve in *r*-*Kz* space

### 3.2.1 *Pandemic-Led Adverse Effects on Entertainment Sector: Fall in* $P_Y$

Suppose '$(1-q)$' is the probability that a sector is *not* affected by the pandemic, $q \in [0, 1]$. In this case, as the probability of exposure is higher due to nature of contact-intensiveness, the higher is the chances of output loss as $q \to 1$ (equivalently, $(1-q) \to 0$). These are non-essential goods, where income elasticity of demand (like luxury goods) is high. Loss of income due to sluggish economic activities will dampen demand too, causing decline in prices for show/performances. Demand will shrink and expenditure will fall, even with lower prices (even if price falls for *Y*-sector, demand inelastic). Ceteris paribus, as $P_y$ falls, *Y*-sector contracts with fall in '$K_y$'. Given the *same* $K_z$, this adverse price shock (with $P_x = 1$ as numeraire) will cause '$r$' to fall and '$AAz$' will shift right downward (Fig. 2). '$K$' released from '$Y$' sector will move to $K_x$ and $K_z$.

As '$K$' moves into $X$ and $Z$, marginal productivity (MP) of labor types in $X$ and $Z$ rises. Now with $\hat{P}_X = 0$, $\hat{P}_Z = 0$ as '$r$' falls, $W_x$ and W rises, while $W_Y$ falls. Thus, three possibilities might emerge as below: (a) $W_X/W_Y$ rises implying changes in inequality in the skilled labor types itself so that intra-skill wage inequality increases depending on respective skill-shares in production; (b) as $W_x$ and W rises, depending on $K$-intensity of these sectors $W_x \geq$, or $\leq W$; (c) $\frac{W_Y}{W}$ falls, improving wage inequality between entertainment and casual sectors. However, if $Y$ is $S_y$ intensive, via Stolper-Samuelson effect $W_y$ falls by more.[4] As $\widehat{Y} < 0$; $\hat{r} < 0 \Rightarrow \widehat{W}_X > 0$, $\widehat{W}_Y < 0$. For SF-subsystem comprising $X$-$Y$ sectors, it is straightforward to write a la Jones (1971), $\hat{W}_Y < \hat{P}_Y < \hat{r} < 0 < \hat{P}_X = 0 < \hat{W}_X$. Thus, skilled performers in the entertainment sectors are worse off, while those in the online sectors with software expertise are better off. For capital owners suffering from decline in price fall are caught in the middle with its real return increasing in terms of the skilled labors in the $Y$-sector, while suffering compared to those in the online.

[4] Here, if *Py* falls, ceteris paribus, we can show that wage inequality aggravates between *X*-*Z* sectors and *X*-*Y* sectors, while for the performance industry, it could suffer—due to abysmally low demand—as workers are chucked off, and hence unemployment generates so that even the unskilled workers gain at the expense of those in the entertainment sector. See Marjit and Das (2021, Cesifo).

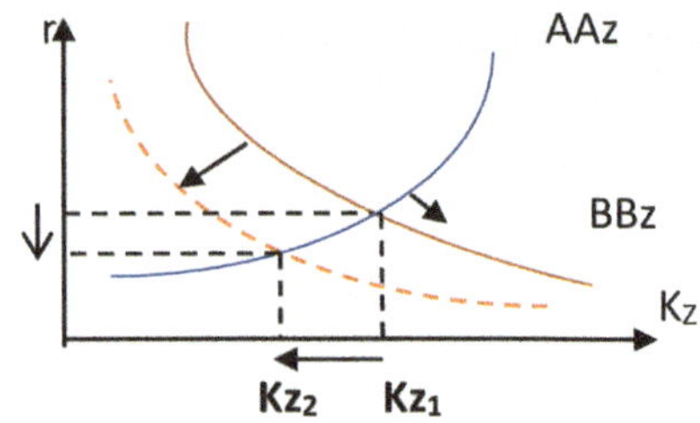


**Fig. 3** Shift of *BB* curve in *r-Kz* space

### 3.2.2 *Adverse Impacts on Casual/Informal Sector: Ceteris Paribus Fall in* $P_Z$

Here, we consider *fall in Pz,* while others remain unchanged. Given *L*, $S_X$, and $S_Y$, output shrinks in this sector and '*W*' falls (if *Z* is *L*-intensive, it will have more pronounced effect). As $K_z$ falls, '*r*' will fall and $(K_x + K_y)$ will rise. *BBz* curve will shift left downward (see Fig. 3).

These changes result in rise in MPs of $S_Y$ and $S_X$, and hence translating into rise in $W_Y$ *and* $W_X$. Depending on share of capital in cost, $W_X$ will rise more than $W_Y$ and $\frac{W_X}{W}$, $\frac{W_Y}{W}$ both rises. This will aggravate wage inequality between skilled and unskilled workers. In this case, unskilled workers are worst affected, while both the skilled occupations gain with more pronounced gainful effects in the skilled sector with higher capital intensity. In both of these cases, here we get interesting impacts with two-pronged nature of wage inequality, viz. between skilled sectors itself as well as between skilled and unskilled. In the context of our chapter, interesting case is the impacts, while both *Y* and *Z* suffer due to pandemic-led policy of social distancing.

### 3.2.3 *Joint Adverse Impact of* $\widehat{P}_Y < 0, \widehat{P}_Z < 0$

Here, we consider with $q \to 1$, $\hat{P}_Y < 0$, $\hat{P}_Z < 0$ conjointly. Definitely, following the preceding discussion, both *AAz* and *BBz* will shift downward. However, impacts on reallocation of '*K*' to other sectors following decline in prices will depend on relative position or relative shifts of the *AA-BB* curves ex post in the *r-*$K_Z$ space. Accordingly, three cases are plausible, viz. (a) $K_Z$ rises, (b) $K_Z$ falls, (c) $K_Z$ does not change. Here, we consider Eqs. (8), (9a), (10a) via shifts of *AAz* and *BBz,* '*r*' falls, triggering alterations in $K_Z$ vis-a-vis *W*/*r* impacts via *AA-BB* shifts (see Fig. 4). Let initially *AA-BB* cross each other at ($K_{z1}$, *r*1). If downward shifts happen in such a way so that $AA_{z1}$ and $BB_{z1}$ intersect that $K_Z$ remains unaltered *(*$\Delta K_Z = 0$*),* then *r*3 < *r*1. Suppose now that the downward shift $AA_{z2}$ is much more than previous case, while BBz1 remains the same ex post, then r falls by more (*r*2 < *r*3 < *r*1), and $\Delta K_Z$ > *0*. Now, think about shifts in $BB_{z2}$ being more pronounced than $BB_{z1}$ so that new $BB_{Z2}$ cuts either $AA_{z1}$ or $AA_{Z2}$ resulting in $\Delta K_Z < 0$. Hence, depending on relative position due to shifts in the wake of fall in $P_Y$ and $P_Z$, $\Delta K_Z \leq 0$, $\Delta K_Z \geq 0$and extent of $\hat{r} < 0$ occurs, and how much $K_Z$ moves matter.

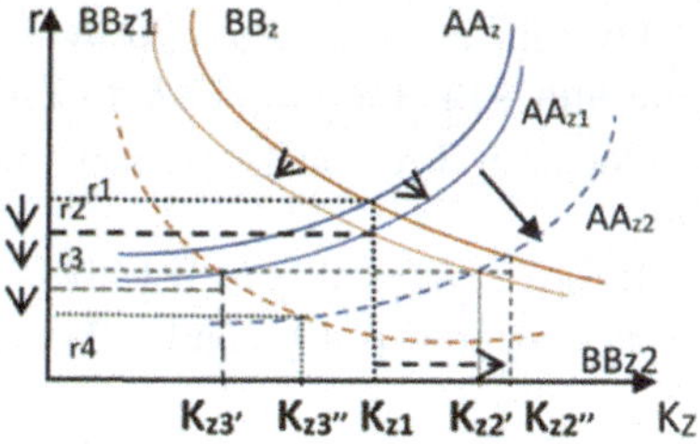


**Fig. 4** Joint shift of *AA-BB* curve in *r-Kz* space

However, movements in '*K*' across sectors trigger changes in MP of labor types and hence, changes in respective wages of skill types vis-à-vis the unskilled ones.

**Proposition 1** Given $\widehat{P}_X = 0$, with q $\rightarrow$ 1, $\widehat{P}_Y < 0$, $\widehat{P}_Z < 0$, it must hold that:

$\left(\widehat{\frac{W_X}{W_Y}}\right) > 0$, but $\left(\widehat{\frac{W_X}{W}}\right)$ and $\left(\widehat{\frac{W_Y}{W}}\right)$ are ambiguous depending on cost share of capital in the respective concerned sectors; however, wage inequality between *X–Y*, *X–Z*, and *Y–Z* sectors would worsen *iff* $\theta_{KX} > \theta_{KY}$ and $\theta_{KY} > \theta_{KZ}$.

***Proof*** Consider first $\widehat{P}_Y < 0 = \widehat{P}_X$, the standard result via SF-subsystem (SFS) implies (Jones, 1971; Samuelson, 1971): $\widehat{W}_Y < \widehat{P}_Y < \hat{r} < 0 < \widehat{W}_X$. Similarly, for $\widehat{P}_Z < 0 = \widehat{P}_X$. case, $\widehat{W} < \widehat{P}_Z < \hat{r} < 0 < \widehat{W}_X$. Thus, movements in real wages for $\widehat{W}_X - \widehat{W}_Y$, $\widehat{W}_X - \widehat{W}$, $\widehat{W}_Y - \widehat{W}$ occur.

- If (i) $\widehat{P}_Y < \widehat{P}_Z < 0 = \widehat{P}_X \Rightarrow \widehat{W}_Y < \widehat{P}_Y < \widehat{P}_Z < \hat{r} < 0 < \widehat{W} < \widehat{W}_X$. Here (*W*/*r*), (*Wx*/*Wy*), (Wx/W) rise along with rise in (*W*/*Wy*).
- On the contrary, if (ii) $\hat{P}_Z < \hat{P}_Y < 0 = \hat{P}_X \Rightarrow \hat{W} < \hat{P}_Z < \hat{P}_Y < \hat{r} < 0 < \hat{W}_Y < \hat{W}_X$. Here (*W*/*r*) falls, but (*Wx*/*Wy*), (*Wx*/*W*) rise along with rise in (*Wy*/*W*).

Now, from Fig. 4, in the presence of joint effect, movements of '*K*' across sectors—from *Y*- and/or *Z*-sectors to *X*—depend on the extent of relative position (or shifts) of $AA_z$–$BB_z$.

In case of (i), we see $\widehat{P}_Y < \widehat{P}_Z < 0 = \widehat{P}_X \Rightarrow \widehat{Y} < 0, \widehat{Z} < 0, \Delta K_Y < 0 \Rightarrow \Delta K_Z > 0, \Delta K_X \geq 0$ because $AA_z$ shifts by more than BBz (see Fig. 3). Thus, $\widehat{W} > \hat{r}, \widehat{W}_X > \widehat{W}_Y, \widehat{W} > \widehat{W}_Y, \widehat{W}_X > \widehat{W}$.

In case of (ii), we see $\widehat{P}_Z < \widehat{P}_Y < 0 = \widehat{P}_X \Rightarrow \widehat{Y} < 0, \widehat{Z} < 0, \Delta K_Y < 0 \Rightarrow \Delta K_Z < 0, \Delta K_X \geq 0$ as $BB_z$ shifts down by more than *AAz* (see Fig. 4). Thus, $\widehat{W} < \hat{r}, \widehat{W}_X > \widehat{W}_Y, \widehat{W}_Y > \widehat{W}, \widehat{W}_X > \widehat{W}$.

However, if $\hat{P}_Z = \hat{P}_Y < 0 = \hat{P}_X$,, then $AA_z$ and $BB_z$ shifts equi-proportionately downward (Fig. 4) so that, $\Delta K_Z = 0, \Delta K_X \geq 0$. Here $\left(\widehat{\frac{W}{r}}\right) = 0$ and $\left(\widehat{\frac{W_X}{W_Y}}\right) > 0$, $\left(\widehat{\frac{W}{W_Y}}\right) > 0$.

Overall, $\widehat{P}_Y < 0, \widehat{P}_Z < 0 \Rightarrow \widehat{Y} < 0, \widehat{Z} < 0$, and relative decline in their prices determines the mobility of $K$ to $Z$ vis-à-vis $X$ sectors and the extent of intersectoral reallocation. Previously, we saw that if $\theta_{KX} > \theta_{KY}, \widehat{W}_X > \widehat{W}_Y > \widehat{W}$ when $\hat{P}_Z < 0$ and.

If $\theta_{KX} > \theta_{KZ}, \widehat{W}_X > \widehat{W}_Y, \widehat{W}_X > \widehat{W} \Rightarrow \widehat{W}_X > \widehat{W} > \widehat{W}_Y$ when $\widehat{P}_Y < 0$.

Now from Eqs. (9a) and (10a), on simplification, we can write:

$$\widehat{W}_Y - \widehat{W} = \left(\widehat{P}_Y/\theta_{SY} - \widehat{P}_Z/\theta_{LZ}\right) + \hat{r}\left(\frac{\theta_{KZ} - \theta_{KY}}{\theta_{SY}\theta_{LZ}}\right) \tag{11a}$$

If $\theta_{KZ} < \theta_{KY}, \hat{r}\left(\frac{\theta_{KZ}-\theta_{KY}}{\theta_{SY}\theta_{LZ}}\right) > 0$. Hence, $\widehat{W}_Y \geq \widehat{W}\, iff\, \widehat{P}_Y/\theta_{SY} \geq \widehat{P}_Z/\theta_{LZ} \Rightarrow \frac{\widehat{P}_Y}{\widehat{P}_Z} \geq \frac{\theta_{SY}}{\theta_{LZ}}$ and vice versa.

Suppose, $\frac{\hat{P}_Y}{\hat{P}_Z}$ > or < 1, accordingly, $\widehat{W}_Y \geq \widehat{W}$ or, $\widehat{W}_Y \leq \widehat{W}$ $\int$ iff $1 \geq \frac{\theta_{SY}}{\theta_{LZ}} \Rightarrow \theta_{LZ} \geq \theta_{SY} \Rightarrow \theta_{KZ} \leq \theta_{KY}$.

Similarly, using Eqs. (8) and (9),

$$\widehat{W}_X - \widehat{W} = \left(-\widehat{P}_Z/\theta_{LZ}\right) + \hat{r}\left(\frac{\theta_{KZ} - \theta_{KX}}{\theta_{SX}\theta_{LZ}}\right) \tag{12}$$

As $\hat{P}_Z < 0$, $\theta_{SX}\theta_{LZ} > 0$, given $\hat{r} < 0$, $\widehat{W}_X > \widehat{W}$ iff $\theta_{KZ} < \theta_{KX}$.Combining these two conditions, we can write: $\widehat{W}_X > \widehat{W}_Y$ iff $\theta_{KX} > \theta_{KY}$ and $\widehat{W}_Y \geq \widehat{W}$ iff $\theta_{KZ} < \theta_{KX}\theta_{KZ} < \theta_{KX}$

$\Rightarrow \widehat{W}_X > \widehat{W}_Y > \widehat{W}$ iff $\theta_{KX} > \theta_{KY} > \theta_{KZ}$.

**Corollary 1** Given, $\widehat{P}_X = 0, \widehat{P}_Y = 0$, with $q \to 1$, $\widehat{P}_Z < 0$, it must hold that: $\widehat{\left(\frac{W_X}{W_Y}\right)} > 0, \widehat{\left(\frac{W_X}{W}\right)} > 0, \widehat{\left(\frac{W_Y}{W}\right)} > 0$. Skill-unskilled wage gap rises; however, wage inequality between $X$- and $Y$-sectors would worsen iff $\theta_{KX} > \theta_{KY}$. See *Appendix for Proof*.

Inequality is most likely to go up against the entertainment industry's skilled performers. Unskilled or semi-skilled workers—although suffering from absolute decline in wage—are relatively better off compared to the skilled professionals in the entertainment activities, unless automation or digitization displaces them or eliminates their occupation. The core model serves as a useful benchmark to compare and contrast how different less stark assumptions about mobility of labor types (and capital) might alter the consequences of the pandemic. Then, different scenarios could evolve with gradual elapse of time when—depending on the movements of 'displaced' workers and capital—there will be transitional phases during which factor returns will also change. Following section captures such scenarios.

# 4 Variants of the Rudimentary Model

## 4.1 Very Short Run: Immobility of 'K'

For the immediate impact, we need to consider 'very short run', which is different from the rudimentary model with specific skills but mobile capital. In the very short run, for capital, it is too short to move across the sectors so that '*K*' is stuck and hence, three sectors will have three different rate of returns, say, $r_x \neq r_y \neq r_z$. Also, $\overline{W_X}, \overline{W_Y}$ are fixed contractually. Now, given specific skills with expertise are necessary to be absorbed in the *X*- and *Y*- sectors, they can—under dire necessity or with nothing to survive—move to the casual sector *Z*, while the unskilled or casual workers with no competence or innate talent or adequate skills to perform works in *X*- or *Y*- sector cannot move. Hence, there is rigid upward mobility (taking far longer time or impossible) of '*L*', while $S_x$ and $S_y$ have more downward mobility because they can do the work in *Z*-sector requiring no special talent to be trained. This makes possible that $W_x$ and $W_y$ could move to *Z* where '*W*' is flexible unlike in *X*- and *Y*-sector with fixed wages to the skilled. In this scenario, we could get disguised unemployment in *Z*-sector where unemployed skilled workers mostly from Y-sector crowd along with the existing worker ('*L*') to push 'W' further down. If for some reason $W_x$ and $W_y$ decline so much that '*W*' exceeds them, this downward mobility could also happen. Now, the model with the following variations is written as:

$$\overline{S_X} - a_{SX}X = SU_X \tag{1a}$$

$$\overline{S_Y} - a_{SY}Y = SU_Y \tag{2a}$$

$$L = a_{LZ}\,Z = \overline{L} \tag{3a}$$

$$a_{KX}.X + a_{KY}.Y + a_{KZ}.Z = \overline{K} \tag{4}$$

As before:

$$K_X + K_Z = \overline{K} - K_Y \tag{4b}$$

Now, competitive equilibrium with zero pure profit condition implies that ($P =$ AC):

$$\overline{W_X}a_{SX} + r_X a_{KX} = 1 \tag{13}$$

$$r_Y a_{KY} = P_Y - \overline{W_Y}a_{SY} \tag{14}$$

$$Wa_{LZ} = P_Z - r_Z a_{KZ} \tag{15}$$

As $K_x$ and $K_y$ are stuck, with fixed $\overline{W_X}, \overline{W_Y}$, we will have $S_X < \overline{S_X}, S_y < \overline{S_Y}$ causing unemployment in both *X*- and *Y*-sectors ($SU_X$, $SU_Y$). 7 variables: *W*, $r_x$, $r_y$, $r_z$ and outputs (*X*, *Y*, and *Z*) are determined via 7 equations Eqs. (13)–(15) and Eqs. (1a)–(4). $r_x$ is determined from Eq. (13) and $r_y$ from Eq. (14). Given $a_{ij}$'s, from Eq. (14), if $P_y$ falls, $r_y$ will fall given $\overline{W_Y}$ and from Eq. (15), given $r_z$, if $P_z$ falls, *W* will decline. As '*W*' is flex, given $P_z$, $r_z$ will determined as residual.

With $\widehat{P}_Y < 0, \widehat{P}_X = 0, \widehat{P}_Z = 0$, $r_y$ will fall. As '*K*' is stuck, $\widehat{Y} < 0$ causes $S_y$ to be chucked off, moving to *Z*-sector (not to *X* as latent skills cannot be instantaneously adjusted or transformed into productive employment at the same level of efficiency alike $S_x$ with longer years of experience). Consequently, unemployment of $S_y$ ($SU_y$) will rise, but that of $S_x$ ($SU_x$) will remain the same as $\hat{P}_X = \hat{r}_X = 0$. '*W*' will have free fall with double whammy. Interesting thing is rising unemployment of $S_y$ with decline in '*W*' for the casual workers. However, if $P_z$ falls W and $r_z$ will fall proportionately, with no incentive for $S_x$ and $S_y$ to crowd in the *Z*-sector. $SU_y$ and $SU_x$ remain the same. Ex post, $\overline{r_x} > r_y(\hat{P}_Y < 0), \overline{r_x} > r_z(\hat{P}_Z < 0)$. This leads to the following proposition:

**Proposition 2** With $K_x$, $K_y$, $K_z$ being stuck in very short run, and $\overline{W_X}, \overline{W_Y}$ being contractually fixed unemployment in *X*- and *Y*-sectors will force $S_x$ and $S_y$ to move to *Z*-sector due to downward mobility so that: (i) $\widehat{W} < 0$; (ii) with $\widehat{P}_Y < 0$, unemployment in *Y* will increase while unemployment in *X* is unaltered; (iii) with $\widehat{P}_Z < 0$, existing unemployment in $S_x$ and $S_y$ prevails without alteration.

***Proof*** See Appendix for formal proof.

## 4.2 *Longer Run or Medium Run: Intersectorally Mobile 'K'*

In this case, as more time elapses after the pandemic hit hard the sector *Y*, with emergence of online commerce as dominant mode with the prospect of flourishing, suppose '*K*' (construed as 'financial capital')[5] is allowed to move across sectors. More leeway is gradually achieved over longer time frame. However, depending on fixity of $\overline{W_X}, \overline{W_Y}$, and changes of $P_y$ vis-à-vis $P_z$, now the mobility of $S_y$ will happen with the possibility of structural changes in the economy. With finite changes, possibility of vanishing *Y*-sector arises (Marjit and Mandal, 2015; Beladi et al., 2013). Thus, we get:

**Proposition 3** With intersectoral mobility of '*K*', two possibilities could arise when $\widehat{P}_Y < 0$ and/or $\widehat{P}_Z < 0$ (i) iff $W_x$ and $W_y$ remain fixed *Y*-sector collapses with finite

[5] K could be a 'wage fund' where financing occurs as if: $K = W_x S_x + W_y S_y + WL$. See Marjit (2020) and Marjit and Das (2021). Here endowment effect could be analyzed. However, it's beyond the scope of this paper.

change so that only $X$ and $Z$ exist; (ii) if gradually $W_x$ and $W_y$ become unstuck, with flexibility of $W_x$, $W_y$ and W the situation will converge to the benchmark model. Capital cost shares will determine the direction of wage inequality as in Propositions 1 and 2.

***Proof*** See Appendix.

## 4.3 Longest Run: No 'Sy'

With the adverse impacts of pandemic looming large over the medium run, the possibilities of unemployment in $Y$-sector casing displacement to $Z$-sector become graver. Hence, the profession loses charm or attraction. With threat of pandemic, there is lack of investments in 'creative sector' or creative talents in opera or ballet or drama with prospective rate of return being low. As people don't acquire these skills, $\overline{S_Y} \to 0$, with no supply of skilled talent in the entertainment industry. Then with finite change, $Y$ will disappear, while $X$ and $Z$ will survive. Then the new model will be a standard specific factor model with 2-sectors and 3 factors—specific factors skilled virtual experts ($S$), unskilled ($L$), and mobile '$K$' as below:

$$W_s a_s + r a_{KX} = P_X \tag{16}$$

$$W a_{LZ} + r a_{KZ} = P_Z \tag{17}$$

$$a_s X = \overline{S} \tag{18}$$

$$a_L Z = \overline{L} \tag{19}$$

$$a_{KX} X + a_{KZ} Z = \overline{K} \tag{20}$$

Thus, we infer:

**Proposition 4** With $\overline{S}_y \to 0, Y \to 0$ so that there will be finite change with vanishing $Y$-sector, while $X$ and $Z$ will survive resulting in polarization with mostly online and some casual sectors. Like in standard specific factor model (Jones, 1971; Samuelson, 1971), inequality results are standard.

***Proof*** With $\widehat{P}_Z < 0$, $\left(\frac{\widehat{W_s}}{W}\right) > 0$, $\widehat{W} < \widehat{P}_Z < \hat{r} < \widehat{P}_X = 0 < \widehat{W}_s$.[6]

---

[6] With quality differentiation among the artists (opera singer. Ballerina or theater personality, etc.), only the superstars with exceptional talents might survive without moving to $Z$-sector. In this case,

# 5 Concluding Remarks

Automation and labor-elimination or labor-displacement or labor-linking; Hybrid work for future where total work is a combination of offline and online modes (e.g., 2 days offline-3 days online and vice versa or, say, 4 days lock down 3 days semi-lockdown or no lock down at all, giving much more freedom for organizing production so that some ailing or dying sectors could revive than with total shut down or lock down.

Opera sector cannot be automated unlike the manufacturing sector where labor-saving technological change/innovation could reduce the demand for labor in that sector with further fall is wage. Although opera sector does not suffer from such potential effects, but demand from viewers fall and demand is inelastic, as price fall does not increase demand. Supply effect is much stronger as price crash will not stimulate demand due to fear of contagion. Skill switching from artist to different professions. For example, then the entertainment sectors could run on offline days or no lock down phases.

Lack of vaccine is an impediment for contact-intensive sectors to perform suboptimally (Deodhar, 2020). It has been reported that vaccination drive could revive contact-intensive sectors, and that could cause reversals of fortune (Press Trust of India, 2021).Digital contact tracing helps in 'fostering participation' so that entertainment sector or CI sectors could adopt such technology to turn the tide in their favor.

# Appendix

## Appendix for Mathematical Proof

### Proof for Corollary 1

Take (9) to get,

$$\widehat{W}_Y = -\frac{\theta_{KY}}{\theta_{SY}}\hat{r} \tag{9a}$$

$$\hat{W} = \left(\widehat{P}_Z/\theta_{LZ}\right) - \frac{\theta_{KZ}}{\theta_{LZ}}\hat{r} \tag{10a}$$

Using (8) and (9a), $\hat{Z} < 0$ and as $\hat{r} < 0$, $\widehat{W}_X > 0$, $\widehat{W}_Y > 0$, $\widehat{W} < 0$ iff $\theta_{LZ} > \theta_{KZ}$. Thus, $\widehat{W}_X > \widehat{W}_Y$ *iff* $\frac{\theta_{KY}}{\theta_{SY}} < \frac{\theta_{KX}}{\theta_{SX}} \Rightarrow \theta_{KY}.\theta_{SX} < \theta_{KX}.\theta_{SY} \Rightarrow \theta_{KY} < \theta_{KX}$ (QED.)

---

the probability of price falling very low is negligible and only high end sophisticated $Y$-firm will survive, others will turn to casual sector. A continuum of quality differentiated creative talent with highest $W_y$ will draw attraction. $P_y$ might not fall.

**Proof for Proposition 2**

Consider the following equations of change a la Jones (1965, 1971):

$$\theta_{SX}\widehat{W}_X + \theta_{KX}\hat{r}_X = 0 \tag{21}$$

$$\theta_{SY}\widehat{W}_Y + \theta_{KY}\hat{r}_Y = \widehat{P}_Y \tag{22}$$

$$\theta\widehat{W} + \theta_{KZ}\hat{r}_Z = \widehat{P}_Z \tag{23}$$

Here, $\overline{W_X}, \overline{W_Y}$ implies $\widehat{W}_X = 0 = \widehat{W}_Y$ so that from Eq. (21), $\hat{r}_X = 0$.

From Eq. (22), $\hat{r}_Y = \widehat{P}_Y/\theta_{KY}$. When, $\widehat{P}_Y \leq 0, \hat{r}_Y \leq 0$, with $\theta_{KY} > 0$.

From Eq. (23), $\widehat{W} < 0$, when $\widehat{P}_Z \leq 0$.

Also, $\hat{r}_Z = \widehat{P}_Z/\theta_{KZ} - \frac{\theta_{LZ}}{\theta_{KZ}}\widehat{W} \Rightarrow \hat{r}_Z = -\frac{\theta_{LZ}}{\theta_{KZ}}\widehat{W} > 0$ when $\widehat{P}_Z = 0$. But $\widehat{P}_Z < 0 \Rightarrow \hat{r}_Z < 0$. (QED).

**Proof for Proposition 3**

**Proof**: (i) Here, from (21) as before, $\widehat{P}_Y < 0, \hat{r}_Y < 0$, with $\theta_{KY} > 0$. As $\widehat{P}_X = 0, \hat{r}_X > \hat{r}_Y$, higher rate of return in $X$ induces $K_y$ to move to $X$. All $Ky$ moves primarily to $X$-sector, and unemployment of $S_x$ will fall having more $K_x$ at their disposal. As long as $W_x$ and $W_y$ remain fixed, unemployment in $S_y$ will rise, all moving to $Z$-sector to join '$L$', causing $\widehat{W} < 0$. Eventually with mobility of '$K$', $r_x = r_y = r_z = r$ (say) will be established. Once '$r$' is determined '$W$' will be determined. Here fixed $W_y$ at high level causes unemployment in $S_y$ to rise, resulting in reallocation of $S_y$ to $Z$ due to large shocks, and will cause transformation at the expense of $Y$-sector, so that all opera artist or theater personality becomes casual worker. Also, Eq. (3a) can be modified to write:

$a_{LZ}.\, Z + a_{sy}.\, Z = \overline{L} + SU_y = L' \Rightarrow \widehat{Z} > 0.$

From Eq. (1a),

$$a_{SX}X = \overline{S_X} - SU_X \Rightarrow \widehat{X} = \frac{d\overline{S_X} - d(SU_X)}{\overline{S_X} - SU_X} = \frac{-d(SU_X)}{\overline{S_X} - SU_X} < 0,$$

as $d(SU_X) < 0 \Rightarrow \widehat{X} > 0$.

Also, from Eq. (2a),

$a_{SY}Y = \overline{S_Y} - SU_Y \Rightarrow \widehat{Y} = \frac{d\overline{S_Y} - d(SU_Y)}{\overline{S_Y} - SU_Y} = \frac{-d(SU_Y)}{\overline{S_Y} - SU_Y} < 0$, as $d(SU_Y) > 0$.

(ii) Suppose $K_x$ rises causing MP of $S_x$ to rise, and if excess demand for online product and services pick up so that demand for $S_x$ shoots up very high, resulting in $\widehat{W}_X > 0$, and $\widehat{W}_Y < 0$. Because $K_y$ moves out, MP of $S_y$ falls causing $W_y$ to decline. As, during this transitional phase, '$r$' goes up, $W_y$ might falls to a much lower level so that $W_Y < \overline{W_Y}, W_X > \overline{W_X}$. Then unemployment of $S_y$ might fall, and the situation will be alike the rudimentary model in Sect. 3.1. $Y$-sector will not suffer from finite change. As before, $\left(\frac{\widehat{W}_X}{W_Y}\right) > 0$, $\left(\frac{\widehat{W}_X}{W}\right) > 0$. $\left(\frac{\widehat{W}_Y}{W}\right) > 0$ depending on $\theta_{KY} > \theta_{KZ}$. with $\widehat{P}_Z < 0$, $\widehat{W} < 0$.

Proof is similar to Proposition 2. (QED).

## References


Adbi, A., Chatterjee, C., & Mishra, A. (2022). How do MNEs and domestic firms respond locally to a global demand shock? Evidence from a pandemic. *Management Science*. Articles in Advance, pp. 1–23.

Baqaee, D. & Emmanuel, F. (2021). Keynesian production networks and covid-19 crisis: A simple benchmark. In *American Economic Association (AEA) Papers and Proceedings* (Vol. 111, pp. 272–276).

Barrero, J, S., Bloom, N., Davis, S. J., & Meyer, B. H. (2021). Covid-19 is a persistent reallocation shock. In *AEA Papers and Proceedings* (Vol. 111, pp. 287–291).

Barrero, J. M., Bloom, N. & Davis, S. J. (2021). Why Working from Home will Stick. *Working Paper 28731*, National Bureau of Economic Research (NBER), April; available at https://www.nber.org/papers/w28731

Bartik, A. W., Bertrand, M., Cullen, Z., Glaeser, E. L., & Luca, M. (2020). The impact of COVID-19 on small business outcomes and expectations. In *Proceedings of the National Academy of Sciences of the United States of America* (PNAS), July 28 (Vol. 117, no. 30, pp. 17656–17666).

Beladi, H. S., Marjit, and S. Kar (2013). Emigration, finite changes and wage inequality. *Economics and Politics, 25* (1), pp. 61–71.

Buera, F., Jaef, R. N. F., Neumeyer, P., Hugo Hopenhayn, & Shin, Y. (2020).The economic ripple effects of Covid-19. *World Bank Policy Research Working Paper 9651*. World Bank

Camera, G., & Gioffre, A. (2021). The economic impact of lockdowns: A theoretical assessment. *Journal of Mathematical Economics., 97*, 102552.

Caves, R. E., Frankel, J. A. & Jones, R. W. (2002). World trade and payments. Addison-Wesley

Court, C. D., Ferreira, J. P., Hewings, G., & Lahr, M. (2021). Accounting for global value chains: rising global inequality in the wake of Covid-19? *International Review of Applied Economics.*

Conley, D., & Johnson, T. (2021). Past is future for the era of COVID-19research in the social sciences. In *Proceedings of the National Academy of Sciences of the United States of America* (PNAS) (vol. 118, no. 13, pp. 1–4). No e2104155118.

Das, G., Marjit, S., & Kar, M. (2020). The impact of immigration on skills, innovation and wages: Education matters more than where people come from. *Journal of Policy Modeling., 42*(3), 557–582.

Das, P., Bisai, S., & Ghosh, S. (2021). Impact of pandemics on income inequality: lessons from the past. *International Review of Applied Economics.*

Deodhar, A. (2020). *Contact-intensity score shows which sectors to take biggest hit from here on.* The Economic Times, September 01; available at: https://economictimes.indiatimes.com/markets/stocks/news/sgx-nifty-up-180-points-heres-what-changed-for-market-while-you-were-sleeping/articleshow/94520897.cms

Earle, P. E. (Ed.). (2020a). *Coronavirus and economic crisis.* American Institute for Economic Research.

Earle, P. E. (Ed.). (2020b). *Coronavirus and economic recovery.* American Institute for Economic Research.

Famiglietti, M., Leibovici, F., & Santacreu, A. M. (2020). The decline of employment during COVID-19: The role of contact-intensive industries. Number 40. https://research.stlouisfed.org/publications/economic-synopses/2020/09/10/the-decline-of-employment-during-covid-19-the-role-of-contact-intensive-industries

Fairlie, R. (2020). The impact of COVID-19 on small business owners: The first three months after social-distancing restrictions. *Working Paper 27462*. National Bureau of Economic Research (NBER).
Glocker, C., & Piribauer, P. (2021). The determinants of output losses during the Covid-19 pandemic. *Economics Letters, 204*, 1–4.
Hardin, C. (2021). Doing economics otherwise, from one crisis to the next. *Journal of Cultural Economy, 14*(1), 1–8. https://doi.org/10.1080/17530350.2020.1846594
Hou, X., Gao, S., Li, Q., Kang, Y., Chen, N., Chen, K., Rao, J., Ellenberg, J. S., & Patz J. A. (2020). Intracounty modeling of COVID-19 infection with human mobility: Assessing spatial heterogeneity with business traffic, age, and race. *117* (30) 17656–17666. https://doi.org/10.1073/pnas.2006991117
Hu, S. & Zhang, Y. (2021). *COVID-19 pandemic and firm performance: Cross-country evidence.* International Review of Economics and Finance.
Jayaram, K., Leke, A., Ooko-Ombaka, A., & Sun, Y. S. (2020). *Finding Africa's path: Shaping bold solutions to save lives and livelihoods in the COVID-19 crisis.* McKinsey Institute, April 2020.
Joyce, R., & Xu, X. (2020). *Sector shutdowns during the coronavirus crisis: Which workers are most exposed?* Institute for Fiscal Studies Briefing Note BN278.
Jones, R.W. (1965). The structure of simple general equilibrium models. *Journal of Political Economy, 73*, 557–572. https://doi.org/10.1086/259084
Jones, R. W. (1971). A three-factor model in theory, trade, and history. In: J. N. Bhagwati et al. (Eds.). *Trade, Balance of Payments, and Growth: Essays in Honor of Charles P. Kindleberger.* North- Holland, Amsterdam.
Jones, R. W., & Marjit, S. (1992). International trade theory and endogenous production structures. In: W. Neuefeind & R. Reizman (Eds.). *Economic theory and international trade—Essays in Honor of T. Rader*. Springer.
Jones, R. W., & Marjit, S. (2009). Competitive trade models and real world features. *Economic Theory, 41*(1), 163–174.
Jones, R. W. (2019). *International trade theory and competitive models: Features, values, and criticisms.* World Scientific Studies in International Economics, vol. 65.
Joji, T. (2021). *Economic characteristics of inter-industry and inter-regional spread of COVID-19 shocks, RIETI, May.*
Kabanda, P. (2018). *The creative wealth of nations. Can art advance development?* Cambridge University Press.
Koren, M., & Peto, R. (2020). Business disruptions from social distancing. *PLOS One.*
Kugler, et al. (2021). *How did the COVID-19 crisis affect different types of workers in the developing world?* IZA DP # 14519, June
Leibovici, F., Santacreu, A. M., & Famiglietti, M. (2020). How the impact of social distancing ripples through the economy. *St. Louis Fed On the Economy Blog, 7*. https://www.stlouisfed.org/on-the-economy/2020/april/impact-social-distancing-ripples-economy
Marjit, S. (1990). *A simple production model in trade and its applications.* Economics Letters.
Marjit, S., & Acharyya, R. (2003). *International trade, wage inequality and the developing economy.* Springer.
Marjit, S., & Mandal, B. (2015). Finite change: Implications for trade theory, policy and development. In "*Development in India*", Mahendra Dev, S., & Babu, P.G., (Eds), Springer.
Marjit, S. (2009). *International trade and economic development. Essays in theory and policy. Oxford Collected Essays.* Oxford University Press.
Marjit, S., Mandal, B., & Nakanishi, N. (2020). *Virtual trade and comparative advantage: the fourth dimension.* Springer Nature.
Marjit, S., Das, G. G., & Mandal, B. (2022). *Virtual trade in a changing world: Comparative advantage, growth and inequality.* Cambridge Elements, Cambridge University Press, forthcoming
Marjit, S., & Das, G. G. (2021). *Contact-intensity, collapsing entertainment sector and wage inequality: A finite change model of covid-19 Impact.* CESifo Working Paper no. 9311.

Marjit, S., & Das, G. G. (2022). *Immunity-driven comparative advantage and its Palliative effect on social health and inequality—A theoretical perspective*. CESifo Working Paper no. 9569.

McCann, P., & Vorley, T. (2021). *Productivity and the pandemic: challenges and insights from Covid-19*. Cheltenham, UK: Edward Elgar Publishing.

Nam, M., & Lee, S. (2021). COVID-19 and employment in South Korea: Trends and comparison with the 2008 Financial Crisis. *IZA DP No., 14101*, 1–44.

Peterson, M. N. (2021). *Why government lockdowns mostly harm the poor*. American Institute for Economic Research (AIER), July 23, Great Barrington, USA. Available at https://www.aier.org/article/why-government-lockdowns-mostly-harm-the-poor/

Press Trust of India. (2021). *Vaccination drive to help revive contact intensive services sector*. Business Standard, January 29, New Delhi; available at https://www.business-standard.com/article/economy-policy/vaccination-drive-to-help-revive-contact-intensive-services-sector-121012901523_1.html

Samuelson, P. A. (1971). Ohlin was right. *Swedish journal of economics*, *73*, 365–84.

Sedik, T. S., & Yoo, J. (2021). *Pandemics and automation: Will the lost jobs come back?* IMF Working Paper.WP/21/11.

Social distancing impacts high-contact industries, UWF. The HAAS Center. https://uwf.edu/centers/haas-center/about-us/news--articles/covid-19-soc-dist-impacts-hi-contact-industries/

Sheridan, A., Andersen, A.L., Hansen, E.T., & Johannesen, N. (2020). Social distancing laws cause only small losses of economic activity during the COVID-19 pandemic in Scandinavia. *PNAS, 117*(34).

# Financing Recovery in the Post-Pandemic Indian Economy

**Abhirup Sarkar and Agnirup Sarkar**

## 1 Prelude

The Indian economy was already going through a state of recession when the COVID-19 pandemic hits the country. Year-on-year growth rate of GDP slipped from 9.5% during the first quarter of 2016–17 to 6% in the first quarter of 2017–18.[1] After registering a temporary recovery in the first quarter of 2018–19 to 8%, the growth rate fell again to 5.1% in the first quarter of 2019–20 and further to 4.5% in the second quarter. It is not difficult to conjecture that the fall in the growth rate in the first quarter of 2017–18 can be attributed to demonetization which was suddenly announced in November 2016. Indeed, apart from demonetization, nothing of economic significance had happened between the period lying between the first quarter of 2016–17 and the first quarter of 2017–18. So, it is but natural to connect the drastic fall in the rate of growth to the unpreparedness of the economy to handle the sudden ban of five hundred and one thousand rupee notes.

The temporary revival of 2018–19 is somewhat dubious. The doubt arises because of a perfunctory treatment of the informal sector in growth rate calculations. Estimates of income produced in the informal sector are based on surveys. But these surveys are infrequent, and it is implicitly assumed that income generated in the informal sector as a proportion of income produced in the formal sector remains constant until another survey is undertaken. This is not a good assumption because demonetization

[1] Unless otherwise specified, all figures are calculated from data available on the Reserve Bank of India website.

A. Sarkar (✉)
Indian Statistical Institute Kolkata, Kolkata, India

A. Sarkar
Indian Institute of Technology Guwahati, Guwahati, India
e-mail: agnirupasar@iitg.ac.in

 
A. Raychaudhuri and A. Ghose (eds.), *Managing Pandemic and Correcting Development Fundamentals*, India Studies in Business and Economics,
https://doi.org/10.1007/978-981-19-8680-2_4

has hurt the informal sector much more severely than the formal sector. The revival of 2018–19 is therefore an overestimation.

Of course, it is possible to argue that as new notes were printed and brought into circulation, the economy got a boost and gradually started getting back to its pre-demonetization track of higher growth. But this does not explain why, after showing a temporary spurt, business activities slid down again to a recessionary mode. Official narratives of the domestic growth trajectory, however, completely dissociate fluctuations in the domestic growth rate from internal factors and point to external disturbances as a more plausible cause. If the official stance is to be believed, one has to accept that neither the fall in the rate of growth in 2017–18 nor the subsequent recovery one year later had anything to do with demonetization.

The world economy was indeed going through a slowdown during the period immediately preceding the pandemic. The IMF in their October World Economic Outlook (2019) had predicted a worldwide growth rate of 3% which was the lowest since the 2008–09 subprime crisis. Combined growth rate in the four biggest economies—United States, Euro Zone, China and Japan—was predicted to be higher than the world average, above 3.5%, while growth rates in emerging economies like Russia, Brazil, Saudi Arabia or Mexico were forecasted to be less than 1%. In contrast, the Indian scenario was envisaged to be better.

Slowdown of the world economy was attributed to reduced international trade. Tariff wars between the US and China, exit of the United Kingdom from the Euro Zone and a general shift of economic ideology away from free trade and globalization, all taken together, led to reduced flow of goods and services across international borders. Tariff wars or Brexit had not only hurt economies of the US, China, the UK and the EU, which were directly hit by these policies, but also their trading partners. But to what extent these external negative shocks on international trade can explain economic fluctuations within India, remained doubtful.

There were several reasons for this doubt. First, economic slowdown had been much less severe in the four largest economies than in the emerging ones. Consequently, the extent of transmission of negative shocks from these large economies onto their trading partners was likely to be small. Second, each of the emerging economies, where growth rate drastically went down, had its own unique problem. In some of these economies, war was ongoing, in some others, there was an explosion of foreign debt, so much so that public confidence in the government had dwindled. In yet others, the banking system had crumbled, while in a fourth category of countries, environmental laws were so oppressive that investors hesitated to invest. In other words, each emerging economy had its own domestic problem to adhere. International shocks could hardly explain their predicament.

One is, therefore, inclined to believe that demonetization had depressed the Indian economy till the onset of the pandemic. The pandemic and the consequent lock down worsened it further.

## 2 Channels of Expenditure for Economic Recovery

Economic hardships during the pandemic are well recorded. Without going into the details of such accounts, it is sufficient to note, for our purpose, that during 2020–21, GDP went down by 7.25% compared with what it was a year earlier. This negative growth was evidently caused by the economy-wide lock down. Economic survey of 2022 predicts a speedy recovery of the Indian economy. It estimates a 9.2% growth of GDP in 2021–22 and forecasts a further growth of 8–8.5% during 2022–23. The high estimated growth of 2020–21 is to a large extent due to a low base. A straightforward calculation reveals that the estimated growth of 9.2% implies a meagre 1.28% growth of GDP in 2020–21 over that of 2019–20. Moreover, given the current world scenario of increasing oil prices and restrictions on trade due to the Russia–Ukraine war, it is unlikely that the projected rate of growth of 8–8.5% in 2022–23 would be achieved. Speedy economic recovery, therefore, is not easy.

One thing is clear though. In the currently suppressed environment, the government must play a greater role in bringing about economic recovery. But a greater role entails higher expenditure. This brings us to the main query of this paper: how can the government finance the higher expenditure required for a speedy recovery of the Indian economy which was already struggling under the effects of demonetization and has been further devastated by the pandemic?

Before we get into the main issue of financing, we need to know the possible channels through which the government is incurring or wishes to incur the expenditure geared towards pulling up the economy from the depths of the COVID-19 crisis. There are a number of possibilities. One possibility is to make direct transfers to those who are hard hit by the pandemic, people like migratory workers or owners of small businesses. Another possibility is to jack-up infrastructural spending which is expected to enhance, directly and indirectly, employment possibilities. A third possibility is subsidization of credit to small business units including support provided through credit guarantee schemes. All three have been tried out in varying degrees.

During the lock down period, direct monetary transfer was not so much resorted to. Instead, households hard hit by the pandemic were provided free ration. Under the Pradhan Mantri Garib Kalyan Yojna (PMGKY), 5 kg of rice or wheat per month was distributed to beneficiaries eligible under the National Food Security Act (NFSA). This entitlement was in addition to the usual monthly quota of subsidized ration. The PMGKY scheme started in March 2020 and was extended till March 2022. The total cost of the scheme has been 2.6 trillion rupees or rupees 2.6 lakh crore[2] till then. According to a statement of prime minister Narendra Modi, 80 crore people were provided free rations during the pandemic through this scheme.[3] Of late, the Union Ministry of Consumer Affairs, Food and Public Distribution has issued a

---

[2] See report in *Business Standard*, November 25, 2021.

[3] Reported in *Hindu Business Line*, August 03, 2021. The figure, however, is more likely to be 80 million.

public statement notifying that the Union Cabinet has decided to extend PMGKY till September 2022.[4]

The resurgent effort lies mostly on infrastructural expenditure. In the 2022–23 budget, there has been a spectacular rise in capital expenditure mostly geared towards enhancing infrastructure. While budgeted total expenditure in 2022–23 over the budgeted total expenditure in 2021–22 has increased by 13.25% and that of revenue expenditure by a meagre 0.86%, expenditure towards grants in aid for creation of capital assets has increased by a whopping 45% and total capital expenditure by 38%. This trend is expected to continue in future.

The increase in capital expenditure is supplemented by targeted credit support to small borrowers and COVID-19 affected sectors. The Reserve Bank of India has taken several measures in this direction. Special refinance facilities to the tune of Rs. 66,000 crore are extended to small borrowers through NABARD, SIDBI and NHB. In the same vein, term loans of Rs. 50,000 crore at the repo rate are made available till 30 June 2022, to ramp up COVID-19-related healthcare infrastructure and services. For contact intensive sectors, an additional on-tap liquidity window of Rs. 15,000 crore is available again up to 30 June 2022. Finally, long-term loans to the tune of Rs. 10,000 crore are made available at the repo rate through Small Finance Banks to small business units, micro and small industries and other unorganized sector entities adversely affected during the second wave of COVID-19.

Along with these measures, the Reserve Bank of India had reduced the repo rate since February 2019 by 250 basis points.[5] As a consequence, the weighted average lending rate of scheduled commercial banks fell by 197 basis points on fresh loans and by 133 basis points on outstanding loans during February 2019 and November 2021 easing the interest burden of borrowers and encouraging them to take more loans. Finally, in June 2021, a Credit Guarantee Scheme was announced through which MFIs can give credit to 25 lakh small borrowers in the urban areas, each getting up to Rs. 1.25 lakh. The money will be provided as credit to the MFIs by the banks for onward lending and such credit will be guaranteed by the government.

Clearly, the measures described above have put substantial pressure on government funds. The easing of interest and credit, on the other hand, has injected liquidity into the system by increasing bank credit.

## 3 Monetization of Public Assets

Part of the fund required for economic recovery was expected to come from selling of public assets. This ranged from total sales, like that of Air India, to partial sales of shares, like that of LIC. Divestment of government companies has attracted a lot of political controversy. In reality, only a very small fraction of total government receipts come from monetization of public assets. In 2020–21, only 1.08% of total receipts

[4] Indian Express, March 27, 2022.

[5] Very recently, however, the repo rate has been increased by 40 basis points to curb inflation.

came from disinvestments. In 2021–22, the government sets an ambitious target of Rs. 175,000 crore to be realized from sales of public assets. This meant that 5.12% of total receipts would comprise proceeds from disinvestment. Revised estimates, however, show that only Rs.78,000 crore could be realized by selling public assets which comprised only 2.16% of total receipts for the year. In the 2022–23 budget, the government has been more pragmatic and targets an amount of Rs. 65,000 crore to be obtained from divestment, which is a meagre 1.64% of total receipts.

From the figures, it appears that monetization of public assets does not go a long way in helping the government meet its financial requirements. Apart from mopping up resources, there must be other stronger reasons for divestment. One reason frequently put forward is efficiency. It is argued that there is a marked efficiency gain when an organization is passed on from public to private ownership. While efficiency gain may be the over-riding argument for privatization of some organizations, for others, it cannot be so. A case in point is privatization of banks and insurance.

In May 2014, a Review Committee headed by P. J. Nayak submitted a report on Banking reforms to the then RBI Governor Raghuram Rajan. The Committee recommended privatization of Public Sector Banks (PSBs) on a number of grounds. Later, these arguments were used to justify privatization of PSBs. The Committee argued that the relative importance of Private Sector Banks (PVBs) is increasing reflecting their relative efficiency, customer-friendliness, better technology and improved domain knowledge in comparison with PSBs. In 2000, 80% market share, in terms of loans advanced, was enjoyed by PSBs, 12% market share by PVBs and the remaining by Foreign Banks. In 2013, PSB's share was 73% and PVB's 21%. The Committee predicted that by 2025, PSB's share will come down to 63% and PVB's share will go up to 32%. In reality, in 2020, PSB share has come down below 60% and PVB's share has gone up above 36%.

A second argument in favour of privatization was in terms of higher profitability of private banks. This, in turn, was the result of a number of factors. PVBs have higher return on assets, more profits per employee, higher interest margin (difference between interest received from advances and interest paid on deposits) and lower staff cost to operating expenses. All this led to higher profitability of private banks.

A third and most important argument was put forward in terms of asset quality, i.e. in terms of the proportion of non-performing assets. In 2013, SBI group had a gross NPA of 6.24% (Non-Performing Assets as a proportion of total advances) and other PSBs had gross NPA of 4.55%. In contrast, new PVBs had gross NPA of 1.96% and old PVBs 2.34%. By 2018–19, the difference had increased. PSB's combined NPA was 11.6% and PVB's combined NPA was 5.3%. The Committee thought that if banks are not privatized, the government will eventually become bankrupt.

There are strong counter arguments though. The Committee's report could have been biased because the composition of the Committee was lopsided. There was just one member from PSB, and the rest, including the chairman, were from the private sector. Therefore, one wonders if the Committee was set up to come up with a conclusion which was already decided upon. More important, PSBs have to perform certain social roles which private banks are under no compulsion to perform.

The social role assigned to the PSBs forces them to open branches in remote and less profitable areas. Again, NPAs are mainly due to big Corporate Defaulters. Most often, these defaulting loans are directed from political quarters. These loans could have been avoided if the governments were more disciplined and transparent.

Indeed, if the government was more vigilant, it is possible to keep NPAs of PSBs within limits. In 2007–08, old PVBs had 2.3% NPA, new PVBs had 2.5% NPA and PSBs had 2.2% NPA. NPA of PSBs had jumped after 2015–16. There is yet another potential danger. If a PSB is bought by a big corporate group, chances are high that most advances will be made to companies within the group. This will increase the risk of lending. Finally, the most important aspect of banking is the security of an ordinary depositor. FRDI, which absolves the bank from all liabilities in case of a run and transfers the risks on to the depositors, will be more lethal if the bank is private.

In conclusion, one can argue that though the banking sector needs to improve its efficiency, this increase cannot be achieved by simply privatizing the entire sector. Public banks still have an important role to play in our economy. So instead of privatizing them, it is a good idea to improve their efficiency by emancipating them from the grips of political control. The same comments would be applicable to the insurance sector which the government is so eager to privatize. It follows, therefore, that the government should not put too much emphasis on monetization of public assets to enhance its financial position.

## 4 Inflation and Monetary Policy

The world is going through an inflationary phase at present. Western countries, which had been experiencing unusually low rates of inflation for a long time, are all facing a reversal, though in varying degrees. Apart from the traditionally inflation-prone Latin America or the recently war-torn Russia, in several European and North American countries, inflation is way above what it used to be. In April 2022, the United Kingdom had a year-on-year inflation rate of 7% and the Euro Area as a whole experienced an inflation of 7.5%. Within the Euro Area, a number of individual countries like Italy (6.2%), Germany (7.4%), Spain (8.3%) and Netherlands (9.6%) experienced inflation above 6%.[6] In North America, Canada (6.7%), Mexico (7.68%) and the United States (8.3%), all had year-on-year inflation rates above 6% in April 2022.

The reason behind this widespread inflation is not hard to find. During the COVID-19 period, countries, in their desperate attempts to fight the pandemic, resorted to monetary expansion without paying much attention to the consequences it might have on future prices. Given the emergency, there was little else one could do. But now that the world economy is gradually coming back to its normal rhythm, inflation needs to be tamed.

[6] Figures within brackets are country inflation rates. Inflation figures are obtained from the website https://tradingeconomics.com/country-list/inflation-rate.

As expected, central banks of inflation affected countries are raising interest rates to curb price rises. The period immediately preceding the pandemic was one of moderately low interest rates. The Federal Funds Rate (FFR), the rate which banks pay to the Fed for overnight borrowing, was pegged between 1 and 1.25% in the beginning of March 2020. As the pandemic broke out and there was widespread drop in employment and output, the Fed eased its monetary policy by reducing the FFR. In April 2020, the band of FFR was reduced to 0–0.25% and remained there till January 2022. Interest rates within the US as well as in other countries, including the United Kingdom and the Euro Zone more or less followed the movement of FFR. Clearly, the low interest rates facilitated bank credit which, in turn, expanded the supply of money followed by inflation. From March 2022, the FFR band has started to increase reaching 0.75–1% in May 2022. Since inflation has not yet been tamed in the US, it is expected that the FFR band will go up further, not only in the US but also in other countries as well.

Let us now look at the Indian scenario. We have already pointed out that during the pandemic, there was sufficient monetary easing through low interest rates, credit guarantee schemes and directed credit schemes. Consequently, the growth rate of money supply went up followed by inflation. Growth of broad money and inflation is shown in Fig. 1. Clearly, money growth and inflation move together. It is also clear that money growth, which temporarily went down in 2019–20, picked up next year to fight the pandemic. More specifically, when the rate of inflation is regressed on a one period lagged money growth, the coefficient of the regressor is positive and large, and the hypothesis that it is non-zero is accepted with 99% confidence. However, money growth alone could explain only a small fraction of the variation in the rate of inflation.

The inflation that followed post-COVID-19 recovery was more from the supply side. First, economic activities increased as the world economy struggled to come back to normal and this increased the demand and the price of oil in the world market. India being a big importer of oil, this had a big repercussion on oil prices in India. With increasing oil prices, transport costs went up and there was a general price rise. Second, disruption in the supply chain due to the pandemic still persisted in some sectors and countries which led to supply shortages and further price rise. Third and most recently, the outbreak of the Russia-Ukraine war has seriously disrupted supply from that part of the world. In addition, sanction on Russian merchandise by Europe and the United States has further aggravated supply bottlenecks, especially that of oil. All these factors, taken together, have increased the rate of inflation in India, as they have increased it elsewhere.

Table 1 presents consumers' price index (CPI) and consumers' food price index (CFPI) year-on-year inflation for April 2022 and April 2021. Three observations are to be made on the inflation figures. First, overall inflation in 2022 is way above overall inflation in 2021, almost double for CPI inflation and more than four times for CFPI inflation. Second, in 2022, rural inflation, both for CPI and CFPI, is higher than urban inflation which is a reversal from what we observe for 2021. Third, food price inflation has been much higher than general inflation in 2022 and one may even say that it is the rise in food prices which is mainly driving up general inflation.

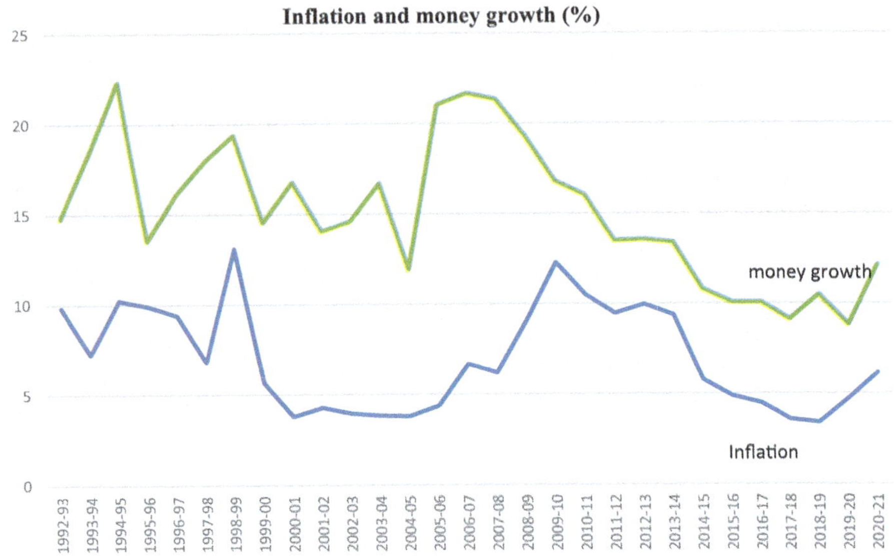


**Fig. 1** Inflation and money growth (%). *Source* Authors calculation from data available on RBI website

Food prices are currently rising at a higher rate both in the rural and urban areas, and the difference in CPI and CFPI inflation rates is more for rural than urban. Once more, this phenomenon is a reversal of 2021 when food price inflation was lower than general inflation, both for urban and rural, food price inflation in the rural areas being really low. An immediate implication of the second and third observations is that the poor are getting more affected by the current inflation than the relatively affluent. This is partly because the proportion of poor in rural areas is higher and partly because the poor spend a higher proportion of their income on food.

Rising oil prices, disruptions in supply chains and increases in the growth of money have all worked together to increase general consumer price inflation. But these factors, individually or collectively, fail to explain why CFPI inflation is higher than CPI inflation or why inflation is higher in rural areas than in urban areas. The explanation lies in the contraction of supply of food grains in the domestic market over the last few years. The contraction, in turn, can be explained by two factors: first, a spectacular rise in the export of food grains from India; second, a substantial

**Table 1** All India inflation based on CPI and CFPI (%)

| Inflation | April 2022 | | | April 2021 | | |
|---|---|---|---|---|---|---|
| | Rural | Urban | Combined | Rural | Urban | Combined |
| CPI | 8.38 | 7.09 | 7.79 | 3.75 | 4.71 | 4.23 |
| CFPI | 8.50 | 8.09 | 8.38 | 1.31 | 3.15 | 1.96 |

*Source* NSO

rise in government procurement to satisfy the needs of implementing PMGKY. We have already described the magnitude and time span of free food distribution through PMGKY. It suffices to talk about the recent trend in rising food grains exports.

Between 2015–16 and 2020–21, the value of food grains exports excluding rice but including wheat has increased 1.66 times. More recently, due to interruptions of supply of wheat from Ukraine, a major exporter of wheat and the consequent scarcity in the world market, the value of Indian export of wheat has exceeded 2 billion US dollars—almost a seven-fold increase compared to 2015–16. At the same time, between 2015–16 and 2020–21, value of rice exports had increased by 50% and increased substantially more in 2021–22. In 2019–20, the value of non-Basmati rice export was 2 million USD which by 2021–22 has become 6.11 billion USD. These fabulous increases in exports of food grains must be compared with a meagre 10% overall increase in the value of exports between 2015–16 and 2020–21. The increase in exports of food grains was bound to reduce supply in the domestic market and increase prices. Since food grains are procured for exports from rural markets, it is not surprising that rural prices are rising faster than urban prices, and the traders also buying in the rural market absorbing a part of the price rise when selling to the urban market.

Of late, the government has put a total ban on export of wheat to increase supply in the local market and restrict speculative hoarding. This may to some extent reduce the rate of rise in the price of food grains. Even before this measure was taken, the RBI increased the Repo rate by 40 basis points to curb inflation. Since the current inflation is coming mostly from the supply side, it is not clear to what extent increasing the rate of interest will serve the purpose of controlling inflation. On the contrary, high interest rates, by restricting demand, may delay economic recovery. Be that as it may, it is sufficiently clear at the moment that given the currently high rate of inflation, easy money policy is not going to be adopted in near future for economic recovery. With monetary policy not available as much of an option, the government is just left with fiscal policy, to which we now turn.

## 5 Fiscal Policy: Prospect of Increasing Public Debt

Two major sources of receipts of the central government are tax revenue and debt. In the union budget (2022), 49% of total receipts are expected to come from net tax revenue which is the amount that remains with the centre after deducting the states' share of taxes from gross tax revenue. Similarly, 42% of receipts are estimated to come from net debt, obtained by deducting repayment of past loans from fresh borrowings of the government. Government attempts at raising funds for economic recovery must centre around these two heads. Though there has been significant growth of tax revenue in the recent past, and the increase seems to be one time, mostly due to the introduction of GST. In other words, the prospect of further big increases in tax revenue appears to be limited. In particular, increases in GST rates are undesirable because tax rate hikes might directly jeopardize economic recovery. Moreover, a rise in tax rate has an uncertain effect on the volume of tax revenue because we do not know which side of the Laffer curve we are in. This leaves the government only with the option of borrowing.

In textbook macroeconomics, two problems are associated with increases in public borrowing. First, in a standard IS-LM framework, an increase in debt-financed expenditure by the government shifts the IS curve to the right. As a result, both output and the rate of interest go up. The rise in the rate of interest, in turn, reduces private investment. Therefore, debt-financed public expenditure crowds out investment made by private firms. It is further argued that government investment is, on an average, less productive than private investment. Therefore, expansion of public debt and the associated rise in the rate of interest hurts the economy.

Second, the Ricardian equivalence literature argues that since the intertemporal budget constraint of the government is balanced, an increase in government debt at present must imply an increase in taxes in future to repay the debt. Future taxes discourage private investment so that once more there is crowding out. Repayment burden also reduces funds available for development. Of course, if the debt burden is too high, it may not be feasible to raise taxes to the required level in which case public debt becomes unsustainable. The underlying assumptions of all these arguments are that the rate of interest is greater than the rate of growth.[7]

Recent literature on public debt argues exactly the opposite.[8] The argument is based on two empirical observations for advanced countries. First, for the last twenty years or so, advanced economies, like the United States, Europe and Japan, while experiencing phenomenal rise in their debt-GDP ratio are also going through a phase of falling interest rates, both nominal and real. That is, contrary to the prediction of the IS-LM model, interest rates have been *falling* in spite of substantial increases in public debt. For example, in the United States, debt-GDP ratio increased from 6% in 2000 to 109% in 2020. Real interest rate was 4.3% in 2000 and fell to 0.1% in 2020. Trends are similar in other advanced countries as well.[9]

The second empirical observation is with respect to relative magnitudes of growth rates and interest rates. In advanced economies over a long period, growth rates have remained above interest rates. In the United States for the period 1950–2008, average nominal interest on *one-year* treasury bills was 4.7%, and on *ten-year* treasury bills 5.6%. On the other hand, average nominal GDP growth was 6.3%. Using same deflator, therefore, average real interest rate was *less than* average growth rate of real GDP. Same trends are observed in other advanced economies.

Two factors are identified as causing the fall in interest rates in spite of rising public debt. First, there has been a rise in the saving ratio. This, in turn, is attributed to three reasons—rising income inequality, longer life expectancy, and increasing uncertainty of future income. Rising inequality shifts income from the poor to the

---

[7] This is a condition for dynamic efficiency and guarantees that the transversality (no Ponzi) condition is satisfied. Classical references in this literature are Diamond (1965) and Barro (1974). For a simple exposition of Ricardian Equivalence, see Heijdra (2017).

[8] Recent work on Public Debt is summarized in Blanchard (2019) and Furman and Summers (2020).

[9] For details, the reader is requested to look at Furman and Summers (2020).

rich who have a higher propensity to save. Similarly, longer life expectancy means longer retirement period which compels an individual to save more for his old age. Finally, with business fluctuations more frequently affecting the world economy, uncertainty of future income has increased. This has also increased the propensity to save.

Coming back to the IS-LM framework, as a result of an increase in saving propensity, the IS curve shifts in. This dampens the effect of an increase in G. Indeed, if the increase in saving propensity is high enough, the effect of an increase in G is outweighed and there is a fall in the rate of interest.

The other reason behind falling interest is scarcity of safe assets in the world market (see Caballero et al. (2017)). Agents all over the world perceive government bonds of developed countries as safe. After the financial crisis, there is a rush to acquire these safe assets, and as a consequence, there has been an increase in their demand. This increase in demand has outstripped the increase in supply (due to expansion of public debt) leading to a rise in the price of these bonds. Since bond price is inversely related to the rate of interest, this, in turn, leads to a fall in the latter variable.

There are two important implications of falling interest rates. First, the possibility of public debt crowding out private investments does not arise. At the same time, growth of income and hence growth of tax revenue exceeds the rate of interest, so that the government's budget constraint does not bind. In other words, it is possible for the government to repay its debt without raising tax rates. Alternatively, the government can roll over its debt without getting into a debt trap.[10]

The falling rates of interest coexisting with rising public debt have led a number of economists to prescribe that without much ado, governments of advanced countries can further expand their debts generously to finance recovery after the COVID-19 crisis. Question is, can the Indian economy follow this prescription?

Nominal interest rates reported in Fig. 2 are average interest rates paid by the central government on its debt in a particular year. Real interest rates are obtained by subtracting the rate of inflation from the nominal interest rate. From Fig. 2, it is clear that nominal interest rates exhibit a downward trend over the years 1992–93 to 2020–21, falling from a peak of 13.75% in 1995–96 to 5.8% in 2020–21. Real interest rates, on the other hand, have fluctuated, becoming negative between 2008–09 and 2013–14 and again in 2020–21, but do not show any discernable trend.

In Fig. 3, the debt-GDP ratio, and the savings ratio for the period 1992–93 to 2019–20 are exhibited. The savings ratio has a clear upward rising trend, increasing from a little over 0.2 in 1992–93 to above 0.3 in 2019–20. The debt-GDP ratio, on the other hand, does not show any trend. The ratio increased up to 2002–03 and then gradually came down presumably due to the adoption of FRBM.

We are concerned with two questions. First, we need know the major factors behind the changes in nominal as well as real rates of interest. Second, we need to see whether and how changes in the debt-GDP ratio affect interest rates, both nominal and real.

[10] When the rate of growth is greater than the rate of interest, the transversality condition is not satisfied and it is possible for the government to play Ponzi, that is, infinitely roll over its debt.

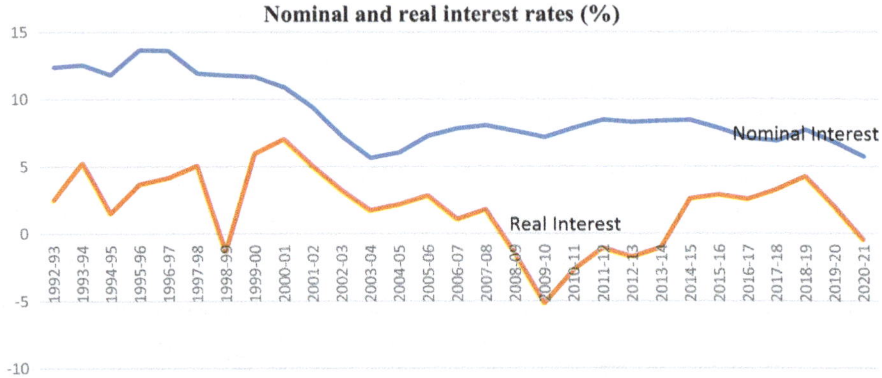


**Fig. 2** Nominal and real interest rates (%). *Source* Authors calculation from data available on RBI website

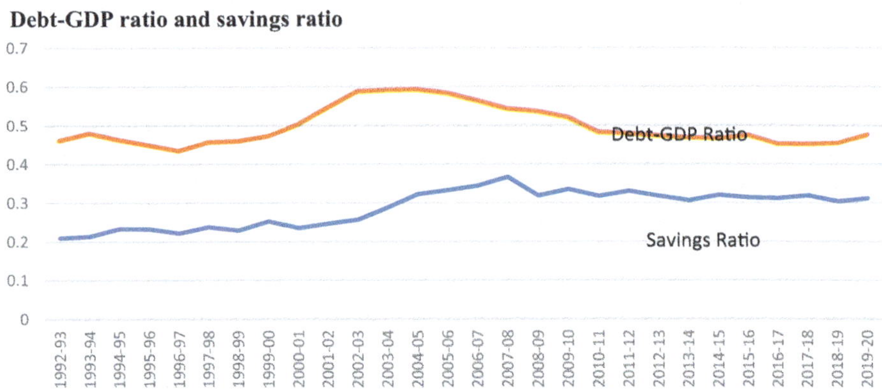


**Fig. 3** Debt-GDP ratio and savings ratio. *Source* Authors calculation from data available on RBI website

Regarding the first question, we hypothesize that apart from savings, inflation and public debt, the stock market can have a bearing on the rate of interest. A priori, the relationship between performance of the stock market and interest rates is likely to be positive. A vibrant stock market induces investors to invest more in equities which reduces the demand for government debt and increases the rate of interest. We measure stock market performance by market capitalization-GDP ratio. The behaviour of this variable over time is exhibited in Fig. 4 below. It has an increasing trend.

We regress nominal interest and real interest on market capitalization-GDP ratio, one-year lagged inflation, gross savings-GDP ratio and debt-GDP ratio. The OLS regression results are presented in the Appendix. The first set of regressions, with nominal interest as the dependent variable, indicate that in all three regressions, lagged inflation and savings/GDP turn out to have significant impacts on the nominal

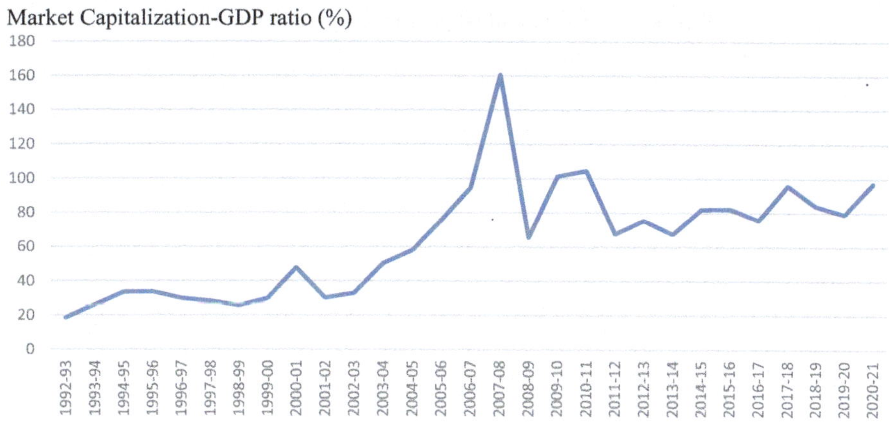


**Fig. 4** Market capitalization-GDP ratio (%). *Source* Authors calculation from data available on RBI website

rate of interest. While lagged inflation has a positive impact on the nominal rate, the savings ratio has a huge negative impact. In the second set of regressions, real interest is regressed on the same set of variables. Once more, lagged inflation and gross savings/GDP are shown by all three regressions to have significant impact on the real rate of interest. However, as opposed to the case of nominal rate, increase in lagged inflation has a negative impact on the real rate as does savings.

Two more observations on the regression results. First, the regressors explain the variations in the nominal rate of interest much better than that of the real rate of interest. This is clear from the $R^2$ and adjusted $R^2$ values.

Second and most important, the regression results suggest that public debt does not have any significant impact on either the nominal or the real rate of interest. If there is any effect, it is small, statistically insignificant and *negative.* There is no obvious explanation of the negative coefficient of public debt in the regression results. But an important implication is that the government can increase its debt without worrying too much about possible rises in the rate of interest. In other words, fiscal policy, and in particular, expansion of public debt, remains a viable option for economic recovery in the post-pandemic Indian economy.

There is another way of looking at sustainability. If the long run rate of growth exceeds the long run rate of interest then we can say that public debt is sustainable. In Fig. 5, the difference between nominal year-on-year GDP growth and nominal interest rate is recorded from 1993–94 to 2020–21. While for most years the difference is positive, for some years, it is negative as well. However, the average annual nominal growth over this period is 11.56%, while the average nominal interest rate is 8.91. This suggests that government debt is not unsustainable.

There is yet another way of checking sustainability of public debt. Let cumulative growth be $G = \prod_0^T (1 + g_t)$ and accumulated interest be $I = \prod_0^T 1 + i_t$ where $g_t$ and $i_t$ are nominal growth rate and nominal interest rate at year $t$. Public debt is sustainable if $G > I$ or equivalently $\ln G > \ln I$. We can calculate the values of these

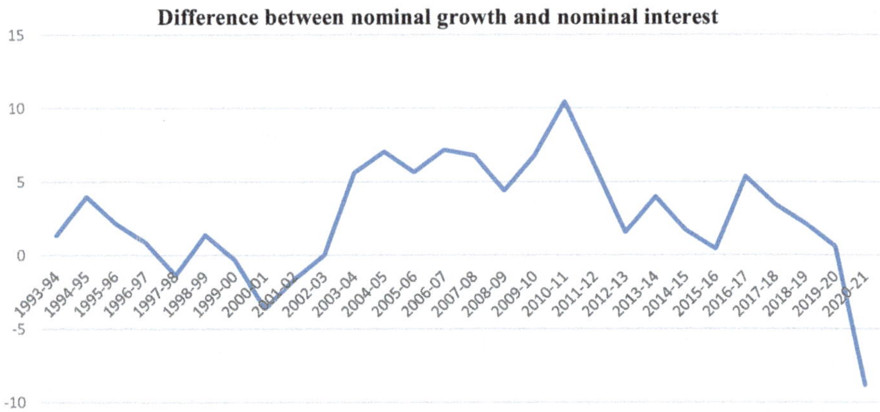


**Fig. 5** Difference between nominal growth and nominal interest. *Source* Authors calculation from data available on RBI website

two variables for $t = 1993\text{–}94$ to $t = 2020\text{–}21$ by noting that $\ln G = \sum \ln(1 + g_t)$ and $\ln I = \sum \ln(1 + i_t)$. It turns out that $\ln G = 3.045$ and $\ln I = 2.384$ for this time horizon, indicating once more that public debt was sustainable.

## 6 Concluding Remarks

In this paper, we considered the different options open to the government for financing economic recovery after the pandemic. Monetization of public assets, monetary policy and fiscal policy were the three possibilities talked about in this context. We came to the conclusion that monetization of assets cannot serve the purpose partly because the amount of money that the government can expect to get by selling public assets is miniscule in comparison with its requirement and partly because many public assets perform important social functions and should not be disposed of at the moment. Again, monetary policy, implying an increase in the supply of money by lowering interest rates was widely resorted to during the pandemic. But given the currently increasing inflation, this is no longer feasible. This leaves the government with fiscal policy, in particular, with expansion of public debt. There is a body of recent literature which argues in favour of increasing public borrowing to finance economic recovery in advanced countries. Looking at the Indian data, we found out that past increases in public debt cannot be associated with increases in the rates of interest which are mainly influenced by savings and inflation. We, therefore, concluded that public debts are sustainable and can be expanded to finance post-COVID-19 recovery.

# Appendix

Regression Results

Dependent Variable: Nominal Interest

| Explanatory variables | Regression I | Regression II | Regression III |
|---|---|---|---|
| Market cap/GDP | 0.02<br>(1.37) | | 0.024*<br>(1.79) |
| One-year lagged inflation | 0.22***<br>(2.87) | 0.22***<br>(2.8) | 0.26***<br>(3.76) |
| Gross savings/GDP | – 0.48***<br>(– 4.48) | – 0.35***<br>(– 7.18) | – 0.53***<br>(– 5.2) |
| Public debt/GDP | – 0.06<br>(– 1.18) | – 0.08<br>(– 1.6) | |
| Intercept | 23.24***<br>(7.5) | 21.7***<br>(7.38) | 20.9***<br>(8.68) |
| $R^2$ | 0.833 | 0.82 | 0.823 |
| Adjusted $R^2$ | 0.8 | 0.79 | 0.8 |
| Number of observations | 28 | 28 | 28 |

*, **, *** imply significance at 0.1%, 0.05% and 0.01% levels respectively.
Numbers in parenthesis indicate $t$-values.

Dependent Variable: Real Interest

| Explanatory variables | Regression I | Regression II | Regression III |
|---|---|---|---|
| Market cap/GDP | 0.02<br>(0.67) | | 0.02<br>(0.78) |
| Lagged inflation | – 0.37*<br>(– 2.07) | – 0.36*<br>(2.11) | – 0.35***<br>(3.76) |
| Gross savings/GDP | – 0.52*<br>(– 2.12) | – 0.37***<br>(– 3.45) | – 0.53**<br>(– 2.27) |
| Public debt/GDP | – 0.02<br>(– 0.2) | – 0.04<br>(– 0.43) | |
| Intercept | 19.64***<br>(2.78) | 17.93**<br>(2.75) | 18.71***<br>(3.5) |
| $R^2$ | 0.39 | 0.38 | 0.39 |
| Adjusted $R^2$ | 0.28 | 0.3 | 0.31 |
| Number of observations | 28 | 28 | 28 |

*, **, *** imply significance at 0.1%, 0.05% and 0.01% levels, respectively.
Numbers in parenthesis indicate $t$-values.

## References

Barro, R. (1974). Are government bonds net wealth? *Journal of Political Economy, 82*(6), 1095–1117.

Blanchard, O. (2019). Public debt and low interest rates. *American Economic Review, 109*(4), 1197–1229.

Diamond, P. (1965). National debt in a neoclassical growth model. *American Economic Review, 55*(5), 1126–1150.

Economic Survey 2021–22. (2022). *Ministry of finance, government of India, New Delhi*. https://www.indiabudget.gov.in/economicsurvey/ebook_es2022/index.html

Furman, J., & Summers, L. (2020). *A reconsideration of fiscal policy in the era of low interest rates, discussion draft*. Available at https://www.brookings.edu/wp-content/uploads/2020/11/furman-summers-fiscal-reconsideration-discussion-draft.pdf

Heijdra, B. (2017). *Foundations of modern macroeconomics* (3rd ed.). Oxford University Press.

National Statistical Office. (2022). Ministry of Statistics and Programme Implementation, Consumer Price Index Numbers on Base 2012=100 for Rural, Urban and Combined for the Month of April 2022. Available at https://pib.gov.in/PressReleasePage.aspx?PRID=1824772

Report of the Committee to Review Governance of Boards of Banks in India, May 2014. Available at https://rbidocs.rbi.org.in/rdocs/PublicationReport/Pdfs/BCF090514FR.pdf

Reserve Bank of India. https://www.rbi.org.in/Scripts/Publications.aspx?publication=Annual

Union Budget. (2022). *Government of India*. https://www.indiabudget.gov.in

World Economic Outlook. (2019). *International Monetary Fund*. https://www.imf.org/en/Publications/WEO/Issues/2019/10/01/world-economic-outlook-october-2019

# Envisioning the Future of Indian Higher Education in the Post-Covid Era: Challenges and Possibilities

**Saumen Chattopadhyay**

## 1 Introduction

With the implementation of the lockdown measures in the wake of the Pandemic, the normal functioning of the colleges and universities came to a halt. The most immediate step taken to overcome the crisis was to shift to online teaching. This disruption played havoc with the teaching–learning process and conduct of research in major parts of the world affected by the Pandemic. India's situation was possibly a little worse than the developed parts of the world due to the poor digital infrastructure and digital divide which made participating in the classroom discussions difficult and expensive. Overcoming the learning loss inflicted on the students will not be easy. The National Education Policy (NEP) GoI (2020a) was announced in July 2020 when the country was in the throes of the First Wave. The NEP envisions a complete restructuring of the Indian higher education regulatory system for the Indian higher education riding on the wave of digital transformation that some parts of the higher education system were witnessing. The big question is whether the plan for total reconfiguration of the Indian higher education sector as mooted in the NEP would be able to deal effectively with the challenges and constraints the sector is faced with and steer the sector toward a new direction impregnated with potentials and possibilities.

This chapter seeks to understand and anticipate the future of the Indian higher education in the Post-Covid era in the wake of the implementation of the NEP. The chapter begins with the conceptualization of the debatable issue of whether higher education as a public good or a common good. This is followed by a brief discussion of the challenges facing the Indian higher education system and how are they being addressed in the proposed NEP. This is followed by a discussion on the possible implications for the two major functions of the universities such

S. Chattopadhyay (✉)
Zakir Husain Centre for Educational Studies, SSS, JNU, New Delhi, India
e-mail: saumen@jnu.ac.in

 
A. Raychaudhuri and A. Ghose (eds.), *Managing Pandemic and Correcting Development Fundamentals*, India Studies in Business and Economics,
https://doi.org/10.1007/978-981-19-8680-2_5

as teaching and doing research with the academic profession being at the center of discussion. We broaden the context of the discussion by bringing in a major force which is gaining momentum, i.e., internationalization. We end this chapter with a discussion on the major issues and objectives, access and equity, conceptualization of quality, autonomy and accountability and the nature of public good character of higher education. We conclude with observations for the evolving market for higher education and the nature of public good character of higher education focusing on inclusive expansion and attainment of quality education.

## 2 Higher Education as a Public Good, and a Common Good

In the UNESCO World Conference on higher education held in Barcelona, Spain during May 16–18, 2022, it was reiterated that higher education should be viewed as a right and higher education is a common good (Sharma et al., 2021; Sharma et al., 2022). This is a very welcome announcement which encapsulates what roles higher education can play to confront the challenges the humanity is faced with and contribute to the consolidation of social and economic order which is inclusive and environmentally sustainable. However, the trajectories of reform opted for by the majority of the countries portends divergence from UNESCO's vision of higher education. The question remains however whether the state or the policymakers would at all be interested in pursuing this objective. The NEP has classified higher education as a quasi-public good. It is imperative in this context to understand what is meant by higher education as a public good or a common good.

While characterizing higher education as a public or a private good, we need to discuss with regard to two specific dimensions of higher education, access to higher education institutions to study and earn certificates and research output or knowledge generated. With respect to the issue of access, there is no rivalry in consumption in the normative sense.[1] However, it is a reality that the admission to an institution is regulated in view of the limited number of seats which makes access to institution excludable. Given the intrinsic property of knowledge in the form of an idea, there is no rivalry either in the use of knowledge. In practice, it may not be so due to patenting and paid access to journal articles while concomitantly, open access domain is gaining popularity. At least with respect to the first dimension, higher education is argued to be a mixed good or a quasi-public good (Chattopadhyay, 2009; Marginson, 2016).

The outcome of learning is embodied in the graduate and the graduate is expected to earn higher stream of incomes because of education than what would have been possible otherwise in absence of an improvement in the cognitive capacity caused by education. Though it is now being increasingly felt (Brown et al., 2020; Marginson, 2016) that the link between education and the job market has become weaker and

[1] It is in this context that it would be worthwhile to trace back to the definition of public good Samuelson (1954) offered and how this definition is able to capture the essence of higher education. Non-rivalry in consumption and non-excludability are the two distinctive features of a public good.

the human capital theory (Becker, 1993) which proposes expenditure on education as a form of investment because of the pecuniary benefits which accrue to the graduates when they start earning. This is the private benefit part of higher education because of the very nature of human capital formed in the process of learning which is embodied in the person and therefore non-separable. The graduate is supposed to be a transformed individual capable of contributing to the maintenance of social and political order through her conduct and approach to life, interventions and engagements in social and political activities which hold the society and the polity together. Marginson (2016) argues that the degree of excludability is determined in a particular socio-political and economic context. The private and the public benefits which are often referred to as generation of externalities which reinforce each other and therefore it is not a zero-sum game. But if we look at the sphere of professional and private education where the students are made to pay high fees, the students are made to feel that pursuit of education is indeed an investment which can potentially diminish the extent of externalities generated because of the possible changes in the students' approach to education and society.

The advocacy for higher education as a public good assumes a new dimension when Locatelli (2018) and Marginson (2016) argue for even treating higher education as a common good. The major distinction between public good and common good with respect to higher education is the solidarity in the community that education inculcates. The externalities or public benefits are generated by the individuals in case of a typical public good. The common good approach to education weaves the society and binds the community together. It also implies access to higher education which is nearly undifferentiated. Though it appears to be a nearly impossible task, but highlighting this approach sets a target of immense significance for the policymakers and the society.

Unlike other economic sectors, the quality of higher education is not an outcome of a well-defined technology which entails conversion of the inputs who are the decision making units like the students and the teachers to university output. Lack of agency, indolence and pursuit of self-interest driven objectives render the existence of an educational production function a difficult proposition (Chattopadhyay, 2012). Because of embodiments of human capital, the quality of inputs are not replicable which makes the attainment of uniform quality across the board nearly impossible. This inherent differentiated nature of the higher education sector will always make it difficult to realize the objective of common good approach to education.

## 3 Challenges Facing Indian Higher Education

As per the All India Survey of Higher Education (AISHE) 2019–20 (GoI, 2020c), with gross enrollment ratio of 27.1%, there were 38.5 million students, 1.5 million teachers engaged in around 1043 universities, 42,343 colleges and 11,779 stand-alone institutions. India is considered to be the second largest higher education system in the world. Around 0.5% of students are enrolled in the PhD program. Though Indian universities do not feature in the global list of the top 100 universities in world ranking, in 2019, with 187,432 scientific papers published by the higher education institutes and research institutes, India stood fourth in the ranking after China, USA and UK (International Facts and Figures 2020). The research productivity is mainly concentrated among the top 100 HEIs as they contribute nearly 70% of the papers with minimal funding for research. Featuring in the list of top 100 universities in the world ranking has now been made to be the mandate of the select Institutions of Eminence (IoEs) and also one of the targets for the Category-I institutions classified under the scheme of Graded Autonomy (GoI, 2018).

The steady rise in gross enrollment ratio (GER) has not been associated with a commensurate expansion in public funding as private participation particularly in the professional education witnessed a rapid rise. For the education sector, public funding is barely 3.1% of GDP (Economic Survey 2021–22: GoI, 2022a). The NEP 2020 noted that the public funding for education as a whole was 4.43% of GDP in 2019–20. The difference in the two estimates of public funding is attributable to the expenditure on skill training and other welfare measures implemented by the various ministries. Quality of higher education has always remained a major concern for the policymakers. The policymakers have shown a distinct preference for benchmarking ranking of the Indian universities with the world ranking tables.[2] As per the QS ranking 2023, the number of Indian higher education institutions in the top 1000 increased to 27 from 22 in QS 2022. The IISc improved its ranking which is followed by eight IITs. The ranking of the IISc was 155 in 2023 compared to 186 in 2022. All seven IITs that came after IISc improved their ranks. However, ranking position of some reputed universities like JNU, University of Delhi, Jadavpur University and Hyderabad Central University declined in 2023 compared to 2022 (The Indian Express: 10 June).[3] In terms of Academic Ranking of World Universities (ARWU), the highest ranking university was in the range of 401–500. The mobility ratios of outbound is much higher than the inbound ratio. This is indicative of Indian students' growing preferences to study abroad. The outbound mobility ratio for India was 1.1 compared 2.2 of China, 0.8 for both South Africa and Brazil (Chattopadhyay, 2021).[4] The inbound mobility ratio for India was only 0.1 compared to 0.4 for China, 3.6 for South Africa and 0.2 for Brazil.[5] The industry has often claimed poor employability of the Indian graduates. There exists a huge disparity in terms of funding by the Centre and the state universities. The inequities in access to education across gender

[2] In the Visitors' conference held …the President of India, Hon'ble Ram LalKovind drew the attention of the Vice Chancellors to the improvement of ranking of the Indian universities in QS 2023 edition. Source :https://pib.gov.in/Pressreleaseshare.aspx?PRID=1831172#

[3] IISc top Indian university, overtakes IITs: QS World University Rankings | Education News, The Indian Express. https://indianexpress.com/article/education/iisc-is-top-indian-university-in-global-rankings-overtakes-iits-7959729/ss.

[4] This is the ratio of students studying abroad and the students enrolled in Indian higher education institutions.

[5] As per the UNESCO estimate nearly 4.4 million students are studying abroad. However as per the estimate of the MEA, the number goes up to 8 million. In comparison, India receives only 49 thousand students from abroad.

and social categories like SC and ST have remained deeply embedded in the Social Structure. Barring a few institutions of excellence, the overall standard of higher education is a matter of concern. The Draft of the NEP (DNEP) (GoI, 2019) put it bluntly that the human resources and physical infrastructure of a majority of Indian HEIs were being sub-optimally utilized. The DNEP claimed that regulation had tried to micromanage the academic activities of the teachers which suffocated and stifled the faculty to be innovative and creative. The unethical practices abound in many realms of functioning of the HEIs starting with faculty recruitment, faculty career advancement schemes, paper setting for examination and evaluation, poor class attendance and financial mismanagement and of course in proliferation of fake journals. The private institutions, barring a few pockets of excellence, have failed to deliver quality education mainly on account of cost-cutting tendencies which led to a serious compromise with the quality (Chattopadhyay, 2021). The poor quality of school education also contributed to the lack of preparedness among the students enrolled in the HEIs.

## 4 A Proposal to Reconfigure Indian Higher Education: NEP 2020

The NEP 2020 (GoI, 2020a) proposes a radical restructuring of the Indian higher education system which have far reaching implications for the inclusivity of the Indian higher education system and the very concept of quality that the policymakers are aiming for. While the focus is now on dealing with the implementation challenges, it is pertinent to reflect and unravel the basic approach toward higher education reform as encapsulated in the NEP. However, we will focus only on some important aspects of the NEP, the regulatory framework, institutionalization of the Academic Bank of Credits (ABC) and funding arrangements. The NEP proposes that the GER should be raised to 50% of the relevant age cohort by 2035 with 50% of them should have exposure to vocational education by 2025 (section 10.8 and 16.5, GoI, 2020a).

### *4.1 The Regulatory Framework*

The NEP has suggested a wide range of reforms which include setting up of an entirely new set of regulatory institutions to overhaul the policy interventions in the Indian higher education system. The overarching authority, Higher Education Commission of India (HECI) as an umbrella institution will be supported by four pillars, the Higher Education Grants Council (HEGC) for funding, the National Higher Education Regulatory Council (NHERC) for regulation, the General Education Council (GEC) for setting quality standards or specifically learning outcomes, and the National Accreditation Council (NAC) as a 'meta-accrediting body'. Based on the diagnosis that regulation has failed to motivate faculty to be innovative and creative, the NEP 2020 advocates for a regime of 'light but tight' regulatory interventions. The private and public should be regulated at par without any distinction between the general and technical education. Successful implementation of the NEP recommendations in a federal structure would require support from the state governments for frictionless coordination between the Union and the states. Given the size of the Indian higher education sector and huge tasks pending for accreditation, the NAC is expected to perform a key role in quality improvement. The General Education Council (GEC) is to be entrusted with the responsibility to oversee the functioning of the 'professional councils' which will act as 'professional standard setting bodies' along with the issue of credit transfer and equivalences to facilitate the students' mobility between the general stream and the vocational stream as well as across the institutions.

## 4.2 ABC and Rising Dependence on Online Education

The proposal to set up an Academic Bank of Credits (ABC) is a major step in the overall reconfiguration of the higher education sector. The ABC will help in consolidation of credits earned by the students which can be stored digitally in the accounts of the students. This will render the learning flexible as the students can learn from 'anywhere and anytime' and any subject of their choice. This has been followed up by the UGC circulars (GoI, 2020b) which allows the students to opt for up to 40% of the credits from other institutions including SWAYAM and other e-platforms. Though this was mooted to be only a panacea to tide over the disruption in teaching–learning during the Pandemic, the implementation of the ABC will entrench online education as the new normal which will be a blended/hybrid mode. This, in fact, will serve two major purposes, one to nurture and promote the culture of multi-disciplinarity as emphasized in the NEP as students can now opt for courses they desire to pursue from other institutions and government promoted e-learning platforms, and two, to enable the students respond to the changing demand for skill in the job market by choosing relevant courses to enhance their employability. The UGC has also signaled that the universities will be allowed to collaborate with the Ed-Tech companies to offer advanced and frontier level courses.

## 4.3 Funding and University Governance

There are three main issues in the debate on university funding in the international context which are relevant for India too: quantum of public funding, mode of funding and purpose of funding, particularly, teaching and/or research. Classification of higher education as a quasi-public good means both public and private sector have legitimate role to play, and in connection with this, it is heartening to note that the NEP reiterates the long standing demand to raise the total budget for education sector to 6% of GDP over a period of ten years. In all likelihood, this is unlikely to materialize as the concern for fiscal crunch will continue to pose challenge for the centre and the states and more so in the Post-Covid era.

There are two sources of public funding as proposed by the Union government, the HEGC as mentioned above and the National Research Foundation (NRF) as the sole body for funding research. Allocation of funds among the HEIs would be made based on their institutional development plan (IDP) duly approved by the Board of Governors (BoGs). There is likely to be a gradual shift from input-based funding to output/performance-based funding.

The NEP has suggested three categories of the HEIs, the Research-university, Teaching-university and the degree granting Autonomous Colleges (ACs). Since funds for research are to be allocated mostly on a competitive basis, the best of the universities are likely to appropriate a chunk of the research funds. While this categorization may be indicative, but the NEP desires that teaching-university and the ACs to strive for excellence to acquire the status of research-university in due course of time. However, given the scarcity of time for doing research and research funds, encouragement for this progression will have very limited effect.

## 5 A State-Regulated Market for Higher Education

Higher education reform world over is mainly informed by neoliberal principles which facilitates market construction with increased private sector participation to gain from competition and university governance reform to achieve efficiency in use of resources. There are three major reasons for the growing dominance of neoliberalism, one, fiscal constraint and two, their assumption about human behavior turning out to be correct. There is hardly any government anywhere in the world which is not faced with fiscal constraint. The dominance of the neoliberal approach to policymaking continues because the behavior of the teachers and students in particular, conform to their ontological assumption that individuals are essentially *homo economicus* and 'manipulatable' by the policy makers. Therefore, broadly speaking, they are not always intrinsically motivated and therefore they are not trust worthy (Olssen et al., 2004). The third factor is the role of mounting expectations from the universities to contribute more prominently and meaningfully to the economy and the societal needs as the traditional mission of the university, disinterested pursuit of knowledge for truth came under scrutiny (McCowan, 2017).

The approach of NEP remains one of market construction as evident from three policy initiatives which support market construction (Chattopadhyay 2020): setting up of an overarching regulatory framework, and giving freedom to the two sides of the market in their decision making, the students through the ABC and the HEIs to evolve as autonomous institutions over a period of ten years. Digital transformation of the university space and the higher education system is playing a crucial role in market construction and a part of it will get integrated with the global with support from a series of measures to promote internationalization. Through the use of technology in the classroom and in the sphere of academic transactions was initiated long ago, the disruption in teaching resulting in a quick transition to online education redefines the concept of space and time associated with university functioning essentially by converting teaching which is in the nature of a service to a digital product which can be reproduced at a minimal cost, stored digitally and shared through the virtual medium with those who are concerned and interested. The four walls of the classroom are transcended with ease, with teaching can now become asynchronous as students can join the classroom potentially from any part of the world anytime. The NEP seeks to construct a state-regulated market for higher education which appears to be different from a typical neoliberal market-based reform in at least three respects. One, the NEP does not approve of commercialization and instead it argues for responsible private sector participation funded by the corporate social responsibility (CSR) to pursue the objective of philanthropy; two, the IDP based reform of university governance which allows for collective participation is not typically akin to NPM and three, channeling of public funds based on university performances rather than providing financial assistance to the students in the form of education vouchers to help develop a market for education.

Given the paucity of funds for the higher education which is a perennial feature for almost every government across the globe, competition among the institutions for maximizing their share in public funding will intensify under the IDP. However, the most important fallout of competition would be eventual discontinuation of many of the courses due to the fall in the number of students leading to even closure of some departments in some colleges and universities over time.

## 6 Policy Implications for Higher Education

In order to trace out the transformation we are witnessing in the higher education sector, we may point out the different functions a university performs (Stiglitz, 1975): teaching, doing research, outreach activities, information generation in the form of certificates and credentials awarded to the students and university experiences which is necessary for self-transformation without which the capacity to contribute to the formation of the social and political order will not materialize. We would however focus on teaching and doing research primarily while drawing attention to the remaining three to round up the discussion on the uses of the university in the age of transformation in the Post-Covid era.

### *6.1 Teaching–Learning*

Transition to online teaching from face to face teaching necessitated by the lockdown measures imposed during the Pandemic is the most fundamental change which has serious implications for the way higher education is going to evolve. Though online delivery of instructions began much before the Pandemic and MOOCs was being popularized by the government, it did not gather steam. The sudden transition to online teaching effectively changed the ball game as the academic, the students and the teachers, the administrators and the policy makers realized albeit often perforce that it had immense potential.

With the restoration of the normalcy which marks a craving for face to face teaching, online teaching would remain a part of the university functioning as blended mode appears to be an acceptable solution by the stakeholders with the implementation of the ABC. The policymakers advocate online teaching because not only does it save cost and improves quality, arguably so, by replicating course content and teaching as classroom lectures can now be digitally stored. This facilitates internationalization measures too as the classroom is now global since the classroom requires virtual presence. Though online teaching limits the possibility of interaction in the classroom, new ways are being explored to give a real time feel to the students in a virtual classroom.

A new category of teaching assistants has emerged who are supposed to help the students in clearing their doubts and in seeking clarifications. This has also made unbundling (McCowan, 2017) of courses possible which marks an increasing tendency toward offering of courses in terms of modules. This has led to the emergence of micro-credentials which link up with the industry's changing demand for skill. The students have to reskill themselves often. With focus on the development of critical thinking and problem solving ability, the students are now best classified as life-long learners.

## *6.2 Rising Importance of the Ed-Tech Companies*

This change has been coterminous with the entry of the Ed-Tech like Coursera, Udemy and EdX (India had 7.1 million students out 58 million of Coursera)[6] (IFC Report, 2020) companies who now peddle course wares which come with the assurance of the latest in the technology to enhance the employability of the students. The universities, both public and private are now actively looking for collaboration with these platforms to offer their courses to the students. These platforms are continuously looking for areas where new demand for skills are emerging accompanied by assessments of skill gaps. The universities have found a new way to respond to the emergence of demand for new skills as the job market is rapidly undergoing a change.

[6] Coursera reaches 58 Million global learners (The IFC Report 2020). Top 5 countries were USA 12.1 Million; India: 7.1 Million; China 3.2 Million; Mexico 3.1 Million; Brazil 2.4 Million. At the end of the previous decade, there were 380 million students opting for 30 thousand rupees, 50 degrees and 1000 universities.

## 6.3 Research and Ranking

Knowledge generated by the university should be made to be useful to the economy and the society through knowledge transfer to the industry and the state. The triple helix model Etakowitz, Webster and Healey (1998) envisaged the role of the university, industry and the government as forming a triangle of cooperation and exchange. Knowledge has the potential to be converted to a patent which would restrict the use of it but at the same time it would incentivize knowledge production. The need of the society is expected to get articulated through the industry's demand for knowledge. However, it has been argued that the private markets for knowledge do not function properly and there is a strong case for public property in the knowledge domain Foray, (2006). The governance of the traditional concept of university which is based on trust reposed on the academic professions to deliver as they were assumed to be intrinsically motivated is contested by the advocates of NPM. The NPM is supposed to ensure improved technical efficiency and value for money for the students who are viewed as customers. Two major elements of NPM are accounting for auditing of the faculty's research performances and its valuation for ordering. This led to an attempt to standardize the faculty performances and the procedures. The UGC Regulations (GoI, 2017) is an example of such an approach (Das & Chattopadhyay, 2014). It is to be seen how the 'light but tight' regulatory regime as suggested by the NEP will be designed and implemented. The problem of straightjacketing which compromises with autonomy and diversity at the faculty level, disciplinary level and at the level of the university is likely to remain (ibid).

The NEP suggests integration of teacher education, 90% of which is in the private sector. With the implementation of the national skill qualification framework (NSQF), there will be a significant boost for vocational education as the students can now freely move between the general and the vocational education. With the rise in demand for reskilling and short term courses, the focus is now on life-long learning.

The challenges that remain to be confronted are simply daunting. The DNEP (GoI 2019) criticized the proliferation of the fake journals which account for an increase in the low quality journal articles. As argued by Bhushan (2019), capacity build-up of the teachers is of paramount importance as this is a necessary condition for valuing scholarship and conduct of good quality research. The trend that we see world over is alarming. Under the pressure of publication as the university is governed in line with the new public management (NPM), instances of taking recourse to unethical practices has also increased (Täljedal, 2013). There has been a rise in phony authorship, paid publications, proliferation of fake journals and a market for buying PhD degrees. Washburn (2005) has argued citing many examples in the context of the USA that how there have been a rising number of cases of collusion between the teachers and the industry in suppressing publications to restrict its dissemination, and manipulation of the research results to ensure easy and unhindered marketing of the drugs developed. Slaughter and Leslie (1997) brought before us many dimensions about academic capitalism which included propertization of knowledge capital.

The policymakers have shown strong preference for embracing world ranking as a way to assess quality as a prerequisite to improve quality. The Graded autonomy (GoI, 2018) has categorized the Indian universities, the THE and QS into three groups based on their NAAC score and/or world ranking[7] of two agencies, the THE and the QS. The Category-I top performing HEIs are bestowed with more freedom in faculty recruitment, admission policy, offering of courses without taking permission from the UGC as long as the courses are self-financing among other measures. The message which comes out loud and clear from this policy is that autonomy can be bestowed as a reward for good performance. But financial autonomy should not be considered as a dimension of autonomy which deserves celebration as it can lead to a compromise with academic autonomy. Institutional autonomy does not necessarily mean faculty autonomy. The main purpose of according the status of Institutions of Eminence (IoEs) to a select set of public and private universities is to set the mandate of these HEIs to feature in the list of global ranking in terms of the THE, QS and additionally Academic Ranking of World Universities (Shanghai Jiao Tong University's ARWU) within a period of ten years by proving them with policy support in terms of autonomy and additional funding particularly to the public funded universities. The setting up of the NIRF is a recognition of the HEIs at the national level and a policy nudge for them to compete and improve ranking as per the NIRF parameters.

As the universities compete in the ranking, the universities strategize to bring about the necessary institutional restructuring by allocating resources (Locke, 2011; Chattopadhyay, 2019). In a way the global ranking has affected the mandate and the university processes of the top ranking universities. As Locke has pointed out the link between marketization and ranking as reputation based on ranking makes an institutions attractive enough to select best of the students, and the faculty and attract funding. This selection based efficiency makes the higher education system more hierarchical. Even though the influence is resisted by some universities, there is a perceptible accommodation in the form of restructuring of university functioning, internalization and institutionalization which 'may produce unintended and undesirable consequences for higher education institutions' (ibid., p. 202). Teichler (2011) raises an important question whether the vertical differences are more important than the horizontal differences and therefore it disregards and undermine the horizontal diversity of the departments.

Recently three universities from China have decided to withdraw themselves from participation in ranking. These universities now will address the national needs as competing in ranking is a distraction.

---

[7] Inclusion in Category I would require NAAC Score of 3.5 and/or featuring in the world ranking within the top 500 as per the THE and QS. Category II would require NAAC score of 3.01–3.49.

### 6.4 Academic Profession

The academic community assumes the central position in the university functioning. A transformation in the academic profession is a prerequisite for transformation in the higher education sector. The graded autonomy allows for incentivisation of the teachers' performance which marks a departure from the existing system which allows for a fixed increment in salary annually almost independent of performances for a given designation. The universities have been given the freedom to pay more to the faculty as long as the extra emoluments are paid out of their own revenues. The industry experts and faculty from universities with ranking in the list of top 100 can also be accommodated within the existing pool of the faculty. These are important policy steps mooted to incentivize and motivate the faculty to do better. The teaching community will not get segregated at the expense of collegiality. There will now be teachers recruited for developing course content, exclusively for teaching, and those only for taking the tutorials. Allocation of funding along with creation of university categories may impede career progression of a majority of the faculty employed in teaching-universities and the Autonomous degree getting colleges. The making of the IDPs collectively by the teachers, students and the non-teaching staffs is likely to avoid the adverse effects of a typical new public management (NPM) guided by the corporate principles. Though this appears to be a bottom up approach as opposed to top down in the NPM, given the resource constraint and stiff competition, the top down approach may prevail over bottom up approach. The implementation of this proposal would require reconstitution of university governance structure which is a daunting exercise. Further, the autonomy needs to be circumscribed as the university teachers are goaded to respond to the industry demand and to write papers keeping in mind the ranking parameters, impact factor of the journals, the list of journals recognized and citation index.

## 7 Globalization and Internationalization

The difference between the two concepts, globalization and internationalization often creates confusion in the policy discourse. The four modes of globalization under the GATS are Mode 1: Cross-border supply of education which involves program mobility; Mode 2: Consumption abroad in the form of student mobility across the border; Mode 3: Commercial or institutional mobility through setting up of branch campuses, and Mode 4: Movement of natural persons. Internationalization refers to the university processes being integrated with the global like curriculum going global, students and the teachers from abroad participating in teaching–learning and research. Globalization as envisaged under the four modes, arguably, seeks to commodify education with the formation of market at the global level. The proponents of internationalization on the other hand (de Wit & Altbach, 2022) argue for internationalization which would be based more on cultural exchanges and foster global citizenship. While globalization often face resistance from the opponents of commercialization and marketization, that is why internationalization is often resorted to globalize with a dose of cultural exchange and collaboration. While the Economic Survey 2021–22 (GoI, 2022a) lists globalization of Indian higher education as one of the policy objectives for higher education reform, the NEP talks about internationalization.

The future market looks more competitive and vulnerable but the only way to go forward is to be inclusive and non-commercial (de Wit & Altbach, 2022). The student mobility across the borders has been steadily rising. The ranking of the universities fosters internationalization at both home and abroad. The ranking agencies like the THE and QS give weightage to the international students studying in the universities.

## *7.1 Internationalization*

The main modalities of internationalization are increased student mobility and research collaborations with the HEIs in other countries. In fact, the focus is more on increasing inbound student mobility by offering education at a relatively lower cost compared to the other global destinations. India being the second in terms of the outbound student mobility in the world, the focus is more on 'internationalization at home'.[8] Given the quality and performance of India's HEIs in the global sphere, the scope of internationalization is likely to be limited in terms of the participating countries.

The NEP recommends opening up of International Branch Campuses (IBCs) in India by the foreign universities in the top 100 list of global rankings. Also, the top Indian universities will be encouraged to open up branch campuses abroad. Recently, media reported about IIT Delhi's willingness to open up branch campuses in Egypt, Saudi Arabia and United Kingdom.[9] The UGC Chairperson revealed that the UGC had contacted 600 foreign universities and 63 foreign envoys posted in India to foster collaboration among the national and foreign universities (The Indian Express 8 June, 2022). Further, the Indian and foreign universities are being encouraged to tie up for twining, dual degree and joint degree programs from AY 2023–24 academic session (GoI, 2022b).[10] However, it is unclear whether the IBCs would be a not-for profit entry as it is required to be the case in the context of India. First, the legal requirement of being a 'not-for profit' is a unique feature of India's education sector. In many

---

[8] Recently, Jindal Global Law School has signed up MoUs with 10 universities in 6 countries for increasing international student mobility. See https://indianexpress.com/article/cities/delhi/jindal-global-law-school-signs-mous-with-10-universities-in-6-countries-for-international-student-mobility-7761885/.

[9] https://www.universityworldnews.com/post.php?story=20211118160358154. https://estudentbook.com/estudenttimes/prestigious-iits-all-set-to-open-branches-in-united-kingdom.

[10] The Indian HEIs to become eligible to tie up should have a NAAC score of above 3.01, or in the top 1000 THE or QS ranking or in the top 100 NIRF ranking. The foreign institutions should feature in the top 1000 of the THE or QS world ranking.

countries, the HEIs are for profit and these rules might hinder them from stepping in the business.

The drive behind India's internationalization policy is mostly rooted in curbing the 'brain-drain' and outward-student mobility and creating an elusive image of being the 'Viswa-Guru' or global leader. The gains from integrating Indian higher education in global higher education would depend on the net outcome of extent of collaboration which opens up a possibility for mutual gains while at the same time, competition and commercial tendencies would tend to commodify higher education and restrict possibilities of higher education becoming a global public good.

## 8 Discussion

### *8.1 Access and Equity*

The spread of online education may widen access but at the same time the system is likely to get more and more differentiated. Category-I and the IoEs have been given freedom to decide admission policy to prioritise merit. It may mean that these top quality institutions have the freedom to deviate from national reservation policy. The structural inequalities remain embedded in the system. With the freedom to charge tuition fees depending on the accreditation score as suggested in the NEP, diminishing public funding and entre of the foreign universities, the cost of education is set to rise. With the increasing differentiation, higher education will further strengthen as a 'positional good' leading to differential treatment in the job market for students coming from various institutions and diverse socio-economic backgrounds.

The overall impact would be accentuation of the existing hierarchy in the higher education sector. This would partially nullify the benefits accruing to the socio-economically disadvantaged groups in the context of massification as the students from the top ranking HEIs stand to gain in the job market as higher education credentials become 'positional goods' (Marginson, 2016). Varghese et al. (2021) pointed out based on empirical evidence that how the inequalities with respect to gender and social groups persist in the context of the massification of Indian higher education.

### *8.2 Quality*

As a select set of universities are being nurtured to feature in world ranking table, excellence seems to be conceptualized and defined by the parameters with weights assigned by the world ranking agencies. What a university can do for the economy and society, what contributions that a university makes to the public good character of higher education and what a university does for self-formation and inculcation of values get relegated in the process. To judge a university only by the parameters set by the world ranking agency would not be proper. The NEP has put a lot of emphasis on the GEC to ensure quality for different professions. The NAC is set to play a major role too. Orientation toward vocational education and the implementation of the ABC will make students think that education is all about doing the necessary credits to earn certificates while the primary purpose of education is to be valued in the job market for possessing the necessary skills. This is one conception of what quality of education is that emerges the policy discourse.

The blended mode would definitely improve access as students from the remotest part of the country can also join as long as the digital divide is overcome with the support from the government. The question remains whether getting access to education will get translated to quality learning outcomes. Foreign collaboration in fact will intensify competition and particularly so for the less reputed middle ranking institutions. With the decline in public funding, the cost recovery tendencies will assume more importance and fee levels are set to rise. So in short, widening access will also be associated with increasing differentiation which will mitigate the possibilities of higher education being upheld as a right and a common good.

One argument often advanced in favor of increasing use of technology is the possibility of replication of the course content and the delivery which are important determinants of quality and learning outcomes. Learning outcomes depend on classroom interaction too. Though the technology is advancing fast to conjure up a real life experience in the classroom, it is likely to have a significant impact on the classroom teaching. For example, it is now possible for someone to think of doing a course on AI to be taught by one of the top experts of the world in that area if one joins a course of Coursera or Udemy. But this is a narrow concept of quality. One significant factor which will determine the quality of Indian higher education is what Marginson (2022) calls 'political culture'. Chattopadhyay (2012) and Chandra (2017) among others drew attention to the adverse effects of corruption on the functioning of the universities and recently Sharma et al. (2021) pointed out the role of students and teachers as political actors is an important element in university governance how the functioning of reputed universities can get affected if the political culture is missing.

## *8.3 Circumscribing Autonomy and Institutionalizing Accountability*

The higher education transformation can be seen as a transition in the spectrum of accountability mechanisms from conscience to market and the state (Trow, 1996). Given the rising importance of strategy making the market is increasingly becoming global and more and more competitive with rising opportunities for collaboration. Exercise of academic autonomy in the Humboldtian sense is more of a utopia now. Only the top performing institutions and the faculty will have autonomy albeit in a limited sense, which is a prerequisite for creativity and innovation, both in teaching and research. Academic freedom in the form of free speech and the public sphere will witness shrinkage. Bureaucratization and states' interference in recruitment and in constitution of committees and choice university leaders should decline otherwise the academic culture and commitment cannot improve. We also need to remember that financial autonomy in the face of reduction in public funding can interfere with the academic autonomy of the institutions which is necessary for rejuvenation of the academia and the universities.

## 8.4 The Public Good Character of Higher Education

Access will expand but because of the limited socialization in the campus, the transformative capacity of education associated with generation of externalities and spread of it within the community will remain limited due to increase in participation and differentiation commensurate with increasing coverage of on line education. In blended mode and the kind of mobility the students are being given in the NEP, there is likely to be a disassociation of the students from the campus and the peer groups. Socialization in the campus is essential from self-formation and to grow into a responsible citizen. At the same time, there is an increasing connection through network and social media.

There is also a focus on competence-based skill development associated with unbundling and award of micro-certificates. How will critical thinking be developed when the peer-based interaction and socialization in the campus are set to wane over time. Protests by the students and teachers and participation in the university activities will gradually decline. The operation of the NPM will make teachers more focused for achieving their research targets. The teaching community will get fragmented more and more and this will restrict their contribution to the making of the students and the campus life.

As ABC gains prominence in the Indian landscape, the possible implications will manifest in the weakening of the teacher–student relations and therefore undermining the emotional connect between university and the students. Informed decision making is difficult given the students' tendency to maximize grades by choosing softer options and uncertainty over course content and efficacy of online instructions.

A major factor for this transformation which is a crucial constraint to imagine and desire the future of Indian higher education is the ubiquitous and perennial fiscal constraint at least with respect to higher education. To gain from the infusion of competitive pressure and a policy nudge for exploring opportunities for collaboration, the foundation has to be strong which requires agency on the part of the teachers and students to build-up their capacities with policy support in the form of regulation and funding support. While appropriate policy support has been envisaged in the NEP and UGC regulations and notifications, the required funding support is unlikely to be forthcoming in the post-Covid era. Chattopadhyay (2022) argues for adopting a public good framework to imagine the future of Indian higher education in the Post-Covid era for achieving human development and social justice.

## 9 Concluding Remarks

This paper looks at the challenges and possibilities as the NEP sets the stage for ushering in major structural changes in the Indian higher education sector. There are challenges which are to be circumvented with the state support and this is necessary to gain from the emerging possibilities both at the national and global level. Capacity building is necessary to gain from competition and collaboration. The NEP 2020 gives the institutions ten years to evolve into truly autonomous multi-disciplinary institutions as the NAC enforces binary grading ostensibly to eliminate the poorly performing institutions. The irreversible changes being effected because of technology and regulations would reduce the fragmentation of the market not only at the national level, but at the global level. The intensity of competition is likely to rise as the institutions compete for funds to survive and the reputed and the well performing institutions take the plunge in the global competition and to create opportunities for research collaboration in pursuit of achieving the status of world class universities. The middle ranking institutions would form clusters and merge with the bigger ones. All these changes will occur when there is a thrust for vocational education. Not sure as of now to what extent the orientation for skill formation will deter self-formation which is at the root of higher education being realized as a public or a common good. It also looks uncertain how the demand for social sciences and humanities will change in view of the freedom being given to the students to choose courses from a larger basket. Though job scarcity will remain, demand for new skills will continue to emerge in the job market. Development in the job markets as demand for new skills emerge, the institutions would have to gear up to respond to the changes. Improvement in quality of school education is absolutely crucial for realizing the benefits of this transformation at the post-secondary level. The multidimensional inequities that exists in the country with respect to region, gender, digital infrastructure and social categories will continue to undermine the issue of access and equity and limit the prospect of transformation of higher education as a public good.

## References

Becker, G. S. (1993). *Human capital: A theoretical and empirical analysis with special reference to education* (3rd ed.). University of Chicago Press (Originally published in 1964).

Bhushan, S. (2019). Contesting the present in the evolution of public higher education. In S. Bhushan (Ed.), *The future of higher education in India*. Springer.

Brown, P., Lauder, H., & Cheung, S. Y. (2020). *The death of human capital?* Oxford University Press.

Chandra, P. (2017). *Building universities that matter: Where are Indian institutions going wrong?* Orient BlackSwan.

Chattopadhyay, S (2009). The market in higher education: Concern for equity and quality. *Economic and Political Weekly, XLIV*(29), 53–61.

Chattopadhyay, S. (2012). *Education and economics: Disciplinary evolution and policy discourse.* Oxford University Press.

Chattopadhyay, S. (2019). World ranking of the universities: What does it entail for the future. In S. Bhushan (Ed.), *The future of the Indian universities*. Springer.
Chattopadhyay, S. (2020). NEP 2020: An uncertain future for Indian higher education. *Economic and Political Weekly, LV*(46), 23–27.
Chattopadhyay, S. (2021). Internationalisation of Indian higher education: Issues and challenges. In S. Chattopadhyay, S. Marginson, & N. V. Varghese (Eds.), *Changing higher education in India*. Bloomsbury.
Chattopadhyay, S. (2022). Higher education in quest of humane development: Envisaging the future in the post-covid era. In B. Dasgupta, P. Sarkhel, A. Ghosh, & B. Ghosh (Eds.), *In quest of human development: Human development, community networking and public service delivery in India*. Springer.
Das, D., & Chattopadhyay, S. (2014). Academic performance indicators: Straight jacketing higher education. *Economic and Political Weekly, 49*(50), 68–71.
de Wit, H., & Altbach, P. A. (2022). The impact of covid-19 on the internationalisation of higher education, revolutionary or not? In C. Raj Kumar, M. Mukherjee, T. Belousova, & N. Nair (Eds.), *Global higher education during and beyond covid-19: Perspectives and challenges* (pp. 219–231). Springer.
Etzkowtiz, H,. Webster, A,. & Healey, P. (1998). Introduction in Etzkowitz,K et al (eds) *Capitalizing Knowledge: New intersections of industry and academia*, State University of New York Press: New York, 1–17
Foray, D (2006). *Economies of Knowledge,* The MIT Press, Cambridge, Massachusetts.
Government of India (GoI). (2017). University Grants Commission (Institutions of Eminence Deemed to be Universities) Regulations 2017. The Gazette of India, 337(4), Part III, Section 4, August 30, 2017. Available at: https://www.ugc.ac.in/pdfnews/5403862_Gazette-Institutions-of-Eminence-Deemed-to-be-Universities.pdf
Government of India. (2018). UGC (Categorisation of Universities (only) for Grant of Graded Autonomy) Regulations 2018. UGC.
Government of India (GoI). (2019). *Draft National Education Policy 2019*. Ministry of Education. Available at: https://www.education.gov.in/sites/upload_files/mhrd/files/Draft_NEP_2019_EN_Revised.pdf. Accessed August 11, 2020
Government of India. (2020a). The National Education Policy 2020. Ministry of Education. Available at: https://www.mhrd.gov.in/sites/upload_files/mhrd/files/NEP_Final_English.pdf. Accessed August 11, 2020
Government of India (GoI). (2020b). *Public notice: Expression of interest (UG Course Mapping/SWAYAM) dated 31.07.2020*. UGC. Available at: https://www.ugc.ac.in/pdfnews/4981711_Public-Notice-EOI.pdf. Accessed August 11, 2020
Government of India (GoI). (2020c). *All India statistics for higher education 2018–19*. Ministry of Education. Available at: https://www.education.gov.in/sites/upload_files/mhrd/files/statistics-new/Budget%20Exp%202017-18%20-27-6-2020c.pdf. Accessed June 28, 2021
Government of India. (2022a). Economic Survey 2021–22.
Government of India (GoI). (2022b). University grants commission academic collaboration between Indian and foreign higher education institutions to offer twining, joint degree, and dual degree programmes) regulations, 2022. https://www.ugc.ac.in/pdfnews/4555806_UGC-Acad-Collab-Regulations.pdf. Accessed June 12, 2022
International Finance Corporation. (2020). Case study: Toward ending educational privilege. IFC-CourseraCaseStudy-May2020.pdf.
IISc top Indian university, overtakes IITs: QS World University Rankings | Education News, The Indian Express.
Locatelli, R. (2018, February). *Education as a public and common good: Reframing the governance of education in a changing context* (UNECSO Education Research and Foresight Working Papers, No. 22). UNESCO. Available at: http://unesdoc.unesco.org/images/0026/002616/261614E.pdf. Accessed June 28, 2021

Locke, W. (2011). The institutionalization of rankings: Managing status anxiety in an increasingly marketized environment in the future of university rankings. In J. C. Shin, R. K. Toutkoushian, & U. Teichler (Eds.), *University rankings: Theoretical basis, methodology and impacts on global higher education*. Springer.

Marginson, S. (2016). *Higher education and the common good*. Melbourne University Press.

Marginson, S. (2022). Challenges and possibilities for higher education in India during and beyond the covid-19 pandemic. In C. M. Raj Kumar, M. Mukherjee, T. Belousova, & N. Nair (Eds.), *Global higher education during and beyond Covid-19: Perspectives and challenges* (pp. 11–22). Springer.

McCowan, T. (2017). Higher education, unbundling and the end of the university as we know it. *Oxford Review of Education, 46*(6), 733–748.

Olssen, M., Codd, J., & O'Neill, A. (2004). *Education policy: Globalization, citizenship and democracy*. Sage Publications.

Samuelson, P. (1954). The pure theory of public expenditure. *Review of Economics and Statistics, 36*(4), 387–389.

Sharma, Y. (2022, May 20). UNESCO reaffirms higher education as a right and a public good. *University World News*. https://www.universityworldnews.com/post.php?story=20220520090907357

Sharma, A., & Chisti, V., Pathak, B. K. (2021). Teachers and students as political actors. In S. Chattopadhyay, S. Marginson, & N. V. Varghese (Eds.), *Indian higher education*. Bloomsbury.

Slaughter, S., & Leslie, L. L. (1997). *Academic capitalism*. The John Hopkins University Press.

Stiglitz, J. E. (1975). The theory of screening, education, and the distribution of income. *The American Economic Review, 65*(3), 283–300.

Täljedal, I.-B. (2013). Publish and Perish: A note on a collapsing academic authorship. In S. Rider, Y. Hasselberg, & A. Waluszewski (Eds.), *Transformation in research, higher education and the academic market: The breakdown of scientific thought*. Springer.

Teichler, U. (2011). The future of university rankings. In J. C. Shin, R. K. Toutkoushian, & U. Teichler (Eds.), *University rankings: Theoretical basis, methodology and impacts on global higher education*. Springer.

Trow, M. (1996). *Trust markets and accountability in higher education: A comparative perspective*. Research and Occasional Paper Series, CSHE.1.96. Centre for Studies in Higher Education, University of California.

Varghese, N. V., Sabharwal, N., & Malish, C. M. (2021). Equity in higher education for inclusive growth: Evidence from India. In S. Chattopadhyay, S. Marginson, & N. V. Varghese (Eds.), *Indian higher education*. Bloomsbury.

Washburn, J. (2005). *University Inc. The corporate corruption of higher education*. Basic Books.

# Trends, Patterns and Regional Variations of COVID-19 Pandemic in India at Sub-national Level: Analysis Based on Spatial Econometric Method

**Sushil Kr. Haldar**

## 1 Introduction

The first COVID-19 case in India was reported on January 30, 2020, in Kerala. Observing the devastating consequences of European countries, the Government of India has declared a nationwide lockdown with a view to stop spreading the COVID-19 on March 24 for three weeks, subsequently it was extended till May 17, 2020, after which phased lockdown for containment zones had been in effect until June 30, 2020. The government implemented a zonal classification of regions in the nation, with each region falling in one of three classes—red zones (hotspots with high doubling rates and high number of active cases), orange zones (non-hotspots with fewer cases) and green zones (regions without confirmed cases or without new cases in the previous 21 days). In addition to nationwide response patterns, various state governments responded to the pandemic with various declarations of emergency, closure of institutions and public meeting places, in addition to other restrictions to contain the spread of the virus. But we could not stop the spreading of COVID-19! India shares about 16.5% of global population, but it shares 8.33% of global COVID-19 infected patients and 8.37% of global death due to COVID-19 as reported by the WHO as on May 13, 2022 (WHO May 2022). Numerous studies have attempted to know the growth pattern and spatial distribution and determinants of COVID-19 pandemic across the countries in the world including India. In order to explore the scope of my study, I try to highlight some of the Indian studies on COVID-19 pandemic.

Using mathematical modeling on real data of COVID-19 across 17 states, Sarkar et al. (2020) have argued that achieving a reduction in the contact rate between uninfected and infected individuals by quarantined the susceptible individuals, can

S. Kr. Haldar (✉)
Department of Economics, Jadavpur University, Kolkata 700032, India
e-mail: sushil.haldar@gmai.com



A. Raychaudhuri and A. Ghose (eds.), *Managing Pandemic and Correcting Development Fundamentals*, India Studies in Business and Economics,
https://doi.org/10.1007/978-981-19-8680-2_6

effectively reduce the basic reproduction number. Their model suggests that the elimination of ongoing COVID-19 pandemic is possible by combining the restrictive social distancing and contact tracing. This is supported by Yadav and Bhattacharjee (2020); their preliminary results reveal that the lockdown was effective in reducing mobility, and urbanization and accessibility do have a role to play in the spread of the virus. But, lockdown cannot continue for indefinite period, as a result social distancing along with COVID protocol becomes relevant to combat the rapid spreading of the virus. Using a standard epidemiological model of growth of COVID-19 till middle of May, Chatterjee et al. (2020) have observed that with the current infection rate and containment measures, the total active infection in India would be maximum at the end of June or beginning of July 2020. Short-term predictions reveal an increasing and worrying trend of COVID-19 cases for all states in India, while the long-term predictions reveal the possibility of oscillatory dynamics (Khajanchi et al., 2020). There exists wide geographical variation in COVID-19 pandemic with a concentration in some major cities and states while disaggregated data at local levels allows understanding geographical disparity of the pandemic (Ghosh et al., 2020; Srivastava et al., 2020). Ghosh et al. (2020) have used COVID-19 data from March 01 to May 31 and observed that the infection rate (IR) is concentrated mainly Western and Northern India, and they are associated with major cities. Tamrakar et al. (2020) have identified hotspot and cold spot districts based on IR using the data on COVID-19 during March 14 to July 31; they have observed that the IR is highly concentrated among nine states in India. They argue that after adjusting the role of socio-economic and health-related factors, the COVID-19 IR was found to be more rampant in districts with a higher population density, a higher percentage of the urban population, a higher percentage of backward castes and with a higher level of testing ratio. This result is more or less supported by Kashif et al. (2020). Initially, there was a sharp contrast between Western and Eastern India but from mid-May, Eastern India has witnessed a steep rise in IR; spatial autocorrelation analysis showed a low autocorrelation initially which is found to be increasing over time; moreover, the hotspot clustering was observed in Western Maharashtra, Eastern Tamil Nadu, Gujarat and around West Bengal especially Kolkata by the second week of August (Gupta et al., 2020). An interesting study was conducted by Basu and Majumder (2021) using the state-level panel data for India, and they have observed that infections are clustered in more urbanized and prosperous states; poorer states show low cases of infection showing evidence of herd immunity of poor which stands in sharp contrast with the developed countries in the world.

## 2 Scope and Objectives of the Study

All the earlier studies are to some extent partial in nature because the above studies could not capture the entire period of data on COVID-19. India has witnessed three waves of COVID-19 pandemic. The first wave was witnessed during September 2020; the second wave was occurred during May 2021, and the third wave was occurred during Feb 2022. The present study is distinct from earlier studies because it considers the entire periods from March 2020 to Feb 2022. The prediction of infection rate in India done by earlier studies does not match with the real picture because of the peculiar features of the virus in one hand and heterogeneous characteristics of our country at the sub-national level. The present study on COVID-19 pandemic considers 27 states in India that covers 99.7% of India's population. Our study takes into account a long period of time (viz. the initial outbreak of pandemic during March 2020 to February 2022)—this will help us to understand the degree of spreading of pandemic during initial phase of lockdown, final phase of lockdown and unlock periods as well. The national level infection rate (CIR) and fatality rate (CFR) are estimated at 3239.992 (per 100 thousand populations) and 1.19 (in percentage), respectively, on March 7, 2022. Does the COVID infection rate (CIR) across states vary uniformly? Are the COVID fatality rate (CFR) same across states? How do the CIR and CFR vary across states over time (viz. initial phase of lockdown, mid of lockdown phase and unlock period)? Is there any relationship between CIR and CFR across states over time? Are the growth patterns of CIR and CFR same across states over time? Does neighborhood effect matter toward spreading of the virus? How do the values of global and local Moran's index respond over three waves of time? What are the socio-economic, demographic and geo-spatial factors responsible toward variations of CIR and CFR across states?

## 3 Data and Methodology

State wise data regarding COVID-19 are collected from the Ministry of Health and Family Welfare, Government of India. Data regarding socio-economic variables and healthcare variables are drawn from NFHS-4 and Census, 2011, and the data are extrapolated for 2020. Population size and its age compositions of states are drawn from population projection report, RGI Government of India. A detailed note pertaining data, abbreviations and data source are given in Appendix.

We have considered two COVID-19 pandemic parameters, which are defined as follows:

$$\text{COVID incidence rate (CIR)} = \frac{I}{P}, \tag{1}$$

and

$$\text{COVID fatality rate} = \frac{D}{I} \tag{2}$$

where $P$ is the total population who are exposed to the risk of being affected by the virus, $I$ be the number of persons who are affected, $D$ stands for total death due to COVID-19. Now, we can estimate CIR and CFR at the specific time or at the particular time interval (may be a week/month/year). This means we can estimate cumulative and non-cumulative figures of CIR and CFR. The CIR and CFR are estimated across states including India from April 1, 2020, to March 2022 considering only the peak time points of three waves. The cumulative values of CIR across states over time look like logistic curve. The parameters of logistic curve may be estimated using the following principle:

$$\text{CIR} = \frac{M}{1 + e^{r(\beta - t)}} \tag{3}$$

where $M$ be the maximum value of CIR, $r$ stands for rate of growth of CIR and $\beta$ represents the time at which the curve becomes skew-symmetric. This means that the point of inflection occurs at $t = \beta$. Therefore, we have three unknown parameters (like $M$, $r$ and $\beta$) to be estimated using appropriate method. In our present paper, we could not estimate the parameters of the logistic growth curve of CIR. However, we plot the growth patterns of CIR across few states considering the five distinct geographical regions in India.

Spatial factors need to be used in order to take into account the impact of neighborhood externalities. We use **Moran's index (MI)** which captures spatial autocorrelation. Following Anselin (1988, 1995) and Hongfei et al. (2007), we define Moran's index (MI) as

$$\text{MI} = \frac{N}{W} \cdot \frac{\sum_i \sum_j w_{ij}(X_i - \overline{X})(X_j - \overline{X})}{\sum_i (X_i - \overline{X})^2}, \tag{4}$$

where $N$ = number of spatial units indexed by $i$ and $j$ (states), $W = \sum_i \sum_j w_{ij}$ = sum of spatial weights, $w_{ij}$ is a matrix of spatial weights with zeros on the diagonal ($w_{ii} = w_{jj} = 0$), $X$ be the variable of interest (viz. CIR or CFR) and $\overline{X}$ = mean of the variable. The spatial weight matrix can be defined in many ways but the Rook's contiguity matrix is assumed to be a better approach (Anselin, 1988). We have adopted Rook's contiguity matrix; by geographic proximity, we construct a binary matrix, in which, $w_{ij} = 1$ if two states share borders, otherwise zero. The weight matrix has been row standardized. Following Anselin (1988), for statistical significance testing, we transform Eq. (4) to $Z$ (normalized value) value.

$$Z_{\text{MI}} = \frac{\text{MI} - E[\text{MI}]}{\sqrt{V(\text{MI})}}, \tag{5}$$

where $E[\text{MI}] = -\frac{1}{N-1}$ and

$$V(\text{MI}) = \frac{NS_4 - S_3 S_5}{(N-1)(N-2)(N-3) \cdot W^2} - (E[\text{MI}])^2$$

where

$$S_1 = \frac{1}{2}\sum_i \sum_j (w_{ij} + w_{ji})^2, \quad S_2 = \sum_i \left( \sum_j w_{ij} + \sum_j w_{ji} \right)^2,$$

$$S_3 = \frac{N^{-1}\sum_i (X_i - \overline{X})^4}{\left[ N^{-1}\sum_i (X_i - \overline{X})^2 \right]^2},$$

$$S_4 = (N^2 - 3N + 3)S_1 - NS_2 + 3W^2, \quad S_5 = (N^2 - N))S_1 - 2NS_2 + 6W^2.$$

The *Z*-scores of MI along with the corresponding "*p*-values" are used for measuring statistical significance whether or not to reject the null hypothesis (of no-spatial autocorrelation); high but positive *Z*-score for a feature indicates that the surrounding features have similar values (either high values or low values). This gives us that the feature is clustered or clubbed geographically (Anselin & Florax, 1995). Similarly, negative *Z*-score for a feature indicates a statistically significant spatial data outlier which means that the feature values are dispersed spatially. Equation (5) is meant for global Moran's index, it measures the extent to which points that are "close together" on average in space having similar values.

However, a local Moran index is suggested that captures the extent to which points that are "close" to a given point having similar values (Anselin & Florax, 1995). This is shown below:

Analysis of local Moran's *I* is very similar to that of global Moran's *I*, as shown in Eq. (6).

$$\mathrm{MI}_i^L = \frac{X_i - \overline{X}}{S_i^2} \sum_{j=1, i \neq j} w_{ij}(X_j - \overline{X}) \tag{6}$$

where $S_i^2 = \frac{\sum_{j=1, i \neq j}^{N} w_{ij}}{N-1} - \overline{X}^2$. For a randomization hypothesis, the expected value is $E(I_i) = -\frac{\sum_{j=1, i \neq j}^{N} w_{ij}}{N-1}$ and the variance of $\mathrm{MI}_i^L$ is given as:

The GMI lets us get an idea of the intensity of the "average" spatial autocorrelation in a given sample for a given variable like CIR or CFR. When the GMI indicates the presence of positive spatial autocorrelation, the measurement is assumed to be identical (on an average) at every point of the space considered. The statistics do not allow us to evaluate the local structure of the spatial autocorrelation. The LMI allows us to identify the individual contributions to the GMI.

The GMI and LMI are basically used for analyzing spatial autocorrelation and identifying clustering but for prediction purposes, we shall use two models like spatial autoregressive model (SAR) and spatial error model (SEM). Following Anselin (1988) and Anselin and Bera (1998), we consider the following two models:

$$y = Wy\rho + X\beta + \varepsilon \tag{7}$$

where $y$ is the vector of dimension $(N \times 1)$ for $N$ dependent variables, the matrix $X$ of dimension $(N \times K)$, $\beta$ is the vector of dimension $(K \times 1)$, $e$ is white noise, $W$ is the spatial weight matrix already defined earlier, $\rho$ is a scalar that measures the mean spill-over effect of nearby individual behaviors on a chosen individual. A similar model is proposed where the disturbance term (error term) is spatially autocorrelated. Disturbance spatial autocorrelation can arise from the omission of a spatially correlated variable or the presence of a form of spatial heterogeneity. This is shown by the following Eq. (8).

$$y = X\beta + (I - \lambda W)^{-1}\varepsilon \tag{8}$$

where $\lambda$ stands for spatial autocorrelation generated from the error term and $I$ be the identity matrix. The other notations are same as defined earlier. The expression (8) is known as spatial error model (SEM). The OLS cannot be applied, rather MLE and GMM are appropriate to estimate the parameters.

## 4 Empirical Analysis

Before analyzing the growth pattern of CIR and CFR across 27 states, we first consider the national picture of CIR and CFR corresponding to the three waves of the pandemic (Tables 1 and 2).

The national picture of CIR gives some interesting results. The growth of CIR was found to be lower during the lockdown period. The lockdown was started on and from March 23, 2020, limiting movement of the entire 1.3 billion population of India as a preventive measure against the COVID-19 pandemic in India. On May 1 the Government of India extended the nationwide lockdown further by two weeks until May 17. The Government divided all the districts into three zones based on the

**Table 1** COVID incidence rate (CIR) in India (per 100 thousand populations)

| Region | Sept 13, 2020 (first wave) | May 11, 2021 (second wave) | Feb 5, 2022 (third wave) | March 7, 2022 |
|---|---|---|---|---|
| India | 358.507 | 1733.773 | 3173.133 | 3239.992 |

*Note* The mid-year projected population in India is used (*source* PRB, USA). *Source* Author's estimation. CIR is estimated per 100 thousand population

**Table 2** COVID fatality rate (CFR) in India (per 100 populations)

| Region | Sept 13, 2020 (first wave) | May 11, 2021 (second wave) | Feb 5, 2022 (third wave) | March 7, 2022 |
|---|---|---|---|---|
| India | 1.653 | 1.087 | 1.191 | 1.199 |

*Source* Author's estimation. CFR is estimated per 100 infected persons

spread of the virus—green, red and orange—with relaxations applied accordingly. On May 17, the lockdown was further extended till May 31 by the National Disaster Management Authority. The success of lockdown to combat the spreading of the virus is clear from Table 1.

Keeping in mind the adverse economic consequences of lockdown, the Government of India on May 30 announced that lockdown restrictions were to be lifted from then onwards, while the ongoing lockdown would be further extended till June 30 for only the containment zones. During the unlock phase, the CIR increases exponentially and it reaches at the maximum level during September 13–19 in the first wave. The CIR of the peak of the second wave is estimated at 1733, which is 4.8 times higher than the first wave; the CIR of the third wave is 3173, which is 1.8 times higher than the second wave! The interesting point is that the CFR is found to be slightly higher initially, but it becomes stable around 1% during the entire pandemic.

Now, in order to understand the growth dynamics of CIR across states, we specifically consider three time points corresponding to the peaks of three waves. During the first wave of the pandemic (Sept 2020), the maximum CIR was found in Puducherry (2325.96) and the minimum was noticed in Himachal Pradesh (126.23). The national average was 308.507.

During the second wave (May 2021), the position of Puducherry remained the same but the minimum infection was found in Bihar (555.17); the national average reached to 1733.77.

In the third wave (Feb 2022), the same picture was found as it was in second wave but the national average reached to 3173.3 (Tables 3 and 4).

The variance of CFR across 27 states is found to be low in all the three waves, the CFR was found to be maximum (2.97) in Punjab followed by Maharashtra (2.81), whereas the minimum CFR was noticed in Assam (0.32). During the second and third waves, Punjab had experienced the maximum CFR, whereas the minimum CFR was found in Telangana. Does higher CIR lead to higher CFR? In order to answer this question, we have carried out the rank correlation between CIR and CFR across 27 states. The values of the rank correlation for three time points are as follows:

Rank correlation between CIR and CFR for T1 (Sept 13, 2020) = 0.2169
Rank correlation between CIR and CFR for T2 (May 11, 2021) = 0.1824
Rank correlation between CIR and CFR for T3 (Feb 5, 2022) = 0.096.

The above results clearly prove that states experiencing higher CIR generally experience higher CFR, but the values are found to be quite low and statistically insignificant. The standard deviation of CIR is quite high in all the three points of time, but it is quite low in case of CFR as noted (Table 5).

How do the infection rates disperse around the national average over time? This can be shown with the help of RADAR diagram as given in Figs. 1, 2 and 3. The dispersion of CIR across states over the national average clearly shows that in all the three waves Puducherry, Goa, Delhi, Maharashtra and Kerala and Karnataka consistently lie above the national average. Only one state like Chhattisgarh lies above the national average during second and third waves of the pandemic.

**Table 3** COVID infection rate (CIR) across 27 states (and UT) over the three waves of the pandemic

| States | Sept 13, 2020 | May 11, 2021 | Feb 5, 2022 |
|---|---|---|---|
| Maharashtra | 825.52 | 4087.90 | 6190.90 |
| Karnataka | 697.95 | 3064.20 | 6017.30 |
| Andhra Pradesh | 613.08 | 1432.20 | 2526.00 |
| Tamil Nadu | 703.89 | 1995.60 | 4810.80 |
| Kerala | 288.76 | 5301.10 | 17,059.00 |
| Delhi | 898.77 | 5610.10 | 7729.10 |
| Uttar Pradesh | 132.15 | 658.86 | 880.73 |
| West Bengal | 206.44 | 1047.90 | 2073.50 |
| Odisha | 335.67 | 1245.10 | 2884.00 |
| Telangana* | 399.10 | 1275.80 | 1966.90 |
| Rajasthan | 131.20 | 1007.30 | 1609.00 |
| Chhattisgarh | 228.19 | 3189.80 | 4198.80 |
| Bihar | 144.60 | 555.17 | 762.72 |
| Haryana | 314.17 | 2167.50 | 3314.70 |
| Assam | 414.91 | 880.70 | 2128.70 |
| Gujarat | 171.17 | 1056.90 | 1818.40 |
| Madhya Pradesh | 104.67 | 829.71 | 1211.50 |
| Punjab | 255.99 | 1497.20 | 2492.50 |
| J&K | 406.66 | 1711.30 | 3444.20 |
| Jharkhand | 171.38 | 829.21 | 1221.20 |
| Uttarakhand | 272.59 | 2244.70 | 3846.80 |
| Goa | 1114.52 | 5606.00 | 11,138.00 |
| Himachal Pradesh | 126.23 | 1857.20 | 3768.20 |
| Puducherry* | 2325.96 | 8729.10 | 19,565.00 |
| Tripura | 474.77 | 958.02 | 2526.70 |
| Manipur | 286.55 | 1326.10 | 4983.10 |
| Chandigarh | 355.42 | 2366.00 | 4263.90 |
| **India** | **358.507** | **1733.773** | **3173.3** |

*Source* Author's estimation

## 4.1 *COVID Infection and Spatial Analysis: Sub-national Level*

The objective of this section is to examine the presence of spatial dependency across states in respect of CIR. We have used global Moran's index and local Moran's index to identify the presence of spatial impact both at the aggregate and disaggregate level. Before going to the empirical analysis, we have represented the geographical

**Table 4** COVID fatality rate (CFR) across 27 states (and UT) over the three waves of the pandemic

| States | Sept 13, 2020 | May 11, 2021 | Feb 5, 2022 |
|---|---|---|---|
| Maharashtra | 2.81 | 1.72 | 1.84 |
| Karnataka | 1.59 | 1.22 | 1.01 |
| Andhra Pradesh | 0.87 | 0.79 | 0.64 |
| Tamil Nadu | 1.67 | 1.39 | 1.11 |
| Kerala | 0.4 | 0.41 | 0.92 |
| Delhi | 2.2 | 1.57 | 1.41 |
| Uttar Pradesh | 1.42 | 1.34 | 1.14 |
| West Bengal | 1.95 | 1.70 | 1.04 |
| Odisha | 0.42 | 0.55 | 0.69 |
| Telangana | 0.61 | 0.54 | 0.53 |
| Rajasthan | 1.21 | 0.81 | 0.76 |
| Chhattisgarh | 0.87 | 1.10 | 1.22 |
| Bihar | 0.52 | 0.57 | 1.48 |
| Haryana | 1.05 | 1.04 | 1.08 |
| Assam | 0.32 | 0.51 | 0.91 |
| Gujarat | 2.85 | 1.39 | 0.89 |
| M. P. | 2.01 | 1.25 | 1.07 |
| Punjab | 2.97 | 2.76 | 2.32 |
| J&K | 1.65 | 1.48 | 1.06 |
| Jharkhand | 0.9 | 0.87 | 1.23 |
| Uttarakhand | 1.33 | 1.63 | 1.77 |
| Goa | 1.18 | 1.37 | 1.54 |
| Him. Pr. | 0.79 | 1.61 | 1.46 |
| Puducherry | 1.9 | 1.58 | 1.19 |
| Tripura | 1.03 | 1.17 | 0.91 |
| Manipur | 0.58 | 1.27 | 1.53 |
| Chandigarh | 1.22 | 1.31 | 1.25 |
| **India** | **1.653** | **1.087** | **1.191** |

*Source* Author's estimation

**Table 5** Standard deviations of CIR and CFR across 27 states over three points of time

| Time | Standard deviation of CIR | Standard deviation of CFR |
|---|---|---|
| Sept 13, 2020 | 447.86 | 0.746 |
| May 11, 2021 | 1933.61 | 0.495 |
| Feb 5, 2022 | 4498.97 | 0.388 |

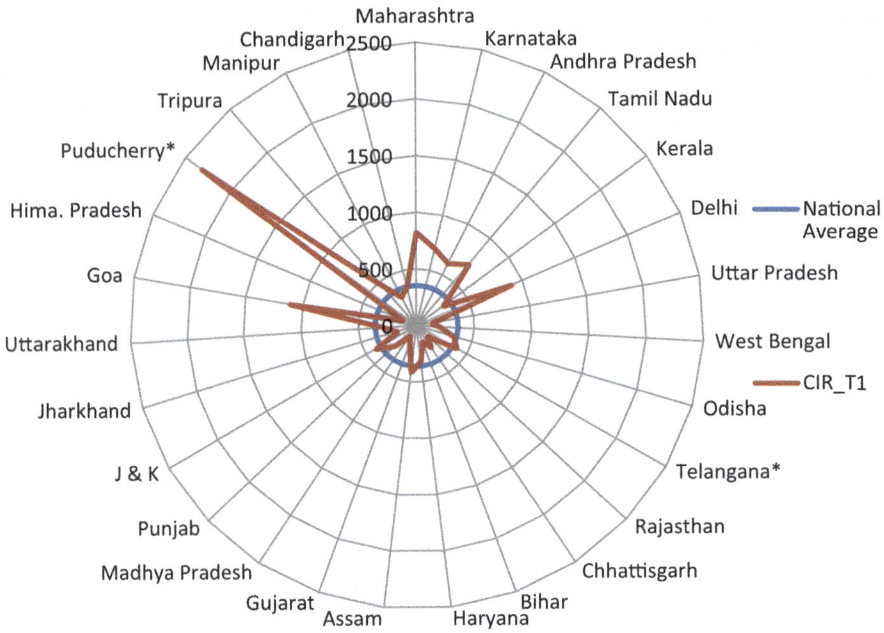


**Fig. 1** Dispersion of CIR of states around national average for first wave (Sep 2020). *Source* Author's calculations

distribution of CIR using the map of India for three waves as mentioned earlier (Fig. 4).

The graphical representation of CIR at first wave shows that states are forming clusters in terms of incidence rate. States from central part of India have similar incidence rate, whereas states from southern part of India are also found to be homogenous. For the graphical representation of the incidence rate, we have classified the distribution into four distinct classes (lower, lower middle, upper middle and high). Deep green color defines lower value, light green color represents the lower middle class, and light red and deep red colors are used to define upper middle and higher class, respectively. In the above figure, clustering in respect of lower and higher value is clear. Incidence rate in these states is influenced by their neighbors; though we have some outlier also.

In second time point (viz. second wave of the pandemic), the clustering of states is also observed. Here, the states are forming clusters in respect lower, lower middle, upper middle and high. Central part of India shows the clustering of states based on lower value; south eastern part shows the clustering in terms of lower middle value. Northern part of India shows the clustering based on upper middle value, whereas southern part has clustering based on higher value. Compare to earlier figure, in this figure, the dependency has increased across states. In third time point (third wave), we have similar result as second time point. The spatial dependency has increased in the third time point (Figs. 5 and 6).

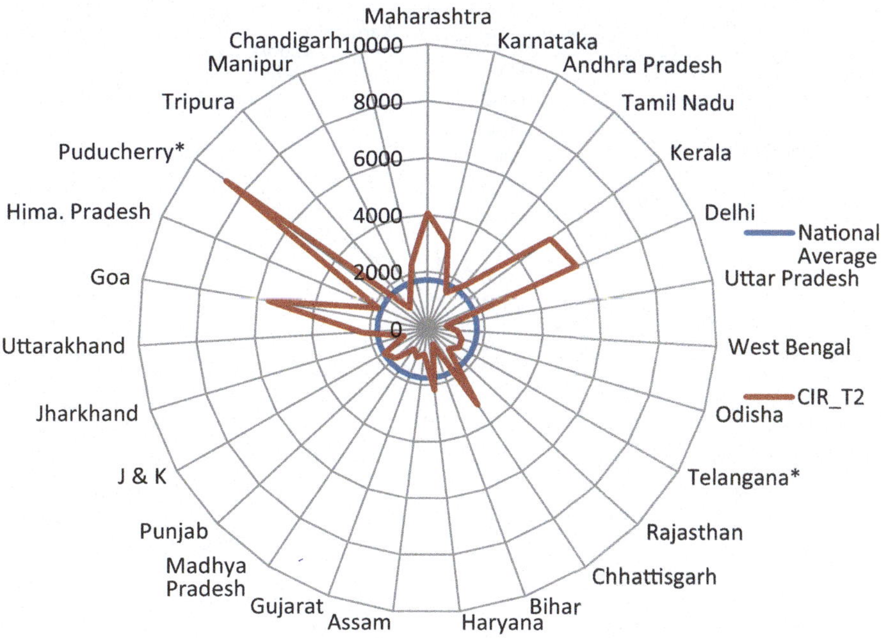


**Fig. 2** Dispersion of CIR of states around national average for second wave (May 2021). *Source* Author's calculations

Based on the distribution of each state in respect of CIR, we have explored the relationship between outcome and performance of a single state with its neighbors over time using the Moran's index as outlined earlier. Here, we have used another graphical plot which clearly portrays that how states are correlated with their neighbors. Following figures consist of four different quadrants, each quadrant has different implication. The top-right quadrant represents the high-high cluster (states with higher values of CIR surrounded by higher values of CIR), top-left quadrant shows low–high cluster (state with lower value surrounded by higher value), bottom-left quadrant defines the low-low cluster (lower states surrounded by lower states), whereas bottom-right quadrant shows that high-low cluster (states with high value surrounded by lower value. The second and fourth quadrants are treated as outliers. The following figures also reflect the average pattern of the relationship of CIR of a state (with its neighbor) using the fitted line.

In each diagram, we have positive fitted line; this implies on an average there exists a positive relationship between states and their neighbors. Over time, the line becomes steeper; this implies an increase in dependency. Now, from each diagram, we can identify the states falling in each quadrant.

In first time point, out of 27 states only six states are in high-high cluster, and 17 states are in low-low clustering. Only few states are playing the role of outliers (Tripura and Delhi are high-low cluster, whereas Telangana and Kerala are in low–high cluster; Fig. 7).

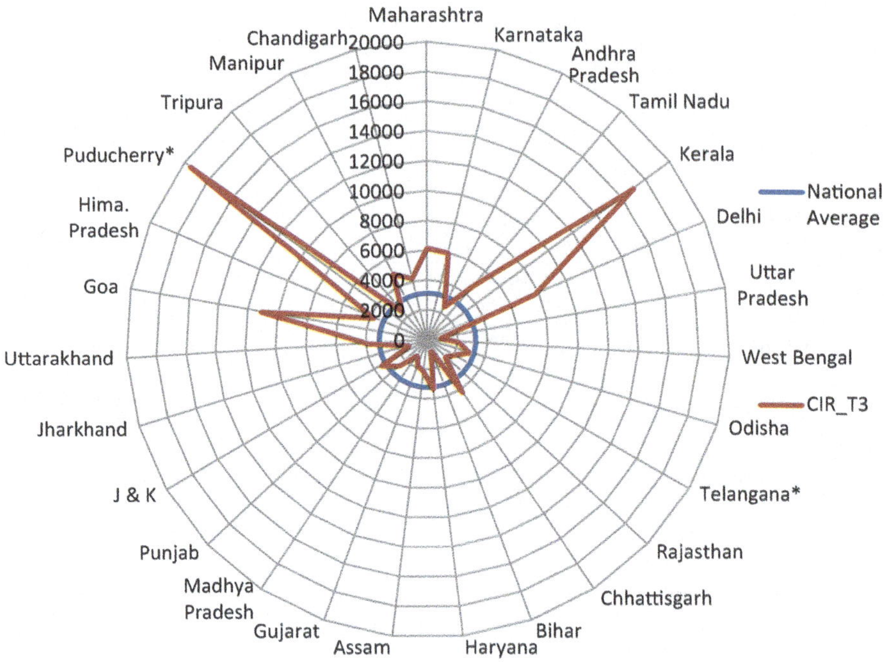


**Fig. 3** Dispersion of CIR of states around national average for third wave (Feb 2022). *Source* Author's calculations

In second time point (second wave), out of 26 states, five states form low-low cluster and 16 states form low-low cluster. Chandigarh, Chhattisgarh and Delhi are in high-low cluster, whereas Telangana, Tamil Nadu and Andhra Pradesh are found to be low–high clustering (Fig. 8).

In the terminal time point (third wave), the number of states of high-high cluster is found to be the same, whereas the number of states in low-low cluster has increased from 16 to 17. Manipur, Delhi and Maharashtra are found to form high-low clustering, and Telangana, Andhra Pradesh are in low–high clustering (Fig. 9).

Table 6 shows the states belonging to different clusters over time. The table also helps us to identify the transitions of states due to spatial spill-over impact. From the result of local Moran's index, we can identify the direction of spill-over effect.

Only three states are stable in high-high cluster, whereas 16 states are stable low-low cluster. The stable states are marked by red colored. Few states from each cluster are unstable due to spatial impact. Table 7 shows the result of global Moran's index across 27 states for three time points. Each index is positive and statistically significant (Table 8).

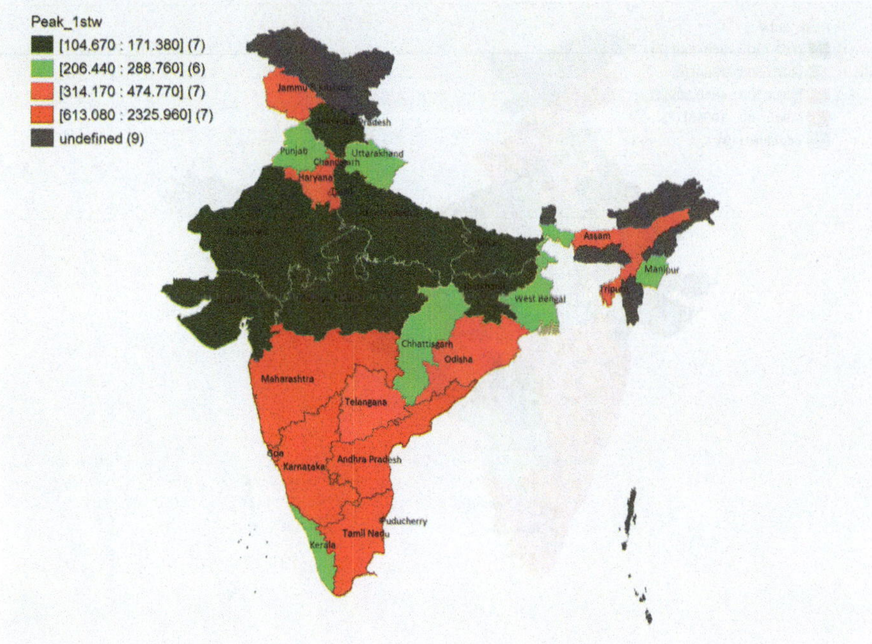


**Fig. 4** Geographical distribution of CIR in the first wave (Sept 2020). *Source* Author's calculations

## 4.2 *Spatial Econometric Results: SAR and SEM*

In Table 9, we have tried to find out the effect of different explanatory variables (along with space) on the variations of CIR. Due to high collinearity among the regressors, we have formulated different models. Basically, collinearity exists among per capita net state domestic product (PCNSDP), per capita education expenditure (PCEE) and per capita health expenditure (PCHE). Here, CIR of a state may get directly affected by its neighboring state's CIR and by their different socio-economic variables like income, education or health expenditure, etc. Therefore, in order to find out the space related spill-over effects of different explanatory variables, we have performed spatial regression as outlined in the methodological section. Here, we consider two types of models—spatial lag or auto-regressive model (SAR) and spatial error model (SEM). The SAR model gives spatial weights or spatial lag to the dependent value of neighbor or its neighbor's neighbor. Similarly, SEM model gives spatial weights to the error term of not only its exact neighbor but its neighbor's neighbor. We find that states spending higher PCEE and PCHE accentuate the CIR. This due to the fact that increase in per capita social expenditure makes a state more aware about the incidence and these states may have greater health infrastructure where people can register their COVID cases. The rail connectivity (rail length per square kilometer)

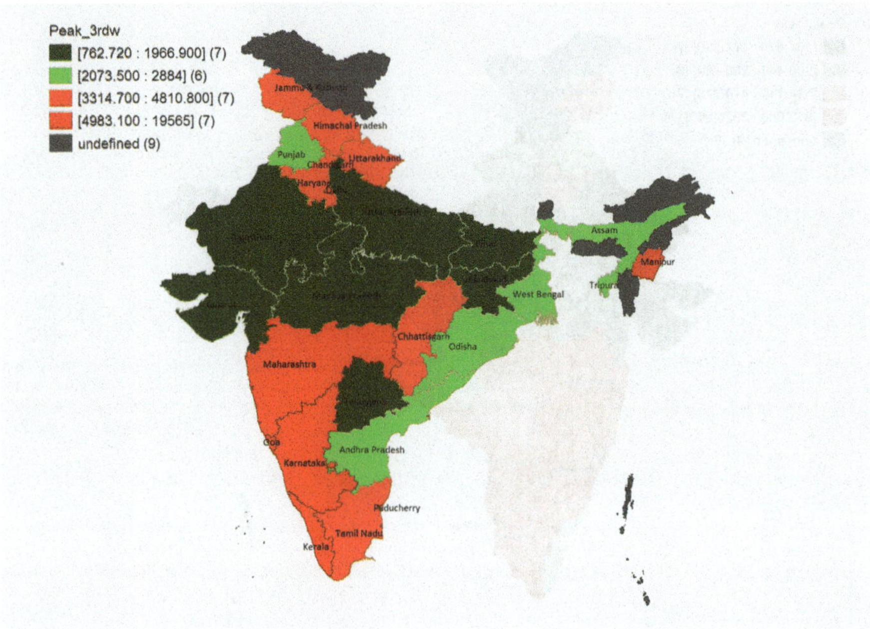


**Fig. 5** Geographical distribution of CIR in the second wave (May 2021). *Source* Author's calculations

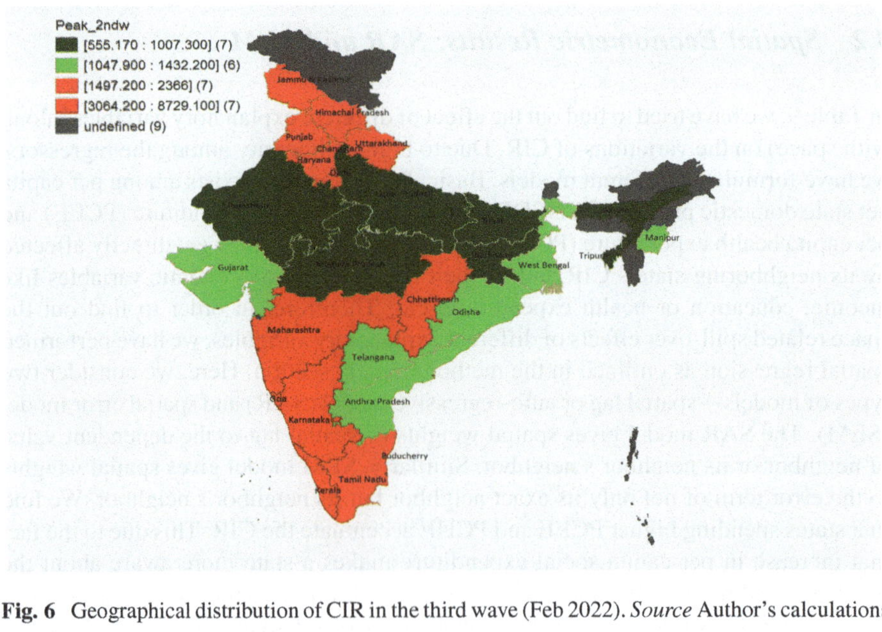


**Fig. 6** Geographical distribution of CIR in the third wave (Feb 2022). *Source* Author's calculations

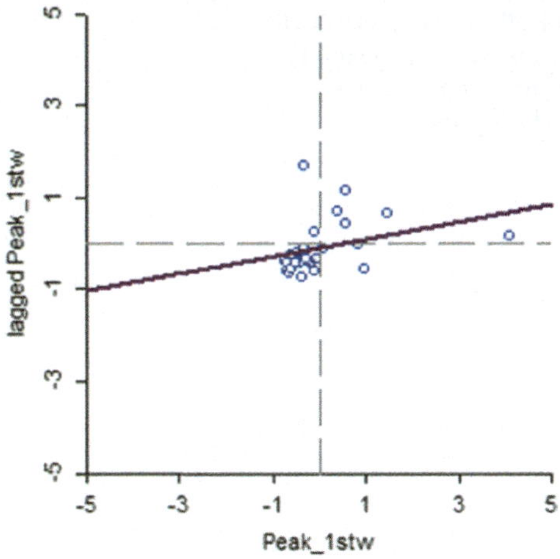


**Fig. 7** Scatter plot of CIR across states in the first wave. *Source* Author's calculations

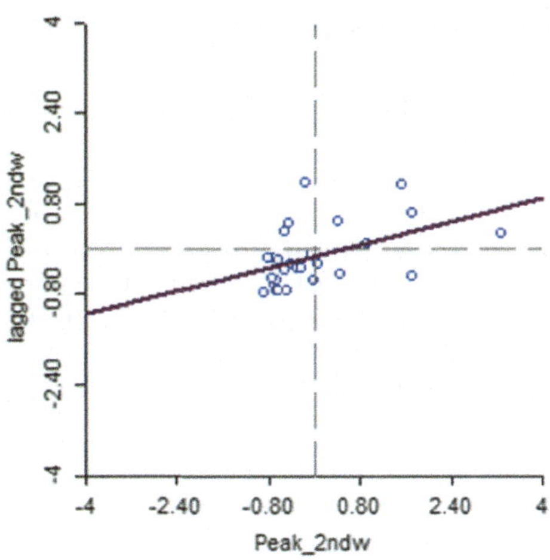


**Fig. 8** Scatter plot of CIR across states in the second wave. *Source* Author's calculations

significantly reduces the CIR. The general awareness about health may be captured by literacy rate (LR); literacy increases the CIR.

Increase in sub-center (SC) significantly reduces the CIR, but an opposite result is found in case of PHC. The testing of COVID is done at the PHC not at the SC, as a result, we find such results because of reporting of COVID infection. However, CHC does not have any significant impact on CIR. The population density (PD) and composition of different age cohort of the population do not show any significant effect on CIR. Both the two parameters $\lambda$ and $\rho$ appear to be statistically significant which clearly proves that space and neighboring effect does play a significant role of spreading the virus.

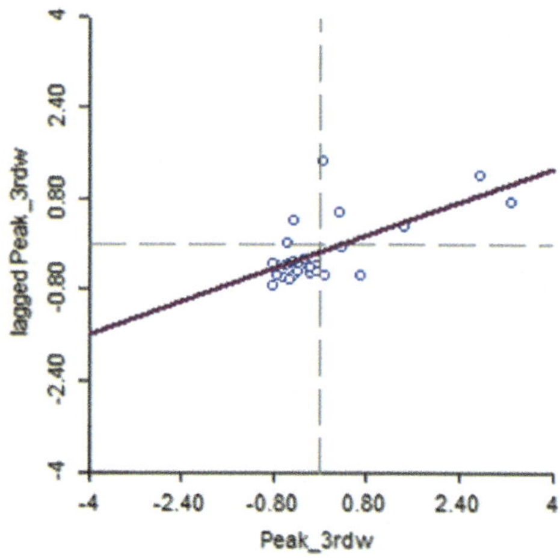


**Fig. 9** Scatter plot of CIR across states in the third wave. *Source* Author's calculations

**Table 6** Cluster of states in three waves of the pandemic

| Clusters | September 13, 2020 (first wave of the pandemic) | May 11, 2021 (second wave of the pandemic) | February 5, 2022 (third wave of the pandemic) |
|---|---|---|---|
| High-high | KAR, GOA, TN, AP, PU, MAH | KAR, KER, GOA, PU, MAH | KER, KAR, GOA, TN, PU |
| Low-low | WB, UP, JHA, HP, HAR, CHH, J&K, OR, GUJ, MP, BI, UK, RAJ, PUN, MANI, CHA, AS | MANI, PUN, TR, UK, BI, MP, GUJ, OR, J&K, HAR, HP, JHA, UP, WB, AS | CHA, PUN, RAJ, TR, UK, BI, MP, GUJ, OR, J&K, CHH, HAR, HP, JHA, UP, WB, AS |
| High-low | TR, DEL | CHA, CHH, DEL | MANI, DEL, MAH |
| Low-high | TEL, KER | TEL, TN, AP | TEL, AP |

**Table 7** Global Moran's index of states in three waves of the pandemic

| | September 13, 2020 | May 11, 2021 | February 5, 2022 |
|---|---|---|---|
| GMI | $0.191^{*}$ | $0.254^{*}$ | $0.363^{**}$ |

*Source* Author's estimation
*Note* * significant at 5% level, ** significant at 1% level.

The SAR (SLM) and SEM results are found to be more or less identical. We have examined the effect of the same explanatory variables on the CFR, the results are reported in Table 10.

It is observed that that an increase in income (PCNSDP), urbanization (Ur) and road length (RD) significantly decreases the CFR. It may be due to accessibility and availability of health infrastructure. On the contrary, availability of rail (RAIL), COVID hospital (CH), community health center (CHC), literacy rate (LR) and population density (PD) significantly increases the CFR. This is not a surprising result.

**Table 8** Local Moran's index of states in three waves of the pandemic

| States | LMI1 (first wave) | LMI2 (second wave) | LMI3 (third wave) |
|---|---|---|---|
| Maharashtra | −0.01175 | 0.085979 | −0.01638 |
| Karnataka | 0.227529 | 0.186991 | 0.179823 |
| Andhra Pradesh | 0.238585 | −0.21828 | −0.19542 |
| Tamil Nadu | 0.614329 | −0.19169**(3) | 0.064532**(1) |
| Kerala | −0.642388**(3) | 1.758925 | 3.283073**(1) |
| Delhi | −0.499086 | −0.76842 | −0.37412 |
| Uttar Pradesh | 0.296361**(2) | 0.121454 | 0.273236 |
| West Bengal | 0.234238 | 0.471301**(2) | 0.346126**(2) |
| Odisha | 0.091843 | 0.191248 | 0.173234 |
| Telangana* | −0.038175 | −0.16867 | −0.01573 |
| Rajasthan | 0.415988**(2) | 0.36314 | 0.381702**(2) |
| Chhattisgarh | 0.100553 | −0.18879 | 0.042987 |
| Bihar | 0.437801**(2) | 0.669095**(2) | 0.590715**(2) |
| Haryana | 0.099456 | 0.005748 | 0.071132 |
| Assam | 0.029162 | 0.446987 | 0.167452 |
| Gujarat | 0.146147 | 0.110931 | −0.2138 |
| Madhya Pradesh | 0.275644 | 0.121277 | 0.270726 |
| Punjab | 0.188238 | 0.104529 | 0.134241 |
| Jammu & Kashmir | 0.067853 | 0.099797 | 0.082187 |
| Jharkhand | 0.345961**(2) | 0.375167 | 0.396051 |
| Uttarakhand | 0.296361**(2) | 0.019477 | 0.083083 |
| Goa | 0.953195 | 1.071241 | 0.466263 |
| Himachal Pradesh | 0.263057 | 0.07824 | 0.072748 |
| Puducherry* | 0.682072 | 0.988797 | 2.516218 |
| Tripura | −0.003307 | 0.5036 | 0.246519 |
| Manipur | 0.036851 | 0.367094 | −0.04435 |
| Chandigarh | 0.087003 | −0.00625 | 0.028061 |

*Source:* Author's estimation
* means significant at 5% level; ** implies significant at 1% level

The share of old age population (POP_60) are more susceptible to infectious disease, and they are assumed to be more vulnerable, as a result their mortality is found to be higher compared to younger population.

**Table 9** Spatial auto-regressive (SAR) model and spatial error model (SEM) (dependent variable: CIR)

| Dep var | CIR | | | | | |
|---|---|---|---|---|---|---|
| Exp var | Mod 1 SLM | Mod2 SEM | Mod 3 SLM | Mod4 SEM | Mod5 SLM | Mod6 SEM |
| PCNSDP | 0.005 (0.012) | 0.005 (0.012) | – | – | – | – |
| PCEE | – | – | 24.43 (33.79) | 58.84* (35.32) | – | – |
| PCHE | – | – | – | – | 94.94 (71.23) | 146.05** (67.16) |
| Ur | 94.25 (59.84) | 25.13 (59.48) | 82.8 (62.55) | −11.57 (57.99) | 56.35 (65.5) | −22.68 (55.142) |
| RD | 3.97 (2.6) | 2.82 (2.47) | 3.55 (2.63) | 2.14 (2.39) | 3.3 (2.57) | 2.36 (2.3) |
| RAIL | −1418.2** (599.02) | − 872.07 (663.75) | −1252* (650.08) | −271.3 (732.72) | −1036.6 (655.7) | −216.8 (672) |
| CH | −16.94 (66.5) | 0.455 (67.42) | −10.04 (66.9) | 40.22 (1.9) | 9.55 (67.7) | 64.2 (70.14) |
| SC | −68.3*** (24.27) | −72.2*** (23.45) | −72.1*** (24.92) | −84.1*** (22.95) | −65.3*** (23.5) | −69.2*** (21.17) |
| PHC | 526.4*** (158.47) | 440.9*** (125.21) | 516.6*** (146.94) | 473.5*** (117.5) | 473.6*** (143.8) | 422.6*** (112.5) |
| CHC | −1528** (622.97) | −727.38 (564.3) | −146**(589.4) | 117.5 (569.13) | −1368.8** (579.7) | −607.5 (533) |
| LR | 254.4** (108.30) | 271.96*** (94.32) | 252.4** (99.86) | 209.9** (95.46) | 249.2*** (94.6) | 213.6 ** (89.4) |
| PD | 0.0698 (0.524) | 0.276 (0.495) | 0.047 (0.52) | 0.193 (0.469) | 0.003 (0.5) | 0.14 (0.45) |
| POP_14 | −15,962.6 (18,180) | −6791.4 (21,027) | −13,011 (20,515) | 2026.3 (8824.8) | −13,930.5 (18,716.3) | −6446.5 (21,748.4) |
| POP_W | −15,567.3 (18,035) | −6650.5 (20,884) | −12,892 (20,352) | 1965.3 (8759.1) | −13,771.5 (18,587.6) | −6386.9 (21,586.7) |
| POP_60 | −16,445.3 (18,203) | −7147.3 (21,059) | −13,529 (20,540) | 1640.2 (8837.3) | −14,437.4 (18,735.9) | −6826.9 (21,772.7) |
| Cons | −11,120.3 (7396.2) | −12,405** (6200) | −11,291* (6818.5) | − 9172 (5998) | −11,831* (6507) | −10,079* (5725.3) |
| *Lambda* | – | 0.077 (1.2) | – | 0.117* (0.066) | – | 0.103* (0.05) |
| *Sigma* | 2417.88 | 2400.4 | 2403.9 | 2294 | 2352 | 2222.7 |
| *Rho* | −0.02 (0.145) | – | −0.17 (0.12) | – | −0.13 (0.12) | – |

*Source* Authors' estimation

* $p < 0.05$, ** $p < 0.01$, *** $p < 0.001$. Values in parentheses represent standard error

**Table 10** Spatial auto-regressive (SAR) model and spatial error model (SEM) (dependent variable: CFR)

| Dep var | CFR | | | | | |
|---|---|---|---|---|---|---|
| Exp var | Mod 7 SLM | Mod8 SEM | Mod 9 SLM | Mod10 SEM | Mod 11 SLM | Mod12 SEM |
| PCNSDP | −1.58e−06 (1.59e−06) | −1.49e−06* (8.08e−07) | – | – | – | – |
| PCEE | – | – | 0.0039 (0.0047) | −0.0007 (0.004) | – | – |
| PCHE | – | – | – | – | 0.006 (0.009) | 0.0001 (0.008) |
| Ur | 0.006 (0.007) | −0.006 (0.005) | −0.0006 (0.007) | −0.01* (0.006) | −0.00008 (0.007) | −0.01* (0.006) |
| RD | −0.0004 (0.0003) | −0.0001 (0.0001) | −0.0005 (0.0003) | −0.0002* (0.0001) | −9.0005 (0.0003) | −0.0002** (0.0001) |
| RAIL | 0.1 (0.083) | 0.21*** (0.04) | 0.165* (0.092) | 0.21*** (0.063) | 0.153* (0.091) | 0.2*** (0.061) |
| CH | 0.008 (0.009) | 0.04*** (0.006) | 0.01 (0.009) | 0.03*** (0.007) | 0.011 (0.009) | 0.03*** (0.007) |
| SC | 0.0009 (0.003) | −0.003 (0.003) | −0.0004 (0.003) | −0.003 (0.004) | 0.0005 (0.003) | −0.003 (0.003) |
| PHC | −0.02 (0.017) | 0.014 (0.01) | −0.011 (0.017) | 0.015 (0.01) | −0.015 (0.016) | 0.016 (0.011) |
| CHC | 0.108 (0.06) | 0.074*** (0.027) | 0.11* (0.067) | 0.05* (0.02) | 0.113* (0.068) | 0.05* (0.03) |
| LR | 0.02* (0.01) | 0.01*** (0.003) | 0.013 (0.013) | 0.01** (0042) | 0.015 (0.012) | 0.01** (0.004) |
| PD | −0.00006 (0.00006) | −0.0001*** (0.00005) | −0.00007 (0.00006) | −0.0001* (0.00006) | −0.00007 (0.00006) | −0.0001** (0.00006) |
| POP_14 | 3.01 (2.46) | 3.23 (2.18) | 2.58 (1.6) | 2.81 (4.16) | 2.77 (2.21) | 3.012 (2.82) |
| POP_W | 3.03 (2.45) | 3.25 (2.17) | 2.62* (1.58) | 2.84 (4.12) | 2.81* (1.48) | 3.032 (2.81) |
| POP_60 | 3.03** (1.46) | 3.26** (1.11) | 2.61* (1.2) | 2.84** (1.16) | 2.8** (1.19) | 3.03*** (0.82) |
| Cons | −1.28 (0.97) | −0.35** (0.14) | −0.548 (0.94) | −0.21* (0.129) | −0.734 (0.9) | −0.21* (0.12) |
| *Lambda* | – | −1.22*** (0.108) | – | −1.27*** (0.136) | – | −1.2*** (0.1382) |
| *Sigma* | 0.31 | 0.14 | 0.31 | 0.15 | 0.31 | 0.15 |
| *Rho* | 0.093 (0.07) | – | 0.038 (0.07) | – | 0.05 (0.06) | – |

*Source* Authors' estimation

* $p < 0.05$, ** $p < 0.01$, *** $p < 0.001$. Values in parentheses represent standard error

## 5 Major Findings

During lockdown phases, the CIR could not spread rapidly. But, there is a sharp increase in CIR witnessed across all the states during September 2020 (unlocking phase of first wave). The CIR varies over time as well as across states.

Spatial impact toward spreading of the virus across states was found to be weak during lockdown phases, it becomes significant during second and third waves. The spatial clustering gains strength over time since we find a positive (roughly 45 degree bisector) straight line. The representation of scatter plots (along with the maps) enables the visualization of the local spatial instability and the identification of the couples of points whose values are judged to be extreme. The L-L and H–H clustering of states do exist in case of aggregate CIR of three waves of the pandemic. The Southern states do form H–H, whereas the Eastern states form L-L clustering. This clearly proves the spatial neighboring effect does exist toward spreading of COVID-19.

The rank correlation between CIR and CFR over different time points across states clearly indicates a weak (but positive correlation). This is because the CFR is stable over time across space (state). We could not study the exact growth pattern of CIR and CFR over time across states, this is a difficult job because majority of the states had experienced three waves of the pandemic with different incidence rates. The GMI and LMI cannot be used for prediction, it helps to analyze or explore the spatial clustering. What are the reasons of such variations of CIR? Certainly, the state specific characteristics do matter. Standard spatial econometric models like spatial autoregressive and spatial error models are estimated using standard spatial weight matrix along with socio-economic characteristics of the states in India. We can conclude that the well-off states do exhibit a higher CIR; probably, the testing is higher in those well-off states compared to poorer states in India. We also find that richer and more urbanized states with better health infrastructure and governance experience a higher CIR. The CFR is found to be more or less stable over the three waves. Keeping in mind the devastating spatial and neighboring effect of the infection rate (CIR), we suggest to ensure and implement of the COVID-19 protocol across the states in India.

## References


Anselin, L. (1988). *Spatial econometrics: Methods and models*. Kluwer Academic Publishers.

Anselin, L. (1995). Local Indicators of Spatial Association—LISA. *Geographical Analysis, 27*(2), 93–115.

Anselin, L., & Florax, R. J. G. M. (1995). Small sample properties of tests for spatial dependence in regression models: some further results. In L. Anselin, & R. J. G. M. Florax (Eds.), *New directions in spatial econometrics*. Advances in Spatial Science. Springer.

Anselin, L., & Bera, A. K. (1998). Spatial dependence in linear regression models with an introduction to spatial econometrics. In A. Ullah & D. E. A. Giles (Eds.), *Handbook of applied economics statistics*. Marcel Dekker.

Basu, P., & Majumder, R. (2021). Regional disparity of covid-19 infections: An investigation using state-level Indian data. *Indian Economic Review, 56*, 215–232. https://doi.org/10.1007/s41775-021-00113-w

Chatterjee, S., Sarkar, A., Chatterjee, S., Karmakar, M., & Paul, R. (2020). Studying the progress of COVID-19 outbreak in India using SIRD model. *Indian Journal of Physics*. https://doi.org/10.1007/s12648-020-01766-8

Ghosh, K., Sengupta, N., Manna, D., & De, S. K. (2020). Inter-state transmission potential and vulnerability of COVID-19 in India. *Progress in Disaster Science, 7*. https://doi.org/10.1016/j.pdisas.2020.100114

Gupta, D., Biswas, D., & Kabiraj, P. (2020). COVID-19 outbreak and Urban dynamics: Regional variations in India. https://doi.org/10.21203/rs.3.rs-84018/v1

Hongfei, L., Catherine, C., & Noel, C. (2007). Beyond Moran's I: Testing for spatial dependence based on the spatial autoregressive model. *Geographical Analysis, 39*(4), 357–375.

Kashif, M., Javed, M. K., & Pandey, D. (2020). A surge in cyber-crime during COVID-19. *Indonesian Journal of Social and Environmental Issues, 1*(2), 48–52. https://doi.org/10.47540/ijsei.v1i2.22

Sarkar, K., Khajanchi, S., & Nieto, J. J. (2020). Modeling and forecasting the COVID-19 pandemic in India. *Chaos Solitons Fractals, 139*, 110049. https://doi.org/10.1016/j.chaos.2020.110049. Epub 2020 Jun 28. PMID: 32834603; PMCID: PMC7321056

Srivastava, A., Tamrakar, V., Moradhvaj, Akhtar, S. N., Kumar, K., Saini, T. C., Nagendra, C., & Saikia, N. (2020). Geographical variation in COVID-19 cases, prevalence, recovery and fatality rate by phase of national lockdown in India, March 14–May 29, 2020. medRxiv preprint, posted June 5, 2020. https://doi.org/10.1101/2020.06.04.20122028

Tamrakar, V., Srivastava, A., Parmar, M. C., Shukla, S. K., Shabnam, S., Boro, B., Saha, A. A., Benjamin Debbarma, B., & Saikia, N. (2020, October 11). District level correlates of COVID-19 pandemic in India. medRxiv preprint. https://doi.org/10.1101/2020.10.08.20208447

Yadav, P., & Bhattacharjee, A. (2020). Impact of COVID-19 on mobility in India: A spatial approach. *Radical Statistics, 126*(56), Special Corona virus Issue.

World Health Organization. (2022, May 13). *Country specific COVID-19 infection and death.*

# The Fundamental Challenges for Development- Poverty, Inequality, Health, Education and External Trade

# Exploring the Significance of Food Insecurity Mediated Poverty and Low Productivity Traps: Furthering Policy by Reconciling Secondary Data with Primary Survey

**Siddhartha Mitra and Paramita Bhattacharya**

## 1 Introduction

Food security is a human right in the sense that "everybody has the right to food security: enough calories for carrying on with the business of life; and a balanced and nutritious diet for sustained physical and mental wellbeing". This makes the incidence of food insecurity, which still exists to a large extent in India and other developing countries, undesirable and research into ways and means for its alleviation and elimination essential.

Such research and writing motivated by the nature of food security as a human right has been going on for a long time. What is less explored is the hypothesis that food insecurity can lead to households getting caught in a poverty trap. This has been neatly summed up in the following statement by Abraham Horwitz (1995)[1] former director of the Pan American Health Organization: *poverty breeds malnutrition and, in turn, malnutrition increases poverty, a vicious circle.*

[1] Interview given in 1995 to a news channel which was then again quoted by S. R. Osmani in the 1st Abraham Horwitz Lecture in 1997.

S. Mitra (✉) · P. Bhattacharya
Department of Economics, Jadavpur University, Kolkata, India
e-mail: siddhartha.mitra@jadavpuruniversity.in

 
A. Raychaudhuri and A. Ghose (eds.), *Managing Pandemic and Correcting Development Fundamentals*, India Studies in Business and Economics,
https://doi.org/10.1007/978-981-19-8680-2_7

However, formal investigation into whether such a poverty trap exists or is at all significant seems to be missing in the literature. The diagram below illustrates the mechanics of this possible poverty trap. First, it is hypothesized that low income or income poverty often leads to a deficiency in calorie intake as well as the intake of one or more essential food groups—for example, proteins, fats, carbohydrates and vitamins—for both adults and children in a family. For adults, it is hypothesized that this implies poor physical health and lack of energy which has a negative impact on their productivity and earning power, given their level of human capital; and for children, it implies poor cognition resulting in drop outs and poor educational achievement, all of which are associated with poor human capital formation. Thus, low levels of human capital replicate themselves generation after generation resulting in a poverty trap characterized by the family trapped in food poverty, a diet poor in calories and nutritional balance.

Though these hypotheses seem obvious, thus implying that such a poverty trap should exist in reality, some doubts can exist. First, it needs to be ascertained whether the incidence of food insecurity among those who are not in income poverty is significantly lower than those who are in income poverty. Moreover, the hypothesized cross-sectional variation in the incidence of food insecurity across expenditure groups does not by itself imply that when income poverty is alleviated by a rise in consumer expenditure, those lifted out of income poverty will use their enhanced income/expenditure to lift themselves out of food insecurity. The reason is that the choice of consumption bundles by individuals is often driven by what others are consuming as well as the changing terms of trade among commodities. If economic growth raises the consumption expenditure of the initially non-poor causing them to consume more of luxury or status goods, then those lifted out of income poverty might tend to follow their example and neglect nutrition. Another reason could be that economic growth may be accompanied by food becoming dearer relative to non-food items, thus preventing food consumption from rising with income due to substitution effects. Second, it needs to be ascertained whether diets that are poor in calories or balanced nutrition actually impede cognition. For example, it is quite possible that the human brain and body might deal with poor nutrition through coping mechanisms which might imply that the expected drop in cognition does not occur.

In the light of the mentioned discussion, we review evidence collated by us which can throw some light on whether the mentioned hypotheses are true. This evidence is presented in Sect. 2. In Sect. 3, we present the objectives of study conducted by us which are derived from the material presented in Sects. 1 and 2. Section 4 provides an elaboration of the methodology employed in the study. Section 5 elaborates on the results of the exercise. Section 6 concludes and discusses both policy implications as well as research possibilities that follow from the conclusions (Fig. 1).

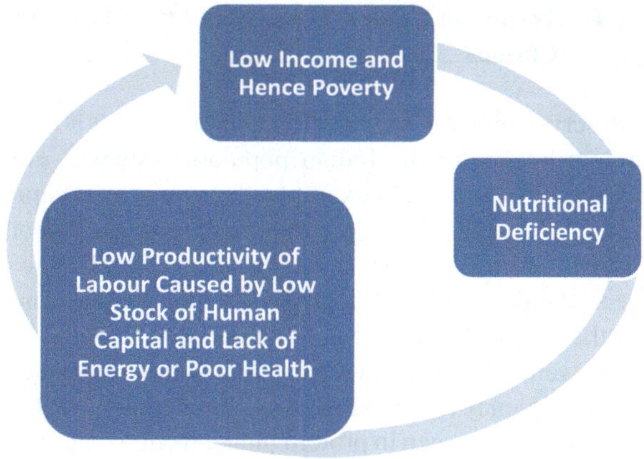


**Fig. 1** Vicious circle of food insecurity led poverty

# 2 Evidence-Based Review of the Hypotheses Underlying the Food Insecurity Mediated Poverty Trap

## *2.1 Food Insecurity and Consumption Expenditure: Review of Evidence*

First, we review how various sorts of nutritional deficiency—calorie, carbohydrate, protein and fat—and their anthropometric manifestations are related to levels of real consumption expenditure or wealth. From our analysis of National Sample Survey (NSS) and National Family Health Survey (NFHS) data, we conclude that calorie, protein, carbohydrate and fat deficiencies and the incidence of their anthropometric manifestations (wasting and stunting) are significantly higher among the poor as compared to the non-poor though for the latter these are not negligible. The incidence of various types of nutritional deficiency by class of monthly per capita expenditure (MPCE) is studied using NSS data for the years, 1999–2000 and 2009–10. The incidence of anthropometric deficiency—stunting (low height for age), wasting (low weight for height) and occurrence of underweight births for groups arranged in ascending order of wealth—is studied using NFHS data for the years, 1998–99 and 2005–06. Note that NFHS ascertains the assets of each sampled household and then uses a weighting procedure based on principal components analysis to arrive at a wealth index. The households are then arranged in ascending order of wealth, this facilitating the ordering of the entire population into quintiles on the basis of wealth.

### 2.1.1 Trends in Calorie Deficiency Over Time and Across Expenditure Classes

It deserves mention that Deaton and Dreze (2009) reveal that per capita calorie and protein intake for the Indian population show a modest declining trend over the period, 1983–2004. For example, the average per capita daily calorie intake declined from 2240 to 2047 cal in rural areas, a modest decline of 8.6% over a period of 21 years, equivalent to an average percentage decline of 0.43% per annum. In urban areas, the decline was from 2070 to 2021 cal, the corresponding percentage figures for the whole period and per annum being 2.3 and 0.1, respectively. Such declines could well be the outcome of mechanization (as suspected by Deaton & Dreze, 2009) and its tendency to encourage a more sedentary life. However, over the same period, a decline was also seen in protein intake from 63.5 to 55.8 g in rural areas per capita per day (total and per annum percentage declines of 12.1% and 0.7%, respectively) and from 58.1 to 55.5 g in urban areas (corresponding percentage figures of 4.6 and 0.2%, respectively). At the same time, there seems to be a shift from protein consumption to fat consumption: in rural areas, the amount of fat consumed increased from 27.1 to 35.4 g per capita per day (the percentage figures in this case are 30.6 and 1.7), whereas, in urban areas, the increase was from an already high 37.1 to 47.4 g per day (the percentage figures being 27.7 and 1.5).

A large number of conclusions emerge from the last paragraph: first, the average calorie intake declined by greater absolute as well as percentage amounts in rural areas than in urban areas. This is expected as mechanization, with its direct implication for physical work in agriculture, should have a greater impact on calorie consumption per capita in rural areas. The mentioned asymmetry in reduction of calorie intake strengthens the case for the argument that calorie intake indeed declined in 1983–2004 due to mechanization. The relative decline in protein intake in urban and rural areas also mirrors this asymmetric impact of mechanization. However, it is seen that in both rural as well as urban areas the decline in protein intake in percentage terms was considerably greater than in calorie intake. This inequality is explained by the almost equal percentage increase in fat consumption in rural and urban areas, with the initial and final levels of fat consumption being much higher in urban areas than in rural areas as the access to fast, junk or restaurant foods is far greater in the former. To conclude, it does seem that the average calorie intake declined in urban as well as rural areas in 1983–2004 due to mechanization. This impact was obviously greater in rural areas as explained. But at the same time there is a change in preferences taking place in both urban and rural areas as a result of which people's preference for fat rich foods is increasing at the expense of protein rich foods. This seems to be a dangerous and unhealthy trend. It might be educative to see whether such trends are there in all deciles of the per capita consumer expenditure ordered population of households. For this, we do a comparison of the results of the NSS surveys of 1999–2000 and 2009–10. However, one has to be cautious as the ten-year period covered has only an intersection of 5 years with the 21-year period covered by the Deaton and Dreze study.

**Table 1** Percentage of calorie deficient population by docile class of MPCE

| Decile | 1999–2000 | | | | 2009–10 | | | |
|---|---|---|---|---|---|---|---|---|
| | Rural | | Urban | | Rural | | Urban | |
| | Mean CD | %Popn | Mean CD | %Popn | Mean CD | %Popn | Mean CD | %Popn |
| 1 | 562.88 | 83.57 | 612.90 | 85.96 | 559.07 | 86.24 | 578.82 | 88.31 |
| 2 | 389.09 | 62.13 | 449.18 | 70.59 | 424.61 | 74.38 | 456.88 | 77.63 |
| 3 | 348.57 | 48.05 | 405.64 | 59.93 | 370.45 | 64.91 | 391.51 | 66.17 |
| 4 | 329.59 | 36.73 | 395.49 | 47.17 | 342.98 | 56.14 | 357.18 | 56.00 |
| 5 | 304.04 | 28.17 | 385.46 | 38.04 | 313.64 | 45.78 | 359.34 | 46.27 |
| 6 | 309.40 | 22.39 | 408.64 | 31.21 | 295.71 | 37.29 | 356.62 | 36.22 |
| 7 | 312.63 | 16.45 | 531.52 | 24.56 | 283.29 | 28.45 | 326.43 | 30.15 |
| 8 | 306.44 | 12.31 | 724.66 | 19.23 | 285.99 | 21.83 | 341.66 | 23.19 |
| 9 | 414.09 | 7.85 | 833.84 | 14.92 | 281.76 | 15.29 | 357.80 | 17.54 |
| 10 | 797.37 | 5.75 | 1133.98 | 11.75 | 316.12 | 9.28 | 418.20 | 14.22 |

In other words, the reduction in calorie intake due to mechanization in 1983–2004, as covered by Deaton and Dreze, might well have petered out in terms of intensity in the period, 1999–2000 and 2009–10.

However, the petering out of increase in calorie deficiency clearly does not happen. In regard to rural areas, we can infer from Table 1 that the mean calorie deficiency rises for the second to fifth decile from the bottom while the fall is negligible for the bottom most decile. For deciles 2–4, the increase is quite large and ranges from 4 to 9%, the corresponding range for the average annual rate of increase being 0.4–0.9%. Such a large increase can be difficult to explain on the basis of mechanization which has after all had a depressing impact on calorie intake since the 1970s[2] and cannot be expected to have an impact of the same intensity over time. If we look at the incidence of calorie deficiency (the proportion of the sub-sample in a consumption expenditure group that is calorie deficient) there is a very significant and large increase in all the deciles. In percentage point terms, it is the highest in the fourth decile (19.41 points) and lowest for the first decile (2.67 points). The first four deciles show substantial percentage point increases in the incidence of calorie deficiency of 2.67, 12.25, 16.86 and 19.41 percentage points, respectively. The relatively low percentage point increase for the first docile is to be expected as the initial incidence is much larger here, 85.96%, as opposed to 62.13, 48.05 and 36.73% for the second, third and fourth deciles. But these large increases in the incidence of calorie deficiency seem difficult to explain on the basis of mechanization, especially for these deciles for which the business of life still involves a lot of physical activity.

[2] See Suryanarayana (2003, 2009) for a discussion of nutrition policies and nutritional norms.

In regard to urban areas, there is again a rise in the incidence of calorie deficiency for all MPCE classes, with the magnitude of the percentage point increase in the incidence of calorie deficiency ranging from 2.35 in the first decile to 8.83 in the fourth decile. The first four deciles again show significant percentage point increases in the incidence of calorie deficiency of 2.35, 7.04, 6.24 and 8.83 percentage points, with the relatively lower increase in the first decile attributable to a much higher incidence of calorie deficiency in the initial period of 85.96% as opposed to 70.59%, 59.93% and 47.17% for the second, third and fourth deciles.

It is seen that the incidence of calorie deficiency in a consumer expenditure class decreases as we move up the expenditure ladder in each of the periods in rural as well as urban areas. But this does not translate to a lowering of the incidence of calorie deficiency when the lower consumption expenditure deciles become wealthier with the reported lowering of income poverty. Of course, increased mechanization over time could be a probable reason for this 'paradox'; another reason could be food items becoming relatively more expensive than non-food items. A third reason could be that the real consumption expenditure in the lower deciles is overvalued by deflating the nominal consumer expenditure in all deciles by a common *consumer price index* (CPI) as in reality the change in the cost of living could well vary significantly as we move from the lower deciles to the higher deciles with the typical consumption basket changing across the deciles. As mentioned, the bite of the impact of mechanization should have worn out since the possible impact of mechanization is being felt for a long time now. Also as explained, it does not seem that the impact of mechanization should in any case be strong for the lower expenditure groups.

A fourth reason is also possible: as economic growth took off in the 1990s the upper expenditure deciles increased their consumption of status goods and the lower expenditure deciles in trying to 'keep up with the Joneses' neglected their calorie intake to the extent that the incidence of calorie deficiency increased rather than decreased with income growth. This sort of explanation is on the lines of status seeking behaviour modelled by Marjit et al. (2016). Thus, individuals are seen to draw utility from the ratio between their status good consumption and average status good consumption; with the rich increasing status good consumption in response to massive income growth after liberalization, the non-rich could have been induced to enhance their status good consumption to the extent that their nutrition suffered.

### 2.1.2 Trends in Protein Deficiency Across Expenditure Classes and Over Time

Let us now look at protein deficiency in various MPCE deciles in 1999–2000 and 2009–10, as revealed by NSS data (see Table 2).

Just as in the case of the calorie deficient households, the incidence of protein deficiency declines in each of the years, 1999–2000 and 2009–10, in the rural and urban areas as we move up the consumption expenditure ladder. However, the incidence of protein deficiency does not decline over time. Quite strikingly, all the deciles show an increase in the incidence of protein deficiency (percentage of households

**Table 2** Percentage of protein deficient population by decile class of MPCE (per consumer unit[3] per diem: 59.07 gms is norm)

| Decile | 1999–2000 | | | | 2009–10 | | | |
|---|---|---|---|---|---|---|---|---|
| | Rural | | Urban | | Rural | | Urban | |
| | Mean PD | %Popn | Mean PD | %Popn | Mean PD | %Popn | Mean PD | %Popn |
| 1 | 13.19 | 74.89 | 14.45 | 78.30 | 13.47 | 80.57 | 14.02 | 84.57 |
| 2 | 8.99 | 48.50 | 10.70 | 58.03 | 10.32 | 65.93 | 11.23 | 71.37 |
| 3 | 8.49 | 34.73 | 9.98 | 47.11 | 9.15 | 55.90 | 9.74 | 58.98 |
| 4 | 8.03 | 25.45 | 9.46 | 36.71 | 8.57 | 46.84 | 8.98 | 48.02 |
| 5 | 7.70 | 18.97 | 10.22 | 27.66 | 7.95 | 37.80 | 9.10 | 40.28 |
| 6 | 7.88 | 14.79 | 11.30 | 22.96 | 7.35 | 30.67 | 8.92 | 31.10 |
| 7 | 8.45 | 10.76 | 16.26 | 18.19 | 6.69 | 22.94 | 8.22 | 25.61 |
| 8 | 8.90 | 7.88 | 21.93 | 15.14 | 6.89 | 16.59 | 8.96 | 19.23 |
| 9 | 12.31 | 5.27 | 26.01 | 11.66 | 7.05 | 10.78 | 9.45 | 14.05 |
| 10 | 24.66 | 4.34 | 33.15 | 10.08 | 8.52 | 6.56 | 12.15 | 10.84 |

that are protein deficient) in the rural as well as urban areas. If we look at the first four deciles there too the increase in incidence is quite striking despite (a) very high levels of initial incidence of protein deficiency—74.89, 48.50, 34.73 and 25.45% in rural areas and 78.30, 58.03, 47.11 and 36.71% in urban areas; (b) alleviation of income poverty of these households; and (c) the relatively small expected impact of mechanization on these households, given their low wealth and ability to benefit from labour saving capital assets. In rural areas, the percentage point increases are 5.68, 17.43, 21.17 and 21.39% points, respectively, whereas, in urban areas, these are 6.27, 13.34, 11.87 and 11.31, respectively, all of which are quite large. Incidentally, the incidence of protein deficiency in each consumption expenditure decile is lower in rural areas than in urban areas in both the considered years, which is to be expected given the more sedentary life in urban areas.

In regard to mean protein deficiency among the protein deprived classes, we see that there is a tendency for it to decline monotonically as we move up the expenditure ladder in the rural areas in both periods from the first to the fifth decile; beyond these deciles, there is no such common monotonic trend. In the urban areas, this monotonic trend is restricted to the first four deciles in both years. By and large, the trends in incidence of calorie deficiency as we move up the expenditure ladder and as each expenditure class benefits from growth in real income are mirrored by trends in the incidence of protein deficiency. The increase in the incidence of protein deficiency among the bottom four deciles also seems to be too large to be explained by mechanization.

---

[3] A normal male person doing sedentary work and belonging to the age group 20–39 is considered to be numeraire, i.e. the embodiment of one consumer unit. A person of given sex, age and activity level is converted into an appropriate number of consumer units based on calorie requirement (NSS Report on Nutritional Intake, 1999–2000) relative to the calorie requirement of the numeraire.

### 2.1.3 Trends in Carbohydrate Deficiency Across Expenditure Classes and Over Time

In this chapter (see Table 3), we proxy carbohydrate deficiency by deficiency in foodgrain consumption, the reason being the high carbohydrate content of foodgrains. The percentage of carbohydrate deficient households in every expenditure class is much lower than the percentage of protein deficient households. As in the case of incidence of protein deficiency, the highest incidence of carbohydrate deficiency in rural areas is observed in the lowest decile in both 1999–2000 and 2009–10, respectively. Further, there is a decrease in the incidence of carbohydrate deficiency as we move up the expenditure ladder from one decile to the next till the sixth (eighth) decile in 1999–2000 (2009–10), beyond which the trend of monotonic decline is broken. In regard to urban areas, the patterns of change in incidence of carbohydrate deficiency as we move up the expenditure ladder are slightly different from those for protein deficiency. Though in 1999–2000, it is the lowest expenditure class which shows the greatest incidence of deficiency, in 2009–10 the ranking changes with the highest expenditure class being characterized by the highest incidence of deficiency (17.64%) followed by the lowest expenditure class (17.43%). In 1999–2000, the incidence of carbohydrate deficiency declines as we move up the expenditure ladder, starting from the lowest decile, till the fourth decile. Beyond the fourth decile, there is an increase in incidence of carbohydrate deficiency till the tenth decile, again probably because of diversification in diets. In 2009–10, a decline in incidence of carbohydrate deficiency also takes place across the first four deciles, beyond which there is no monotonic trend.

How does the incidence of carbohydrate deficiency change as economic growth takes place and households in each decile benefit from an increase in income, the

**Table 3** Percentage of foodgrain deficient population by decile class of MPCE (per consumer unit per diem: 287 gms is norm)

| Decile | 1999–2000 | | | | 2009–10 | | | |
|---|---|---|---|---|---|---|---|---|
| | Rural | | Urban | | Rural | | Urban | |
| | Mean FD | %Popn | Mean FD | %Popn | Mean FD | %Popn | Mean FD | %Popn |
| 1 | 62.66 | 9.57 | 76.04 | 18.37 | 48.59 | 9.59 | 46.90 | 17.43 |
| 2 | 51.13 | 3.88 | 52.93 | 12.50 | 39.92 | 6.24 | 49.29 | 12.92 |
| 3 | 49.51 | 3.35 | 61.40 | 12.19 | 33.57 | 5.09 | 51.34 | 12.37 |
| 4 | 53.42 | 3.28 | 63.78 | 10.92 | 39.91 | 4.95 | 79.63 | 11.45 |
| 5 | 49.46 | 2.96 | 71.52 | 11.31 | 51.10 | 4.09 | 86.55 | 11.92 |
| 6 | 62.18 | 2.82 | 80.59 | 11.89 | 65.37 | 3.78 | 86.81 | 12.12 |
| 7 | 62.72 | 2.85 | 106.76 | 12.89 | 65.33 | 3.52 | 115.01 | 11.15 |
| 8 | 68.57 | 2.62 | 122.34 | 14.42 | 71.00 | 3.24 | 117.65 | 13.76 |
| 9 | 91.86 | 2.93 | 120.81 | 15.01 | 71.01 | 3.31 | 90.31 | 13.05 |
| 10 | 100.19 | 4.32 | 134.57 | 16.83 | 84.19 | 3.84 | 95.31 | 17.64 |

natural outcome of which is a decline in income poverty? In rural areas, there is an increase in incidence of carbohydrate deficiency for each of the expenditure deciles, save the top most decile. However, the changes are small and range from 0.02% points for the first decile to 2.36% points for the second decile. These can easily be explained as a result of diet diversification and a very small response to increase in mechanization. For the top most decile, there is a decrease by 0.48% points. In the case of the urban population, there are both positive and negative changes in incidence of carbohydrate deficiency but these are all small and the range is −1.96 to 0.81% points.

The broad conclusion is that in both rural and urban areas, income growth did not bring about much of a change in the incidence of carbohydrate deficiency. Overall, for rural areas, there is an increase in the incidence of carbohydrate deficiency from 3.86 to 5.23%, a mere change of 1.37% points. For urban areas, the corresponding change is from 12.38 to 13.89, a magnitude of 1.51% points. Every MPCE class is marked in rural as well as urban areas by a small change in the mentioned incidence. An increase in incidence over time is not unexpected given an unchanged norm for calculating such deficiency and the observed decrease in carbohydrate needs resulting from mechanization and income growth induced food diversification. However, the very small magnitude of the increase in incidence of carbohydrate deficiency points to mechanization also leading to a decline in energy requirement that does not exceed a small magnitude. Compare this to the much larger changes in incidence of protein deficiency from 27.18 to 37.74% or 10.56% points for the entire rural population of households, 33.41 to 43.91% or 10.50% points for the entire urban population, and similar large changes for individual expenditure classes in rural or urban areas. It is quite obvious that such large changes cannot be solely or predominantly explained by mechanization. This is especially true because the impact of mechanization on carbohydrate requirement should be greater than that on requirement of proteins, which in comparison with carbohydrates are an insignificant source of human energy, the need for which is directly impacted by mechanization.

Note that the overall increases in incidence of calorie deficiency are slightly smaller than those in the incidence of protein deficiency, 9.47% points (36.70–46.17%) for rural areas and 8.26% points (42.74–51.00%) but much larger than the overall increase in carbohydrate deficiency.

### 2.1.4 Trends in Fat Deficiency Across Expenditure Classes and Over Time

Given that increase in the incidence of calorie deficiency is associated with larger observed increases in incidence of protein deficiency and smaller increases in the incidence of carbohydrate deficiency, the results (see Table 4) for the incidence of fat deficiency over the studied period of 10 years are hardly surprising: a decline from 15.29 to 9.62% in rural areas (5.67% points) and almost no change in urban areas with incidence barely increasing from 5.02 to 5.58% points.

**Table 4** Percentage of fat deficient population by decile class of MPCE (per consumer unit per diem: 19.69 gms is norm)

| Decile | 1999–2000 | | | | 2009–10 | | | |
|---|---|---|---|---|---|---|---|---|
| | Rural | | Urban | | Rural | | Urban | |
| | Mean FatD | %Popn | Mean FatD | %Popn | Mean FatD | %Popn | Mean FatD | %Popn |
| 1 | 5.21 | 63.34 | 4.62 | 30.69 | 4.41 | 38.21 | 3.54 | 18.47 |
| 2 | 3.42 | 29.56 | 4.13 | 7.05 | 3.20 | 12.30 | 3.53 | 4.37 |
| 3 | 3.10 | 14.42 | 7.34 | 3.09 | 3.19 | 5.96 | 3.11 | 1.40 |
| 4 | 3.17 | 7.93 | 8.98 | 2.16 | 3.63 | 3.40 | 4.49 | 1.00 |
| 5 | 3.06 | 3.91 | 13.94 | 1.86 | 3.25 | 1.80 | 12.75 | 1.04 |
| 6 | 4.27 | 1.83 | 14.72 | 2.23 | 3.26 | 1.11 | 13.88 | 0.85 |
| 7 | 5.50 | 1.19 | 17.07 | 3.40 | 3.55 | 0.78 | 11.80 | 0.69 |
| 8 | 8.30 | 0.85 | 16.19 | 4.40 | 3.67 | 0.46 | 13.69 | 0.73 |
| 9 | 12.38 | 0.82 | 17.03 | 3.93 | 4.91 | 0.31 | 14.52 | 0.76 |
| 10 | 14.34 | 1.38 | 16.14 | 4.71 | 7.91 | 0.32 | 11.30 | 0.73 |

It is interesting to see how the secular trends for the overall rural and urban populations in regard to fat deficiency are explained by the MPCE class wise trends. In the rural population, there are massive decreases in incidence of deficiency in the first four deciles (25.13, 17.26, 8.46 and 4.53% points from the initial levels of 63.34, 29.56, 14.42 and 7.93%, respectively) and near stationarity thereafter, with the initial incidence of fat deficiency being too small to allow for any major decrease. For the urban population, a major decrease occurs in the first decile only (12.22 from a level of 30.69%, respectively). Every other decile too shows a decrease which is small in absolute terms but large in proportional terms given that the initial incidence of deficiency is small to start with.

What does this tell us about the diets of how the lower income groups changed in response to income poverty diminishing economic growth? There were very significant increases in the incidence of calorie deficiency as well as protein deficiency and equally significant decreases in fat deficiency. On the other hand, the changes in the incidence of carbohydrate deficiency were small. Had mechanization been an important reason for the reduction in the incidence of calorie deficiency, given the stationarity in nutrition norms, the changes in the incidence of carbohydrate deficiency would not have been negligible. Therefore, there has to be an explanation other than mechanization with the three candidates being (a) an overestimation of income poverty alleviation; (b) a movement in the terms of trade between food and non-food items and (c) an increase in status good consumption by the non-poor following massive income growth causing the poor to neglect their own nutrition and indulge in buying status goods.

## 2.2 Anthropometric Evidence and Wealth Status: Review of Evidence

We now review the evidence in regard to anthropometric indicators in the light of our findings about nutritional intake mentioned above. We look at the NFHS data highlighting three anthropometric indicators: 'stunting' (low height for age), the percentage of children that are underweight for their age and 'wasting' (low weight for height). Note that these anthropometric indicators are an outcome of both nutritional intake and absorption with the latter being determined by, among others, the access to improved sanitation facilities and sources of drinking water. Research (e.g. that by Martorell et al., 2010; Waber et al., 2014) shows that child malnutrition, as revealed by these indicators, has adverse implications for adult IQ, school attainment and formation of human capital. Clearly, anthropometric deficiency and associated poor human capital formation, and the consequent impact on earnings and nutrition of the next generation can form a causal loop that keeps successive generations of a household mired in poverty apart from acting as a constraint on growth of per capita incomes.

The NFHS data classifies households according to a wealth index, computed on the basis of their ownership of assets and appropriate weights given to such ownership worked out through robust principal components analysis. The households are arranged in ascending order of wealth, as measured by the index, into quintiles and named in that order as *poorest*, *poorer*, *middle*, *richer* and *richest*. We proceed to analyse trends in these three anthropometric indicators for the population as a whole and for each economic class.

It is very clear from Tables 5, 6, 7, 8, 9 and 10 that the incidence of the three mentioned indicators of anthropometric deficiency (stunting, occurrence of underweight children and wasting) is very large in the bottom two wealth quintiles and distinctly larger than that in the other three quintiles in both NFHS-2 (1998–99) and NFHS-3 (2005–06) in rural as well as urban areas, the only exception being the slight increase in 'wasting' marking the transition from the 'poorer' to the 'middle' quintile in urban areas in NFHS-2. These findings imply that the food insecurity mediated poverty trap is likely to be very common with low wealth and poor human capital formation driven by malnutrition perpetuating poverty.

Tables 5, 6, 7, 8, 9 and 10 also indicate that the percentages of children that are (a) stunted and (b) underweight (for their age) have decreased across all economic classes from NFHS-2 to NFHS-3 in both rural and urban areas. However, 'wasting'

**Table 5** Percentage of stunted children (under 3) in rural areas

| | Poorest | Poorer | Middle | Richer | Richest | Total |
|---|---|---|---|---|---|---|
| NFHS-2 | 60.86 | 58.13 | 52.11 | 43.96 | 32.32 | 52.22 |
| NFHS-3 | 55.16 | 49.73 | 42.80 | 34.62 | 21.44 | 44.31 |
| Percentage point change | −5.7 | −8.4 | −9.31 | −9.34 | −10.88 | −7.91 |

**Table 6** Percentage of stunted children (under 3) in urban areas

| | Poorest | Poorer | Middle | Richer | Richest | Total |
|---|---|---|---|---|---|---|
| NFHS-2 | 61.54 | 59.54 | 52.51 | 44.55 | 31.61 | 40.12 |
| NFHS-3 | 54.44 | 51.74 | 46.85 | 38.62 | 24.69 | 35.19 |
| Percentage point change | −7.1 | −7.8 | −5.66 | −5.93 | −6.92 | −4.93 |

**Table 7** Percentage of underweight children (under 3) in rural areas

| | Poorest | Poorer | Middle | Richer | Richest | Total |
|---|---|---|---|---|---|---|
| NFHS-2 | 55.28 | 48.24 | 40.40 | 30.54 | 19.93 | 41.94 |
| NFHS-3 | 53.89 | 46.26 | 35.48 | 26.84 | 15.96 | 39.56 |
| Percentage point change | −1.29 | −1.98 | −4.92 | −3.97 | −3.97 | −2.38 |

**Table 8** Percentage of underweight children (under 3) in urban areas

| | Poorest | Poorer | Middle | Richer | Richest | Total |
|---|---|---|---|---|---|---|
| NFHS-2 | 62.72 | 49.34 | 47.74 | 36.01 | 20.75 | 31.03 |
| NFHS-3 | 53.67 | 47.9 | 37.35 | 29.99 | 17.71 | 27.72 |
| Percentage point change | −9.05 | −1.44 | −10.39 | −6.02 | −3.04 | −3.31 |

**Table 9** Percentage of wasted children (under 3) in rural areas

| | Poorest | Poorer | Middle | Richer | Richest | Total |
|---|---|---|---|---|---|---|
| NFHS-2 | 27.11 | 21.53 | 17.97 | 14.24 | 10.73 | 19.54 |
| NFHS-3 | 29.49 | 24.69 | 20.20 | 16.32 | 12.60 | 22.32 |
| Percentage point change | 2.38 | 3.16 | 2.23 | 2.08 | 1.87 | 2.78 |

shows an increase in the considered period across all the economic classes in both rural and urban areas except for the 'middle' income class in urban areas which shows a slight decline.

It is important for a story of anthropometric and nutritional change in India in the period, 1990–2010 to reconcile the decrease in the incidence of stunting and percentage of children that are underweight with the increase in the incidence of 'wasting' as well as rise in the incidence of 'calorie deficiency' revealed by NSS data.

**Table 10** Percentage of wasted children (under 3) in urban areas

| | Poorest | Poorer | Middle | Richer | Richest | Total |
|---|---|---|---|---|---|---|
| NFHS-2 | 25.44 | 21.05 | 21.36 | 16.42 | 11.90 | 15.18 |
| NFHS-3 | 32.43 | 24.13 | 19.71 | 18.38 | 14.22 | 17.60 |
| Percentage point change | 6.99 | 3.08 | −1.65 | 1.96 | 2.32 | 2.42 |

It is crucial in this regard to recognize that the period was marked by increase in access to improved drinking water as well as sanitation facilities (IIPS, 2000, 2007)[4] leading to better absorption of nutrients by children[5] as well as an expansion of the scale and scope of the supplementary nutrition programme for pregnant women, lactating mothers and children in the age group of 0–6 years through the Integrated Child Development Services (ICDS) Scheme launched in 1975. Supplementary nutrition to pregnant and lactating mothers as well as small children ranged from calorie rich carbohydrates and fats to eggs, milk, food fortified with micronutrients and tablets containing supplements such as iron, folic acids and vitamins. These not only help to alleviate calorie deficits but also provide nutrients such as phosphorus, calcium, magnesium, sulphur and various vitamins which are crucial for preventing stunting.

Our hypothesis about expansion in scale and scope of the supplementary nutrition programme under ICDS is based on data on programme coverage which indicated significant expansion in the period lying between the two studied NFHS surveys, as well as comparison of a limited number of snapshots of the programme, culled from the literature, at different points of time which indicated a trend of qualitative improvement (Sachdev & Dasgupta, 2001; Programme Evaluation Organisation, GOI, 2011). The improvement in supplementary nutrition as well as better absorption of nutrients on account of access to improved drinking water and sanitation can help resolve the puzzle of greater incidence of calorie deficits being accompanied by reduction in stunting and percentage of children that were underweight but increase in the incidence of wasting. We draw the attention of the reader to the fact that the overall decrease in the incidence of stunting was identically equal to (a) decrease in stunting contributing to decrease in the proportion of children that were stunted and underweight and (b) the decrease in stunting contributing to decrease in the proportion that were not underweight but stunted. Given the improvement in supplementary nutrition, the mentioned improved absorption of nutrients and the observed decrease in the proportion of children that were underweight it is highly likely that decreases of both types were positive. Moreover, some of the decrease in each category, but not all, most likely contributed to an increase in 'wasting': as the proportion of children fulfilling the genetic potential in regard to linear growth rose, possibly because of a better intake of minerals crucial for such growth such as phosphorus, calcium, magnesium, sulphur, vitamins D, K and C and copper[6] and/or better absorption of nutrients, the proportion of children that were wasted but not underweight for their age (children with height greatly in excess of the maximum height consistent with stunting but only a little above the maximum weight consistent with being 'underweight') rose.

---

[4] From NFHS-2 to NFHS-3, only a 7 year period, the percentage of households with no access to toilets and resorting to open defecation went down from 64 to 55%; the percentage with access to piped water supply went up from 38.7 to 42% and the percentage of households which treated water to purify it before drinking went up from 31.6 to 34.4%.

[5] Rah et al. (2015) and Spears et al. (2013) provide discussions relating to the beneficial impact that improved drinking water and sanitation have on absorption of nutrients by children.

[6] See Briend et al. (2015) who attribute stunting without wasting to a deficiency in these nutrients.

The validity of the above narrative hinges on the decrease in the incidence of stunting being associated with an increase in the incidence of wasting and a decrease in the percentage of underweight children of lower magnitudes. Indeed, this is what we observe, from Tables 5, 6, 7, 8, 9 and 10, in rural and urban areas on scrutinizing the percentage point changes in incidence of stunting, wasting and the proportion of children that were underweight.

In regard to stunting and wasting, we observe that the negative percentage point change in the former exceeds the positive percentage change in the latter in magnitude for the rural as well as urban populations, as well as each economic class within these populations apart from the 'middle' class in urban areas which is marked by a decrease in 'wasting' but again of a lower magnitude than the decrease in 'stunting'. In regarding to stunting and the percentage of underweight children, we see that the magnitude of decrease in the former exceeds that in the latter for the rural as well as urban population taken as a whole and each economic class within the rural population. However, this inequality does not hold for each economic class within the urban population possibly because of movement of households from one economic class to another in the course of the 7 years that separated the two NFHS surveys as well as the dynamic nature of the urban population because of rural–urban migration. Thus, when we study the anthropometric changes that took place in the urban population between 1998–99 and 2005–06, we are not only observing changes that took place due to women and children from households already living in urban areas in 1998–99 being exposed to different conditions through the evolution of the ICDS and access to better drinking water and sanitation but also changes occurring in that population through rural–urban migration. For example, the decline in the percentage of children in the 'poorest' class who are underweight by as much as 9.05% points may be accounted for partially by migration of families characterized by incidence of underweight children far lower than what was observed in NFHS-2 for that class (62.72%).

The above is mainly an attempt to construct a story of nutrition and anthropometric change in the period 1990–2010 that is consistent with all the major findings emerging from the mentioned NSS and NFHS datasets, under the implicit assumption that both datasets are accurate. In short, we infer that though this period was marked by an enhanced incidence of deficiency in calorie intake, it was most probably true that a supply of key nutrients to children and pregnant and lactating mothers through the ICDS as well as enhanced access to improved drinking water and sanitation, leading to greater absorption of nutrients, caused a decrease in the incidence of stunting and underweight children. However, the incidence of wasting registered an increase as better intake of key nutrients often got translated into height increases without matching weight increases.

On the basis of our findings, we can also speculate about what would have happened if the increase in incidence of calorie deficiency, observed across all deciles of MPCE for both rural and urban areas in the period between 1999–2000 and 2009–10, had not taken place: a decrease in incidence of wasting instead of the observed increase and much higher decreases in the incidence of stunting as well as the percentage of children that were underweight. The change in trends would have been marked for the population belonging to the bottom three quintiles of the wealth distribution which were, it seems, in reality characterized by a huge increase in the incidence of calorie deficiency: NSS data reveals an increase in the incidence of calorie deficiency in the second to seventh deciles of the rural monthly per capita expenditure distribution ranging from 12 to 19.41% points; in the urban areas, increase in the incidence of calorie deficiency in the second to sixth deciles was smaller but still very significant, ranging from 5.01 to 8.83% points. Note the great room for anthropometric improvement in these three quintiles in rural and urban areas, as revealed by NFHS-3: an incidence of wasting ranging from 19.71 to 32.43%; a percentage of underweight children ranging from 35.48 to 53.89% and an incidence of stunting ranging from 42.80 to 55.16%. Thus, the foregone improvement in the mentioned anthropometric indicators on account of the observed increase in calorie deficiency is very large. There is a need to ascertain the reasons behind this increase which took place even when the economy was registering high growth. This would ensure that the future is marked by more rapid and more balanced improvement in anthropometric indicators.

### *2.3 The Literature on the Causality Running from Income Poverty or Malnutrition to Poor Human Capital Formation*

Even when a poor child is given equal opportunity to education, he or she may not be able to increase her human capital to the same extent as a child from a non-poor family. This is because low incomes might have an adverse impact on cognitive power through poor nutrition or poor parenting.

One of the pioneers in relating cognition to income is Kimberly Noble. Noble (2017) reviews the work done in this regard by her and other neuroscientists, for example Noble et al. (2015) and Noble et al. (2007), and highlights the following facts: (a) Children from low income families do significantly worse on IQ and other tests; (b) an examination of brain structure and size reveals smaller hippocampi for children of low income families, lower cortical surface area for adolescents coming from low income classes and a faster reduction of cortical thickness with age. Note that a larger hippocampus would be better at conversion of short-term memory into long term memory, in other words, converting what is taught or read into a larger effective non-temporary increase in human capital; a higher cortical surface area is associated with better impulse control and comprehension, such as that of language and therefore can be, ceteris paribus associated with a higher level of human capital; and a slower reduction of cortical thickness implies that the ability to learn or adjust to changes in the environment, i.e. plasticity of the brain or the ability of the brain to generate new human capital—declines more solely with age.

What is responsible for this adverse association between brain structure and size and low income? Noble (2017) points out that it is difficult to disentangle nutritional, environmental and genetic influences, given that we can currently draw upon results of a study of brain structure and size for different socio-economic classes at only one point of time. For example, even an explanation that the poor are poor because their genes result in lower cognitive ability and not because their poverty results in poor environments and nutrition cannot be ruled out. The reasoning goes as follows: though poverty might be highly associated with malnutrition and poor security for children it might also be associated with genes that are not suitable for human capital formation. Therefore, poorer brain size and structure associated with poverty could be a result of one or more of these factors—poorer genes, malnutrition, lower security or poor parenting—with us not being to identify one or more factors as significant determinants or even rule out that the entire result is driven by genetic influences, unless randomized control trials (RCTs) are performed.

For example, Noble (2017) herself suggests the following types of RCT: identifying a group of poor children with very similar socio-economic backgrounds and dividing these randomly into two groups, providing the parents of the first group with income supplements and leaving parents of the second group to fend totally for themselves. The changes in the brains of children in these two groups could be studied to see whether cognitive powers in the first group grow significantly faster than those in the second group. If that is indeed the case, we can say that higher income indeed produces changes in environmental factors such as parenting, security and nutrition which have a beneficial effect on the brain and therefore on cognition. It can be further argued that a big push given through income supplements could enhance cognition and hence human capital formation among the children of the poor to such a significant extent that their ability to earn incomes when they grow up is enhanced, thus lifting poor families permanently out of the poverty trap with no income supplements needed after a certain period of time. Thus, the policy advice emerging out of such a positive finding would be to give a big push for a limited amount of time to poor families in the form of income supplements.

The results of the RCTs suggested by Noble are not yet in the public domain. It is possible that income supplements will not work, especially if parents are given a free hand in the spending of incomes and end up splurging on frivolous and non-essential consumption, even those labelled by social scientists as 'sins' such as cigarettes and liquor. Second, even if these do work there would be a fair degree of uncertainty about the channels through which the beneficial impact of income supplements is transmitted and their relative and absolute significance. For example, we would not know exactly why income supplements act leave a positive impact on cognition: it could be because of higher security, better parenting or better child nutrition or one or more of the factors.

If nutritional supplements for poor children do help to enhance cognition of poor children and the other factors such as improved parenting and security are not significant determinants, then there is a case for providing nutritional supplements and not income supplements. This would provide a better bang for the government buck, i.e. the human capital augmenting effect of government expenditure would be raised. There is therefore a strong case for doing RCTs, involving a study of how brain structure and size respond to nutritional supplementation for those who are poor and malnourished. Further, one could easily test whether a given amount of expenditure on nutrition supplementation has a statistically significant greater or lower impact on cognition than an equal amount on income supplementation and ascertain whether such statistical significance is associated with economic significance, i.e. the difference in magnitudes of impacts is large.

Two other groups of researchers have investigated the link between malnutrition and cognition development. The first group consists of nutrition scientists. Plaza et al. (2001) mention findings of suboptimal head circumference, an indication of malnutrition, being associated with poor scholastic achievement and Intelligence Quotient (IQ). However, this does not rule out the argument that children inherit genes which make for poorer cognition from their parents and such genes also lead to low parental incomes and thus child malnutrition, with the last outcome causing low head circumference, thus leading to the observed high association between low head circumference and IQ or scholastic achievement. The second group consists of those researching in paediatrics. Liu et al. (2003) find that malnutrition, as indicated by various physical indicators, is seen to cause deficits in cognition among young children even after controlling for various kinds of psychosocial adversity such as lack of education of father and/or mother, employment of parents in unskilled or semiskilled occupation which would be highly associated with the incidence of low income, large family size and overcrowding at home. This study seems more convincing than the one by nutrition scientists and seems to suggest that malnutrition does significantly affect cognition. It, however, does not tell us much about whether malnutrition has a bigger impact on cognition than the other adverse influences of poverty on cognition working through parenting, security, etc. Therefore, the question of whether government efforts should concentrate on nutritional supplements rather than income supplements remains unresolved.

It should be noted that the effect of nutritional supplements or income supplements on cognition, as demonstrated by RCTs, can possibly misinform us about the impact of income poverty alleviating economic growth on human capital formation among those lifted out of income poverty, even in cases where all income classes have an equal opportunity of accessing education facilities. This is because such alleviation of income poverty associated with economic growth may also be accompanied by (a) a movement in terms of trade which might make non-food items cheaper than food items; and (b) an increase in status good consumption by the rich causing copycat status good consumption among the lower income classes. Factors (a) and (b) might imply that malnutrition might not be alleviated to any significant effect, and therefore, human capital formation among the poor might not be induced by economic growth. In other words, economic growth can possibly be accompanied by changes in the socio-economic environment which ensure that the pure effect of income/nutritional supplementation does not materialize equivalently or at all. This is possibly true of the Indian experience during the first decade of the twenty-first century, a period which saw significant reported alleviation of income poverty and growth of incomes among the lower income classes but also an increase in deficiencies in nutritional intake.

Income poverty alleviation in the absence of human capital augmentation implies that such poverty alleviation is being brought about purely by (a) changes in physical infrastructure or availability or physical capital and/or (b) greater demand resulting from growth in incomes of the non-poor. Those lifted above the poverty line or brought closer to the poverty line by such developments might find it difficult to enhance their incomes, further in the absence of human capital formation. Thus, the bite of poverty or low productivity traps might continue to persist.

## 3 Research Objectives

Using RCTs to examine the effect of income or nutrition supplements on cognition was outside the scope of the study underlying this paper because of limited finances. However, certain related important questions can be asked or answered in regard to the Indian case without undertaking the mentioned costly RCTs.

First, we need to know whether household income per capita is a significant enough determinant of nutritional status. This is equivalent to asking the following questions: (a) Ceteris paribus, would a child belonging to a high income household be associated with a probability of malnutrition which is significantly lower, both statistically and economically, than another child belonging to a low income or poor household? (b) How does the effect of caste or religion on nutritional status compare with that in terms of magnitude to the effect of income? We answer these questions with the help of the data collected from our primary survey.

The second set of questions relates to whether food insecurity leads to significantly poorer educational achievement (lower human capital formation) due to poorer cognition. Note that the identification of this phenomenon is a necessary condition for the food insecurity mediated poverty trap to occur. We look at this question again with the help of primary data.

The third set of questions relates to the apparent paradox of income poverty alleviating economic growth being associated with greater deficiency in nutritional intake and incidence of some dimensions of anthropometric deficiency in the lower income classes. This phenomenon has been explained in detail above but through use of data we look to identify the real explanation of the phenomenon out of a set of possible explanations: (a) the consumer price index understating the true rate of inflation of prices affecting the lower income classes, thus implying that significant reported poverty alleviation has not actually occurred; (b) non-food inflation being much lower than food inflation for the period under consideration thus leading to substitution of food consumption by non-food consumption; and (c) economic growth fuelled additional status good consumption among the rich inducing copycat consumption among the poor and thus neglect of nutrition by the poor. We answer this set of questions with the help of NSS data pertaining to 1999–2000 and 2009–10.

# 4 Methodology

## *4.1 The Primary Survey*

Given the limited funds available, a small sample of 150 households was surveyed. The entire sample came from two villages in South 24 Paraganas district of West Bengal: *Madhya Narayanpur* and *Purba Narayanpur* in Canning Block. The villages were chosen so that there was a high degree of variation in socio-economic identity in the sample: (a) while the majority of households sampled were Hindu there was a large Muslim minority, and within the Hindu households there was enough representation from scheduled castes and other backward classes; and (b) there was also enough variation in economic status. In short, the villages were selected so that the sampled households would provide us with enough variation in regard to the variables of interest.

A questionnaire was administered (see Appendix) to the households which not only tried to determine their current income and educational status but also their food habits and intake now and 15 years back (through a process of recall). An effort was also made to ascertain whether factors such as the availability of education facilities, mid-day meals for school children and sanitation are adequate now and whether such availability has changed over the past 15 years. The data collected helps us to reflect upon the following questions/problems:

(a) Whether nutritional status is significantly impacted by socio-economic identity
(b) Whether a poverty trap arising out of poor nutrition status actually exists
(c) Ways to get out of the poverty trap, if one or more exist, by enhancing nutritional or *income status.*

## *4.2 Secondary Data-Based Study*

As mentioned, we use secondary data to resolve the paradox of increased deficiency in nutritional intake occurring with economic growth and associated income poverty alleviation in the first decade of the twenty-first century. This deficiency proved costly, curbing the decline in stunting and occurrence of underweight children and resulting in an increase in wasting among the poor. We use NSS data for the following years: 1999–2000, 2004–05, 2009–10 and 2011–12.

In order to achieve our objective, we break the NSS sample ordered by monthly per capita expenditure into four parts: the bottom three deciles are classified as 'poorest'; deciles 4–6 are classified as 'poorer'; deciles 7–9 are considered as belonging to the 'middle class' and finally, the 10th decile is considered as the 'rich class'. Within each class, the average per capita consumption of each consumed item in the base year is calculated to construct the representative bundle of that class. It is this consumption bundle which is used to calculate the price index for each of the mentioned years and the average annual rate of inflation experienced by the class during the two periods, 1999–2004 and 2004–10.

Our methodology involves determining class wise price indices for food and non-food items. The class wise determination of overall price indices is driven by the observation that the typical consumption bundle consumed varies by economic class—poorest, poorer, middle and rich—and therefore, its implication that we should deflate the expenditure or income in each class by a different deflator to see whether real per capita income or expenditure has grown in that class. The separate determination of food and non-price indices is driven by two different considerations: first, we wish to determine whether each class, especially the bottom income classes, has been impacted in its nutritional choices by a movement in the price of food relative to that of non-food items; second, this is made necessary by the data we have as some of the non-food items such as education and health are marked by data on just expenditures and not quantities and prices.

We define the food price index of class $j$ in the $k$th period as follows:

$$\mathrm{FPI}_{jk} = \frac{\sum_{i=1}^{n_F} q_{0ij}^F * p_{ki}^F}{\sum_{i=1}^{n_F} q_{0ij}^F * p_{0i}^F} * 100$$

where $n_F$ denotes the total number of food items that have ever been consumed in positive quantities in any one of the years under study, $q_{0ij}^F$ denotes the quantity of $i$th food item consumed per capita in the base period (1999–2000) in class $j$; $p_{0i}^F$ denotes the price of the $i$th food item in the base period and finally $p_{ki}^F$ denotes the price of the $i$th food item in the $k$th period.

In the case of non-food items, we do not have price or quantity data for health and education. We therefore define one unit of education/health for any class as that obtained from the education/health expenditure per capita in that class, i.e. we consider the representative individual in that class as consuming 1 unit of education with price equal to the magnitude of expenditure per capita. However, the use of quantity weights does not make sense under such an assumption as there would be no variation across classes. Therefore, we use the average expenditure share of items in total non-food expenditure as weights. We follow a similar weighting scheme for all non-food items in order to be consistent. Thus, non-food price index for class $j$ in period $k$ is given by

$$\mathrm{NPI}_{jk} = \frac{\sum_{i=1}^{n_N} E_{0ij} * p_{ki}}{\sum_{i=1}^{n_N} E_{0ij} * p_{0i}} \times 100$$

where $n_N$ denotes the number of non-food items that have ever been consumed in positive quantities in any one of the years being studied; $E_{0ij}$ the share of the $i$th non-food item in non-food expenditure per capita in class $j$ in the base period; $p_{0i}$ the price of the $i$th non-food item in the base period and finally, $p_{ki}$ the price of the $i$th non-food item in the $k$th period.

Once the food and non-food price index numbers are generated these can be combined to yield the overall price index for class $j$ in period $k$ in the following manner:

$$\mathrm{CPI}_{jk} = E_{j0}\mathrm{FPI}_{jk} + (1 - E_{jo})\mathrm{NPI}_{jk}$$

where $E_{j0}$ is the share of food expenditure in total expenditure in the base period for class $j$.

## 5 Results

### *5.1 Results from the Secondary Survey*

Tables 11 and 12 capture the economic class wise average rural and urban annual rates of inflation for food items for the three periods, 2000–05, 2005–10 and 2010–12 on the basis of food price indices calculated from NSS data for the four years, 1999–2000, 2004–05, 2009–10 and 2011–12. Tables 13 and 14 do the same for non-food rates of inflation. The rural and urban food price and non-food price indices are then used to calculate class wise overall price indices for rural and urban areas for the four mentioned years. This data is then used to calculate the class wise average annual rates of overall inflation, i.e. the average annual change in the average price level for food and non-food items combined.

If we compare the class wise food inflation rates to the non-food inflation rates in rural and urban areas for the periods 2005–10 and 2000–05, we observe that for the bottom two classes—'poorest' and 'poor'—the former is greater than the latter in all but one of the eight cases, that corresponding to the 'poor' category in urban areas in 2005–10 where the food and non-food inflation rates are roughly equal. This

**Table 11** Average annual rates (%) of food inflation (rural)

| | Poorest | Poor | Middle | Rich |
|---|---|---|---|---|
| 2010–2012 | 9.02 | 14.30 | 20.62 | 22.70 |
| 2005–2010 | 10.63 | 11.80 | 12.10 | 12.74 |
| 2000–2005 | 2.00 | 2.81 | 2.81 | 2.80 |

**Table 12** Average annual rates (%) of food inflation (urban)

| | Poorest | Poor | Middle | Rich |
|---|---|---|---|---|
| 2010–2012 | 14.88 | 18.53 | 17.01 | 15.72 |
| 2005–2010 | 11.22 | 11.90 | 12.17 | 12.38 |
| 2000–2005 | 2.10 | 2.56 | 2.98 | 3.20 |

**Table 13** Average annual rates (%) of non-food inflation (rural)

| | Poorest | Poor | Middle | Rich |
|---|---|---|---|---|
| 2010–2012 | 42.19 | 36.40 | 21.87 | −19.77 |
| 2005–2010 | −2.98 | −2.15 | −1.91 | −2.85 |
| 2000–2005 | −2.89 | −0.33 | 4.37 | 43.71 |

**Table 14** Average annual rates (%) of non-food inflation (urban)

| | Poorest | Poor | Middle | Rich |
|---|---|---|---|---|
| 2010–2012 | 16.98 | 8.62 | 0.69 | −10.11 |
| 2005–2010 | 8.03 | 12.03 | 8.43 | 1.61 |
| 2000–2005 | −7.34 | −2.67 | 7.03 | 39.69 |

implies that non-food items in general became cheaper relative to food items for the two mentioned classes for the mentioned periods, a phenomenon which could explain the substitution of food items by non-food items by these two classes and therefore an increase in deficiency in nutritional intake. Note that this trend does not hold good for 2010–12.

To end this section, we look at the findings regarding overall inflation rate by classes. Again, the periods of interest are 2000–2005 and 2005–10, the larger periods. For 2000–05, we see that the inflation rates for the 'poorest' and 'poor' classes are significantly lower than that for the other two classes and for all classes combined. Thus, the argument that use of a single CPI led to overestimation of income poverty alleviation does not go through. This argument, however, goes through in 2005–10 as the direction of the inequality is reversed (Tables 15 and 16).

**Table 15** Average annual rates of overall inflation (rural) for the most recent periods

| | Poorest | Poor | Middle | Rich | All classes |
|---|---|---|---|---|---|
| 2010–2012 | 15.147 | 19.400 | 21.009 | −4.598 | 11.370 |
| 2005–2010 | 6.691 | 6.942 | 5.823 | 0.662 | 4.533 |
| 2000–2005 | 0.319 | 1.308 | 3.481 | 25.361 | 7.270 |

**Table 16** Average annual rates of overall inflation (urban) for the most recent periods

| | Poorest | Poor | Middle | Rich | All classes |
|---|---|---|---|---|---|
| 2010–2012 | 15.616 | 14.079 | 7.839 | −3.438 | 8.041 |
| 2005–2010 | 7.842 | 8.272 | 6.555 | 2.774 | 6.259 |
| 2000–2005 | −0.347 | 0.543 | 2.873 | 12.638 | 3.88 |

**Table 17** Percentage of population that is food poor

| 15 years ago | | | Now | | |
|---|---|---|---|---|---|
| Carbohydrates only (0) | Carbohydrates and vegetables (1) | Total (0 + 1) | Carbohydrates only (0) | Carbohydrates and vegetables (1) | Total (0 + 1) |
| 20.67 | 3.33 | 24.00 | 18.00 | 2.00 | |

## 5.2 *Results from the Primary Survey*

The population surveyed is around 70% Hindu and 30% Muslim while more than 40% of the Hindu population is schedule caste. This along with the income diversity makes for enough socio-economic diversity to analyse the effect of socio-economic status and identity on nutrition.

From Table 17, we see that the incidence of 'food poverty', defined here as poor quality of diet or a totally protein deficient diet, is quite high in the surveyed villages. It was as high as 24% fifteen years ago with 20.67% of the population getting their nutrition from carbohydrates only. In 15 years, these numbers have gone down marginally to 20% and 18%, respectively, but are still very high.

Persistent food poverty is also a major phenomenon. The percentage of households that were food poor 15 years ago and are also food poor now is as high as 14.67%. Thus, more than 60% of originally food poor households continue to be food poor today. The reasons for this could be diverse: the food poverty trap arising out of income poverty or cultural reasons born out of caste and religion which keep the households in food poverty.

It is seen that roughly only 46% of the food poor households now belong to the bottom 50% of the income distribution. This seems to suggest that the association between economic status and nutritional status is poor, and there are other more important determinants of nutritional status. However, a more accurate idea of the impact of economic status on nutritional status can be obtained if we control for factors such as caste, religion and education through a regression. Further, we see that the association between food poverty 15 years back and income poverty now is poor as well. Only about one-third of the originally food poor households are income poor now, suggesting again that food poverty often does not lead to income poverty, possibly because endowments rather than productivity drive incomes and diets are determined more by caste, religion, education, etc., than income levels.

If we do not control for other factors the incidence of food poverty is definitely lower among Hindus than among Muslims (see Table 18); it has also been going down among Hindus but remained constant for Muslims. In regard to caste (see Table 19), the *Hindu general* category (non-SC or non-OBC) shows the lowest incidence of food poverty in both periods; *Hindu general* and SC categories show a distinct decline over time whereas for OBCs, the result is exactly the opposite.

**Table 18** Religion and food poverty (percentage that is food poor)

| Religion | Now | 15 years ago |
|---|---|---|
| Hindu | 15.38 | 21.15 |
| Muslim | 30.43 | 30.43 |

**Table 19** Caste and food poverty (percentage that is food poor)

| Caste | Now | 15 years ago |
|---|---|---|
| SC | 22.22 | 35.56 |
| OBC | 29.69 | 25 |
| General | 2.78 | 11.11 |

Next, we come to the logistic regression (see Table 20), which when estimated using maximum likelihood techniques, informs us about the sensitivity of the probability of being food poor to each of the probable determining variables. Though the effect of income is statistically significant at the 1% level, we find that an increase in income by Rs. 1000 decreases the probability of being food poor by only 6% points. On the other hand, if we consider *Hindu general* as the base category, then *ceteris paribus*, the probability of Muslims being food poor is lower by 27.85% points and of *Hindu SCs* being food poor is less by 26.90% points. The difference in probabilities between each of these two categories and the *Hindu general* category is statistically significant at the 1% level. This is not true of the difference between the *Hindu OBC* and *Hindu general* category.

Next, we look at the households with a male member in the age group 16–30. Table 21 shows a decomposition of this household population, which comprises 58% of the total population of all households and have exactly one such member each,

**Table 20** Estimates of a logistic regression for identifying the determinants of the probability of a household being food poor

| Variables | Marginal impact of explanatory variable on food poverty at the means of observations | Std. Err | $P > z$ |
|---|---|---|---|
| Per capita income ($y$) | −0.00006 | 0.00002 | 0.003 |
| Education dummy ($E$) | 0.2063 | 0.1197 | 0.085 |
| *Socio-religious-identity* | | | |
| Hindu SC (SC) | −0.2690 | 0.0677 | 0.000 |
| Hindu OBC (OBC) | −0.0415 | 0.0352 | 0.239 |
| Muslims (M) | −0.2785 | 0.0803 | 0.001 |

*Note* If $p$ is the probability of the household being food poor, then the estimated regression equation is $\ln\left(\frac{p}{1-p}\right) = 6.609 - 0.0005y + 1.813E - 4.217\text{SC} - 2.180\text{OBC} - 4.264\text{M}$. The value of pseudo $R$-square is 0.1897

**Table 21** Sub-sample of households with positive number of males in 16–30 years age group (in percentage)

| Diet category | Education | |
|---|---|---|
| | Without higher secondary degree | With higher secondary degree |
| 0 (only carbohydrates) | 13.79 | 1.15 |
| Not 0 | 65.52 | 19.54 |

**Table 22** Estimates of logistic regression with probability of the sole male member in the age group 16–30 possessing a higher secondary degree as dependent variable (p*)

| Dependent variable: education dummy | Marginal effects ($dp^*/dx$) | Std. Err | $P > z$ |
|---|---|---|---|
| Diet dummy ($D$) | 0.1415 | 0.0813 | 0.082 |
| Per capita income ($y$) | 2.30e−06 | 0.00001 | 0.857 |
| *Socio-religious-identity* | | | |
| Hindu dummy (SC) | −0.1398 | 0.1771 | 0.430 |
| Hindu OBC dummy (OBC) | −0.1733 | 0.1853 | 0.350 |
| Muslim dummy (M) | −0.2829 | 0.1782 | 0.112 |

*Note* If $p^*$ is the probability of the household having a male in the age group 16–30 with a higher secondary degree, then the estimated regression equation is $\ln\left(\frac{p^*}{1-p^*}\right) = -2.324 + 0.00003y + 1.759D - 0.802\text{SC} - 1.071\text{OBC} - 3.063\text{M}$. The value of pseudo $R$-square is 0.1393

on the basis of the possession of a higher secondary degree by the male member of focus and the characteristic of being food poor.

The table above shows that only about 7% of total number of food poor households in category 0 (only carbohydrates) that have a male member in the age group 16–30 is characterized by that male member possessing a higher secondary degree. For others who are food non-poor and have such a male member the proportion is above 21%. Similar results are obtained from the logistic regression (see Table 22): not being food poor (not being in 0 category) enhances the probability of the said male not possessing a higher secondary degree by 14.15%, with the diet dummy being statistically significant at the 10% level of significance. This highlights the fact that food poverty does indeed have implications for human capital formation.

## 6 Conclusions and Implications for Policy and Future Research

The contribution of this work lies in value drawn by juxtaposing the specific findings emerging from primary surveys against the more general findings for the whole of India emerging from secondary (National Sample Survey and National Family Health Survey) data. First, it establishes on the basis of a review of literature and secondary data that the food security mediated poverty trap is indeed a highly probable phenomenon as malnutrition, often an implication of income poverty, has negative implications for human capital formation. Second, it establishes, on the basis of secondary data which clearly shows a significantly higher nutritional and anthropometric deficiency among the poor that for India as a whole the incidence of this poverty trap is high. Yet the primary data-based study of two villages in West Bengal reveals malnutrition to be driven more by cultural factors born out of caste and religious affiliation than income poverty, thus highlighting the significant incidence of a malnutrition mediated low productivity trap and the less significant incidence of a malnutrition mediated poverty trap.

These findings show that policies relating to malnutrition, poverty and low productivity might have to be fine-tuned to the specific needs of different regions. Where cultural factors drive malnutrition to a greater extent than low income it is necessary that the government devotes more attention to generation of dietary awareness. This yields the maximum bang for the buck: income supplements in such cases might not yield desired results because of cultural predispositions encouraging unbalanced dietary intake; and both cash and nutritional supplements might prove to be more expensive than an information programme which simply spreads dietary awareness. However, given our general findings, there are sure to be regions where the incidence of the food insecurity driven poverty trap is significant and in those areas a programme based on nutritional and/or income supplements would obviously be more apt because of the origins of malnutrition in low purchasing power. There, however, needs to be more research as to whether income supplements should be used instead of nutritional supplements, the reverse, or a programme which assigns positive weights to both types of supplements. While the effect of nutritional supplements is certain, income supplements might be associated with certain leakages born out of the use of the supplement for frivolous consumption. Yet at the same time income supplements can be impact cognition positively through multiple channels: not just better nutrition but also better security for the child and better parenting born out of parents enjoying better economic security. The relative efficiency of these two supplements needs to be determined through further research based on randomized control trials at different levels of supplementation. This would yield information regarding how the marginal efficiency of income supplements/nutritional supplements varies at the household level with the scale of expenditure on the supplement, thus helping us to ascertain the correct weights to be given to income (nutritional) supplements, with possible weights ranging from 0 (1) to 1 (0).

The study also warns against complacency that economic growth can solve nutritional and anthropometric problems: secondary data yields evidence that income poverty alleviation born out of economic growth has been associated with a rise in such deficiency, the probable significant explanations for such behaviour being the poor trying to match the enhanced status good consumption of the rich, induced by growth of incomes in the upper end of the distribution, in a classic case of ‘catching up with the Joneses’; and the observed phenomenon of food inflation exceeding non-food inflation leading to substitution away from food in favour of non-food items. It is also possible that an overestimation of poverty alleviation in the second half of the first decade of this century has made this paradoxical phenomenon seem larger than what it really is. There is a chance such phenomena might be associated with future economic growth though safeguards can be taken in the form of a close watch on the relative magnitudes of food and non-food inflation with the government stepping in with a suitable tax-subsidy programme in case the former type of inflation exceeds the latter.

**Acknowledgements** This paper is based on the findings of a project initiated by the *Planning and Development Unit, Jadavpur University* and funded by *NITI Aayog, Government of India* as well as related unpublished parts of the doctoral dissertation of Paramita Bhattacharya.

## Appendix: Questionnaire for Primary Survey

1. Village name
2. Are there any children in the household in the age group of 16–20 years?
3. Name, age and gender of head of household
4. Household size
5. Age and gender of other members of the household, their relationship with the head of the household, and the monthly income of the income earners.

| Sl. No. | Name | Age | Gender | Highest level of education attained till date | Relation with head of household | Income earner or not | Average monthly income of the income earners |
|---|---|---|---|---|---|---|---|
| | | | | | | | |
| | | | | | | | |
| | | | | | | | |
| | | | | | | | |
| | | | | | | | |
| | | | | | | | |
| | | | | | | | |
| | | | | | | | |
| | | | | | | | |
| | | | | | | | |

6. Identify members using Sl. No in the table above whose principal source of income is the following:

   i. Government, public sector or private sector job.
   ii. Self-employment in agriculture
   iii. Wage employment in agriculture
   iv. Others

7. Religion
8. Classify the households in terms of the following categories if Hindu

i. SC
ii. ST
iii. OBC
iv. General

9. In case the household is Hindu and is placed in the first three categories (above), does it possess a relevant certificate?
10. In case the household is non-Hindu and SC/ST does it have a relevant certificate?
11. Identify the children aged 16 to 18 years who are not in school by Sl. No. (in 5).
12. Against the possible reasons for not being in school list the relevant Sl. Nos, thus pointing out the reason for each child identified in 11 for not being in school.

i. Dropped out voluntarily due to family facing financial hardship
ii. Dropped out because of poor performance or failure
iii. Other (explain):

13. Present consumption of food in the household

| Sl. No. | Timings at which various meals are taken in the household even if some or all of the meals are marked by absentees | Food Items Consumed | | | | | |
|---|---|---|---|---|---|---|---|
| | | Adult Males (>18 Years) | Adult Females (>18 Years) | Male Child <12 Years | Female Child <12 Years | 12-18 Years (Male) | 12-18 Years (Female) |
| | | | | | | | |
| | | | | | | | |
| | | | | | | | |
| | | | | | | | |
| | | | | | | | |

14. Food consumption in the household 15 years back

| Sl. No. | Timings at which various meals were taken in the household even if some or all of the meals were marked by absentees | Food Items Consumed | | | | | |
|---|---|---|---|---|---|---|---|
| | | Adult Males (>18 Years) | Adult Females (>18 Years) | Male Child <12 Years | Female Child <12 Years | 12-18 Years (Male) | 12-18 Years (Female) |
| | | | | | | | |
| | | | | | | | |
| | | | | | | | |
| | | | | | | | |
| | | | | | | | |
| | | | | | | | |

15. Monthly consumption of major food items and expenditures on these (now and 15 years back if there has been a significant change between then and now):

| Food items | Quantity being consumed now (monthly) | Current expenditure (monthly) | Quantity consumed 15 years ago (monthly) | Expenditure 15 years ago (monthly) |
|---|---|---|---|---|
| Cereals | | | | |
| Pulses | | | | |
| Vegetables | | | | |
| Oil | | | | |
| Milk and milk products | | | | |
| Non-vegetarian food | | | | |
| Fruits | | | | |
| Sugar/gur | | | | |
| Tea/coffee | | | | |
| Pan/tobacco products | | | | |

16. Is there a good primary government school that is accessible from the village now? What about middle and secondary schools? Compare with the situation 15 years back
17. Comment on the quality of the mid-day meal programme now and 15 years back as well as provide details regarding how much it helps/helped to supplement the food consumption of the household
18. Compare the state of accessible government health facilities (health centres/dispensaries/hospitals) at present to that 15 years back?
19. Do you access private health facilities now? What about 15 years back?
20. What are/were the expenditures on health and education now/'15 years ago'?
21. Name the goods (and their quantities) which you consume as a result of (a) home production, transfers from relatives or friends outside the household, and (b) access to nature (forests/lakes/trees, etc.)? Compare this to the situation 15 years back.
22. Do you use the PDS? If yes, provide monthly quantity of purchases and expenditures on these. What was the scenario 15 years ago?
23. Wealth now and 15 years ago

    i. Amount of land owned
    ii. Nature of home ownership: owned/rented/relative's house
    iii. Type of household: Kuccha/Pucca
    iv. Type of flooring
    v. Type of roofing
    vi. Number of rooms
    vii. Number of household members sleeping per room.
    viii. Drinking water source
    ix. Type of toilet facility
    x. Ownership of a bank or post office account
    xi. Ownership of durable goods (list and visually inspect)

24. What is the source of drinking water? Is it treated before consumption? Compare with the situation 15 years back.
25. How active are/were Anganwadis 15 years back?

## References

Briend, A., Khara, T., & Dolan, C. (2015). Wasting and stunting—Similarities and differences; policy and programmatic implications. *Food and Nutrition Bulletin, 36*(1), S15–S33.

Deaton, A., & Dreze, J. (2009). Food and nutrition in India: Facts and interpretation. *Economic and Political Weekly, XLIV*(7), 42–65.

International Institute for Population Sciences (IIPS) and ORC Macro. (2000). *National Family Health Survey (NFHS-2), 1998–99: India*. IIPS.

International Institute for Population Sciences (IIPS) and Macro International. (2007). *National Family Health Survey (NFHS-3), 2005–06: India* (Vol. I). IIPS.

Liu, J., Raine, A., Venables, P. H., Dalais, C., & Mednick, S. A. (2003). Malnutrition at age 3 years and lower cognitive ability at age 11 years: Independence from psychosocial adversity. *Archives of Pediatrics and Adolescent Medicine, 157*(6), 593–600.

Marjit, S., Santra, S., & Hati, K. K. (2015). Relative social status and conflicting measures of poverty: A behavioral analytical model. *Journal of Quantitative Economics, 13*(1), 77–86.

Martorell, R., Melgar, P., Maluccio, J. A., Stein, A. D., & Rivera, J. A. (2010). The nutrition intervention improved adult human capital and economic productivity. *Journal of Nutrition, 140*(2), 411–414.

Noble, K. G. (2017, March). Brain trust. *Scientific American, 31*(3), 44–49.

Noble, K. G., et al. (2015). Family income, parental education and brain structure in children and adolescents. *Nature Neuroscience, 18*, 773–778.

Noble, K. G., McCandliss, B. D., & Farah, M. J. (2007). Socioeconomic gradients predict individual differences in neurocognitive abilities. *Developmental Science, 10*(4), 464–480.

Plaza, B. L., et al. (2001). The impact of malnutrition on brain development, intelligence and school work performance. *Archivos Latinoamericanos de Nutricion, 5*(1), 64–71.

Programme Evaluation Organisation, Planning Commission, Government of India. (2011). *Evaluation study on Integrated Child Development Schemes (ICDS)* (Vol. 1).

Rah, J. H., Cronin, A. A., Badgaiyan, B., Aguayo, V. M., Coates, S., & Ahmed, S. (2015). Household sanitation and personal hygiene practices are associated with child stunting in rural India: A cross-sectional analysis of surveys. *British Medical Journal Open, 2015*, 5.

Sachdev, Y., & Dasgupta, J. (2001). Integrated Child Development Services (ICDS) scheme. *Medical Journal Armed Forces India, 57*(2), 139–143.

Spears, D., Ghosh, A., & Cumming, O. (2013). Open defecation and childhood stunting in India: An ecological analysis of new data from 112 districts. *PLoS ONE, 8*, e73784.

Suryanarayana, M. H. (2003). Policies for nutrition: How imperative are they? In S. M. Dev, K. P. Kannan, & N. Ramachandran (Eds.), *Towards a food secure India: Issues & policies* (pp. 406–432). Institute for Human Development.

Suryanarayana, M. H. (2009). *Nutritional norms for poverty: Issues and implications*. Concept Paper. http://planningcommission.nic.in/reports/genrep/surya.pdf

Waber, D. P., Bryce, C. P., Girard, J. M., Zichlin, M., Fitzmaurice, G. M., & Galler, J. R. (2014). Impaired IQ and academic skills in adults who experienced moderate to severe infantile malnutrition: A forty-year study. *Nutritional Neuroscience, 17*(2), 58–64.

# State-Level Exports: An Alternate Estimate

**Simontini Das and Saikat Sinha Roy**

## 1 Introduction

The process of trade liberalization in India gained momentum since 1991. In post-liberalization period, Indian states have started to recognize the importance of international trade. The states have taken initiatives to reframe their respective commercial policies to gain from trade liberalization. In this regard, *Export Preparedness Index 2020* published by the NITI Aayog shows the preparedness of Indian states with regards to global positioning. The importance of state-level trade performance and trade promotion policies has become all the more important when states are designing initiatives to come out of economic recession and be a part of the post-pandemic global revival.

The existing literature highlights the importance of physical and social infrastructure, foreign direct investment, state policy, among other factors, in determining the state-level export performance.[1] For instance, Coughlin and Cartwright (1987), Limao and Venables (2001), Sun (2001), Wu (2011), Coughlin (2012), Zhang and Felmingham (2010), and Perez and Wilson (2012) explain variations in export performance across regions in terms of state-level trade promotion policy, technical efficiency, foreign direct investment, proximity to port and variations in regional economic growth. The importance of availability of infrastructure in determining regional competitiveness is also highlighted in the existing literature (Coughlin & Fabel, 1987; Coughlin, 2012; Bougheas et al., 2000; Wilson et al., 2003; Francois & Manchin, 2007; Iwanow & Kirkpatrick, 2009; Perez & Wilson, 2012). Geographical advantage and agglomeration, among other factors, are important in determining

[1] Sinha Roy et al. (2015) provide a detailed review of literature on this subject.

S. Das (✉) · S. Sinha Roy
Department of Economics, Jadavpur University, Kolkata 700032, India
e-mail: simontini@gmail.com

 
A. Raychaudhuri and A. Ghose (eds.), *Managing Pandemic and Correcting Development Fundamentals*, India Studies in Business and Economics,
https://doi.org/10.1007/978-981-19-8680-2_8

regional specialization and trade (Steinle, 1992).[2] Sinha Roy et al. (2015) show that trade facilitation index, FDI, per capita NSDP, ASIDE funds are important in explaining state-level export performance in India. Pradhan and Das (2012) analyze state-level export performances and show that availability of better infrastructure enhances the export potentiality of Indian states. However, the major constraint in undertaking research on export performance at the sub-national level is the availability of consistent time-comparable state-level export data.

In India, the Directorate General of Commercial Intelligence and Statistics (DGCI&S), Kolkata, Government of India, has recently started providing data on state-level exports. The DGCI&S uses information from the customs, collected at ports, to estimate and arrive at the state-level export database. Sinha Roy et al. (2015) have identified the gaps in this database. The main problem relates to the identification of the correct state of origin of exports, known as attribution error (Smith, 1989). Even though the exporters are required to provide their state of origin code in case of single shipment bill, they often mention either their state location, location of their registered office, and the state from where the product is procured or the location of the port of shipment as the state of origin of exports. Further, production of any exportable may involve two or more states. Besides, there is no provision to mention about different states for different products in case of shipping bill with multiple invoices and with various goods (Sinha Roy et al., 2015). A substantial number of exporters also do not mention the state of origin in their shipping bills, leading to under-reporting of state-level export data. Above all, the DGCI&S data on state-level exports are not validated.

To avoid the problem of identification of state, alternate database, like CMIE-Prowess or ASI unit-level data, can be used. Firm-level data provide the state location of production, from where the state of origin of the export can be easily identified. Pradhan and Das (2012) use CMIE-Prowess firm-level database to minimize the identification problem related to origin of state. Sinha Roy et al. (2015) have mentioned about other possible sources using which estimates of state-level exports can be arrived at. Marjit et al. (2007) construct regional trade openness index using industry-level ASI database. On the whole, data unavailability hinders the research related to state-level export performance in India.

There is however no attempt as yet to estimate state-level exports using ASI unit-level database. ASI unit-level database, which is more comprehensive and larger sample size than the corresponding CMIE database, provides statistical information on several manufacturing production-related variables including exports. Another advantage of using ASI database is that it provides information related to National Industrial Classification (NIC) which is easily comparable with Indian Trade Classification (ITC). Consequently, ASI provides reliable industry-specific

[2] This is somewhat similar to a large literature explaining variations in growth across regions. For instance, Ahluwalia (2000), Besley and Burgess (2004), Amin and Mattoo (2008), Aghion et al. (2008), Kumar and Subramanian (2012), Ghate and Wright (2013), and Singh and Bhanumurthy (2014) analyze the impact of labor market, institutions, population growth, urbanization, literacy rate, share of organized manufacturing, and infrastructure on inter-state variations in economic growth.

export database, which is difficult to arrive at from CMIE-Prowess database. The new export database thus arrived at along with the state-wise production database has immense implications for state-level export policy.

The paper is structured in the following way. Section 2 delineates ASI unit-level data. Section 3 describes detailed methodology and complete enumeration of data. Sections 4 and 5 discuss the sub-national-level export structure and its association with state-level production structure, respectively. The last section concludes.

## 2 ASI Unit-Level Data Description

Annual Survey of Industry (ASI) data are collected annually by the Central Statistical Office (CSO), Government of India, for the entire country covering all the states and union territories using a detailed questionnaire. ASI unit-level database provides the information on the state location of the factories registered under Sections 2(m)(i) and 2(m)(ii) of the Factories Act, 1948. The ASI sample frame is the list of registered factories or units maintained by Chief Inspector of Factories (CIF) in each state. The ASI frame is revised and updated periodically. All the factories under updated frame are divided into two sectors: census and sample. Census sector includes

a. all industrial units of Manipur, Meghalaya, Nagaland, Tripura, Sikkim, and Andaman & Nicobar Islands,
b. factory units having 100 or more workers and all the factories covered under the Joint Returns from the rest of 25 states or UTs,
c. after excluding the abovementioned census sector units, all other units belong to the strata (State by 4-digit of NIC-08) having less than or equal to 4 units.

The sample sector includes the remaining units after excluding the census sector units from total number of units. Sample sector units are arranged in order to their number of workers and classified into various strata (State X Sector X 4-digit NIC). Sample is drawn from each stratum for all the states. The sample proportion is 20%. An even number of units with a minimum of 4 are selected and evenly distributed in two sub-samples. The three sectors are Bidi, manufacturing, and electricity. Central sample consists of census sector and sample sector. After selecting the central sample, the remaining factories are considered as the residual frame for selection of state sample units. Residual units are regrouped into various strata (District X 3-digit NIC). Sample is drawn from each stratum. The sample proportion is 10% in general. Central sample is used to estimate state-level characteristics, whereas state sample units pooled with validated state-wise unit-level data of central sample are used to estimate sub-state-level characteristics. ASI unit-level data provide the data on the share (%) of product/by-product directly exported by the industrial units.

**Table 1** Census and sample firm composition of ASI unit-level data over the year 2008–09 to 2014–15

| Year | Total number of firms | No. of census firms | No. of sample firms | Information not available |
|---|---|---|---|---|
| 2008–2009 | 54,349 | 20,228 (37.22%) | 34,120 (62.78%) | 1 |
| 2009–2010 | 57,113 | 19,838 (34.73%) | 37,275 (65.27%) | |
| 2011–2012 | 52,778 | 21,483 (40.70%) | 31,292 (59.29%) | 3 |
| 2012–2013 | 59,162 | 42,231 (71.38%) | 16,931 (28.62%) | |
| 2013–2014 | 57,968 | 39,042 (67.35) | 18,926 (32.65%) | |
| 2014–2015 | 63,296 | 22,960 (36.27%) | 40,336 (63.73%) | |
| Total | 344,666 | 165,782 (48.10%) | 178,880 (51.90%) | |

*Source* Authors' calculation on the basis of ASI unit-level dataset

The state of origin of exports can, thus, be identified precisely from the ASI database. 29 Indian states are considered[3] here. In this exercise, ASI unit-level data are considered for the years 2008–09, 2009–10, 2010–11, 2011–12, 2012–13, 2013–14, and 2014–15. We have tabulated the state-level export data of organized manufacturing sector for these years with the sole exception of 2010–11. In 2010–11, the number of units reporting positive exports is disproportionately low at only four firms (with DSL 23,549, 24,740, 35,470, and 68,951). Table 1 gives an account of the coverage of firms, census and sample, which has improved over the years albeit fluctuations. Further, it can be noted that, except for a couple of years, the majority of the firms covered are sample firms.

## 3 Detailed Methodology and Export Data Generation

The value of exports can be tabulated at the firm level. This firm-level export data can be used to estimate state-level export data. State-level export data can be estimated by using the following steps:

- **Step 1**: Multiplication of the share of exports with the total sales value of the firm to arrive at value of exports in Indian Rupees at the firm level.

[3] The project includes the complete enumeration of all union territories; however, the paper excludes union territories Chandigarh, Daman & Diu, Dadra & N. Haveli, and Andaman & Nicobar Island.

- **Step 2**: Identification of the firms according to their state location (following ASI state code).
- **Step 3**: Identification of census and sample firms according to ASI scheme.
- **Step 4**: Export of the census firms is aggregated at individual state level. Let $E_{Ci}$ is the export of the $i$th state contributed by the census firms. In this regards, it should be mentioned that Manipur, Meghalaya, Nagaland, Tripura, and Sikkim only have census firms. For these five states, $E_i = E_{Ci}$ where $i =$ Manipur, Meghalaya, Nagaland, Tripura, and Sikkim
- **Step 5**: State-wise sample firms are clustered according to NIC 2008 4-digit classification. Exports of the sample firms of $j$th strata (State X 4 Digit NIC) are aggregated to obtain $E_{Sij}$ (export of the $i$th state contributed by the sample firms of $j$th strata). However, samples are drawn from the population. $E_{Sij}$ is to be inflated to get total contribution of state-level exports by the sample firms. ASI provides the sample frame for each year. On the basis of the available sample frame, multiplier (or weight) for each strata is calculated. Say $\lambda_j$ is the multiplier of the $j$th strata.

  Let exports of the $i$th state by the sample firms $= E_{Si}$. If they are compared, then

$$E_{Si} = \sum_{j=1}^{k} \lambda_j E_{Sij},$$

where $k =$ number of strata available in $i$th state,

$\lambda_j$ is the blowing up factor used by the ASI to estimate state-level variables from firm-level information for the sample scheme. This multiplier is the reciprocal of the sample proportion. The population distribution, sample distribution, and sample structure are not given by ASI unit-level data. Hence, instead of estimating the multiplier, we use the multiplier provided by ASI for each sample firm.

- **Step 6**: Let $E_i$ is the aggregate export of the $i$th state, then $E_i = E_{Ci} + E_{Si}$
- **Step 7**: The firms thus identified are according to the NIC2000 2-digit classification. Thereafter, firm-level exports are aggregated on the basis of 2-digit industrial classification to obtain state-level industry-specific exports.

One lacuna of this methodology is that the sample composition varies over the years. ASI does not provide sample frame for each year. Hence, it is not possible to compare the distribution pattern of production firms and exporter firms. The proportion of exporting and non-exporting firms under the sample scheme also changes from one year to another year. One year may have higher proportion of exporting firms relative to non-exporting firms resulting in over-estimation for the year. The opposite may happen in some other years.

Table 2 puts forth the new state-level aggregate manufacturing export data for the period 2008–09 to 2014–15 with exception of 2010–11. India's northeastern states like Sikkim, Arunachal Pradesh, Nagaland, Manipur, Tripura, and Meghalaya are found not to export regularly during the time period under consideration. Telangana, the new state, is added in 2011–12.

This newly enumerated state-level export data, like the corresponding DGCI&S data, has varied over the years. However, it is worth mentioning here that this set of state-level export data based on ASI unit-level records is free from the state of origin identification problem, as the state-specific geographical location of the firms is explicitly given in the ASI unit-level database. Here, the point of production is identified accurately. However, ASI covers only the organized manufacturing sectors leaving aside informal sector, agriculture, mining, and mineral sectors. Agricultural exports, export from informal sectors, mining, and mineral exports are thus excluded in this exercise.

Table 3 shows the ranking of the states on the basis of their manufacturing exports arrived at from ASI unit-level records. Data exploration shows that, despite fluctuations, Maharashtra, Tamil Nadu, and Gujarat secure the top three positions. In 2009–10, Kerala secures the top position followed by Maharashtra and Tamil Nadu. Uttar Pradesh and Telangana maintain their respective positions during the period. There is an improvement in the ranking, based on newly enumerated state-level export data in this exercise, for nine states including Karnataka, Haryana, Punjab, Kerala, Rajasthan, Uttarakhand, Chhattisgarh, and Himachal Pradesh during the time period from 2008–09 to 2014–15. In particular, Karnataka is found to have improved manufacturing export performance over the years and secures the 4th position in 2014–15. In sharp contrast, Andhra Pradesh, West Bengal, Madhya Pradesh, Odisha, Delhi, Goa, Jharkhand, Jammu & Kashmir, Bihar, and Assam experience a decline in similar ranking over time. Some states experience moderate fall whereas for some others, the fall is sharper. However, it needs to be highlighted here that northeastern states including Sikkim, Manipur, Nagaland, Arunachal Pradesh, Tripura, and Meghalaya, on the basis of this enumeration, are not involved in exporting from the organized manufacturing sector on a regular basis during this period.

## 4 State-Level Export Structure

Having estimated the exports in organized manufacturing sector and deciphering their respective ranks in the country, it is important to identify the state-level export structure. Table 4 shows the pattern of export diversification at the sub-national level. It can be observed that the top five product groups (at the 2-digit level) consist of more than 50% in individual state's export basket. This is true despite some of the states having a diversified export basket. Detailed examination shows that the share of top five export items is more than 90% of the total export basket in the states with relatively lower degree of diversification. In Orissa, this share is more than 99%. The share of top five items in total export basket is also high in Jammu and Kashmir, Assam, and Jharkhand. Conversely, this share is moderately high in industrially developed states like Punjab, Haryana, Gujarat, Maharashtra, Karnataka, and Tamil

**Table 2** State-level exports estimated from ASI unit-level data (in Rs. lakhs)

| State code | Name of the state | 2008–09 | 2009–10 | 2011–12 | 2012–13 | 2013–14 | 2014–15 |
|---|---|---|---|---|---|---|---|
| 1 | Jammu and Kashmir | 30,511.53 | 16,802 | 11,626.34 | 11,766 | 105,000 | 31,500 |
| 2 | Himachal Pradesh | 8382.59 | 11,499.83 | 195,483.7 | 189,160 | 376,000 | 148,000 |
| 3 | Punjab | 504,645.4 | 607,715.4 | 1,047,840 | 1,201,510 | 2,050,000 | 1,840,000 |
| 4 | Uttarakhand | 142,817.7 | 157,734.9 | 88,526.38 | 69,942 | 125,000 | 607,000 |
| 5 | Haryana | 1,456,360 | 1,870,660 | 2,665,960 | 3,240,840 | 2,230,000 | 3,420,000 |
| 6 | Delhi | 214,137.8 | 238,450.7 | 470,086 | 380,773.5 | 375,000 | 429,000 |
| 7 | Rajasthan | 306,052.9 | 560,670.7 | 1,217,090 | 1,893,640 | 1,290,000 | 1,370,000 |
| 8 | Uttar Pradesh | 1,769,220 | 1,831,460 | 2,526,410 | 3,244,870 | 3,810,000 | 3,750,000 |
| 9 | Bihar | 974.79 | 60.15 | 725,545.5 | 2873.75 | 2090 | 3830 |
| 10 | Sikkim | 0 | 0 | 0 | 0 | 136 | 0 |
| 11 | Arunachal Pradesh | 0 | 0 | 0 | 0 | 0 | 0 |
| 12 | Nagaland | 0 | 0.19507 | 0 | 0 | 0 | 300 |
| 13 | Manipur | 0 | 0 | 1388.51 | 0 | 0 | 0 |
| 14 | Tripura | 0 | 0 | 0 | 0 | 0 | 0 |
| 15 | Meghalaya | 0 | 0 | 0 | 3800 | 0 | 0 |
| 16 | Assam | 7415.19 | 2635.09 | 53,177.72 | 73,084.16 | 5340 | 1970 |
| 17 | West Bengal | 682,903.8 | 631,796.7 | 1,152,900 | 822,654.3 | 1,000,000 | 933,000 |
| 18 | Jharkhand | 21,242.39 | 19,079.71 | 11,303.86 | 39,342.3 | 29,900 | 34,200 |
| 19 | Odisha | 456,708.7 | 7419.292 | 273,205.8 | 193,753 | 461,000 | 639,000 |
| 20 | Chhattisgarh | 46,483.31 | 2134.7 | 145,949.2 | 54,522.31 | 115,000 | 277,000 |
| 21 | Madhya Pradesh | 575,737.4 | 170,596.8 | 346,300.4 | 3,759,220 | 675,000 | 804,000 |
| 22 | Gujarat | 2,875,370 | 1,389,660 | 3,401,780 | 18,950,200 | 7,630,000 | 4,140,000 |
| 23 | Maharashtra | 6,409,410 | 6,147,820 | 7,819,040 | 8,081,230 | 10,400,000 | 8,770,000 |
| 24 | Andhra Pradesh | 1,565,560 | 1,175,350 | 1,989,180 | 1,254,470 | 1,700,000 | 1,360,000 |
| 25 | Karnataka | 1,649,900 | 678,515.7 | 1,753,060 | 1,704,430 | 1,590,000 | 4,080,000 |
| 26 | Goa | 81,574.04 | 40,303.16 | 230,001.5 | 198,280 | 124,000 | 200,000 |
| 27 | Kerala | 675,164.3 | 9,445,960 | 971,374.2 | 812,550.7 | 1,120,000 | 1,410,000 |
| 28 | Tamil Nadu | 3,185,860 | 3,213,720 | 4,751,720 | 7,094,200 | 5,610,000 | 7,020,000 |
| 29 | Telangana | 0 | 0 | 0 | 688,880.1 | 1,070,000 | 971,000 |

*Source* Authors' calculation based on ASI unit-level records

**Table 3** Ranking of the Indian States based on export performance

| Name of the state | 2008–09 | 2009–10 | 2011–12 | 2012–13 | 2013–14 | 2014–15 |
|---|---|---|---|---|---|---|
| Maharashtra | 1 | 2 | 1 | 2 | 1 | 1 |
| Tamil Nadu | 2 | 3 | 2 | 3 | 3 | 2 |
| Gujarat | 3 | 6 | 3 | 1 | 2 | 3 |
| Karnataka | 5 | 8 | 7 | 8 | 8 | 4 |
| Uttar Pradesh | 4 | 5 | 5 | 5 | 4 | 5 |
| Haryana | 7 | 4 | 4 | 6 | 5 | 6 |
| Punjab | 11 | 10 | 10 | 10 | 6 | 7 |
| Kerala | 9 | 1 | 11 | 12 | 10 | 8 |
| Rajasthan | 13 | 11 | 8 | 7 | 9 | 9 |
| Andhra Pradesh | 6 | 7 | 6 | 9 | 7 | 10 |
| Telangana | – | – | – | 13 | 11 | 11 |
| West Bengal | 8 | 9 | 9 | 11 | 12 | 12 |
| Madhya Pradesh | 10 | 13 | 14 | 4 | 13 | 13 |
| Odisha | 12 | 19 | 15 | 16 | 14 | 14 |
| Uttarakhand | 15 | 14 | 19 | 19 | 17 | 15 |
| Delhi | 14 | 12 | 13 | 14 | 16 | 16 |
| Chhattisgarh | 17 | 21 | 18 | 20 | 19 | 17 |
| Goa | 16 | 15 | 16 | 15 | 18 | 18 |
| Himachal Pradesh | 20 | 18 | 17 | 17 | 15 | 19 |
| Jharkhand | 19 | 16 | 22 | 21 | 21 | 20 |
| Jammu and Kashmir | 18 | 17 | 21 | 22 | 20 | 21 |
| Bihar | 22 | 22 | 12 | 24 | 23 | 22 |
| Assam | 21 | 20 | 20 | 18 | 22 | 23 |
| Nagaland | 25 | 23 | 26 | 27 | 26 | 24 |
| Sikkim | 23 | 24 | 24 | 25 | 24 | 25 |
| Arunachal Pradesh | 24 | 25 | 25 | 26 | 25 | 26 |
| Manipur | 26 | 26 | 23 | 28 | 27 | 27 |
| Tripura | 27 | 27 | 27 | 29 | 28 | 28 |
| Meghalaya | 28 | 28 | 28 | 23 | 29 | 29 |

*Source* Authors' calculation based on ASI unit-level records

Nadu. In West Bengal, the top five items consist of 78.2% share in the state's export basket.

Another interesting feature of state-level export performance is discernible if observations are at a disaggregated level. 14 states out of 23 are found to have more than 20 items in their respective export baskets. These states are Punjab, Uttarakhand, Haryana, Delhi, Rajasthan, Uttar Pradesh, West Bengal, Madhya Pradesh, Gujarat, Maharashtra, Karnataka, Kerala, Andhra Pradesh, and Tamil Nadu. The extent of

**Table 4** State-wise export diversification and top five item of exports

| States | Number of exported item(s) | Share of top 5 export items (in %) |
|---|---|---|
| Jammu and Kashmir | 11 | 93.43 |
| Himachal Pradesh | 18 | 81.63 |
| Punjab | 23 | 72.71 |
| Uttarakhand | 21 | 61.47 |
| Haryana | 23 | 75.78 |
| Delhi | 21 | 88.09 |
| Rajasthan | 22 | 65.7 |
| Uttar Pradesh | 24 | 58.17 |
| Bihar | 10 | 74.8 |
| Assam | 13 | 90.53 |
| West Bengal | 22 | 78.2 |
| Jharkhand | 7 | 93.93 |
| Odisha | 10 | 99.54 |
| Chhattisgarh | 16 | 87.14 |
| Madhya Pradesh | 22 | 80.4 |
| Gujarat | 24 | 69.23 |
| Maharashtra | 24 | 59.95 |
| Andhra Pradesh | 23 | 70.46 |
| Karnataka | 24 | 55.69 |
| Goa | 17 | 78.2 |
| Kerala | 23 | 87.64 |
| Tamil Nadu | 24 | 64.44 |
| Telangana | 19 | 86.35 |

*Source* Authors' calculation

export diversification is high in these states. For instance, export basket of West Bengal consists of 22 items despite decline in the state's overall ranking over time. This is in contrast to the lack of diversification in export basket for Jammu and Kashmir, Bihar, Jharkhand, and Orissa. In particular, Jharkhand exports only 7 items during the period 2008–09 to 2014–15. Even in Assam, a single food product accounts for about 26% of total export. In Himachal Pradesh and Goa, pharmaceutical products account for a large proportion of respective state-level total exports.

## 5 Comparison Between Export and Production Structures at the Sub-national Level

To examine the compatibility between export structure and production structure at the sub-national level, rank correlation between the two is checked. For state-level, export share and production share of different 2-digit industries are calculated for each year. Industry-wise average export share and average production share are calculated at individual state level. Based on ranking of industries within each state, being ranked according to respective state-level, export share and production share, Spearman rank correlation and Kendall's tau-a rank correlations are calculated for all 23 states. Northeastern states Sikkim, Arunachal Pradesh, Nagaland, Manipur, Tripura, and Meghalaya are not included here.

Table 5 shows that Bihar, Jammu and Kashmir, Jharkhand, Rajasthan, and Uttar Pradesh do not exhibit any significant correspondence between export and production structures. The rest 18 states have significant positive correlation between inter-industry export ranking and production ranking, but the degree of association varies across the sub-nations. We consider Kendall's tau-a rank correlation coefficient as it is more appropriate for small number of observations. Gujarat and Madhya Pradesh have high-degree positive association between industry-wise export and production structures over the period. This association is moderately high in Assam, Haryana, Maharashtra, Odisha, and Tamil Nadu (0.6–0.7). The rank correlation coefficient is lower between 0.5 and 0.6 for Delhi, Punjab, and Uttarakhand. The remaining states, including Andhra Pradesh, Chhattisgarh, Goa, Himachal Pradesh, Karnataka, Kerala, Telangana, and West Bengal, show positive association between export structure and production structure, but the degree of association is low (below 0.5).

Detailed industry-specific study reveals some interesting observations. Table 6 identifies state-wise top five industries[4] in export basket as well as in production basket along with their respective shares. State-wise disaggregate level study shows that pharmaceuticals, medicinal, and botanical products are the most important exported product group in Himachal Pradesh, Madhya Pradesh, Goa, and Telangana. Food product is the most important exportable in Jammu and Kashmir, Haryana, Uttar Pradesh, Assam, Andhra Pradesh, and Kerala. Textile occupies first position in Punjab, whereas it has high export share in Jammu and Kashmir, Uttarakhand, and in Rajasthan. Wearing apparel industry has the highest export share in Delhi and Karnataka. It also contributes substantially in the export baskets of Tamil Nadu, Uttar Pradesh, and Haryana. Chemical product industry contributes highest share in export basket in Rajasthan and Gujarat. It occupies second position in Goa. Motor vehicles and transport equipment industry is the most important exportable industry in Tamil Nadu. It is also important in Haryana. Motor vehicles, trailers, and semi-trailers industry is the top most exportable from Tamil Nadu; it is also an important export item for Haryana. Basic metal product industry occupies the first position

[4] Top five industries in export basket and production basket are considered as they jointly contribute more that 60% in both the baskets.

**Table 5** Rank correlation between export and production structures across states

| State | No. of observation | Spearman's rho | *P*-value | Correlated | Kendall's tau-a | *P*-value | Correlation |
|---|---|---|---|---|---|---|---|
| A.P. | 23 | 0.6929 | 0.0002 | Yes | 0.4822 | 0.0014 | Yes |
| Assam | 13 | 0.8187 | 0.0006 | Yes | 0.641 | 0.0028 | Yes |
| Bihar | 10 | 0.297 | 0.4047 | No | 0.2 | 0.4743 | No |
| Chhattisgarh | 16 | 0.5882 | 0.0165 | Yes | 0.4833 | 0.0103 | Yes |
| Delhi | 21 | 0.6481 | 0.0015 | Yes | 0.5143 | 0.0012 | Yes |
| Goa | 17 | 0.5604 | 0.0193 | Yes | 0.4044 | 0.026 | Yes |
| Gujarat | 24 | 0.9296 | 0 | Yes | 0.7681 | 0 | Yes |
| H.P. | 18 | 0.4757 | 0.046 | Yes | 0.3725 | 0.0339 | Yes |
| Haryana | 23 | 0.8745 | 0 | Yes | 0.6996 | 0 | Yes |
| J&K | 11 | 0.5455 | 0.06666 | No | 0.303 | 0.1926 | No |
| Jharkhand | 7 | 0.1071 | 0.8192 | No | 0.1429 | 0.7639 | No |
| Karnataka | 24 | 0.6258 | 0.0011 | Yes | 0.4529 | 0.0021 | Yes |
| Kerala | 23 | 0.6439 | 0.0009 | Yes | 0.4664 | 0.002 | Yes |
| M.P. | 22 | 0.8735 | 0 | Yes | 0.7056 | 0 | Yes |
| Maharashtra | 24 | 0.7997 | 0 | Yes | 0.6123 | 0 | Yes |
| Odisha | 10 | 0.8303 | 0.0029 | Yes | 0.6889 | 0.0073 | Yes |
| Punjab | 23 | 0.7964 | 0 | Yes | 0.5968 | 0.0001 | Yes |
| Rajasthan | 22 | 0.3721 | 0.0881 | No | 0.2641 | 0.0907 | No |
| Tamil Nadu | 24 | 0.7697 | 0 | Yes | 0.6196 | 0 | Yes |
| Telangana | 19 | 0.5511 | 0.0145 | Yes | 0.386 | 0.0229 | Yes |
| U.P. | 24 | 0.313 | 0.1364 | No | 0.2319 | 0.1181 | No |
| Uttarakhand | 21 | 0.6779 | 0.0007 | Yes | 0.5048 | 0.0015 | Yes |
| West Bengal | 22 | 0.563 | 0.0064 | Yes | 0.4459 | 0.004 | Yes |

*Source* Authors' calculation

in the export basket in West Bengal, Jharkhand, Uttarakhand, Orissa, and Chhattisgarh; it is also an important export item in Maharashtra and Andhra Pradesh. The above detailing of facts shows that the pattern of export diversification has varied across states, which indicate varying patterns of state-level comparative advantage. In order to understand the pattern of comparative advantage, it is important look into respective state-level production structure.

In Himachal Pradesh, Gujarat, Madhya Pradesh, and Odisha, four industries out of five are common in export basket and in production basket, but with different ranking. These common industries for some of the states include:

- Himachal Pradesh: Pharmaceutical industry, electrical equipment industry, textile and chemical product industry
- Gujarat: Chemical industry, Coke and refined petroleum industry, basic metal industry, textile industry

**Table 6** State-wise top five industries in export and production baskets

| States | Share of top 5 export items (in %) | Name of the top five exportable items | Share of individual export (in %) | Name of the top five industry | Share of individual industry in production (in %) | Share of top 5 industries (in %) |
|---|---|---|---|---|---|---|
| Jammu and Kashmir | 93.43 | Food products (1) | 38.93 | Chemicals and chemical products | 28.83 | 72.03 |
| | | Textiles (2) | 21.92 | Pharmaceuticals, medicinal chemical and botanical products | 15.28 | |
| | | Electrical equipment (3) | 16.48 | Basic metals | 12.55 | |
| | | Rubber and plastics products (4) | 9.75 | Rubber and plastics products | 7.75 | |
| | | Pharmaceuticals, medicinal chemical and botanical products (5) | 6.36 | Food products | 7.63 | |
| Himachal Pradesh | 81.63 | Pharmaceuticals, medicinal chemical and botanical products (1) | 45.6 | Pharmaceuticals, medicinal chemical and botanical products | 22.94 | 64.64 |
| | | Electrical equipment (2) | 10.24 | Chemicals and chemical products | 14.87 | |
| | | Leather and related products (3) | 10 | Electrical equipment | 10.72 | |
| | | Textiles (4) | 9.52 | Textiles | 8.36 | |
| | | Chemicals and chemical products (5) | 6.27 | Other non-metallic mineral products | 7.75 | |
| Punjab | 72.71 | Textiles (1) | 27.89 | Textiles | 21.11 | 61.6 |
| | | Food products (2) | 19.53 | Food products | 15.47 | |
| | | Fabricated metal products, except machinery and equipment (3) | 9.02 | Basic metals | 10.23 | |

(continued)

**Table 6** (continued)

| States | Share of top 5 export items (in %) | Name of the top five exportable items | Share of individual export (in %) | Name of the top five industry | Share of individual industry in production (in %) | Share of top 5 industries (in %) |
|---|---|---|---|---|---|---|
| | | Wearing apparel (4) | 8.24 | Machinery and equipment n.e.c | 7.88 | |
| | | Other transport equipment (5) | 8.03 | Chemicals and chemical products | 6.91 | |
| Uttarakhand | 61.47 | Basic metals (1) | 18.22 | Motor vehicles, trailers and semi-trailers | 12.66 | 51.16 |
| | | Textiles (2) | 17.09 | Other transport equipment | 11.96 | |
| | | Rubber and plastics products (3) | 10.9 | Machinery and equipment n.e.c | 9.74 | |
| | | Electrical equipment (4) | 7.91 | Chemicals and chemical products | 8.98 | |
| | | Food products (5) | 7.35 | Electrical equipment | 7.81 | |
| Haryana | 75.78 | Food products (1) | 21.99 | Motor vehicles, trailers and semi-trailers | 32.96 | 76.42 |
| | | Wearing apparel (2) | 18.04 | Other transport equipment | 15.4 | |
| | | Motor vehicles, trailers and semi-trailers (3) | 17.27 | Basic metals | 12.77 | |
| | | Basic metals (4) | 10.49 | Food products | 9.14 | |
| | | Textiles (5) | 8.01 | Machinery and equipment n.e.c | 6.14 | |
| Delhi | 88.09 | Wearing apparel (1) | 65.48 | Food products | 41.32 | 72.08 |
| | | Food products (2) | 7.03 | Wearing apparel | 14.6 | |
| | | Fabricated metal products, except machinery and equipment (3) | 6.2 | Chemicals and chemical products | 7.35 | |

(continued)

**Table 6** (continued)

| States | Share of top 5 export items (in %) | Name of the top five exportable items | Share of individual export (in %) | Name of the top five industry | Share of individual industry in production (in %) | Share of top 5 industries (in %) |
|---|---|---|---|---|---|---|
| | | Chemicals and chemical products (4) | 5.74 | Tobacco products | 4.54 | |
| | | Textiles (5) | 3.64 | Electrical equipment | 4.27 | |
| Rajasthan | 65.7 | Chemicals and chemical products (1) | 27.33 | Other non-metallic mineral products | 20.11 | 57.92 |
| | | Textiles (2) | 16.66 | Textiles | 10.44 | |
| | | Rubber and plastics products (3) | 7.89 | Chemicals and chemical products | 9.45 | |
| | | Other manufacturing (4) | 7.14 | Basic metals | 9.13 | |
| | | Wearing apparel (5) | 6.69 | Food products | 8.79 | |
| Uttar Pradesh | 58.17 | Food products (1) | 16.1 | Food products | 19.65 | 59.83 |
| | | Wearing apparel (2) | 15.36 | Coke and refined petroleum products | 17.59 | |
| | | Leather and related products (3) | 12.68 | Chemicals and chemical products | 8.35 | |
| | | Fabricated metal products, except machinery and equipment (4) | 7.87 | Computer, electronic and optical products | 7.41 | |
| | | Computer, electronic and optical products (5) | 6.17 | Motor vehicles, trailers and semi-trailers | 6.82 | |
| Bihar | 74.8 | Paper and paper products (1) | 16.67 | Coke and refined petroleum products | 72.07 | 93.66 |

(continued)

**Table 6** (continued)

| States | Share of top 5 export items (in %) | Name of the top five exportable items | Share of individual export (in %) | Name of the top five industry | Share of individual industry in production (in %) | Share of top 5 industries (in %) |
|---|---|---|---|---|---|---|
| | | Electricity, gas, steam and air-conditioning supply (2) | 16.63 | Food products | 10.16 | |
| | | Machinery and equipment n.e.c. (3) | 14.75 | Tobacco products | 6.94 | |
| | | Other non-metallic mineral products (4) | 13.41 | Other non-metallic mineral products | 2.39 | |
| | | Rubber and plastics products (5) | 13.34 | Beverages | 2.11 | |
| Assam | 90.53 | Food products (1) | 26.24 | Coke and refined petroleum products | 65.91 | 92.33 |
| | | Coke and refined petroleum products (2) | 22.56 | Food products | 15.37 | |
| | | Pharmaceuticals, medicinal chemical and botanical (3) | 20.38 | Chemicals and chemical products | 6.16 | |
| | | Other non-metallic mineral products (4) | 12.46 | Other non-metallic mineral products | 2.94 | |
| | | Basic metals (5) | 8.88 | Tobacco products | 1.96 | |
| West Bengal | 78.2 | Basic metals (1) | 28.63 | Basic metals | 26.35 | 77.77 |
| | | Leather and related products (2) | 18.12 | Coke and refined petroleum products | 22.62 | |
| | | Textiles (3) | 11.89 | Chemicals and chemical products | 13.11 | |
| | | Food products (4) | 10.68 | Food products | 10.06 | |

(continued)

**Table 6** (continued)

| States | Share of top 5 export items (in %) | Name of the top five exportable items | Share of individual export (in %) | Name of the top five industry | Share of individual industry in production (in %) | Share of top 5 industries (in %) |
|---|---|---|---|---|---|---|
| | | Wearing apparel (5) | 8.88 | Textiles | 5.63 | |
| Jharkhand | 93.93 | Basic metals (1) | 46.02 | Basic metals | 61.6 | 92.06 |
| | | Other non-metallic mineral products (2) | 16.11 | Motor vehicles, trailers and semi-trailers | 15.45 | |
| | | Machinery and equipment n.e.c. (3) | 14.11 | Coke and refined petroleum products | 6.11 | |
| | | Computer, electronic and optical product (4) | 10.33 | Other non-metallic mineral products | 5.28 | |
| | | Chemicals and chemical products (5) | 7.36 | Machinery and equipment n.e.c | 3.62 | |
| Odisha | 99.54 | Basic metals (1) | 80.97 | Basic metals | 66.89 | 89.68 |
| | | Other non-metallic mineral products (2) | 13.09 | Chemicals and chemical products | 11.07 | |
| | | Food products (3) | 4.96 | Other non-metallic mineral products | 6.01 | |
| | | Chemicals and chemical products (4) | 0.28 | Food products | 3.04 | |
| | | Electrical equipment (5) | 0.23 | Electricity, gas, steam and air-conditioning supply | 2.67 | |
| Chhattisgarh | 16 | Basic metals (1) | 51.81 | Basic metals | 78.57 | 95.11 |
| | | Food products (2) | 15.98 | Other non-metallic mineral products | 9.6 | |
| | | Textiles (3) | 7.97 | Fabricated metal products, except machinery and equipment | 2.66 | |

(continued)

**Table 6** (continued)

| States | Share of top 5 export items (in %) | Name of the top five exportable items | Share of individual export (in %) | Name of the top five industry | Share of individual industry in production (in %) | Share of top 5 industries (in %) |
|---|---|---|---|---|---|---|
| | | Other non-metallic mineral products (4) | 6.36 | Food products | 2.64 | |
| | | Machinery and equipment n.e.c. (5) | 5.01 | Electricity, gas, steam and air-conditioning supply | 1.63 | |
| Madhya Pradesh | 80.4 | Pharmaceuticals, medicinal chemical and botanical products (1) | 33.12 | Food products | 16.65 | 56.58 |
| | | Coke and refined petroleum products (2) | 14.49 | Other non-metallic mineral products | 12.8 | |
| | | Food products (3) | 13.82 | Coke and refined petroleum products | 12.22 | |
| | | Other non-metallic mineral products (4) | 11.13 | Electrical equipment | 7.58 | |
| | | Textiles (5) | 7.84 | textiles | 7.33 | |
| Gujarat | 69.23 | Chemicals and chemical products (1) | 28.63 | Coke and refined petroleum products | 47.3 | 79.37 |
| | | Coke and refined petroleum products (2) | 15.83 | Chemicals and chemical products | 14.95 | |
| | | Other manufacturing (3) | 9.96 | Basic metals | 6.94 | |
| | | Basic metals (4) | 7.89 | Food products | 6.26 | |
| | | Textiles (5) | 6.92 | Textiles | 3.91 | |
| Maharashtra | 59.95 | Other manufacturing (1) | 20.23 | Coke and refined petroleum products | 20.25 | 59.7 |
| | | Basic metals (2) | 14.48 | Basic metals | 11.96 | |

(continued)

**Table 6** (continued)

| States | Share of top 5 export items (in %) | Name of the top five exportable items | Share of individual export (in %) | Name of the top five industry | Share of individual industry in production (in %) | Share of top 5 industries (in %) |
|---|---|---|---|---|---|---|
| | | Pharmaceuticals, medicinal chemical and botanical products (3) | 9.61 | Motor vehicles, trailers and semi-trailers | 10.22 | |
| | | Chemicals and chemical products (4) | 9.07 | Food products | 9.06 | |
| | | Food products (5) | 6.55 | Chemicals and chemical products | 8.21 | |
| Andhra Pradesh | 70.46 | Food products (1) | 26.07 | Coke and refined petroleum products | 21.59 | 66.9 |
| | | Basic metals (2) | 15.55 | Food products | 14.53 | |
| | | Pharmaceuticals, medicinal chemical and botanical products (3) | 14.16 | Basic metals | 13.36 | |
| | | Tobacco products (4) | 7.69 | Other non-metallic mineral products | 8.93 | |
| | | Coke and refined petroleum products (5) | 6.99 | Chemicals and chemical products | 8.5 | |
| Karnataka | 55.69 | Wearing apparel (1) | 15.4 | Coke and refined petroleum products | 20.79 | 59.61 |
| | | Coke and refined petroleum products (2) | 10.58 | Basic metals | 14.21 | |
| | | Basic metals (3) | 10.21 | Other manufacturing | 9.12 | |
| | | Pharmaceuticals, medicinal chemical and botanical products (4) | 9.87 | Food products | 8.46 | |

(continued)

**Table 6** (continued)

| States | Share of top 5 export items (in %) | Name of the top five exportable items | Share of individual export (in %) | Name of the top five industry | Share of individual industry in production (in %) | Share of top 5 industries (in %) |
|---|---|---|---|---|---|---|
| | | Food products (5) | 9.64 | Motor vehicles, trailers and semi-trailers | 7.03 | |
| Goa | 78.2 | Pharmaceuticals, medicinal chemical and botanical products (1) | 33.45 | Chemicals and chemical products | 23.27 | 68.79 |
| | | Chemicals and chemical products (2) | 15.5 | Pharmaceuticals, medicinal chemical and botanical products | 16.63 | |
| | | Food products (3) | 10.41 | Basic metals | 10.85 | |
| | | Basic metals (4) | 9.57 | Rubber and plastics products | 10.2 | |
| | | Computer, electronic and optical products (5) | 9.27 | Electrical equipment | 7.84 | |
| Kerala | 87.64 | Food products (1) | 55.29 | Coke and refined petroleum products | 55.21 | 83.85 |
| | | Other manufacturing (2) | 15.86 | Food products | 12.14 | |
| | | Textiles (3) | 7.15 | Chemicals and chemical products | 6.4 | |
| | | Rubber and plastics products (4) | 4.92 | Rubber and plastics products | 5.9 | |
| | | Computer, electronic and optical products (5) | 4.42 | Other manufacturing | 4.2 | |
| Tamil Nadu | 64.44 | Motor vehicles, trailers and semi-trailers (1) | 22.46 | Motor vehicles, trailers and semi-trailers | 22.54 | 56.76 |

(continued)

**Table 6** (continued)

| States | Share of top 5 export items (in %) | Name of the top five exportable items | Share of individual export (in %) | Name of the top five industry | Share of individual industry in production (in %) | Share of top 5 industries (in %) |
|---|---|---|---|---|---|---|
| | | Wearing apparel(2) | 17.77 | Coke and refined petroleum products | 12.72 | |
| | | Textiles (3) | 9.69 | Textiles | 7.73 | |
| | | Leather and related products (4) | 9.36 | Basic metals | 7.44 | |
| | | Food products (5) | 5.15 | Food products | 6.33 | |
| Telangana | 86.35 | Pharmaceuticals, medicinal chemical and botanical products (1) | 63.41 | Pharmaceuticals, medicinal chemical and botanical products | 21.62 | 60.02 |
| | | Food products (2) | 10.51 | Other non-metallic mineral products | 11.45 | |
| | | Chemicals and chemical products (3) | 5.54 | Food products | 10.98 | |
| | | Machinery and equipment n.e.c. (4) | 4.23 | Electrical equipment | 9.77 | |
| | | Wood and products of wood and cork, except furniture; manufacture of articles of straw and plaiting materials (5) | 2.65 | Rubber and plastics products | 6.21 | |

*Source* Authors' calculation. Figure in parenthesis indicates ranking of the product in export basket

- Madhya Pradesh: Pharmaceutical product industry, Coke and refined petroleum industry, food product industry, other non-metallic mineral product industry
- Odisha: Basic metal industry, other non-metallic mineral product industry, food product industry, chemical product industry.

Pharmaceutical industry has the highest average share in both exports and production in Himachal Pradesh. While the industry has the highest average share of 33.12%

in export basket in Madhya Pradesh, it is not among the top five in the production basket. In Gujarat, chemical industry has the highest share in the export basket (around 28.63%), whereas its share in production basket is lower at 14.95%. Basic metal industry is important for Odisha both in the export as well as in production baskets.

Thirteen states, for instance J&K, Haryana, Delhi, Assam, West Bengal, Jharkhand, Chhattisgarh, Maharashtra, Andhra Pradesh, Karnataka, Kerala, Goa, and Tamil Nadu, have three common items in their export basket as well as in production basket. These common product groups can be deciphered as given below:

- Jammu & Kashmir: Food product industry, rubber and plastic product industry, pharmaceutical industry
- Haryana: Food product industry, motor vehicles trailer and semi-trailer industry, basic metal product industry
- Delhi: Wearing apparel industry, food product industry, chemical product industry
- Assam: Food product industry, coke and refined petroleum product industry, other non-metallic mineral product industry
- West Bengal: Basic metal product industry, Textile industry, food product industry
- Jharkhand: Basic metal product industry, other non-metallic mineral product industry, machinery and equipment industry
- Chhattisgarh: Basic metal product industry, food product industry, other non-metallic mineral product industry
- Maharashtra: Basic metal product industry, chemical product industry, food product industry
- Andhra Pradesh: Food product industry, basic metal product industry, coke and refined petroleum product industry
- Karnataka: Coke and refined petroleum product industry, basic metal product industry, food product industry
- Kerala: Food product industry, other manufacturing product industry, rubber and plastic product industry
- Goa: Pharmaceutical industry, chemical product industry, basic metal product industry
- Tamil Nadu: Motor vehicles trailer and semi-trailer industry, textile product industry, food product industry.

For the remaining six states, however, fewer common products in export and production baskets can be observed. For instance, while Punjab, Rajasthan, Uttar Pradesh, and Telangana have two common products, Uttarakhand and Bihar have only one common product.

- Punjab: Textile industry and food product industry
- Rajasthan: Chemical product industry and textile industry
- Uttar Pradesh: Food product industry and computer, electronic and optical product industry
- Telangana: Pharmaceutical industry, food product industry
- Uttarakhand: electrical equipment industry

- Bihar: other non-metallic mineral product industry.

Industry-specific detailed state-level analysis exhibits that wide heterogeneity persists between the export and the production baskets despite high-rank correlation coefficients between the two. On the whole, one-to-one concordance between export and production structure is not clearly observed from this data series. The above exercise based on alternate data source clearly identifies the pattern of state-level comparative advantage.

## 6 Conclusions

The paper estimates a new state-level export data series for the organized manufacturing sector for the period 2008–09 to 2014–15 and ranks Indian states on the basis of newly estimated export data series. The new state-level export data series are free from the identification of state of origin problem. However, this database includes only organized manufacturing sectors exports. Agriculture, mining and mineral sectors, unorganized manufacturing and service sectors are excluded from this exercise. Maharashtra, Tamil Nadu, and Gujarat are the top three exporting states, despite fluctuations. While Andhra Pradesh, West Bengal, Madhya Pradesh, Odisha, Delhi, Goa, Jharkhand, Jammu & Kashmir, Bihar, U.P. and Assam experience a fall in state-level ranking, Karnataka, Haryana, Punjab, Kerala, Rajasthan, Chhattisgarh, and Himachal Pradesh have emerged more important in this respect.

Diversity in the export basket varies across the states. Punjab, Uttarakhand, Haryana, Delhi, Rajasthan, Uttar Pradesh, West Bengal, Madhya Pradesh, Gujarat, Maharashtra, Karnataka, Kerala, Andhra Pradesh, and Tamil Nadu have high diversity, and Jammu and Kashmir, Bihar, Jharkhand, and Orissa have a more concentrated export basket. Comparison between state-wise production and export structures reveals varying results. Spearman rank correlation and Kendall's tau rank correlation show that majority of Indian states have significant positive association between production and export structures. Gujarat and Madhya Pradesh have high-degree positive association between industry-wise export structure and production structure, whereas Bihar, Jammu & Kashmir, Jharkhand, Rajasthan, and Uttar Pradesh do not have significant rank correlation. However, product-wise one-to-one matching exhibits wide heterogeneity between the export and the production baskets. The above exercise based on alternate data source clearly identifies the pattern of state-level comparative advantage. In the post-pandemic period, in their individual endeavor to promote exports, states need to formulate export promotion policies based on comparative advantage. Alternate export data series can be useful source information in this exercise.

**Acknowledgements** The authors are indebted to Professors Ajitava Raychaudhuri, Rajat Acharyya, Ranajoy Bhattacharyya, Rajendra P. Kundu, and others for their comments on an earlier draft of the paper. The paper is based on the final report of the project titled "State-level Exports: An

Alternate Exploration Using ASI Unit Level Data" funded by the Planning Commission Endowment Unit, Jadavpur University, Kolkata, in 2018.

## References


Aghion, P., Burgess, R., Redding, S. J., & Zilibotti, F. (2008). The unequal effects of liberalization: Evidence from dismantling the License Raj in India. *American Economic Review, 98*(4), 1397–1412.

Ahluwalia, M. S. (2000). Economic performance of states in post-reform-period. *Economic and Political Weekly, 35*(6).

Amin, M., & Mattoo, A. (2008). *Human capital and the changing structure of the Indian economy* (Policy Research Working Paper Series 4576). The World Bank.

Besley, T., & Burgess, R. (2004). Can Labor Regulation hinder economic performance? Evidence from India. *The Quarterly Journal of Economics, 119*(1), 91–134.

Bougheas, S., Demetriades, P. O., & Mamuneas, T. P. (2000). Infrastructure, specialization, and economic growth. *Canadian Journal of Economics, 33*(2), 506–522.

Coughlin, C. C. (2012). *Extensive and intensive trade margins: A state-by-state view* (Working Paper 2012-002A). Federal Reserve Bank of St. Louis. http://research.stlouisfed.org/wp/2012/2012-002.pdf

Coughlin, C. C., & Fabel, O. (1987). Manufacturing export performance at state level 1963–1980. Working Paper: Federal Reserve Bank of St. Louis 1987-008A.

Coughlin, C. C., & Cartwright, P. A. (1987). An examination of state foreign export promotion and manufacturing exports. *Journal of Regional Science, 27*(3), 439–449.

Francois, J., & Manchin, M. (2007). *Institutions, infrastructure, and trade* (Policy Research Working Paper No. 4152). World Bank. https://openknowledge.worldbank.org/handle/10986/7201. License: CC BY 3.0 IGO.

Ghate, C., & Wright, S. (2013). Why were some Indian states so slow to participate in the turnaround? *Economic and Political Weekly, XLVIII*(13).

Iwanow, T., & Kirkpatrick, C. (2009). Trade facilitation and manufactured exports: Is Africa different? *World Development, 37*(6), 1039–1050.

Kumar, U., & Subramanian, A. (2012). Growth in India's state in the first decade of 21st century: Four facts. *Economic & Political Weekly, XLVII*(3).

Limao, N., & Venables, A. J. (2001). Infrastructure, geographical disadvantage, transport costs, and trade. *The World Bank Economic Review, 15*(3), 451–479.

Marjit, S., Kar, S., & Maiti, D. (2007). Regional trade openness index and income disparity: A new methodology and the Indian experiment. *Economic and Political Weekly, 42*(9), 757–769.

Perez, A. P., & Wilson, J. S. (2012). Export performance and trade facilitation reform: Hard and soft Infrastructure. *World Development, 40*(7), 1295–1307.

Pradhan, J. P., & Das, K. (2012). Regional origin of manufacturing exports: Inter-state patterns in India. *Journal of Regional Development and Planning, 1*(2), 117–167.

Singh, P., & Bhanumurthy, N. R. (2014). Infrastructure development and regional growth in India. In A. N. Ghosh & A. K. Karmakar (Eds.), *Analytical issues in trade, development and finance* (pp. 321–341). Springer.

Sinha Roy, S., et al. (2015). *State-level export performance: Competitiveness, determinants and policy implications*. Jadavpur University.

Smith, T. (1989). Regional exports of manufactured products. *Economic Review, 74*(1), 21–31.

Steinle, W. (1992). Regional competitiveness and single market. *Regional Studies, 26*, 307–331.

Sun, H. (2001). Foreign direct investment and regional export performance in China. *Journal of Regional Science, 41*(2), 317–336.

Wilson, J. S., Mann, C. L., & Otsuki, T. (2003). Trade facilitation and economic development: New approach to quantifying the impact. *The World Bank Economic Review, 17*(3), 367–389.
Wu, Y. (2011). Export performance in China's regional economies. *Applied Economics, 39*(10), 1283–1293.
Zhang, Q., & Felmingham, B. (2010). The role of FDI, exports and spillover effects in the regional development of China. *The Journal of Development Studies, 38*(4), 157178.

# Subaltern Culture and Happiness in Tribal Communities of West Bengal

**Bidisha Chakraborty and Dedipya Basak**

## 1 Introduction

> The vicious cycle of political-economic deprivation and social alienation continues to keep the Adivasis subjugated to the ruling modern. The politics of dominance, economics of immediate gain, and social outlook of separateness have charted out for the Adivasis as well as others a very different path. (Rana et al. 2020)

The tribal people are the original inhabitants of India prior to the coming and settlement of the Aryans to this country. Gradually, the indigenous people were forced to move to isolated areas in forests and mountains. Tribal people exhibit family, social, and cultural values and practices that are clearly different from the mainstream population in India. The Government of India has classified most of the tribal communities as "scheduled tribes" for administrative purposes to confer certain constitutional privileges and protection to these backward and disadvantaged group of people. The scheduled tribes are also called the "Adivasis".

There are not much scientific studies dealing with the well-being of tribal communities. A research report titled "Living world of the Adivasis of Bengal" compiled by Prof. Sen's Pratichi Institute and Asiatic Society, illustrated a picture of lack of understanding and appreciation about the humanity and culture of Adivasis. In the preface of that report, Prof. Sen said that as early as the third century BC Emperor Ashoka pointed to the need to pay attention to the rights of "forest people," but that much needed attention had hardly bestowed. In the introduction to the report, Prof. Sen writes that deprivations of the Adivasis arise not merely from their lack of private resources, "but also from the neglect of their interests in the governmental distribution of public facilities".

There are many tribal communities in Indian Subcontinent. According to 2011 census, the tribal population in India is 104 million or 8.6% of total Indian population.

B. Chakraborty (✉) · D. Basak
Department of Economics, Jadavpur University, Kolkata, India
e-mail: bidisha.chakraborty@jadavpuruniversity.in

 
A. Raychaudhuri and A. Ghose (eds.), *Managing Pandemic and Correcting Development Fundamentals*, India Studies in Business and Economics,
https://doi.org/10.1007/978-981-19-8680-2_9

Only the state West Bengal has about 40 tribal groups. Tribal population of over five million people form 5.8% of the total population of the West Bengal. The diversity of culture, community structure, and language differentiates one tribal community from another. To some communities, the fire is the main god, whereas some are worshippers of trees. Some communities are matriarch, but some are not. Some live on animals, while some live on vegetation. But, few things are common to them—poor economic condition, deprivation of dignity, and inabilities to access the opportunities.

Tribal people often have very rich cultural tradition and beautiful creative features. In spite of having differences in cultural practices, they have one thing in common. Their well-being and respective cultural practices are very closely knitted. This project attempts to find out how different aspects of cultural practices or community involvement and modern outlook of three major tribal communities of South West-Bengal—Shabar, Bhumij, and Santhal—impacts their well-being. For measuring well-being of tribal communities, we resort to economics of happiness. It is an approach to assess welfare by combining the approach of economists and psychologists and relying on more expansive notions of utility and welfare than conventional economics. This project measures well-being of tribal people by their self-reported indicators of happiness comprising the aspects personal happiness, worth of life, safety for future, personal relationships with spouse and other family members, loneliness, and anger.

There exists substantial literature dealing with culture and happiness. Chang (2009) has suggested that with greater community involvement, the happiness level may increase; a "more" social person is happier than an isolated one. In his research, Wang (2015) has identified that individuals who live close to their native motherland are happier and healthier compared to their relocated counterparts. All of these researchers identify that native culture and its practice puts a positive impact on an individual's socio-economic and mental well-being. But, there is evidence too, where native cultural bias has been considered negative for socio-economic and mental growth. While one group of researchers identify that valuing one's own culture leads the person to a higher level of happiness (Dockery, 2003; Wang, 2015) then another group of scientists are against this "exaggerated" evaluation and confinement toward someone's own culture. They argue that cross cultural encounters make a person happier (Chakraborty et al., 2015; Lu & Gilmore, 2004; Mathews, 2012). The empirical research of Gilmour and Lu (2004) based on Chinese and American respondents conclude that in spite of having vast differences in cultural practice both the community is dependent on culture for their respective well-being. Though cultural practice plays a major role in tribal life, there are very few studies on the well-being and cultural practice of tribal people. A research, conducted on Australian aboriginal cultural practices by Dockery (2003) reveals that a strong attachment toward traditional culture instead of dragging down, emphatically boosts the socio-economic well-being of the Individual(s) and has the potential to enhance quality lifestyle of individuals. Snodgrass et al. (2017) conduct an anthropological research on the Sahariya tribe of Rajasthan and Madhya Pradesh and also argue that cultural practice improves the mental well-being of the individuals. Ghosh et al. (2004) study psychiatric morbidity among a tribal community named Toto in sub Himalayan region.

BoroBaski (2019) opines that govt. policies should aim at development of tribal people keeping intact their cultural practices. Nandi et al. (1977) did a comparative study of mental morbidity between upper caste and tribal communities. They find that neurotic disorder, anxiety, and obsession are almost absent tribes. The rate of morbidity among Brahmin are four times that among tribes. Nandi et al. (1992) study urbanization and mental morbidity in West Bengal and find that urbanization brings in stress and depression among tribal population, but it may also reduce mental retardation. But, this study did not employ any econometric tool, used only statistical tool.

In this context, we are interested in finding out how modern outlook vis a vis traditional cultural practices of tribal communities of West Bengal influences the self-reported indicators of their happiness. The present paper is organized as follows. Section 2 describes the objectives and testable hypotheses. The information related to data collection, the questionnaire, and the overview of samples are described in Sect. 3. Section 4 presents the statistical analysis. Section 5 concludes.

## 2 Objectives and Testable Hypotheses

The objective of this project is to find out how along with other socio-economic variables, modern outlook and attachment to own culture impact the happiness of Santhal, Shabar, and Bhumij people of Purulia and Jhargram. This project tests the following hypotheses:

1. Age, gender, income, food sufficiency, modern outlook, marital status, and other socio-economic conditions significantly influence the happiness of the tribal people.
2. Modern outlook vis a vis attachment to traditional subaltern cultural practice plays a crucial role in determining happiness of tribal population of South West Bengal.

## 3 Data

While collecting the necessary information from the samples in consideration, we adopted the direct interview method using questionnaire. In order to collect data, questionnaire was framed to collect the data on happiness, cultural practices, and socio-economic condition of Shabar, Bhumij, and Santhal people of West Midnapore (Jhargram) and Purulia Districts of West Bengal. We adopted convenience sampling. Our sample consists of the respondents coming from both genders. Our overall sample size is 237.

Two districts with highest tribal population in South West Bengal were identified.

Table 1 shows seven districts with highest percentage of tribal population of West Bengal.

**Table 1** Seven districts with highest percentage of tribal population of West Bengal

| Districts | Tribal population (%) |
|---|---|
| Malda | 7.87 |
| Bankura | 10.25 |
| West Midnapore and Jhargram | 14.88 |
| South Dinajpur | 16.43 |
| Purulia | 18.45 |
| Jalpaiguri | 18.89 |
| Darjeeling and Kalimpong | 21.52 |

First, a pilot survey was conducted. We undertook a sample survey of 35 Santhal household representatives in the Purulia district of West Bengal in the month of September, 2019. A set of questions were asked from the questionnaire and we strictly monitored whether any of the respondents is having any problem or discomfort in answering the questions. The final survey was carried out in November 2019–February 2020. We collected data from those villages where availability of our tribal communities is comparatively abundant. Some of these tribal villages (Tolas) from which the respondents participated in the survey are Jhardihi, Balukundi, Jhogruti, Charuti, Panchnanguda, Khanakul, Tapoban, Baradihi, JamunaBandh, Paharshole, Champahati, and Khatra.

During this survey, the respondents did not face any problem. All questions were clearly understandable to most of the respondents. In few cases, respondents had the language barrier. In such cases, the local guide explained the questions in their native language to the respondent. All data has been collected directly from the field.

## 4 The Questionnaire

Our project is based on a very general questionnaire which does not ask for any confidential personal details from the respondents.

The entire questionnaire is divided into four sub-sections. The first part named as "Socio-economic and Demographic Questions" (Question Nos. 01–23) asks some basic information like age, gender, representing community, working status, religion, personal and family income, and marital status. We also include some questions to understand the economic status of the respondents—whether they own land, patta, and enjoy the infrastructural facilities like electricity, water, and sanitation. We asked about the nature of their houses they live in (sometimes provided by the govt. under Indira AwasYojana) number of assets like bicycle, television, computer, and mobile phone they own.

In the second section, 'Cultural Aspects', we asked whether the respondent is able to speak and/or write his/her native language, has any cultural association outside the community, is playing an important role inside the community, consuming traditional food, whether believes in banking system, whether he is willing to accept modern lifestyle, etc.

In the third section, we asked about whether the respondent is living a happy and worthy life, considers the time is safe for future, having a good relationship with spouse and other family members etc.

To determine happiness level of the respondent, we have used seven statements where in each statement a respondent were asked to choose any one from the five options: Strongly disagree, Disagree, Neither disagree nor agree, Agree, Strongly agree.

To understand the overall mental state of the respondent, we have included some of the positive and negative feelings into this section. We asked whether the respondent, feeling depressed in life, feeling lonely, and feeling angry. In each question, we provided four options starting from always to never.

To construct the happiness score, we assigned quantitative value on each option. In most of the cases, they are equal to the value of the serial number of the respective option—if the "strongly agree" comes as 5th option then our assigned quantitative value for this option is '05'.

In order to measure happiness, five different globally acclaimed techniques are being used: Emotional Regulation method, Engagement and Meaning method, Flourishing method, Life-satisfaction method, Meaning of Life Method. All of these five, measure the person's Happiness as a certain level or a score. All these methods rely on the individual's assessment of self. In our study, we use the life-satisfaction method of measuring happiness. We ask the respondent about his personal and familial life and ask him to choose an option from five (in some cases four) varying levels: Strongly Disagree, Disagree, Neither agree nor Disagree, Agree, Strongly Agree (Always, Most of the times, Sometimes, Not at all).

Detailed questionnaire is given in Appendix of this chapter.

## 5 Framework of Regression Analysis

### *5.1 Indexation*

The responses received for personal happiness and well-being have been assigned values in increasing order based on agreement level of the pursued happiness by the respondent to facilitate analysis. The assigned values are

- Strongly Disagree—1
- Disagree—2
- Neither Agree nor Disagree—3
- Agree—4
- Strongly Agree—5.

The responses received for negative emotions (like anger and loneliness) have been assigned values in increasing order based on agreement level of the pursued negativity by the respondent to facilitate analysis. The assigned values are

- Always—1
- Most of the Time—2
- Sometimes—3
- Never—4.

We have measured cultural attachment by the respondent's ability to speak and write his/her native language, to what extent the respondent consumes traditional food, whether the respondent participates in local performing art etc. Please note that we have constructed modern outlook score or lack of cultural attachment. While constructing modern outlook index, living condition index, and happiness index, we used the formula:

$$\text{index}_j = 1 - \frac{\text{Max} - \text{Actual}_j}{\text{Max} - \text{Min}}$$

where max is the maximum score among all individuals for that sub category (culture/happiness/living condition), actual $j$ is the actual score of $j$th individual, and min is the minimum score. For the questions marked by underline and italics (question nos. 3, 5, and 9 in cultural aspects section and question no. 5 in happiness and well-being-related questions of the questionnaire given in Appendix) the marking system is opposite.

## *5.2 Field Survey Observations/Overview of the Sample*

The survey was conducted on Shabar, Santhal, and Bhumij community of tribal people of southern West Bengal. The sample size of the survey is 237—consisting of 79 household representatives from each community. We have tried to adequately represent various income levels, property levels, age, gender, etc., in our project. A brief outlook of the entire sample survey is presented in Tables 2 and 3 and Figs. 1 and 2.

Community-wise gender participation in survey and community-wise participation in workforce can be seen from Figs. 1 and 2, respectively.

The Monthly Family Income Distribution of Shabar Community, Bhumij Community, and Santhal Community can be visualized from Figs. 3, 4, and 5, respectively.

The situation regarding community-wise food sufficiency level can be visualized from Fig. 6.

The facts about the community-wise holding of agricultural land and the distribution of patta can be gathered from Figs. 7 and 8, respectively.

**Table 2** A brief outlook of the entire sample survey

| Description | Shabar | Bhumij | Santhal |
|---|---|---|---|
| No. of sample observations | • Jhargram—46<br>• Purulia—33 | • Jhargram—46<br>• Purulia—33 | • Jhargram—46<br>• Purulia—33 |
| Gender | • Male—45<br>• Female—34 | • Male—41<br>• Female—38 | • Male—62<br>• Female—17 |
| Age | • Min—18<br>• Max—60<br>• Range—42 | • Min—19<br>• Max—60<br>• Range—41 | • Min—18<br>• Max—60<br>• Range—42 |
| Education level | • Illiterate—49<br>• Primary—18<br>• Secondary—11<br>• H. S—Nil<br>• Graduate—01<br>• P.G—Nil | • Illiterate—25<br>• Primary—12<br>• Secondary—34<br>• H. S—04<br>• Graduate—02<br>• P.G—02 | • Illiterate—32<br>• Primary—10<br>• Secondary—20<br>• H. S—10<br>• Graduate—06<br>• P.G—01 |
| Work participation | • Overall—56<br>• Male—33<br>• Female—23 | • Overall—56<br>• Male—32<br>• Female—24 | • Overall—55<br>• Male—43<br>• Female—12 |
| Monthly family income | • < 1000—02<br>• 1000 to < 5000—54<br>• 5000 to < 10,000—22<br>• 10,000 above—01 | • < 1000—10<br>• 1000 to < 5000—44<br>• 5000 to < 10,000—21<br>• 10,000 above—03 | • < 1000—01<br>• 1000 to < 5000—50<br>• 5000 to < 10,000—18<br>• 10,000 above—10 |
| Food sufficiency | • Yes—33<br>• No—46 | • Yes—35<br>• No—44 | • Yes—38<br>• No—41 |
| Alcohol consumption | • Yes—43<br>• No—36 | • Yes—06<br>• No—773 | • Yes—33<br>• No—46 |
| Tobacco consumption | • Yes—59<br>• No—20 | • Yes—44<br>• No—35 | • Yes—43<br>• No—36 |
| Own agricultural land | • Yes—31<br>• No—48 | • Yes—44<br>• No—35 | • Yes—58<br>• No—21 |
| Having patta of agricultural land | • Yes—51<br>• No—28 | • Yes—04<br>• No—75 | • Yes—31<br>• No—48 |
| Brick made house | • N.A—30<br>• Indira Awas—47<br>• Own house—02<br>• Mansion—00 | • N.A—49<br>• Indira Awas—28<br>• Own house—02<br>• Mansion—00 | • N.A—52<br>• Indira Awas—26<br>• Own house—01<br>• Mansion—00 |
| Sanitation type | • Open air—51<br>• Primitive—05<br>• Modern—23 | • Open air—65<br>• Primitive—01<br>• Modern—13 | • Open air—52<br>• Primitive—04<br>• Modern—23 |
| Availability of electricity | • Yes—38<br>• No—41 | • Yes—48<br>• No—31 | • Yes—49<br>• No—30 |
| Drinking water facility in home | • Yes—08<br>• No—71 | • Yes—09<br>• No—70 | • Yes—15<br>• No—64 |

(continued)

**Table 2** (continued)

| Description | Shabar | Bhumij | Santhal |
|---|---|---|---|
| Marital status | • Single—01<br>• In relation—00<br>• Married—71<br>• Divorced—03<br>• Widow/widower—04 | • Single—11<br>• In relation—01<br>• Married—65<br>• Divorced—03<br>• Widow/widower—09 | • Single—06<br>• In relation—06<br>• Married—64<br>• Divorced—01<br>• Widow/widower—03 |
| Faced social discrimination | • Yes—20<br>• No—59 | • Yes—05<br>• No—74 | • Yes—07<br>• No—72 ara> |
| Receives community support in need | • Always—09<br>• Mostly—16<br>• Sometimes—26<br>• Never—28 | • Always—19<br>• Mostly—17<br>• Sometimes—25<br>• Never—18 | • Always—13<br>• Mostly—19<br>• Sometimes—17<br>• Never—30 |
| Receives govt. medical support | • Yes—50<br>• No—29 | • Yes—49<br>• No—30 | • Yes—57<br>• No—22 |
| Availed the benefit of ST reservation | • Yes—02<br>• No—77 | • Yes—03<br>• No—76 | • Yes—11<br>• No—68 |

**Table 3** Summary statistics

| Statistics | Family income (in Rs 1000) | Modern outlook score | Food sufficiency | Happiness index | Age |
|---|---|---|---|---|---|
| Mean | 3.976 | 0.539 | 0.447 | 0.725 | 38.86 |
| Range | 17.5 | 1 | 1 | 0.721 | 42 |
| Sd | 3.096 | 0.168 | 0.498 | 0.117 | 60 |
| Max | 18 | 1 | 1 | 1 | 12.17 |

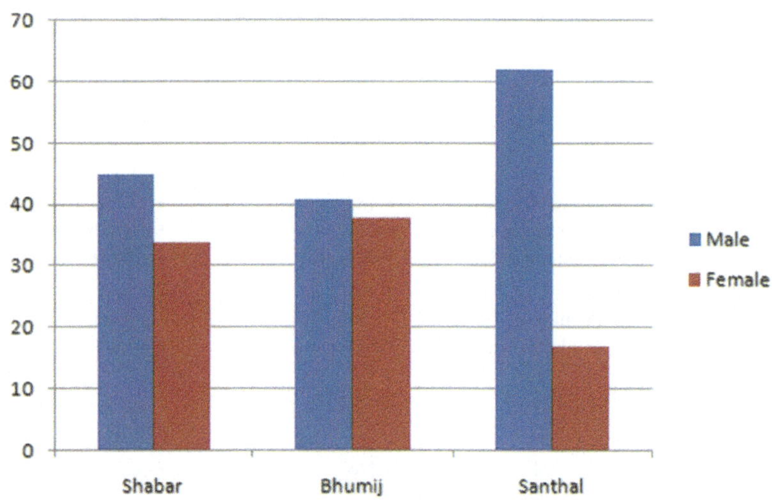


**Fig. 1** Community-wise gender participation in survey

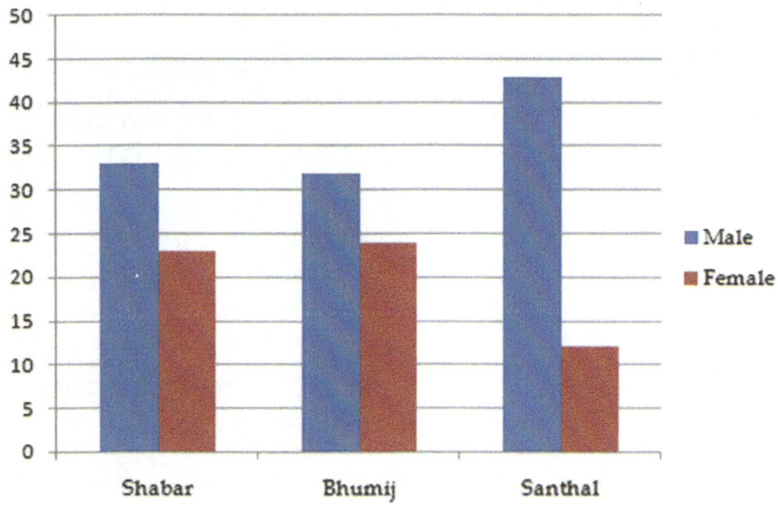


**Fig. 2** Community wise participation in workforce

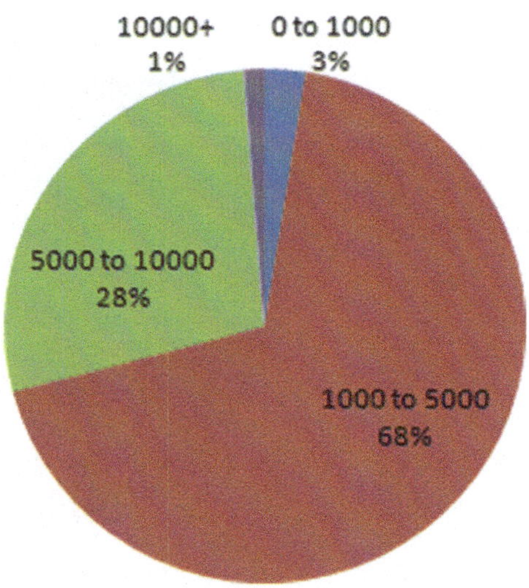


**Fig. 3** Monthly family income distribution of Shabar community

Figures 9, 10, and 11 depict the scenario regarding the availing houses under Indira Awas Scheme, drinking water facility inside home, and availing electric facility inside home.

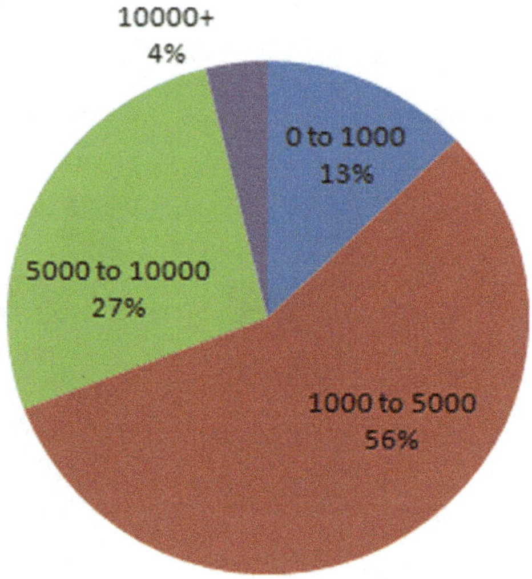


**Fig. 4** Monthly family income distribution of Bhumij community

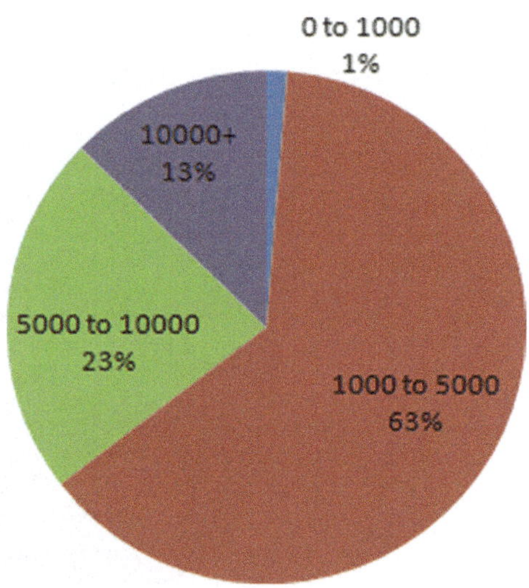


**Fig. 5** Monthly family income distribution of Santhal community

## *5.3 Statistical Analysis*

### 5.3.1 Correlation Between Different Important Variables

The correlations among different variables are represented in Table 4.

The Pearson product-moment correlation coefficient (or Pearson correlation coefficient, for short) is a measure of the strength of a linear association between two variables. We find that only personal income and work dummy (whether employed or unemployed) have correlation coefficient above 0.5. We also find that both modern

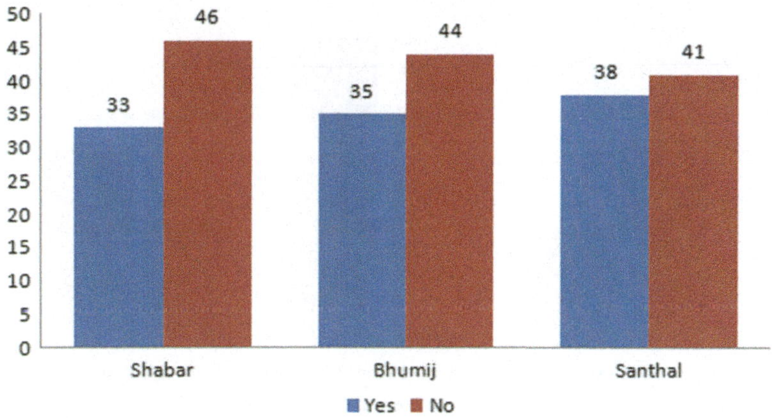


**Fig. 6** Community-wise food sufficiency level

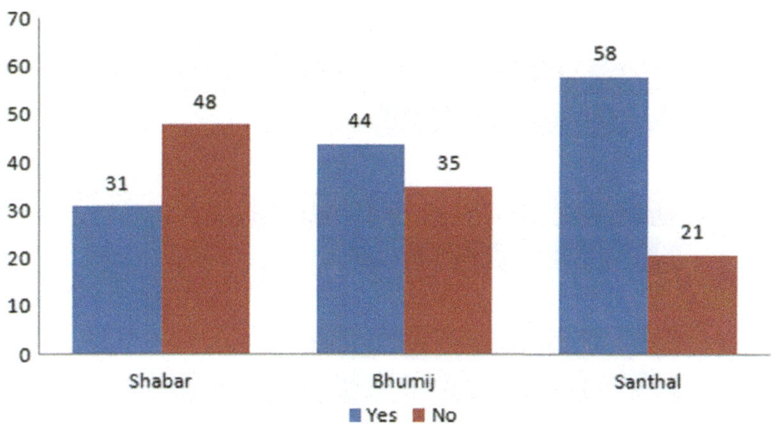


**Fig. 7** Community-wise holding of agricultural land

outlook score and happiness index are negatively correlated with age. Modern outlook score is negatively correlated to happiness index, family income, and food sufficiency, while happiness index is positively correlated to government support index, family income, and food sufficiency. However, values of all these correlation coefficients are very low.

### 5.3.2 Regression Analysis

To estimate happiness equation, we used Ordered Probit model. The Ordered Probit model is formed indexing individuals by the subscript $i$

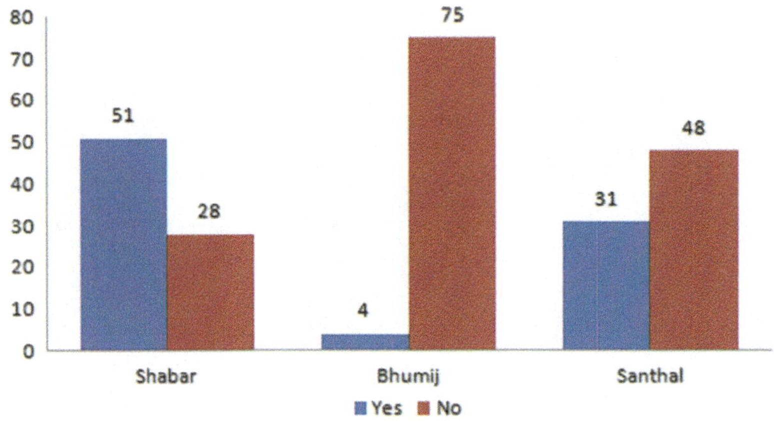


**Fig. 8** Community-wise distribution of patta

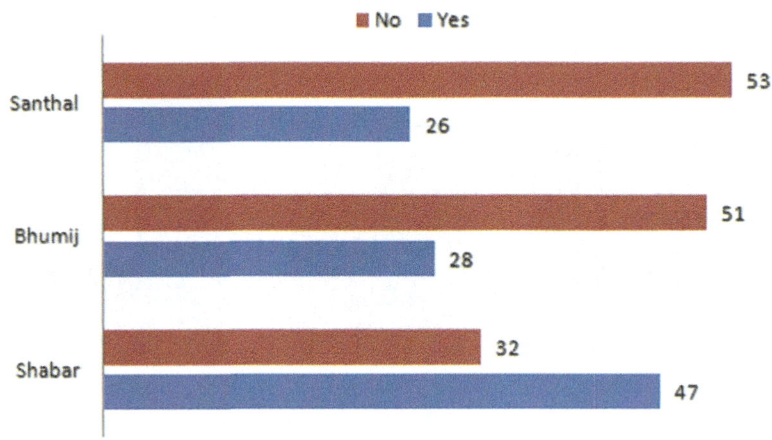


**Fig. 9** Availing houses under Indira Awas Scheme

$$H_i^* = \mu_j + \sum_{k=1}^{K} \beta_k X_{ik} + \varepsilon_i \quad (1)$$

where $H_i^*$ is latent happiness level of individual $i$, and the $\beta$ is the associated linear coefficient of the variable $X$; $\mu_j$ denotes the cut points or threshold values; $K$ denotes the number of regressors excluding the intercept; and $\varepsilon$ denotes the error term, the cumulative distribution of error is assumed to follow normal distribution.

The categorical variable $H_i$ is formed in the following way. From the data, it is observed that for very few people happiness index is less than 0.5. About 0.725 being the mean score of happiness index, it is considered another cutoff point.

$H_i = 0$ if $H_i^* < 0.5$—very unhappy.

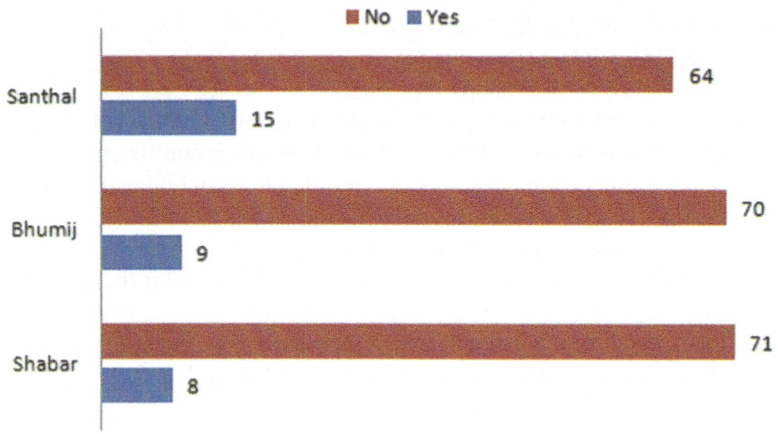


**Fig. 10** Drinking water facility inside home

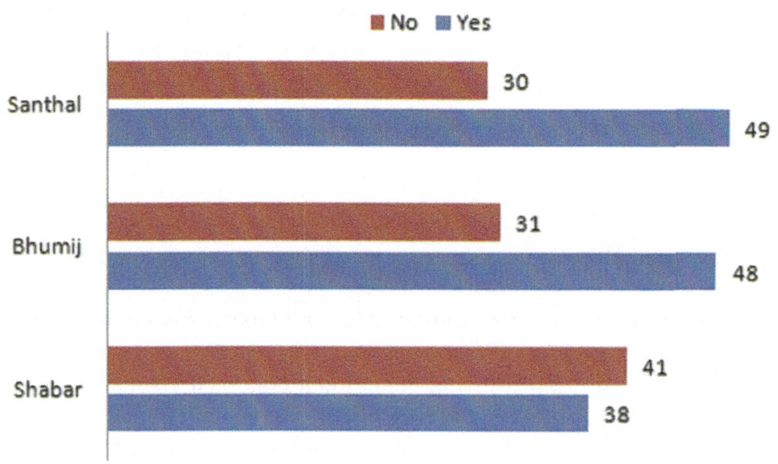


**Fig. 11** Availing electric facility inside home

**Table 4** The correlations among different variables

| | Happiness index | Modern outlook score | Govt. support index | Age | Family income | Food sufficiency |
|---|---|---|---|---|---|---|
| Happiness index | 1.0 | −0.185 | 0.085 | −0.124 | 0.059 | 0.158 |
| Modern outlook score | | 1.0 | 0.067 | −0.026 | −0.066 | −0.103 |

$H_i = 1$ if $0.5 < H_i^* < 0.725$—unhappy.
$H_i = 2$ if $0.725 < H_i^* < 0.9$—happy.
$H_i = 3$ if $0.9 < H_i^*$—very happy.

We run several ordered Probit regression and in all the ordered Probit regressions modern outlook score enters with negative and significant coefficient (both simple coefficient and marginal coefficient in predicting happiness of highest category. In the following table, Model 1 represents the regression results of ordered Probit model.

We also run Probit regression considering $H_i$ as binary variable. $H_i$ assumes the value 1 if the latent variable takes the value less than 0.7 and 0 if the latent variable takes the value above 0.7. In this case, we consider individuals to be happy if their happiness index is above 0.7 and unhappy if their happiness index is below it. In the following table, model 2 represents the results of Probit model.

We estimate the regression equation:

$$\begin{aligned} H_i = {} & \alpha_0 + \beta_1 \text{Age}_i + \beta_2 \text{Gender dummy}_i + \beta_3 \text{Modern outlook}_i \\ & + \beta_4 \text{Living condition index}_i + \beta_5 \text{Discrimination}_i + \beta_6 \text{Drinking Alcohol}_i \\ & + \beta_7 \text{Food Sufficiency}_i + \beta_8 \text{Food sufficiency}_i * \text{Family income}_i \\ & + \beta_9 \text{Wealth index}_i + \beta_{10} \text{ Wealth index with patta}_i \\ & + \beta_{11} \text{Government support index }_i + \varepsilon_i \end{aligned}$$

### 5.3.3 Regression Results

Table 5 shows the impact of age, cultural index and other socio-economic variables on the overall happiness level of respondents.

In both the regressions, possessing modern outlook vis a vis traditional cultural view is found to have negative significant effect. The natural habitat of Adivasis is far away from modern urban life in spirit and in practice. Modern outlook (belief in banking system, modern pattern of agriculture) makes one person aware of urban life that involves complexity. Knowing the complexity may develop stress among the indigenous people (Nandi et al., 1992). With modern outlook, tribal people develop goals and aspirations. When aspirations are not achieved, that may result into frustrations and unhappiness. For the same reason, we are obtaining the result that food sufficiency alone (in Model 1) enters with positive and significant coefficient, but the interaction of food sufficiency and family income enters with negative significant coefficient. It implies that once the families have sufficient food to eat, increase in family income decreases the happiness of tribal community.

In both the regressions, depression is found to be negatively related to the happiness of tribal community. Since ages, tribal communities have been facing discrimination from people belonging to upper caste communities. We, in our study, find that facing discrimination reduces their happiness significantly. This justifies the privileges and protection provided to "scheduled tribes" of India.

**Table 5** Regression results

| Explanatory variables | Model 1<br>OPROBIT HI category | Model 2<br>PROBIT HI binary<br>(cutoff 0.7) |
|---|---|---|
| Age | −0.007 (−0.00066) | −0.0095 (−0.003) |
| Gender (female = 0, male = 1) | −0.2135 (−0.018) | −0.507** (−0.179**) |
| Modern outlook index (lack of cultural attachment) | −1.034** (−0.086**) | −0.9804* (−0.339*) |
| Living condition index | 0.3763 (0.0314) | |
| Discrimination faced | −0.147* (−0.123*) | −0.389** (−0.135**) |
| Drinking Alcohol | 0.3311** (0.0277*) | 0.478** (0.165**) |
| Food sufficiency | 0.2915* (0.024*) | |
| Interaction of food sufficiency and family income | | −1.73*** (−0.599***) |
| Wealth index | −0.305 (−0.0255) | |
| Wealth index with patta | | 1.29* (0.4467*) |
| Govt. support index | 0.4524 (0.038) | 1.417*** (0.4905***) |

*Notes* Marked with '***', '**' and '*' are significant at 0.001, 0.05, and 0.1 confidence interval, respectively, marginal effects are mentioned in parentheses

Drinking alcohol is found to have positive significant effect on happiness of tribal community in both the regressions. Consumption of alcohol is a part of social rituals in many tribal communities. At the national level, about half of Scheduled Tribe men (51%) aged 15–54 years, consume some form of alcohol. The prevalence of alcohol consumption was found to be much lower among non-Scheduled Tribe men (30%) (High level committee report, 2014). While collecting data we found that many a times, tribal people drink alcohol to forget hunger. Even they feed alcohol to their babies so that they do not cry out of hunger!

In both regressions, gender enters with negative coefficient. However, it is significant only in Probit model when happiness index is considered as binary variable. The result implies that the female population of tribal community is happier than their male counterpart. There are many studies that support the hypothesis that tribal women face less discrimination compared to majority of non-tribal Indian women (Mitra, 2008).

In Model 2, when happiness index is considered as binary variable and we run Probit regression wealth index with patta and government support index enters with highly positive and significant coefficient. Government support index is constructed based on whether healthcare facilities are provided by the government, whether required medicines and treatments are available at health care centers, benefits of job reservation received. Government should also make an arrangement to give patta for the land owned by them. This result points out to the necessity of strengthening government support to marginalized tribal communities staying at interior locations.

## 6 Policy Prescriptions and Conclusion

Based on our survey, we find that 45% of our respondents do not get sufficient food to eat. In our regression model, **food sufficiency** is found to have a positive, significant role in determining happiness of the indigenous population. So, there is an urgent need of distributing free food among these tribal people unless a "food for work" scheme is introduced for them—so that they do not fall victim of starvation and hunger and can remain physically strong and mentally happy.

Since it is found that the negative impact of **modern outlook vis a vis traditional cultural practices** on happiness is significant and robust-economic development, keeping their traditional culture intact should be the primary objective of the government. Sometimes, tribal people are actively engaged in practicing traditional art form. In this era of globalization, the beautiful art form created by them may be marketed and publicized, globally. Having a modern outlook is an inevitable outcome of development. With modern outlook, ambitions and aspirations are expected to grow within the tribal population. So the government should foster an environment-creating access to job opportunities and services such as Govt. schools, healthcare system, banks, and the Government's social safety net for the tribal people so that they can fulfill their aspirations.

In this study, we find that **alcohol consumption** makes people happier. Alcohol consumption is definitely harmful for health. Since our survey results indicate that the tribal people consume alcohol to forget the pangs of hunger, so it is believed that once food and employment are available to them, alcohol consumption would be lower.

The Constitution of India prohibits **discrimination** on grounds of religion, race, caste, sex and place of birth, and provides the right to equality. Articles and special schedules of constitution are paternalistic and protective toward Scheduled Tribes. Yet, after 70 years of existence of the Constitution, tribal people are looked down upon by people of higher caste and they have to struggle for equal treatment from the society. In this study, we find that facing discrimination has a significant negative impact on the happiness of tribal individuals. So, it is prescribed that the government should try to ensure social equality and justice for the tribal population so that they do not have to fall victim to any caste-based humiliation. There is a dire need to set up a caste-based harassment cell. Any kind of harassment, humiliation or violence—verbal, behavioral, or physical should be a punishable offence.

It is very important to strengthen and widen the **government support** provided to these indigenous people in the form of employment generation, infrastructure development improved (water, sanitation and housing), and health care facilities. Most of the respondents we have surveyed have not been benefitted by job reservation policies. So, it is important that the benefits of job reservation policy should reach the rural tribal communities. To make these people prepared for employment it is important not only to increase number of schools and but also school quality should be enhanced. Government should also make necessary steps **to issue patta (land deed)** to the tribal individuals who own lands.

To conclude, food, social equality and access to basic necessities of life—these are what our tribal brothers and sisters want. It is a responsibility on the part of the government to create an environment to satisfy these basic requirements of tribal communities.

This study suffers from few limitations. To start with, our sample size is small. We initially had plans to collect more data. But, due to the COVID-19-driven lockdown, we could not do so. Further, the word "culture" has a vast implication. In this study, we could not include many aspects of tribal culture—such as norms, values, habits, morals, shared meanings, patterned ways of behaving, thinking and acting. In spite of its limitations, this is the first work that studies happiness of indigenous people of India.

**Acknowledgements** We acknowledge the financial support received by Planning and Development Unit, Department of Economics, Jadavpur University. This research paper is an outcome of a project funded by it. We are grateful to the participants of the online Seminar on presentations of ongoing projects of the Planning and Development Unit, JU, held on October 2, 2020 for their valuable comments.

## Appendix: Questionnaire

### Culture and Happiness

### Socio-economic and Demographic Questions

1. Age
2. Gender
3. Religion
4. District
5. Village/Locality
6. Family income
7. Working/ Non-working

   If working, answer questions 8–10, otherwise skip to question 11.
8. Occupation
9. Own income
10. Government job/private job/Self-employed
11. Do you own any property/land? Yes No
12. Do you have patta of land? Yes No
13. **What is the marital status of the respondent?**

    1. Unmarried
    2. Unmarried but has a partner
    3. Married
    4. Divorced
    5. Widow

14. **How many members are there (including minors) in the family of the respondent?**

    1. Number of family members staying at native place -
    2. Number of family members staying away -

15. **Does the respondent get Food sufficiency?**

    1. Gets sufficient food to eat everyday
    2. Doesn't get sufficient food to eat everyday

16. Consumes tobacco Yes No
17. Drinks alcohol Yes No
18. **What is the Education level of the respondent?**

    1. Cannot read and write.
    2. Less than equal to Primary Education level.
    3. More than Primary but less than equal to Secondary Education level.
    4. More than Secondary but less than equal to Higher Secondary Education.
    5. More than Higher Secondary but not graduate.
    6. Graduate and above.

19. **What is the nature of living place of the respondent?**

    1. The respondent lives in Primitive House (made of straw, wood, mud).
    2. The Respondent lives in Brick- Made small houses under Indira-Awas-Yojna.
    3. The Respondent lives in his own brick-made house.
    4. The Respondent lives in a villa.

20. Does the respondent have electricity at your residence? Yes No
21. **How many of these does the respondent have?**

    - Mobile -
    - TV -
    - Radio -
    - Computer -
    - Bicycle -
    - Car -

22. **What kind of sanitary system does the respondent use in his house?**

    1. There is no sanitary system in the house and the respondent uses open air sanitation.
    2. He has a sanitary system in the house but still goes to open air.
    3. He has primitive type sanitary system and he uses it.
    4. He has a modern sanitary system and he uses it.

23. **How does the respondent access drinking water facility?**

    1. Within household premise

2. Near household premise
3. Away from house

**Cultural Aspects**

1. **To what extent the respondent speaks native language? (modern outlook/lack of cultural attachment increases with increase in rank)**
    1. Only speaks native language.
    2. Speaks native and broken in other Language.
    3. Equally strong in Native and Language.
    4. Broken in native Language and strong in other regional Language.
    5. Only speak other regional Languages.
2. **To what extent the respondent writes native language? (modern outlook/lack of cultural attachment increases with increase in rank)**
    1. Only writes native language.
    2. Can write native and little other Language.
    3. Equally strong in Native and other Language.
    4. Little native Language and strong in other Language.
    5. Only writes other Languages.
3. ***To what extent the respondent is comfortable outside his/her community?***
    1. Soundly believe and participate in other culture and rituals.
    2. Only knows other culture and rituals.
    3. Has a little idea about other cultures.
    4. Does not know about it.
4. **How far the respondent is attached with the community? (modern outlook/lack of cultural attachment increases with increase in rank)**
    1. Leader and/or playing any other major role in the community.
    2. Actively participate in different program organized by community but not a leader.
    3. Sometimes joins the program organized by the community.
    4. Occasionally joins the program organized by the community.
    5. Not interested at all.
5. ***How many times the respondent attended any social gatherings of own community (Puja/festival/ cultural function, marriage, death and etc) in the last six months?***

    –
6. **To what extent the respondent does consume his/her traditional food? (modern outlook/ lack of cultural attachment increases with increase in rank)**
    1. Eats every-day.
    2. Eats only during holidays and at weekends.

3. Eats in social gatherings.
4. Does not eat at all.

7. **What is the nature of fuel the individual uses for cooking? (modern outlook/lack of cultural attachment increases with increase in rank)**

    1. Smoke emanating fuel (Fire-wood/Crop residue/Cow-dung cake/Coal, Charcoal)
    2. non smoke emanating fuel (Kerosene/LPG/PNG/Electricity)

8. **What is the agricultural pattern the respondent does follow? (modern outlook/lack of cultural attachment increases with increase in rank)**

    1. Follows the traditional agricultural pattern only.
    2. Follows both the traditional and modern mode of farming.
    3. Only follows the modern pattern of agriculture.

9. ***How far the respondent does believe the usual banking system?***

    1. He is a bank account holder, maintains it and if necessary, will borrow from the bank only.
    2. He has a bank account but does not maintain it and believes in other money lending institutions.
    3. Has no idea about banking system and only borrow from other money lending institutions.

10. **Does the respondent engage himself/herself in any kind of (performing or non-performing) traditional art-form? (modern outlook/lack of cultural attachment increases with increase in rank)**

    1. The respondent is a performance artist and often being paid for his/her performance.
    2. The respondent is a performance artist but unpaid and still struggling.
    3. Only perform inside the community.
    4. Does not perform at all.

11. **What kind of lifestyle is the respondent willing to accept? (modern outlook/lack of cultural attachment increases with increase in rank)**

    1. He is not willing to accept a modern lifestyle and happy in a complete primitive lifestyle.
    2. He is willing to accept a modern lifestyle but has very less or no access to it.
    3. He is willing to accept a modern lifestyle and has access to it and is happy in it.
    4. He has access to modern life style, but thinks that would be happier in primitive life.

12. **To what extent do you receive help and support from others of your community when you need it? (modern outlook/ lack of cultural attachment increases with increase in rank)**
    1. Always
    2. Most of the times
    3. Sometimes
    4. Never
13. **Have you faced any disrespect/ discrimination for belonging in a tribal community in last six month? If yes, how many times?**

Ans:-

**Happiness and Well-Being-related Questions**

1. **In general, the respondent considers him-self a very Happy person:**
    1. Strongly Disagree
    2. Disagree
    3. Neither agree nor Disagree
    4. Agree
    5. Strongly Agree
2. **In General the respondent thinks that he is leading a worthy life?**
    1. Strongly Disagree
    2. Disagree
    3. Neither agree nor Disagree
    4. Agree
    5. Strongly Agree
3. **The respondent considers his present overall situation is very safe for his future generation.**
    1. Strongly Disagree
    2. Disagree
    3. Neither agree nor Disagree
    4. Agree
    5. Strongly Agree
4. **Some people are generally very happy. They enjoy life regardless of what is going on, getting the most out of everything. This character describes the respondent best.**
    1. Strongly Disagree
    2. Disagree
    3. Neither agree nor Disagree
    4. Agree
    5. Strongly Agree

5. ***Some people are generally not very happy. Although they are not depressed, they never seem as happy as they might be. These Characteristics describe the respondent most.***
    1. Strongly Disagree
    2. Disagree
    3. Neither agree nor Disagree
    4. Agree
    5. Strongly Agree
6. **In general, I feel very positive. How far this statement describes the respondent most**
    1. Strongly Disagree
    2. Disagree
    3. Neither Agree nor Disagree
    4. Agree
    5. Strongly Agree
7. **How lonely do you feel in your daily life?**
    1. Always
    2. Most of the times
    3. Sometimes
    4. Not at all
8. **In general, how often do you feel angry?**
    1. Always
    2. Most of the times
    3. Sometimes
    4. Not at all
9. **To what extent have you been feeling loved?**
    1. Not at all
    2. Sometimes
    3. Most of the Time
    4. Very much
10. **How satisfied are you with your personal relationships?**
    1. Not at all
    2. Sometimes
    3. Most of the Time
    4. Very much

**Government Support**

1. **What kind of Govt. support does the respondent Receive?**

    **Ans –**

2. **What kind of Govt. support does the respondent want/recommend?**

   Ans –

3. **The respondent and his family (including Olds, minors and pregnant women and new mothers) members receive a strong healthcare service from the government. Is the respondent agreeing with the statement?**

   1. Strongly Disagree
   2. Disagree
   3. Neither agree nor disagree
   4. Agree
   5. Strongly Agree

4. **Is there availability of required medicines and treatment at health centers all the time?**

   - Yes, most of the times available
   - No, most of the times it is not available

5. **Does the job/seat reservation policy enhances your well-being substantially?/Has job reservation policy benefited you?** Yes No

## References

Bijoy, C. R. The Adivasis of India—A history of discrimination, conflict and resistance. https://www.researchgate.net/publication/295315229

BoroBaski. (2019). Is "brick house" the only sign of development?—West Bengal. https://indiantribalheritage.org/?p=29829#gsc.tab=0

Chakraborty, S., Thompson, J. C., & Yehoue, B. E. (2015). Culture and development. *The World Bank Economic Review, 29*, 238–246.

Chang, W.-C. (2009). Social capital and subjective happiness in Taiwan. *International Journal of Social Economics, 36*(8), 844–868.

Dockery, M. A. (2003). Culture and wellbeing: The case of indigenous Australians. The Center for Labour Market Research Discussion Paper Series 09/01.

Ghosh, A. B., Banerjee, G., & Biswas, D. (2004). Psychiatric morbidity in sub-Himalayan tribal community: An epidemiological study. *Indian Journal of Psychiatry, 46*, 324–332.

Gilmour, R., & Lu, L. (2004). Culture and concept of happiness: Individual oriented and social oriented SWB. *Journal of Happiness Studies, 5*, 269–291.

Lu, L., & Gilmour, R. (2004). Culture and conceptions of happiness: individual oriented and social oriented swb. *Journal of Happiness Studies: An Interdisciplinary Forum on Subjective Well-Being, 5*(3), 269–291. https://doi.org/10.1007/s10902-004-8789-5

Mathews, J. (2012). Happiness, culture, and context. *International Journal of Wellbeing, 2*(4), 299–312.

Mitra, A. (2008). The status of women among scheduled tribes in India. *The Journal of Socioeconomics, 37*, 1202–1217.

Nandi, D. N., Mukherjee, S. P., Boral, G. C., Banerjee, G., Ghosh, A., Ajmany, S., Sarkar, S., & Biswas, D. (1977). Prevalence of psychiatric morbidity in two tribal communities in certain villages of West Bengal—A cross cultural study. *Indian Journal of Psychiatry, 19*(3), 2–12.

Nandi, D. N., Banerjee, G., Chowdhury, A. N., Banerjee, T., Boral, G. C., Sen, B., et al. (1992). Urbanization and mental morbidity in certain tribal communities in West-Bengal. *Indian Journal of Psychiatry, 34*(4), 334–339.

Rana, K., et al. (2020). *Living world of Adivasis of West Bengal: An ethnographic exploration*. The Asiatic Society and The Pratichi Institute.

Report of the high level committee on socioeconomic, health and education status of tribal communities of India. Ministry of Tribal Affairs, Government of India, May 2014.

Snodgrass, G. J., Lacy, G. M., & Upadhyay, C. (2017). Developing culturally sensitive affect scales for global mental health-research and practice: Emotional balance, not named syndromes, in Indian Adivasi subjective well-being. *Social Science & Medicine, 187*, 174–183.

Wang, J. H. (2015). Happiness and social exclusion of indigenous peoples in Taiwan—A social sustainability perspective. *PLoS ONE*. https://doi.org/10.1371/journal.pone.0118305

# Is the GST Reform Pro-poor in India?

**Poulomi Roy**

## 1 Introduction

In the short run, economic policy change affects the income levels of different income/social groups mainly through the prices of commodities they consume or via an income transfer mechanism. However, the effectiveness of the income transfer mechanism depends on the information on the distribution of well-being. The distribution of well-being of the poor is often not known to government agencies, which makes indirect taxation a predominant tool for social welfare policy.

In July 2017, India moved to the goods and service tax (GST) system from the pre-existing value-added tax (VAT) system. VAT reform was an improvement over the central excise duty and state sales tax system. The newly introduced goods and services tax (GST) is the next logical step towards complete indirect tax reform in India.

*GST* is an indirect tax imposed on goods and services. With GST, the government intended to implement one tax for the entire nation. Different taxes such as service tax, excise duty, VAT, luxury tax, octroi duty, central sales tax, entertainment tax, and state excise duty are all clubbed into GST. In the existing VAT system, taxes were assigned in the state of origin where production or sale happened, and the GST is collected at the destination where goods and services are consumed. Thus, GST is a destination-based tax. Many manufacturing states voiced their concern regarding the probable revenue loss due to this shift in the system. Goods and service tax act 2017 states compensation will be provided to the states for the loss of revenue. It was further stated that the states facing the revenue loss problem would receive compensation for the five years from the date of implementation of GST in that state. It is expected that industry, consumers, and the government will benefit from implementation.

---

P. Roy (✉)
Department of Economics, Jadavpur University, Kolkata 700032, India
e-mail: poulomi.roy@gmail.com



A. Raychaudhuri and A. Ghose (eds.), *Managing Pandemic and Correcting Development Fundamentals*, India Studies in Business and Economics,
https://doi.org/10.1007/978-981-19-8680-2_10

As mentioned above, it is expected that other things remaining unchanged in GST will reduce the burden of taxation on consumers and benefit consumers. The question is whether the GST reform favours poor consumers or rich consumers, or both. The present study focuses on the impact of GST on the consumers, especially the poor consumers only.

The objective of the present study is to test the hypotheses that the grouping of commodities under different tax rates satisfies the distributive rule. If the items consumed by poor people are taxed at a lower rate, and pro-rich items are taxed at higher rates, we can say that the GST reform in India is pro-poor.

Poverty occurs when some families are too deprived of attaining a basic minimum living standard. It is essential to identify who is "poor," which is reached by selecting a level of income or expenditure as the poverty line and classifying all households who fall below the cutoff level. The most important aim of the government's development efforts is to reduce poverty. Poverty reduction, to a large extent, depends on the government's budgetary policies, that is, expenditure and revenue-raising policies. This chapter focuses on the effect of revenue-raising policies of the government on poverty in India.

On the other hand, faced with a severe revenue crisis, most developing countries have introduced different tax reform measures. Tax reform measures are also responsible for determining how different groups of citizens share the burden of taxes.

It is argued that the income tax reforms are implemented more on efficiency and equity ground and are not an instrument of a poverty reduction strategy as the poor are not liable for personal income tax (Gemmell & Morrissey, 2002). The same study also suggests that the principal taxes paid by the poor are sales taxes and tariffs on the goods they consume. The tax system could be made pro-poor if pro-poor items are zero rated or subsidised. Indirect taxes are the main source of tax revenue for many countries, particularly for sub-national governments in developing countries. Sahn and Younger (1999) and Gemmell and Morrissey (2002) suggest that some indirect taxes, particularly taxes such as sales tax or VAT, can be quite progressive or regressive and can potentially affect poverty or inequality in developing countries.

Deaton et al. (1992) for Pakistan; Yitzhaki (1994) for Israel; Yitzhaki and Lewis (1996) for Indonesia; Sahn and Younger (1999) for Africa; Younger et al. (1999) for Madagaskar; Muñoz and Cho (2003) for Ethiopia; Jäntti (2005) for Finland and Prasada (2005) for Sri Lanka, Roy et al. (2010) for India are a few to be mentioned. The present study considers the Engel curve to analyse the impact of GST reform in India on the poor. The combinations of commodities purchased by the poor and rich households differ; any tax reform that reduces the price of pro-poor products will have a larger effect on the welfare of poor households. Our primary hypothesis is that GST reform in India satisfies the distributive principle.

The rest of the paper will be organised as follows. Section 2 will provide the data and outline the methodology of the study. In Sect. 3, we elucidate the empirical models and summarise the findings. Section 4 comments on policy implications and concludes the paper.

## 2 Methodology and Data Source

The Engel curve describes how the share of household expenditure on a particular good or servi10. ce depends on total household expenditure. Engel's law states that the poorer a family is, the larger its budget is spent on food items. Therefore, the basic work evaluates the relationship between a household's expenditure on a particular commodity and the total household per capita monthly expenditure. When compared with GST rates, it helps us in understanding whether pro-poor commodities are taxed at a lower rate or not. Theoretically, an Engle curve can be either negatively sloped or positively sloped. (i) A negatively sloped Engel curve indicates that the share of expenditure on that commodity falls as the income of the household increases. Thus, the commodity must be taxed at a lower rate, and (ii) A positively sloped Engel curve suggests that the commodity is mainly consumed by the rich class and can be taxed at a higher rate. (iii) A concave-sloped Engel curve can describe two possibilities: one that either the particular good is consumed by both the groups; second, it may indicate that the consumption reaches a saturation point it starts declining.

Engel curve will determine what type of commodity the households consume. Thus, we can group the commodities into necessary, luxury, and common goods depending on the shape and slope of the Engel curve. Suppose the necessary goods are taxed at a higher rate, whereas the luxury good is taxed at a lower rate. Then definitely, we can argue that the commodity tax grouping is not based on the distributive principle.

The data we use are taken from unit-level survey data on consumer expenditure in India. The National Sample Survey Organization (NSSO) in India conducts and publishes such data. The survey was carried out between July 2011 and June 2012. NSSO adopted a stratified multi-stage design for the survey. Census villages of 2001 are used as the first stage units (FSU) for the rural and urban sectors. The Urban Frame Survey blocks are used as FSUs. Households are ultimate stage units, but some data at the individual level are also available.

Our analysis is based on data at the individual and the household level. The variables that reflect individual-level information are age, sex, and education level. Information on household size, total monthly consumption expenditure, and total monthly expenditure on various commodities are available at the household level.

NSSO carries out a consumer expenditure survey every five years and the latest large-scale unit-level data on consumer expenditure in India is the NSSO 68th round data (2011–2012) (NSSO (2013)).

## 3 Descriptive Analysis

The report on GST, status, and concepts published by the revenue department of the government of India reveals that the following items are not to be considered either as good or services:

1. Services by an employee to the employer concerning his employment.
2. Services by any court or Tribunal established under any law for the time being in force.
3. 
   (a) the functions performed by the Members of Parliament, Members of State Legislature, Members of Panchayats, Members of Municipalities, and Members of other local authorities;
   (b) the duties performed by any person who holds any post in pursuance of the provisions of the Constitution in that capacity, or
   (c) the duties performed by any person as a Chairperson or a Member or a Director in a body established by the Central Government or a State Government or local authority and who has not deemed an employee before the commencement of this clause.
4. Services of funeral, burial, crematorium, or mortuary, including transportation of the deceased.
5. Sale of land and, subject to clause (b) of paragraph 5 of Schedule II, sale of the building.
6. Actionable claims, other than lottery, betting, and gambling.
7. [Supply of goods from a non-taxable territory to another place in the non-taxable territory without such goods entering India.
   (a) Supply of warehoused goods to any person before clearance for home consumption;
   (b) Supply of goods by the consignee to any other person, by the endorsement of documents of title to the goods, after the goods have been dispatched from the port of origin located outside India but before clearance for home consumption.]

Other than the items mentioned above, alcohol and five petroleum products, such as petrol, diesel, crude oil, natural gas, and aviation turbine fuel, are kept outside GST initially. In the 122nd amendment bill, only, alcoholic liquor for human consumption is outside GST. It is proposed that GST covers the above-mentioned five petroleum products from the date of recommendation of the GST council.

During several deliberations held by the GST council in India, it was decided that there will be seven groups of commodities under GST, namely:

| | |
|---|---|
| Nil: | Exempted from taxation |
| 0%: | Zero-rated exports |
| 3%: | Gold |
| 5%: | Essential goods |
| 12%: | Basic necessity products |
| 18%: | Revenue neutral rate |
| 28%: | Demerit goods |
| Not covered: | Petroleum products, alcohol. |

Table 1 represents the change in tax rates from the pre-GST to the post-GST scenario for various NSSO commodity groups [1]. We observe that taxes on necessary goods such as cereals, pulses, cereal substitutes, milk (liquid), salt and beverages, spices, edible oil, foot ware (of value Rs. 1000), egg, fish, meat, fruits, vegetables, firewood, kerosene, and LPG have either remained unchanged or decreased marginally in the post-reform period. Taxes on bad commodities such as tobacco group commodities have been increased. In contrast, alcohol is kept outside GST as state governments were uncertain about the probable impact of increasing tax on alcohol on their revenue. Alcohol is one of the major sources of revenue for the various state governments. Educational and medical goods and services are two necessities of citizens. GSTs on these two groups of commodities either remain unchanged or reduced. Toilet articles are also commonly used commodities, but taxes on most of the commodities of this group either remained unchanged or increased in the post-reform period. Taxes on other commodity groups such as entertainment, other consumables (such as electric bulbs and fans), clothing, and bedding have been increased in the post-reform period.

From the NSSO classified commodity groups, we have constructed 11 commodity groups, namely, food (consisting of cereals, pulses, and cereal substitutes), milk and milk products, sugar, salt and beverages, spices, edible oil, other food (comprising of vegetables, fruits, egg, fish, meat and pulses), clothing and bedding, footwear, fuel and light, tobacco, pan, and intoxicants, others (comprising services, durable goods, conveyance, etc.). The commodity groups are aggregated over different qualities and varieties. Table 2 reports the shares of average monthly expenditure on various commodity groups in India. An Indian household, on average, spends 26% on food and other food. Shares of expenditure on fuel and light, milk and milk products, and clothing and bedding are 10%, 8%, and 5%, respectively. Expenditure on footwear is the least (only 1%), and that on others is the highest, that is 36%. Taxes on the majority of the food groups have either decreased or remained unchanged. The taxes on the commodity groups like footwear (of value Rs. 1000 and above), milk products, others, tobacco, and intoxicants have increased.

As policymakers claimed, we find that the overall grouping of commodities followed the rule distributive rule because necessities are either exempted from taxation or taxed at lower rates. The bad commodities, namely tobacco, are taxed at a higher rate.

Next, we used the Engel curve approach to identify whether a particular commodity group is mainly consumed by the poor individuals or the rich individuals, or by both. In Figs. 1, 2, 3, 4, 5, 6, 7, 8, 9, 10 and 11, we have plotted how the shares of expenditure on certain commodity changes with the change in the monthly per capita expenditure of a household. We find that Engle curves for food, other food, salt, sugar and beverages, spices, fuel and light, and edible oil are negatively sloped, indicating these commodities are more consumed by the poor than the rich. So, we classify them as pro-poor goods.

Interestingly, Fig. 9 shows that the Engel curve for the tobacco and intoxicant groups is low and negative. Thus, poorer households are very much addicted to tobacco and intoxicants, and they are not spending much on purchasing milk and

**Table 1** Direction of tax change from pre-GST to post-GST

| Commodity group | Tax rate (GST) | Tax rate (Pre-GST) |
|---|---|---|
| Cereals and cereal substitutes | 0–5 | 0–5 |
| Pulses and pulses products | 0–5 | 0–5 |
| Milk and milk products | 0–18 | 0–5 |
| Salt and sugar | 0–5 | 0–5 |
| Beverages | 5–18 | 4–12 |
| Spices | 5 | 0–6 |
| Edible oil | 5, 18 | 4–6 |
| Egg, fish, and meat | 0, 5 | 0 |
| Vegetables | 0, 5 | 0 |
| Fruits (fresh) | 0, 5 | 0 |
| Fruits (dry) | 12, 5 | 12–18 |
| Pan | 0, 28 | 0 |
| Tobacco | 5, 28 | 12.5–40 |
| Intoxicants | 0, 18 | 12–15 |
| Fuel and light | 0–18 | 4–14.5 |
| Clothing | 18 | 5 |
| Bedding | 18 | 0–12.5 |
| Footwear | 5, 18 | 0–21 |
| Education | 0, 12, 18 | 0–27 |
| Medical institutional | 12 | 15 |
| Medical non-institutional | 0, 12 | 15 |
| Entertainment | 18–28 | 15 |
| Minor durable-type goods | 12, 28 | 18 |
| Toilet articles | 12–28 | 12.5–27 |
| Other household consumables | 12–18 | 5–12 |
| Consumer services excluding conveyance | 18 | 15 |
| Conveyance | 0, 5, 12 | 15 |
| Packaged processed food | 12, 18 | 12.5–65 |
| Served processed food | 12 | 5–12 |
| Durable goods | 12–18 | 26–31 |

*Source* https://cbec-gst.gov.in/gst-goods-services-rates.html (CBIC (2019))

milk products. Till 2.3 times the official poverty line, we find the Engel curve of milk and milk product is positively sloped. Thus, milk and milk products are luxury goods for poor households whose monthly per capita expenditure is 2.3 times the official poverty line. Clothing and bedding, others (services, durables, etc.), and footwear are pro-rich commodity groups. Ideally, more milk and milk products and less tobacco

**Table 2** Shares of expenditure on various commodities with corresponding GST and VAT rates

| Commodity | Share in total monthly expenditure | GST rate | VAT rate |
|---|---|---|---|
| Footwear | 0.013 | 18 | 9 |
| Spices | 0.023 | 5 | 5 |
| Tobacco, pan, intoxicants | 0.024 | 28 | 12.5 |
| Edible oil | 0.037 | 5 | 5 |
| Salt, sugar, and beverages | 0.038 | 5 | 5 |
| Clothing and bedding | 0.054 | 18 | 12.5 |
| Milk and milk product | 0.080 | 12 | 5 |
| Fuel and light | 0.101 | 5 | 12.5 |
| Other food | 0.111 | 5 | 5 |
| Food | 0.154 | 0 | 0 |
| Others | 0.365 | 28 | 12.5 |

*Note* Reported tax rates are rates applicable for the majority of the commodities within a particular group

and intoxicant should be on a budget for poor people. Poor households receive more utility by consuming more tobacco and intoxicants and less milk and milk products.

***Engle Curves Analysis for Different Commodities***

See Figs. 1, 2, 3, 4, 5, 6, 7, 8, 9, 10 and 11.

Our policymakers have considered tobacco as a bad commodity and milk as a good commodity while deciding upon the GST rates of these commodities. However, there

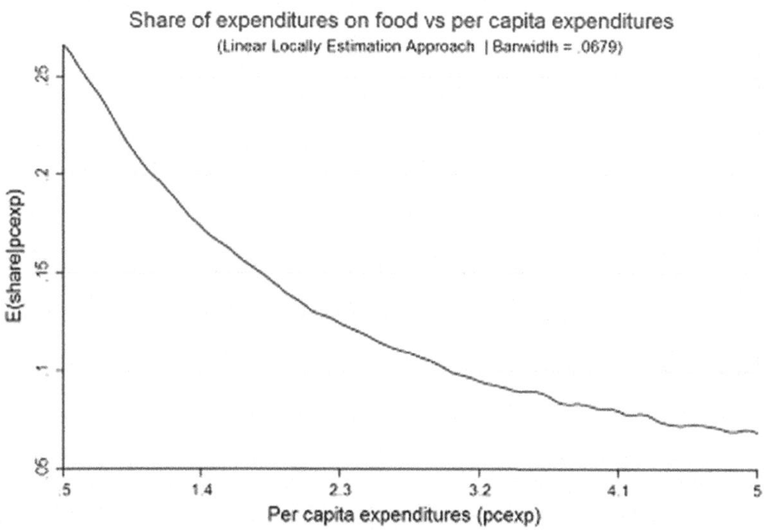


**Fig. 1** Engel curve for food (cereal, pulses, and cereal substitutes)

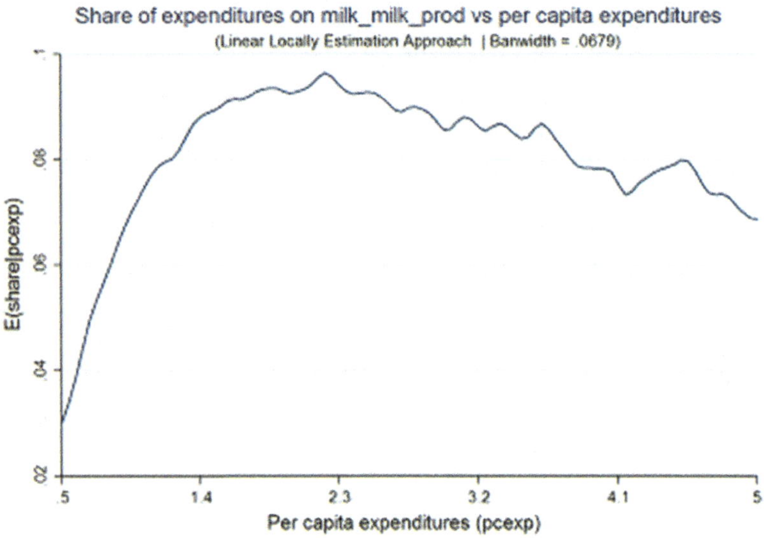


**Fig. 2** Engel curve for milk and milk product

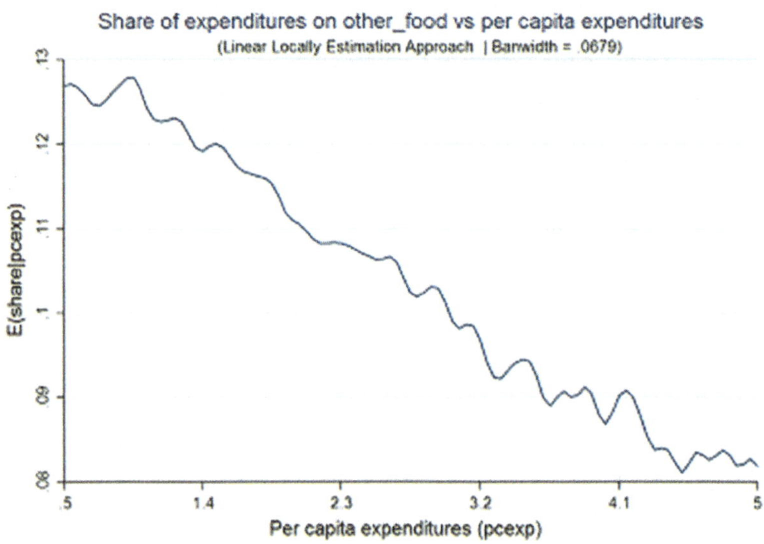


**Fig. 3** Engel curve for other food items

is a conflict between policymakers' choices and individual choices. We observe that poorer households give more weight to so-called bad commodities and less weight to milk while making their own choice. Next, we check how each commodity's consumption pattern changes with monthly per capita expenditure change. Thus, the

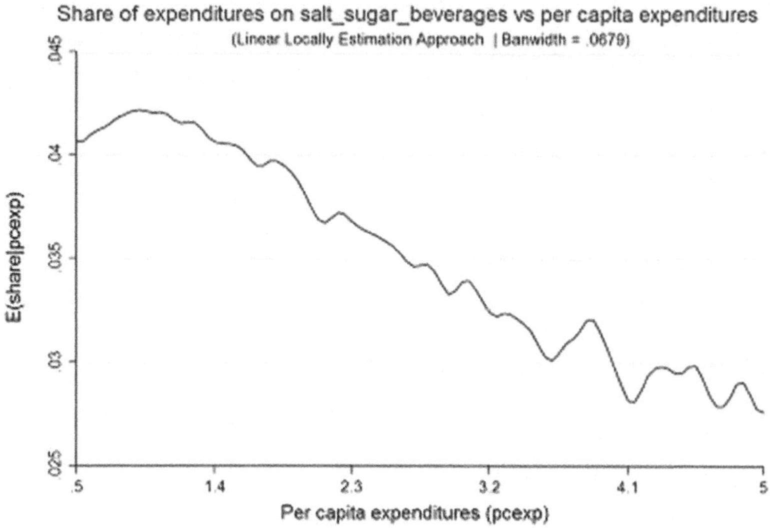


**Fig. 4** Engel curve for salt, sugar, and beverages

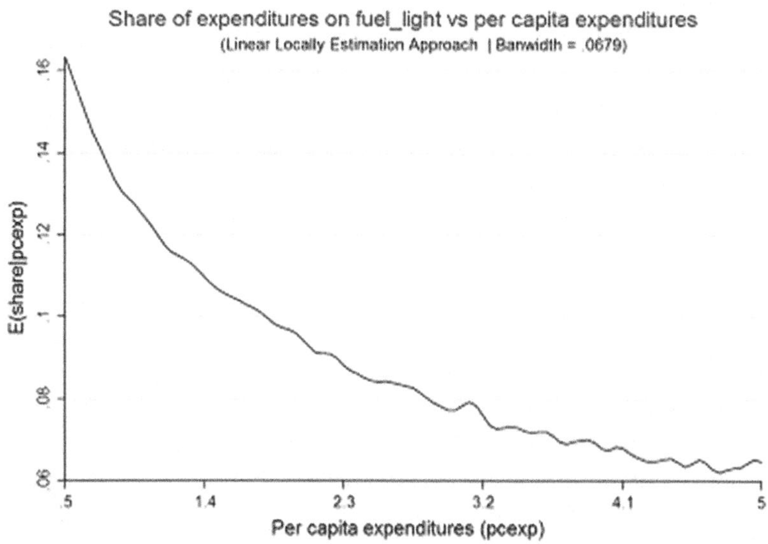


**Fig. 5** Engel curve for fuel and light

slopes of the Engel curves help us identify a pro-poor, pro-rich, and undefined group of commodities within the broad group of commodities as specified by the NSSO.

Cereals, pulses, coal, coke, firewood, kerosene (PDS), kerosene (non-PDS), LPG*, matchbox, edible oil, egg, fish, meat, vegetables, tea leaf, salt, sugar, beer,

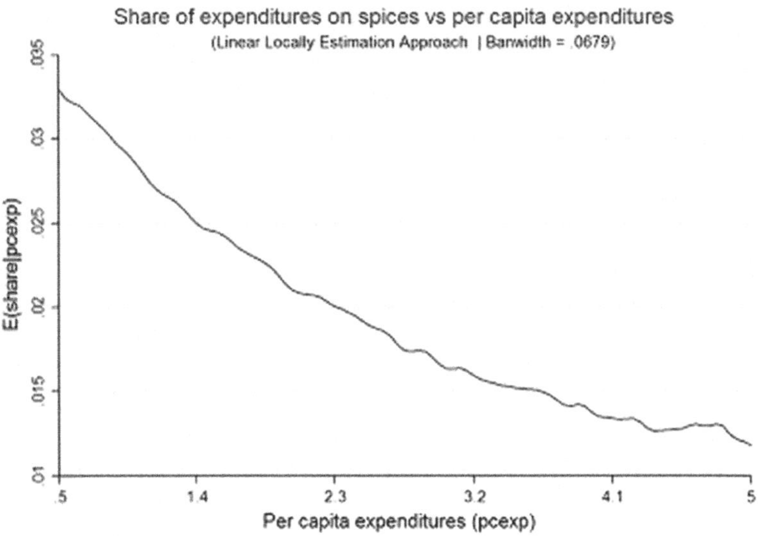


**Fig. 6** Engel curve for spices

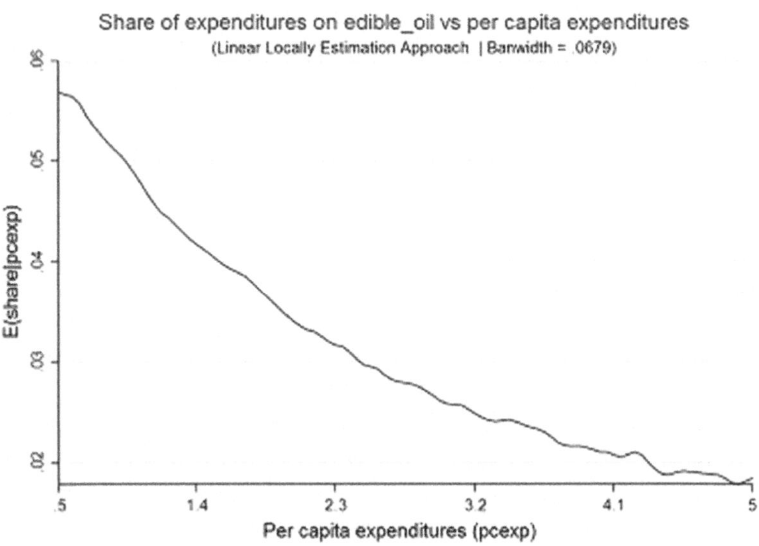


**Fig. 7** Engel curve for edible oil

country liquor, ganja, bidi, cheroot, hookah, tobacco leaf, toilet articles, etc., are identified as pro-poor goods. In contrast, honey, ghee, fresh fruits, foreign liquor, toddy, curd, butter, coffee, coffee powder, cold beverages, fruit juice, mineral water, tea, utensils and crockery, ornaments, clothing, bedding, electricity, electric fan,

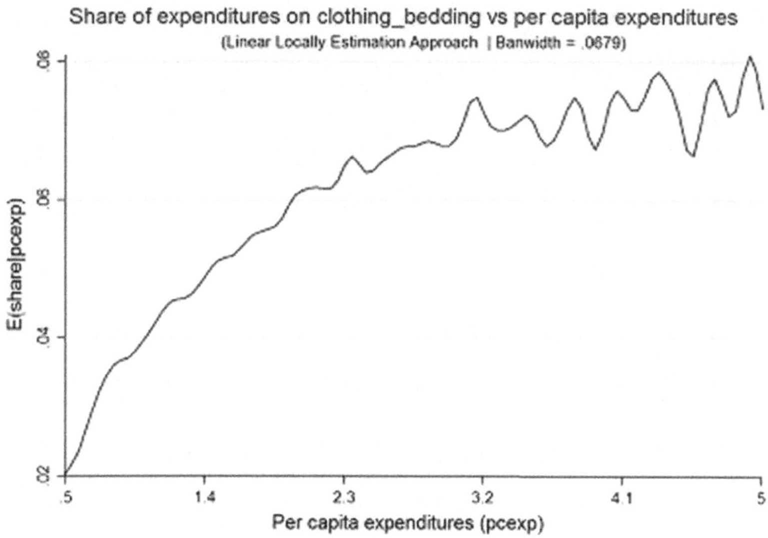


**Fig. 8** Engel curve for clothing and bedding

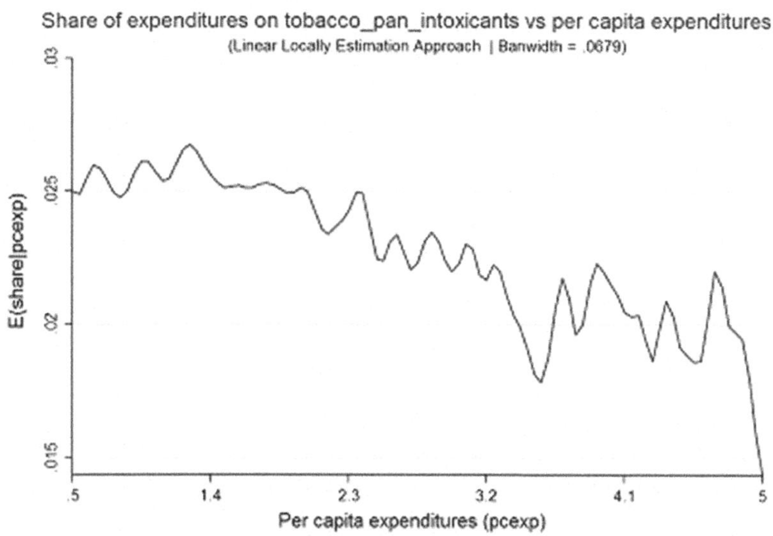


**Fig. 9** Engel curve for tobacco, pan, and intoxicants

cosmetics, AC and cooler, clock and watches, electric bulbs and tube lights (CFL), cigarettes, entertainment, recreational services, durable goods, furniture, education, health, medical, conveyance, etc., are found to be pro-rich commodities. We could not find any clear trend in the slopes of the Engel curves for a few commodities. We define them as an undefined group. Cereal substitutes, milk (liquid), biscuits,

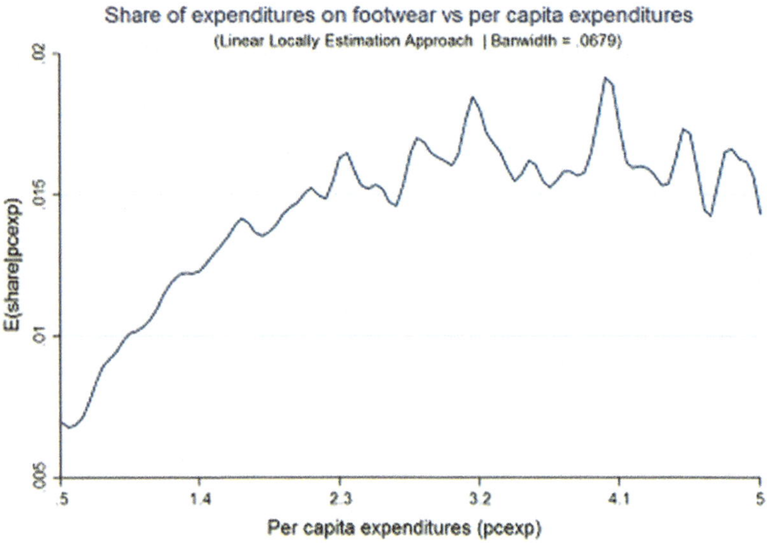


**Fig. 10** Engel curve for footwear

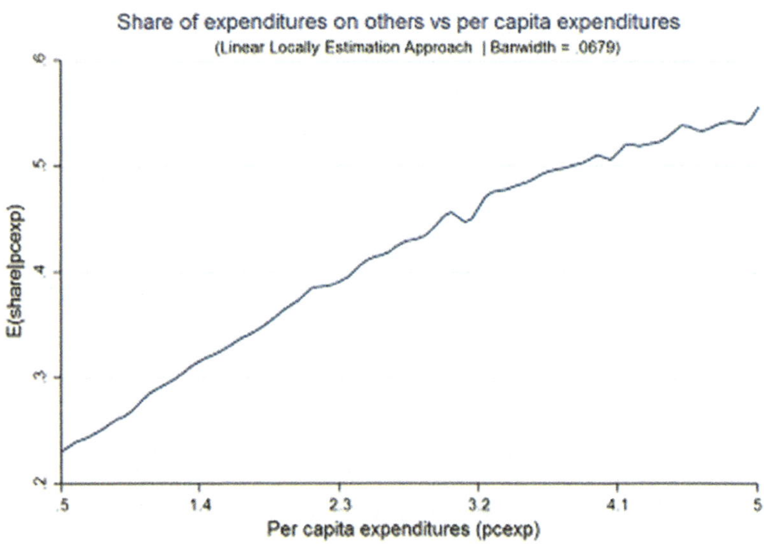


**Fig. 11** Engel curve for all other items

sevai/noodles, newspapers, books and journals, milk powder, baby food, candle, diesel, petrol, etc., fall into this group.

Intragroup analysis of pro-rich commodities reveals that some are taxed at a lower rate, or policymakers kept them out of GST. Foreign liquor, toddy, and electricity are exempted from GST, but they are pro-rich commodities. Again, articles of gold, silver, and precious metals, including jewellery made of gold, silver, and precious metals, are taxed at a 3% rate though they are also pro-rich commodities.

One of the objectives of this study is to check whether the design of the GST structure in India is pro-poor or not. We check whether all the pro-poor commodities are exempted from taxation or not. We find that pro-poor commodities such as tea leaf, sugar, spices, LPG, coal, and kerosene are taxed at 5%; toilet articles are taxed at 12% or 18% rates; bidi, cheroot, tobacco leaf, hookah are taxed at 18%. Policymakers should revise the GST rates for tea leaf, LPG, coal, kerosene, and toilet articles such as soap and toothpaste. Further reduction in taxes on these commodities will improve the social welfare of poor individuals. The policymakers chose alcohol to keep outside GST but tobacco at the 18% tax group. Both are bad commodities, so they should be treated equally. The difference in tax rates for tobacco and intoxicants may shift the household consumption towards alcohol. However, as they are good for addiction, it is less likely they will reduce consumption of these bad. Given the limited income of the poor households, this will indirectly affect the household members' consumption of the food items.

## 4 Conclusion and Policy Prescriptions

The present work is an effort to understand the nature of marginal GST tax reform undertaken by the government of India. Although GST is a better tax regime in general since it avoids cascading, does it benefit the poor more than the rich? This study has addressed this question based on 616 commodities and services subsumed under 11 commodity and services groups. We find that the tax grouping of commodities under GST reform is largely poverty-reducing, but the direction of the tax change is not always right. There is further scope for improvement in the design of the GST system in India. The intragroup analysis suggests that there should be a reduction in taxes on a few commodities consumed by poor people.

Taxes on pro-poor commodities like tea leaf, LPG, kerosene (non-PDS), toilet articles, spices, sugar, edible oil, etc., should be reduced further. Again, alcohol, electricity, jewellery made of gold, silver and precious stones, coffee, coffee powder, and cigarettes should be taxed at a higher rate.

## Appendix: Figures for the Intra Group Study: Classification of Pro-poor and Pro-rich Commodities

**Food**

See Figs. 12, 13, 14 and 15.

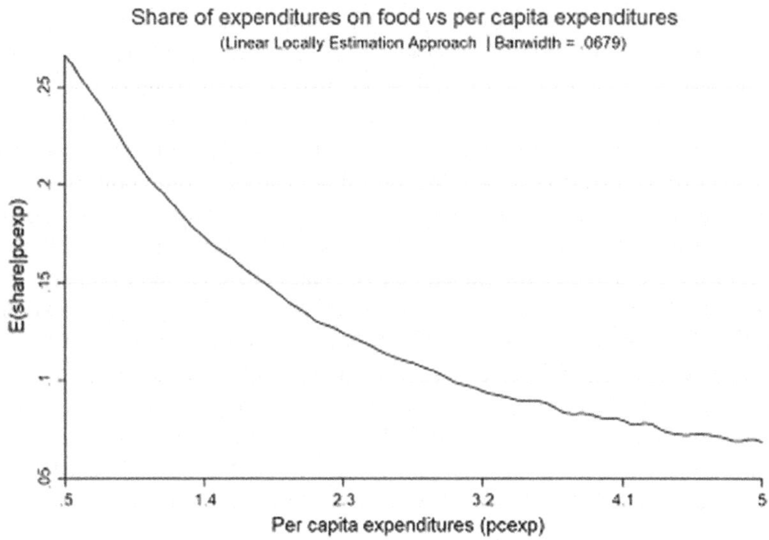


**Fig. 12** Engel curve for food

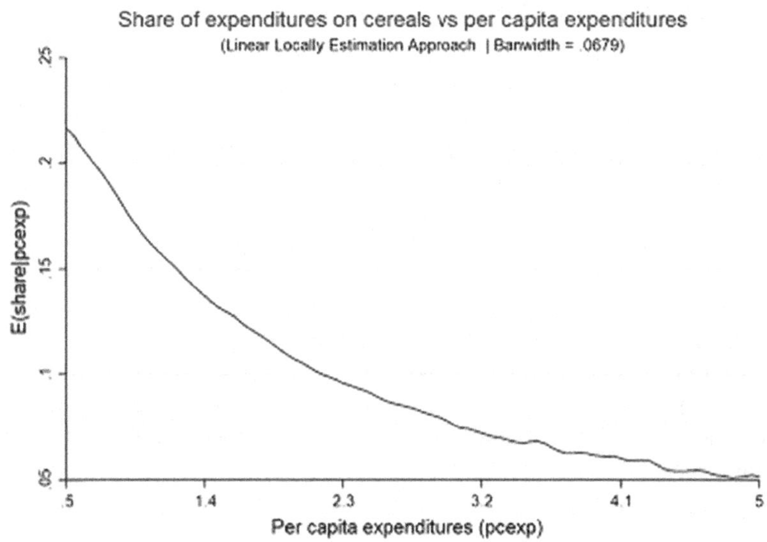


**Fig. 13** Engel curve for cereals

## Milk-Milk-Products

See Figs. 16, 17, 18, 19, 20 and 21.

## Fuel-Light

See Figs. 22, 23, 24, 25, 26, 27, 28, 29, 30, 31, 32 and 33.

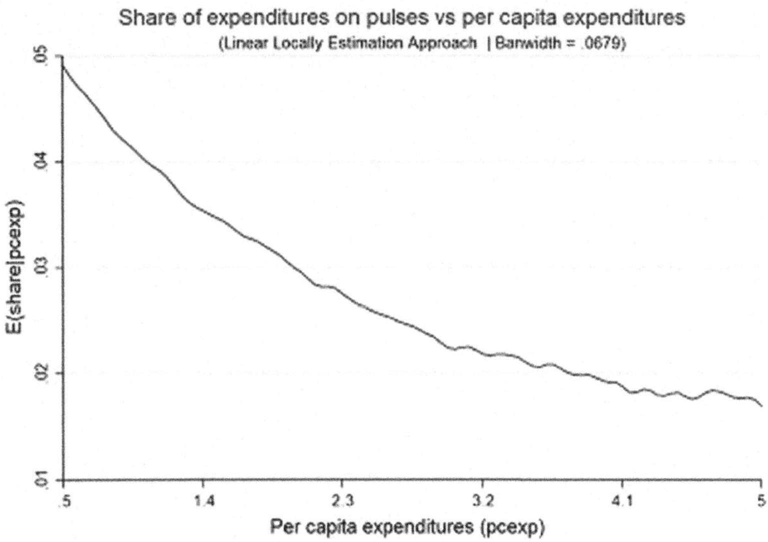


**Fig. 14** Engel curve for pulses

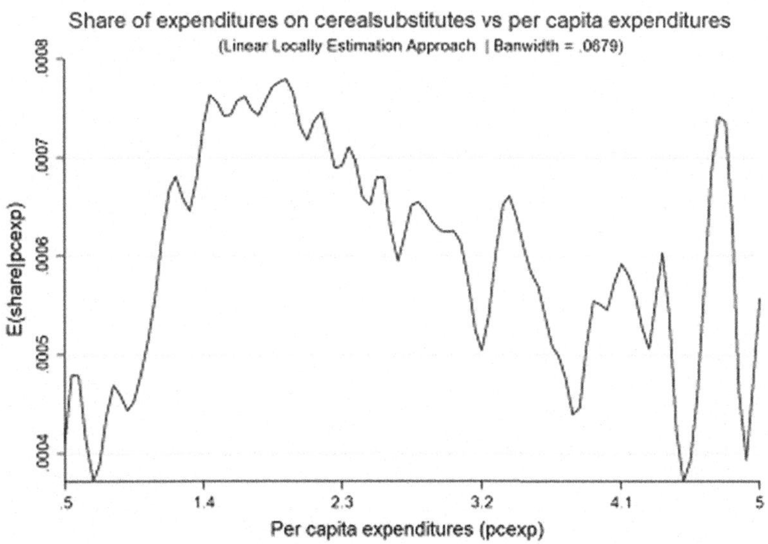


**Fig. 15** Engel curve for cereal substitutes

**Clothing-Bedding**
See Figs. 34 and 35.

**Other Food**
See Figs. 36, 37, 38 and 39.

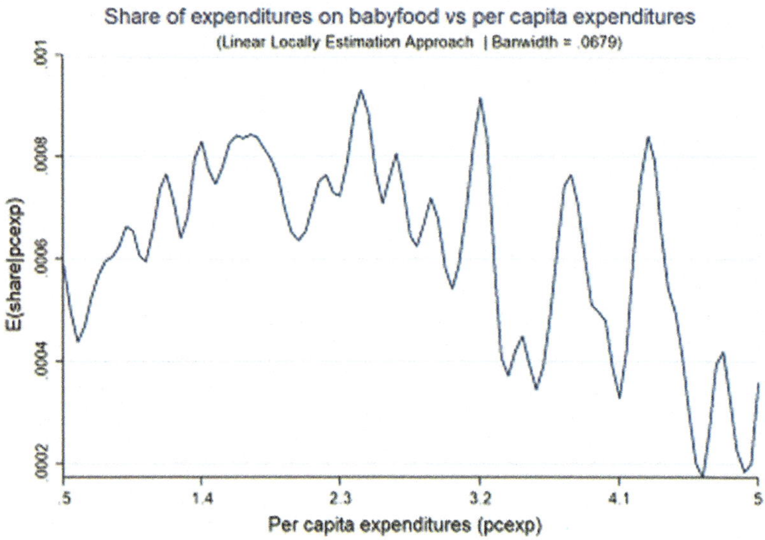


**Fig. 16** Engel curve for baby food

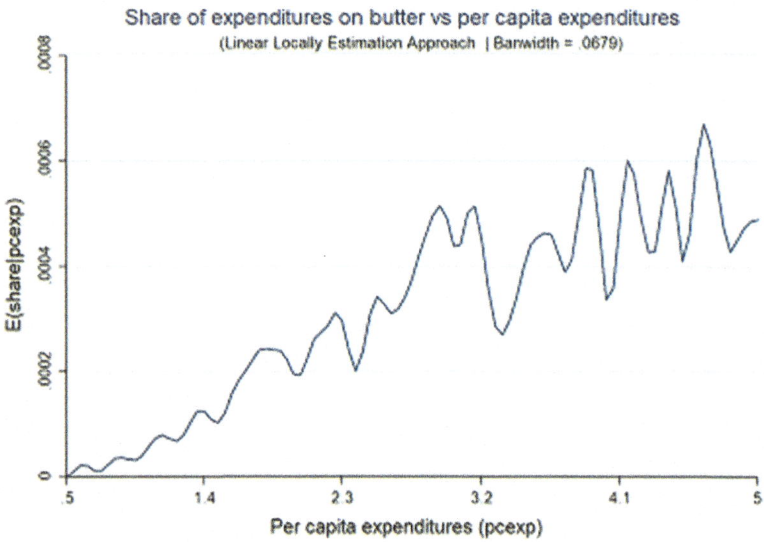


**Fig. 17** Engel curve for butter

**Salt-Sugar-Beverages**
See Figs. 40, 41, 42, 43, 44, 45, 46, 47 and 48.

**Tobacco-Pan-Intoxicants**
See Figs. 49, 50 and 51.

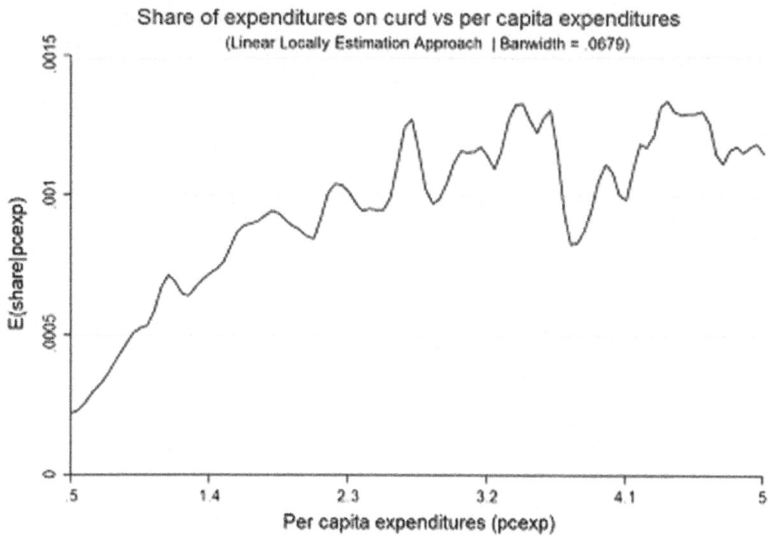


**Fig. 18** Engel curve for curd

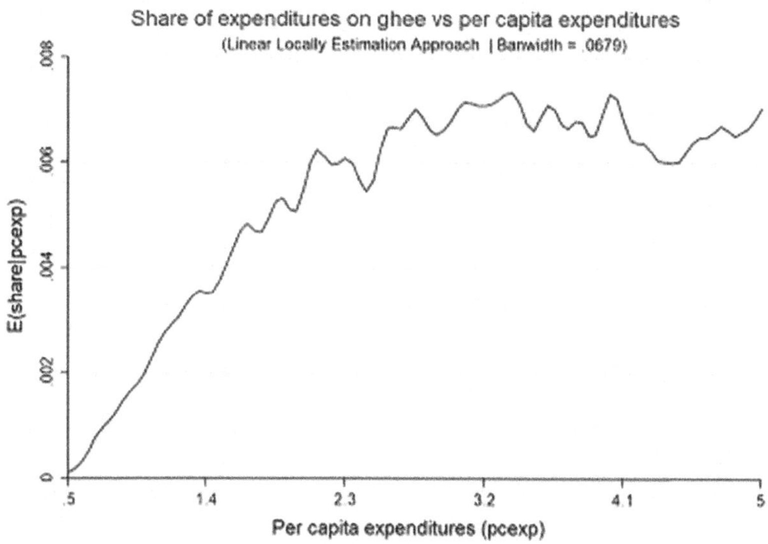


**Fig. 19** Engel curve for ghee

**Sub-group: Intoxicants**
See Figs. 52, 53, 54 and 55.

**Sub-group: Tobacco-Pan**
See Figs. 56, 57, 58, 59, 60, 61, 62, 63 and 64.

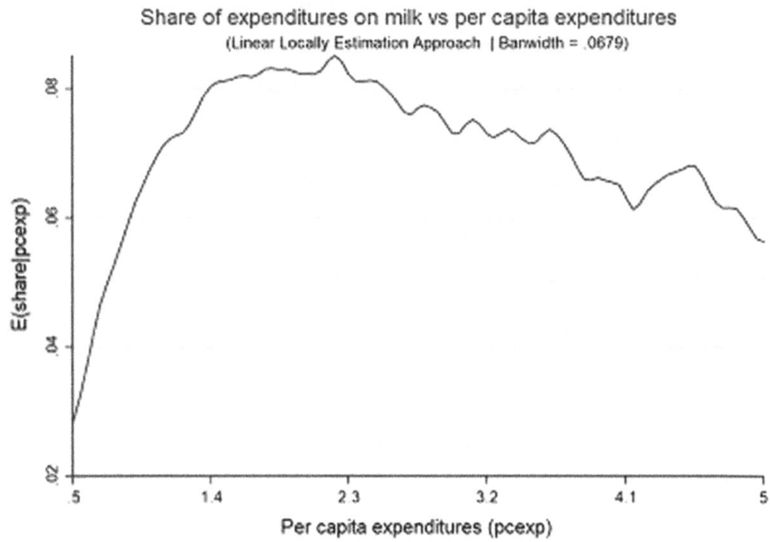


**Fig. 20** Engel curve for milk

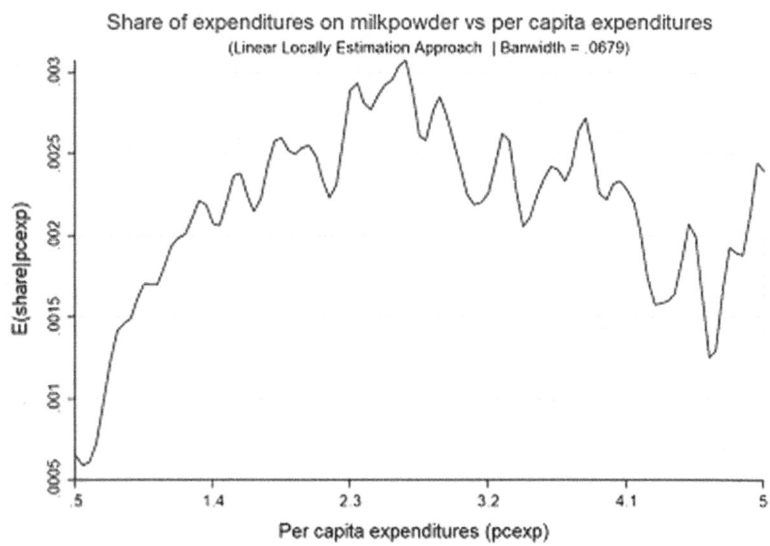


**Fig. 21** Engel curve for milk powder

## Others

See Figs. 65, 66, 67, 68, 69, 70, 71, 72, 73, 74, 75, 76, 77, 78, 79, 80, 81, 82, 83, 84 and 85.

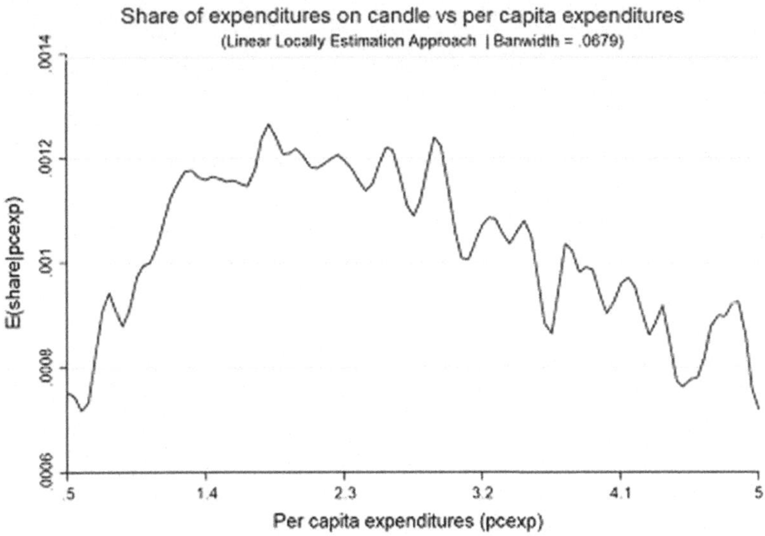


**Fig. 22** Engel curve for candle

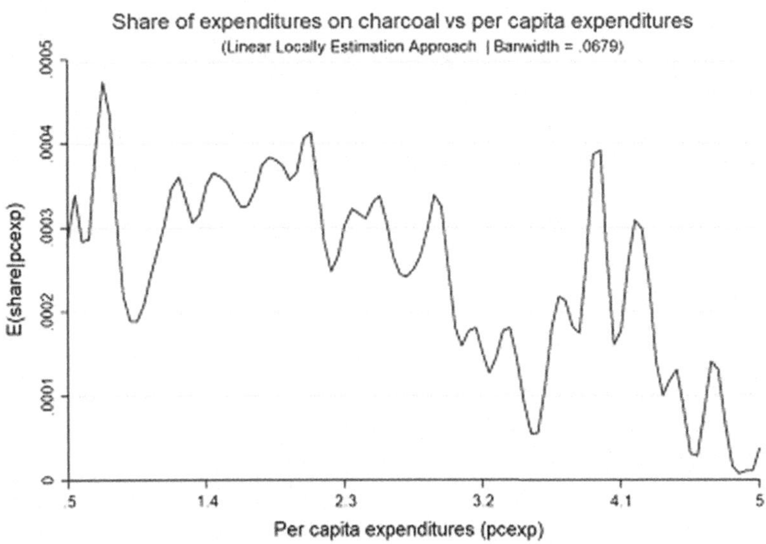


**Fig. 23** Engel curve for charcoal

[1] National Sample Survey Organisation (NSSO), from 1972 to 73, conducts surveys on a large household sample to collect information on household consumer expenditure every five-year interval. The present study is based on NSSO unit-level consumer

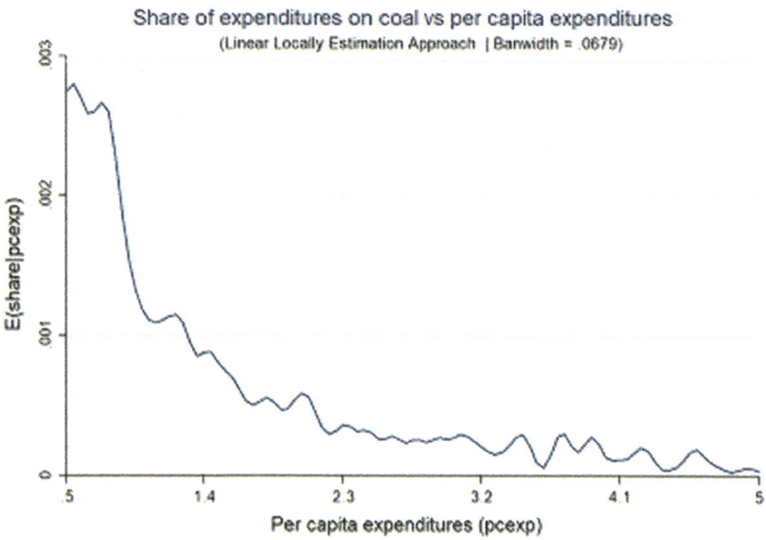


**Fig. 24** Engel curve for coal

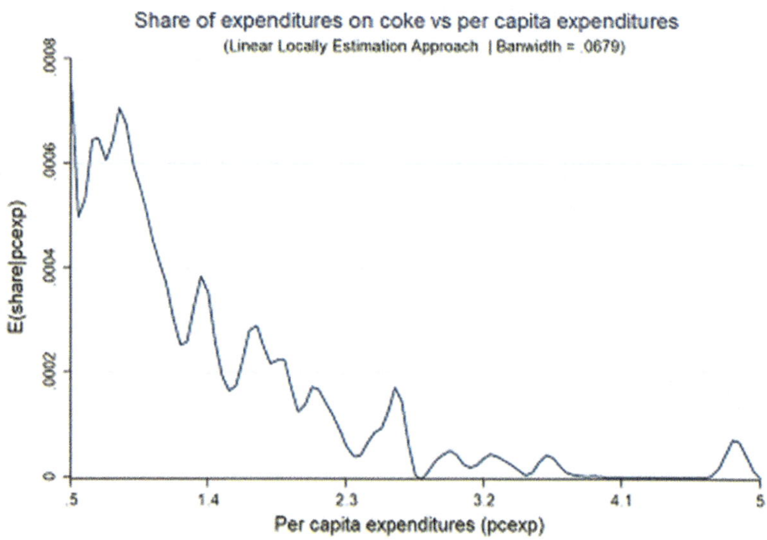


**Fig. 25** Engel curve for coke

expenditure survey data of 2011–12 (68th round), so we consider the NSSO classification of commodity groups and commodities. NSSO reports households' consumption expenditure on 616 commodities varying over 31 commodity groups.

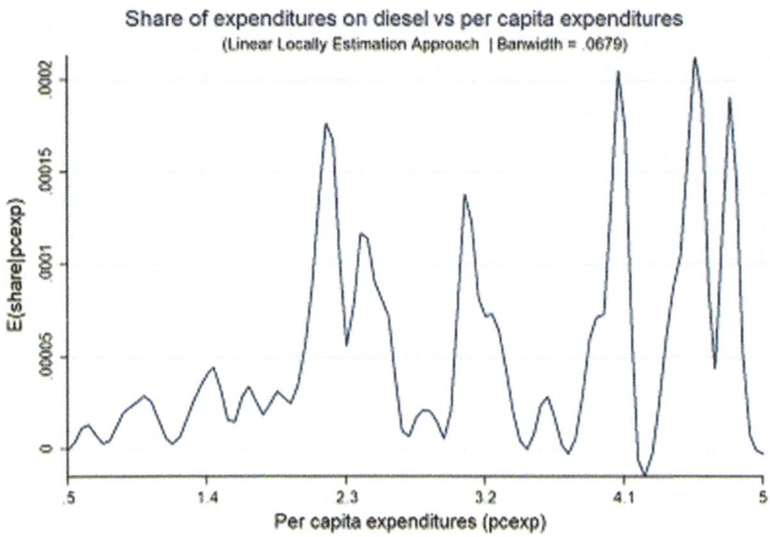


**Fig. 26** Engel curve for diesel

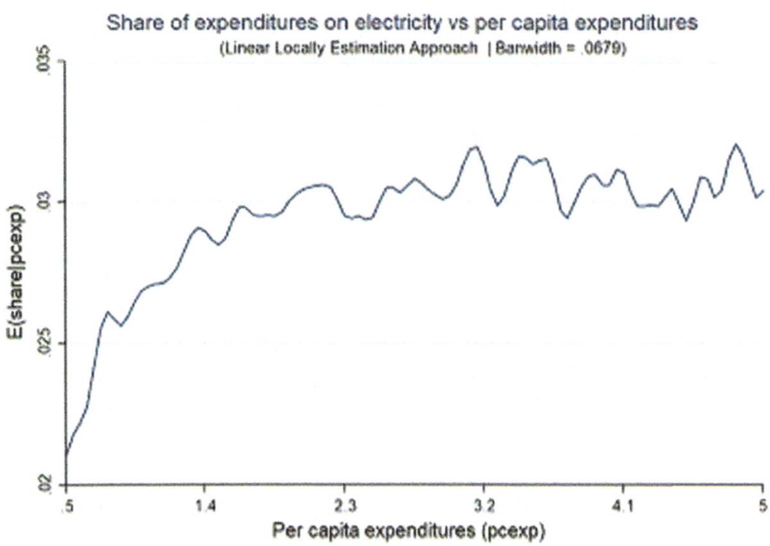


**Fig. 27** Engel curve for electricity

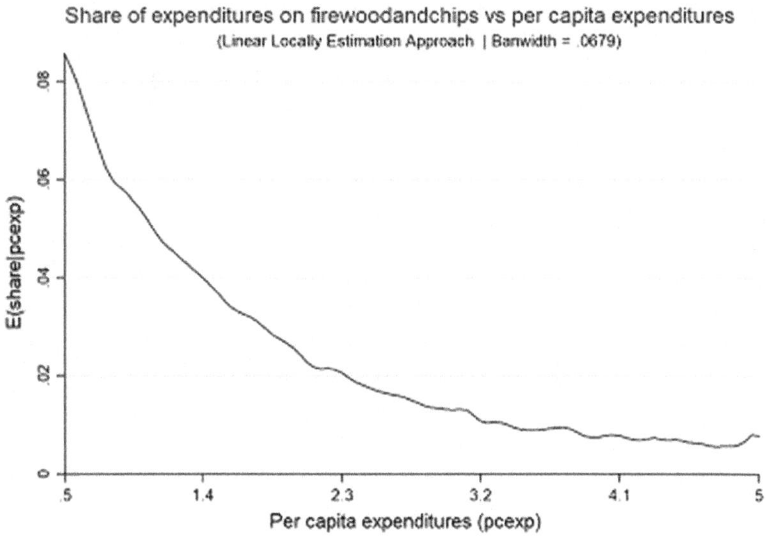


**Fig. 28** Engel curve for firewood and chips

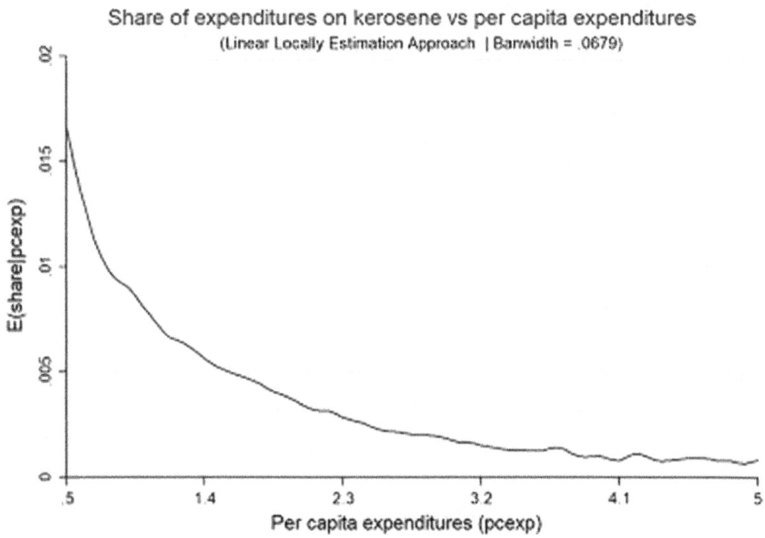


**Fig. 29** Engel curve for kerosene

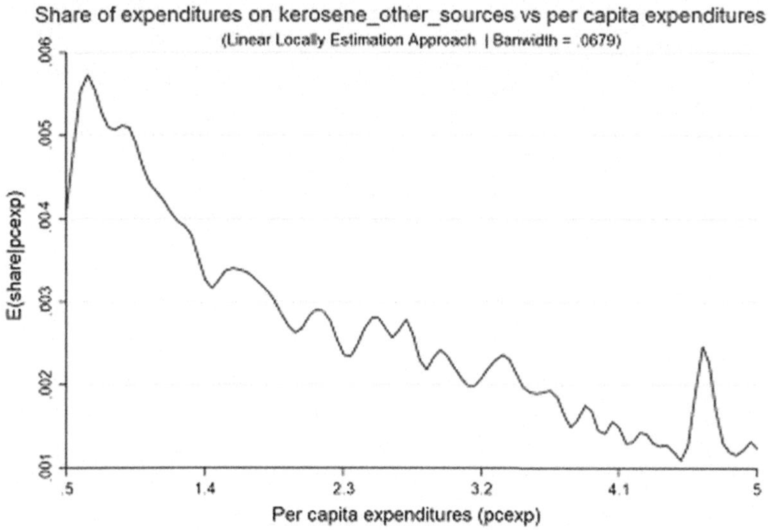


**Fig. 30** Engel curve for kerosene (PDS)

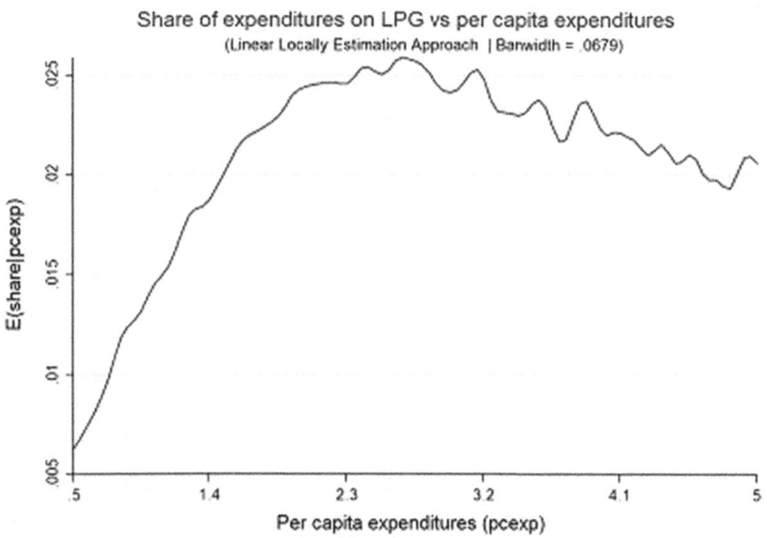


**Fig. 31** Engel curve for LPG

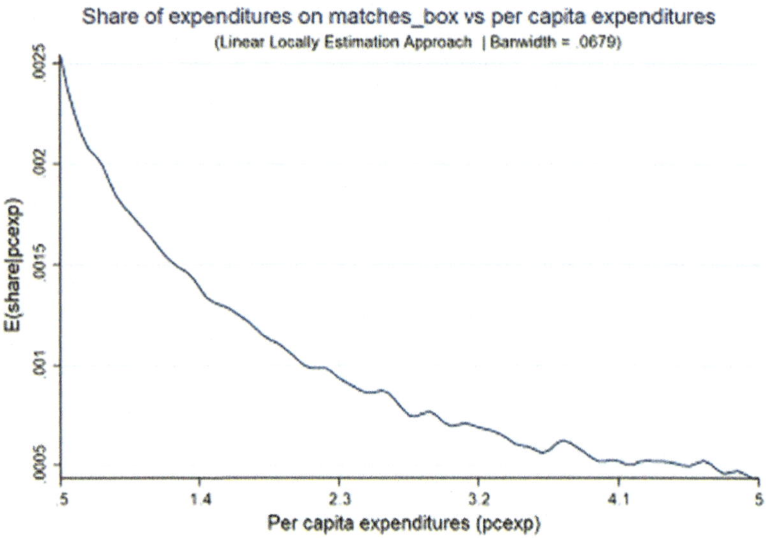


**Fig. 32** Engel curve for matches

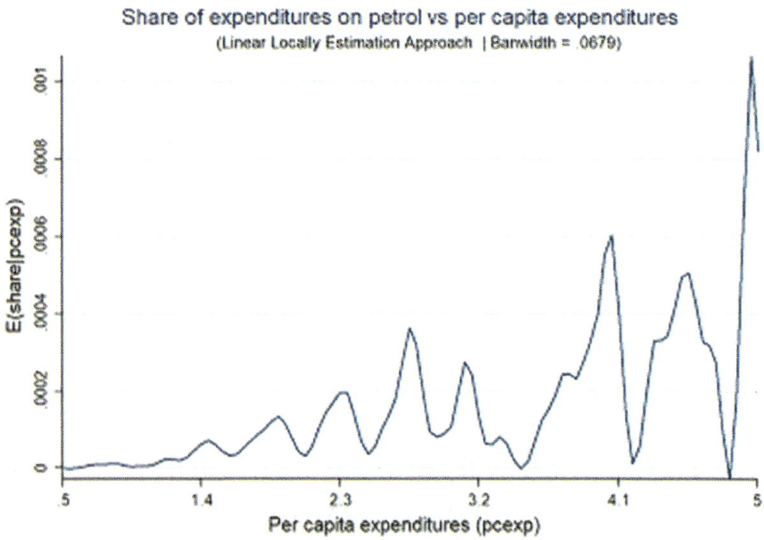


**Fig. 33** Engel curve for petrol

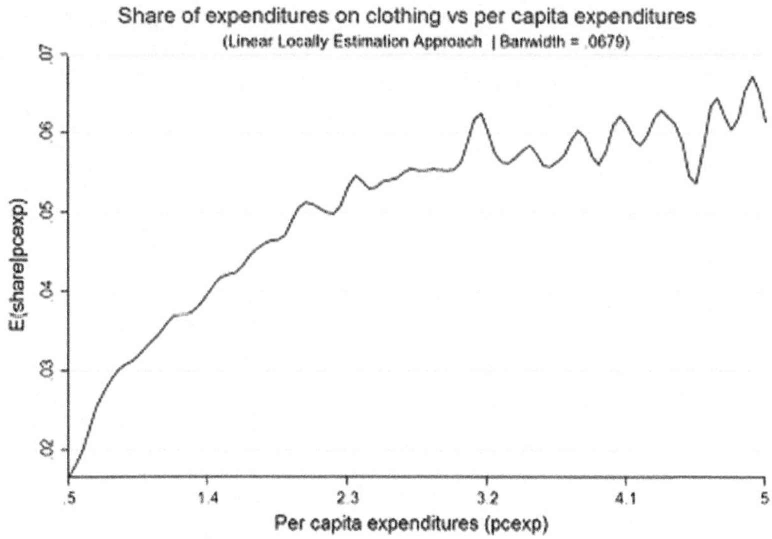


**Fig. 34** Engel curve for clothing

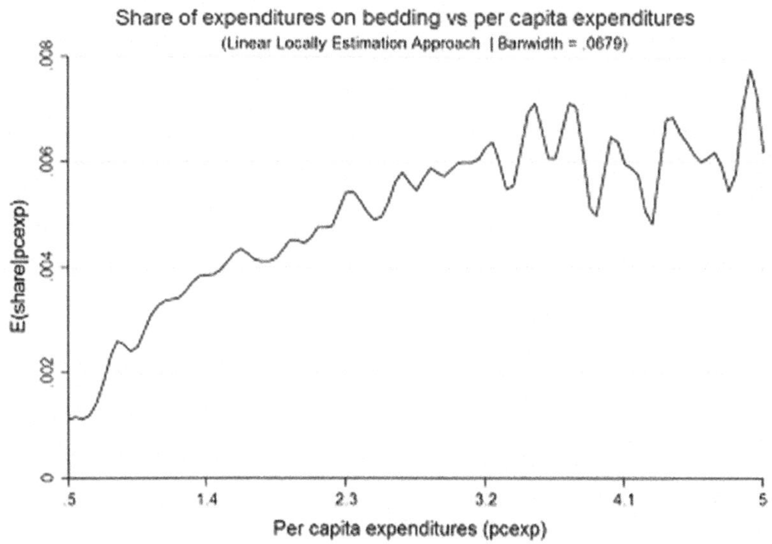


**Fig. 35** Engel curve for bedding

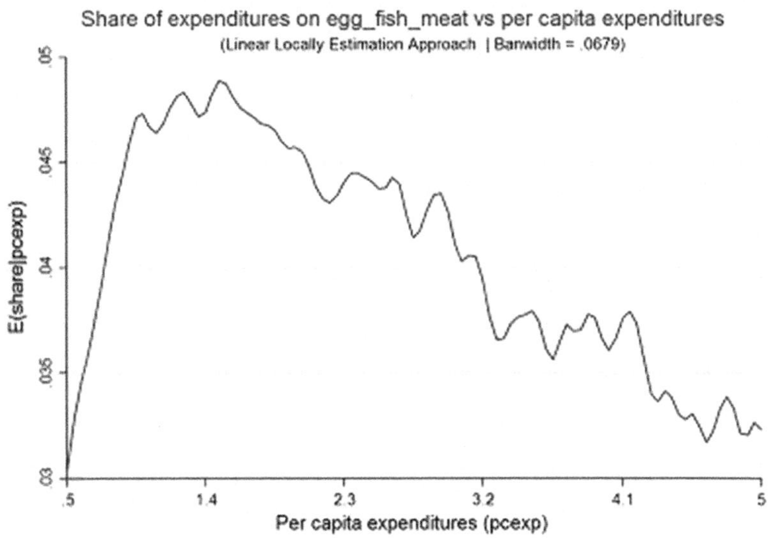


**Fig. 36** Engel curve for egg, fish, and meat

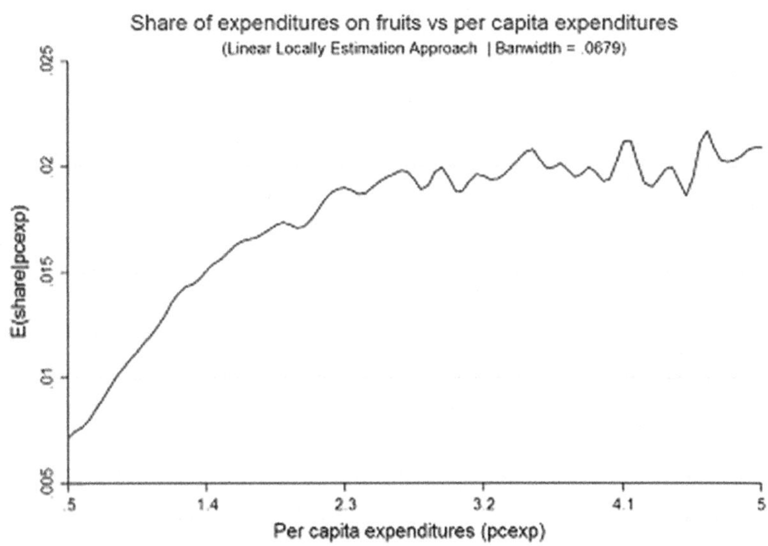


**Fig. 37** Engel curve for fruits

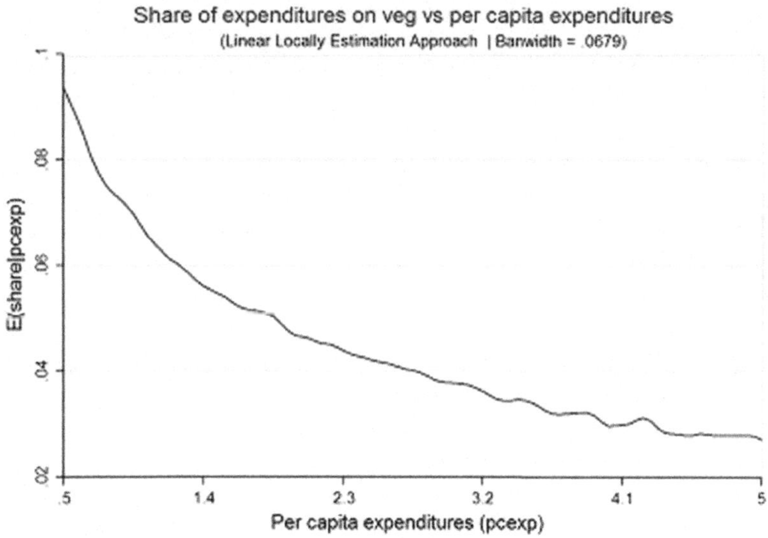


**Fig. 38** Engel curve for vegetables

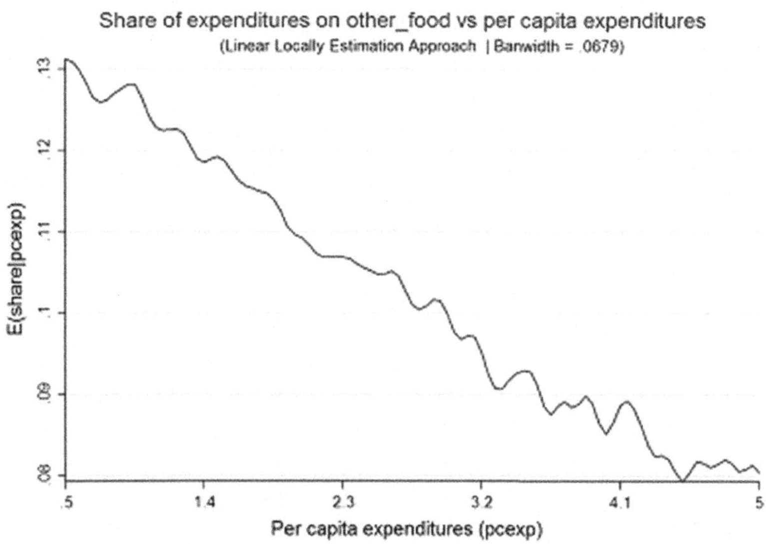


**Fig. 39** Engel curve for other food

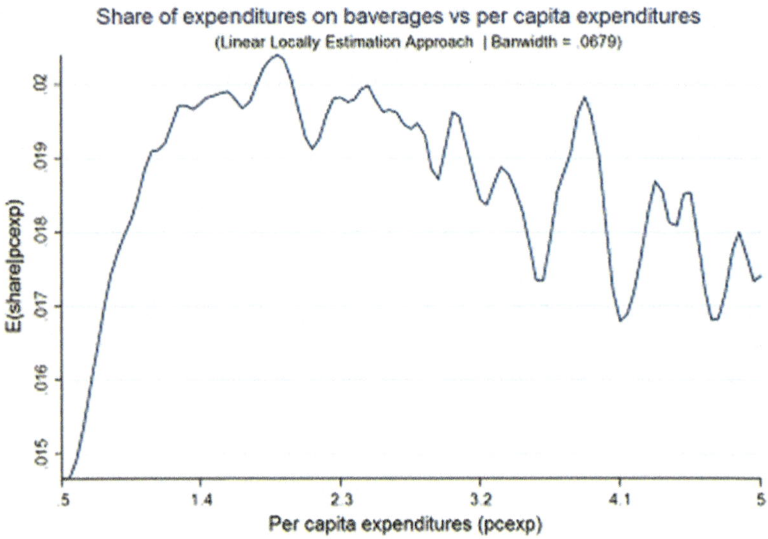


**Fig. 40** Engel curve for beverages

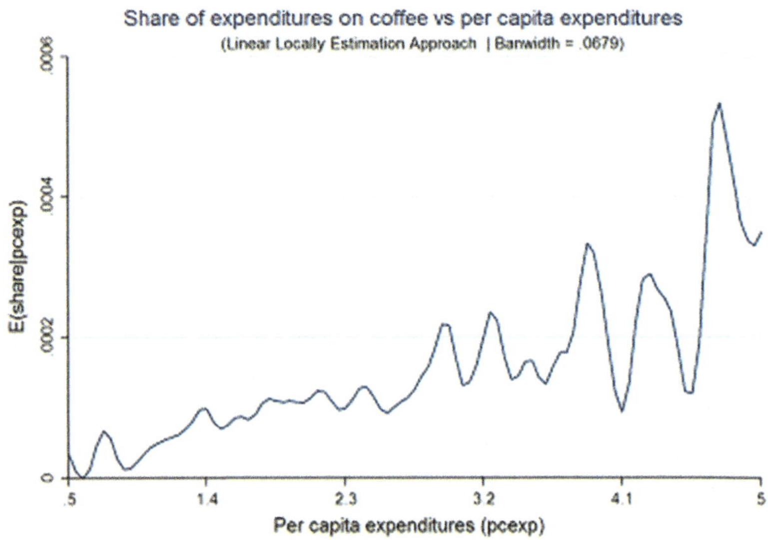


**Fig. 41** Engel curve for coffee

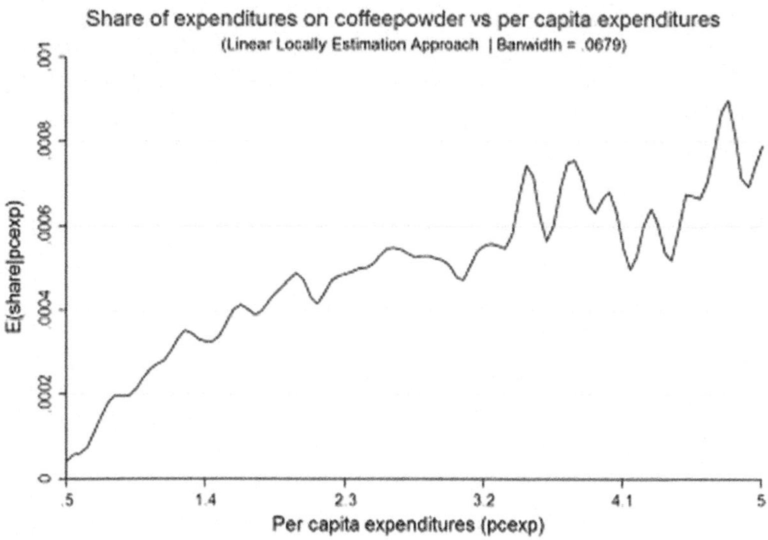


**Fig. 42** Engel curve for coffee powder

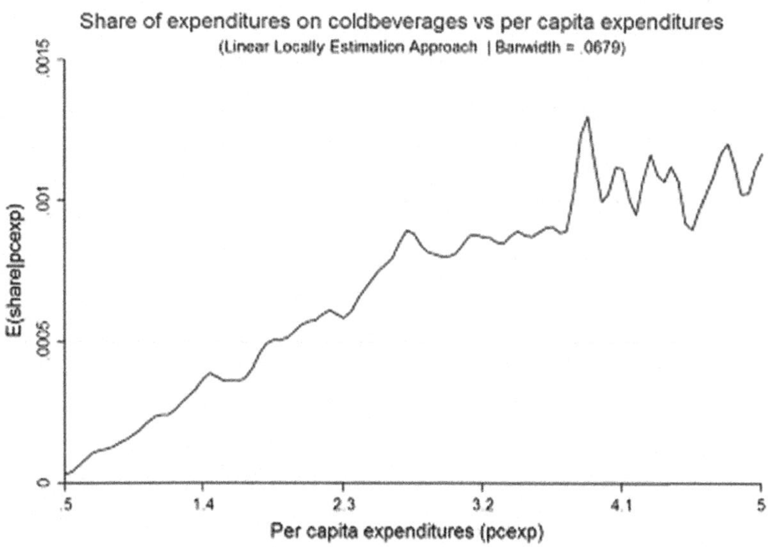


**Fig. 43** Engel curve for cold beverages

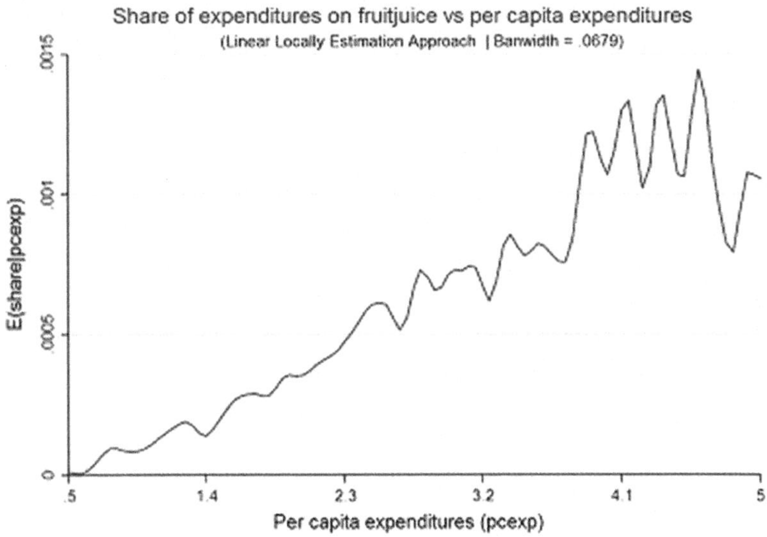


**Fig. 44** Engel curve for fruit juice

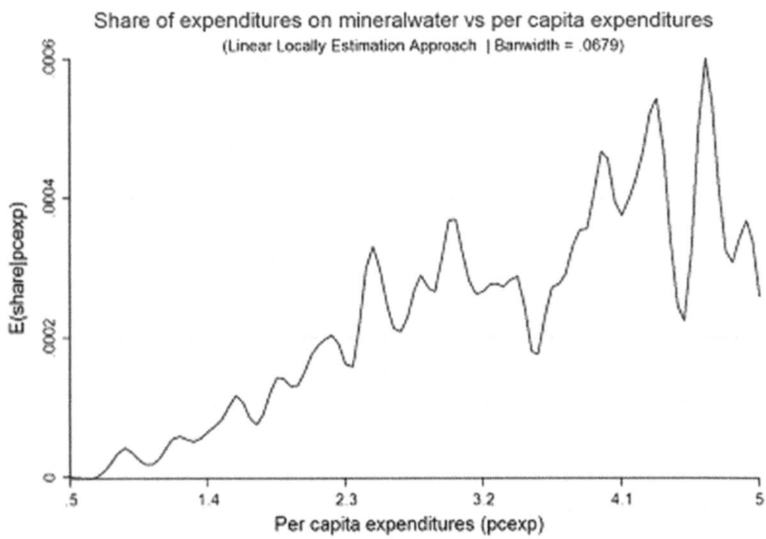


**Fig. 45** Engel curve for mineral water

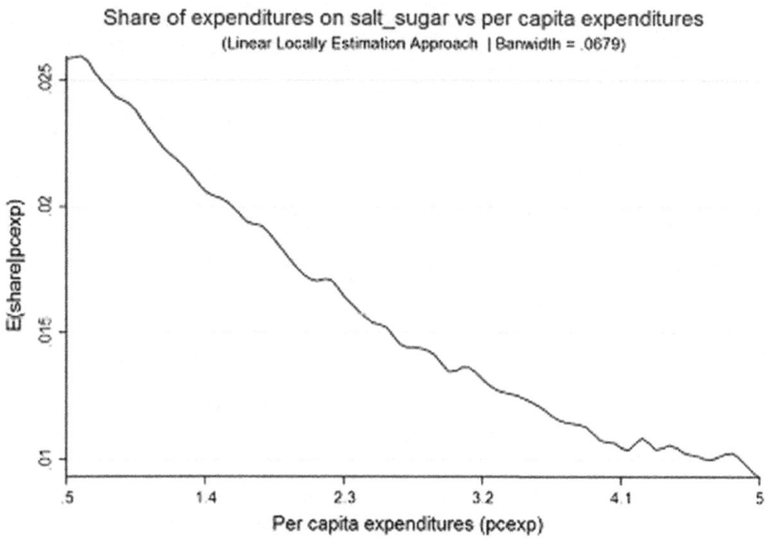


**Fig. 46** Engel curve for salt and sugar

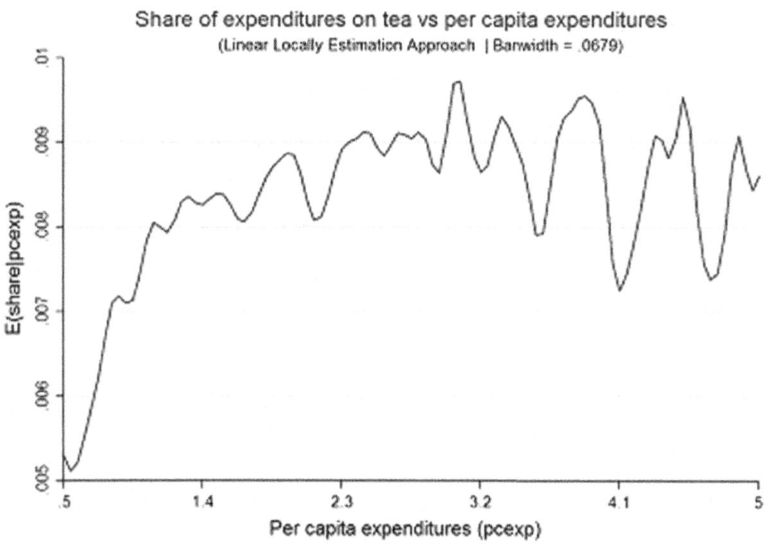


**Fig. 47** Engel curve for tea

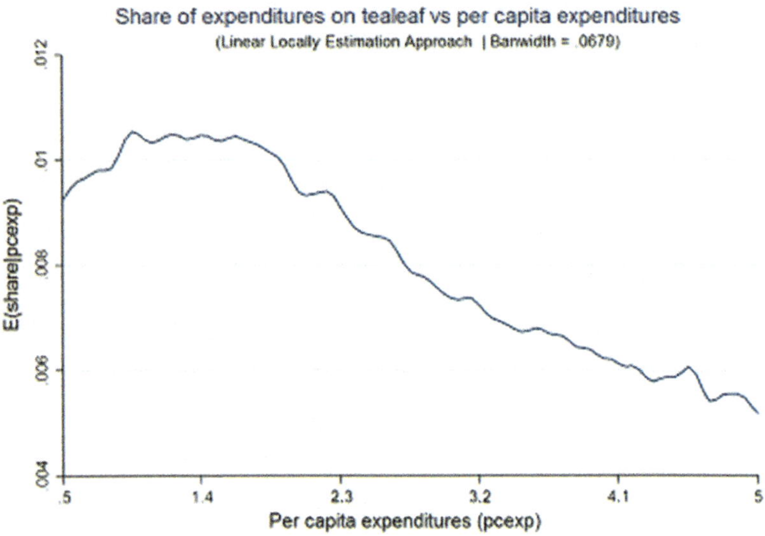


**Fig. 48** Engel curve for tea leaf

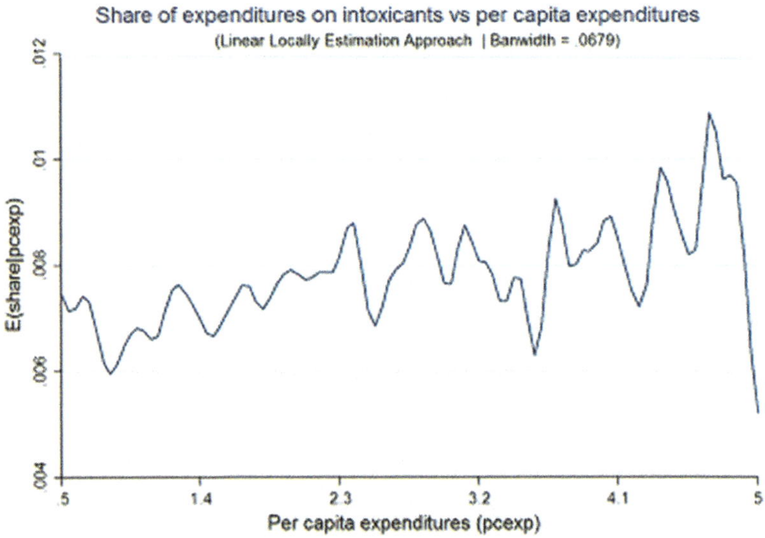


**Fig. 49** Engel curve for intoxicants

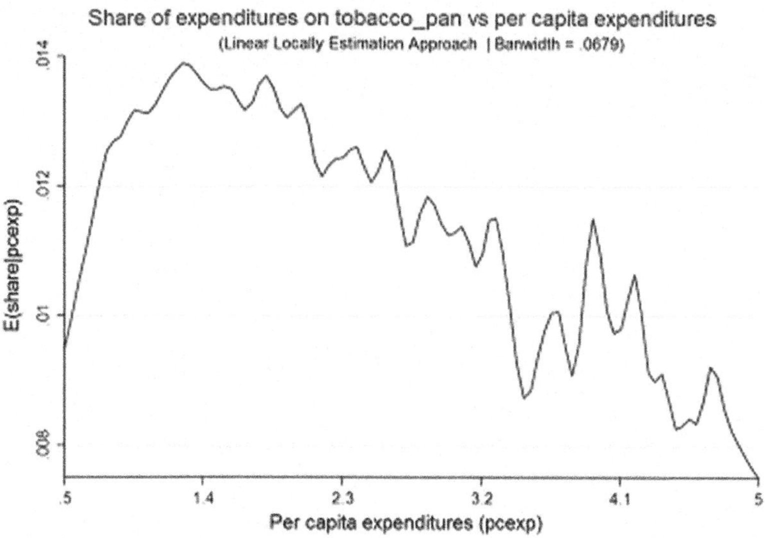


**Fig. 50** Engel curve for tobacco and pan

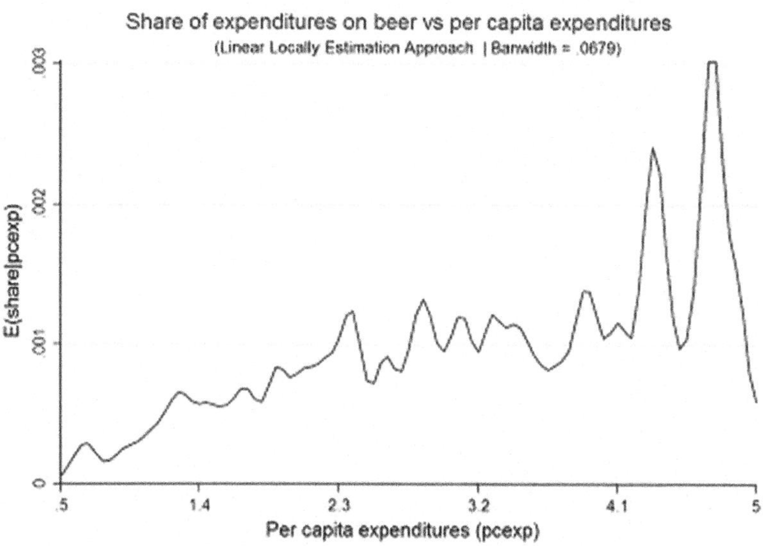


**Fig. 51** Engel curve for beer

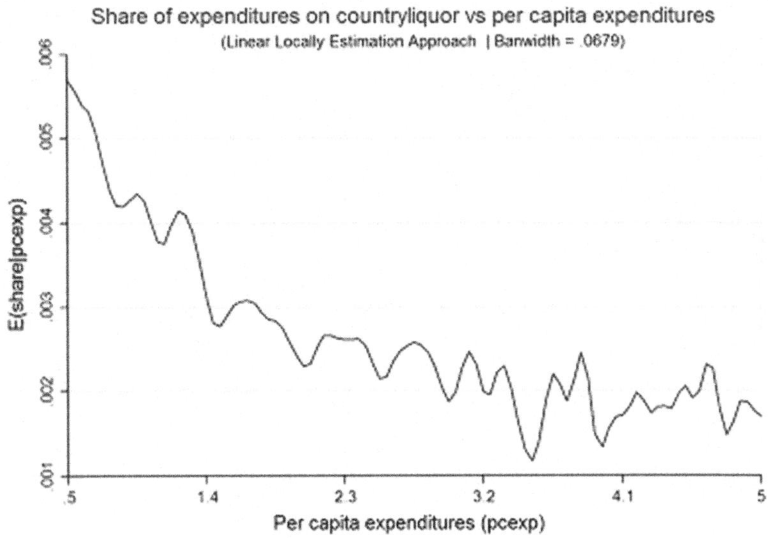


**Fig. 52** Engel curve for country liquor

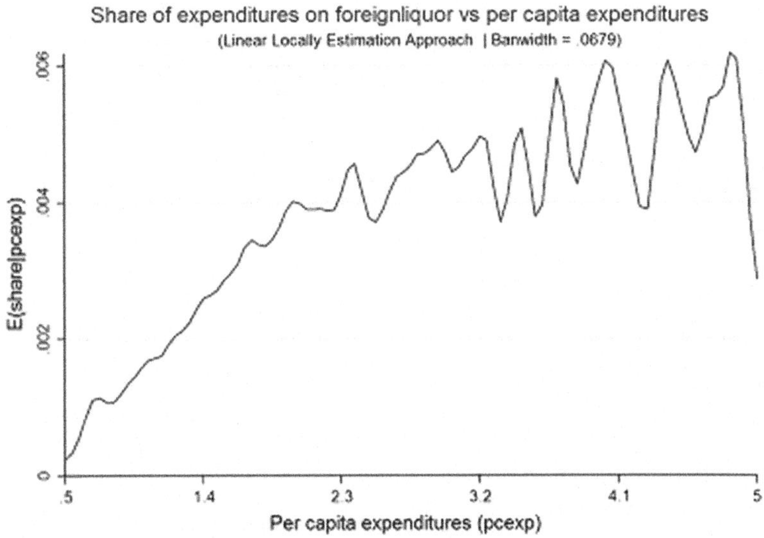


**Fig. 53** Engel curve for foreign liquor

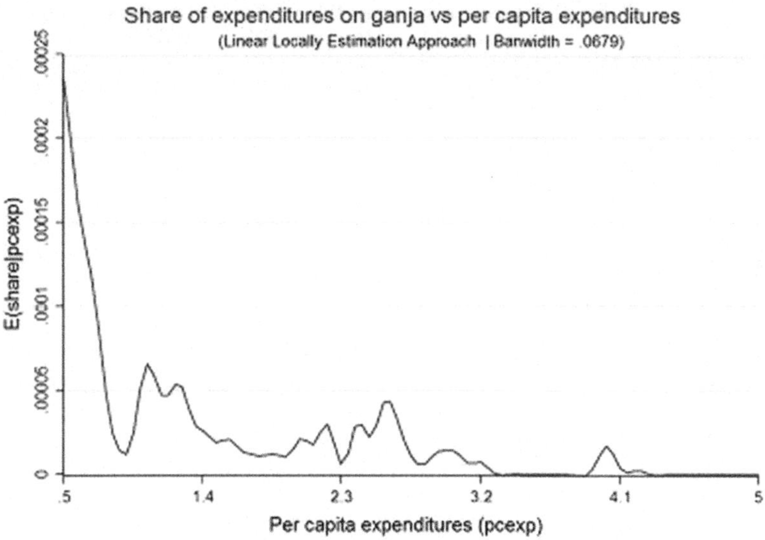


**Fig. 54** Engel curve for ganja

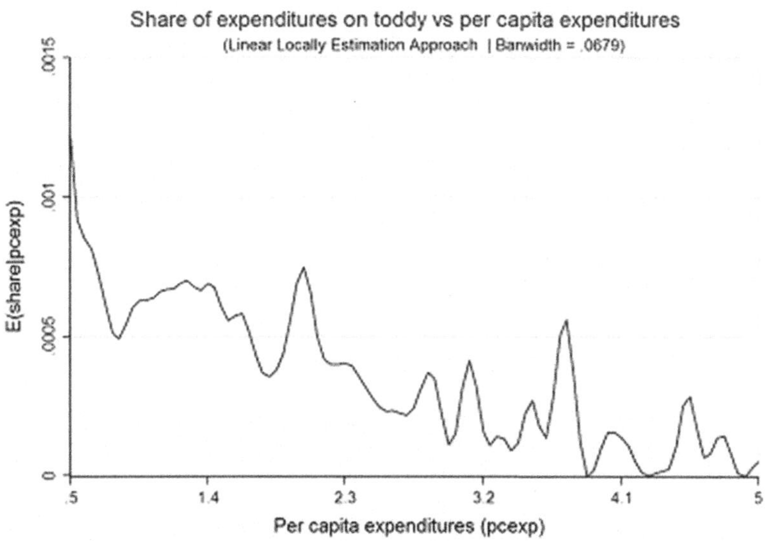


**Fig. 55** Engel curve for toddy

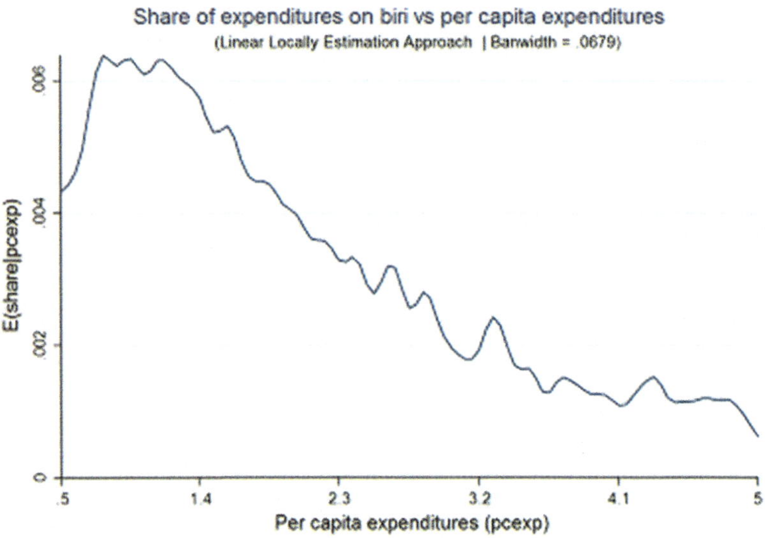


**Fig. 56** Engel curve for bidi

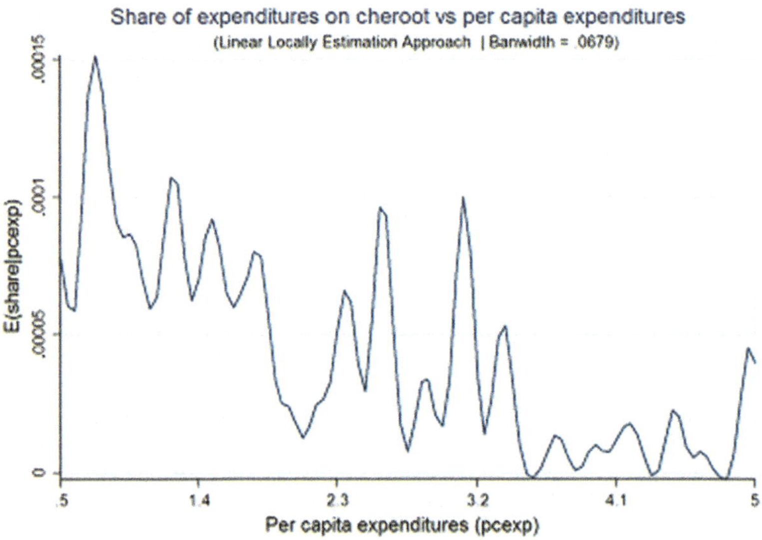


**Fig. 57** Engel curve for cheroot

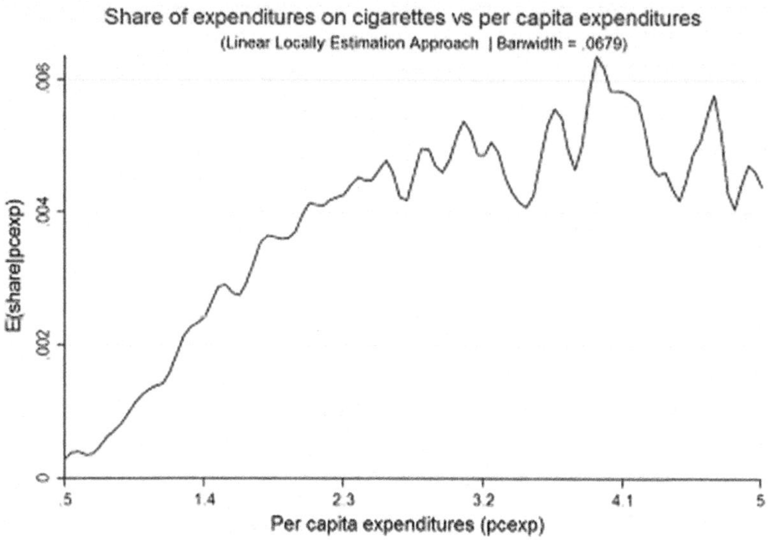


**Fig. 58** Engel curve for cigarettes

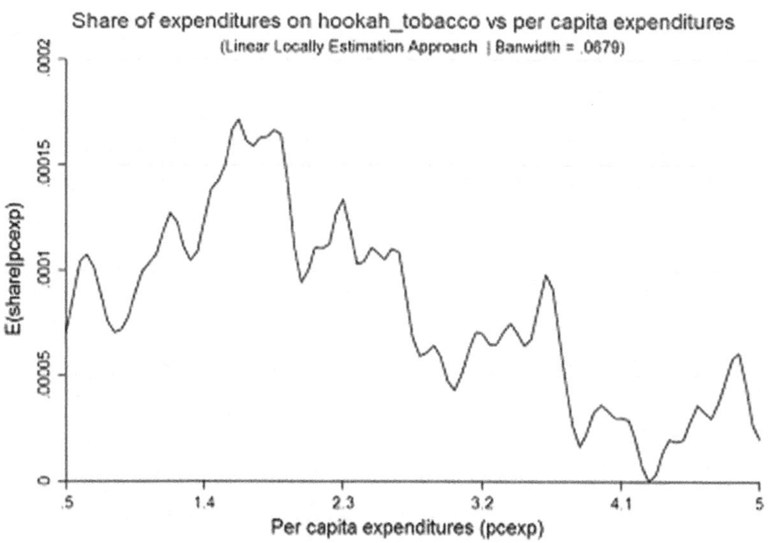


**Fig. 59** Engel curve for hookah and tobacco

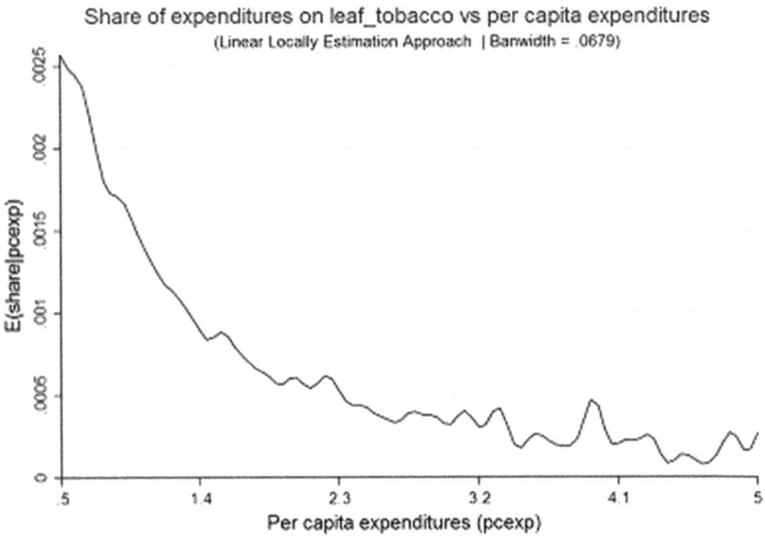


**Fig. 60** Engel curve for leaf tobacco

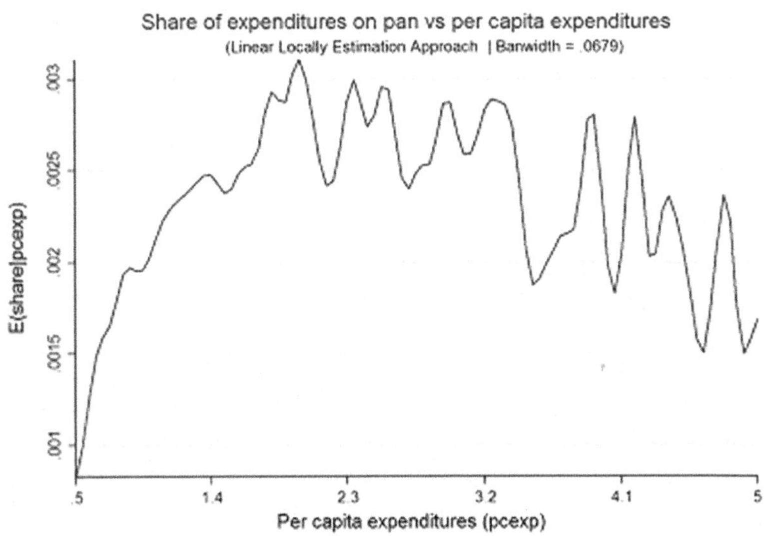


**Fig. 61** Engel curve for pan

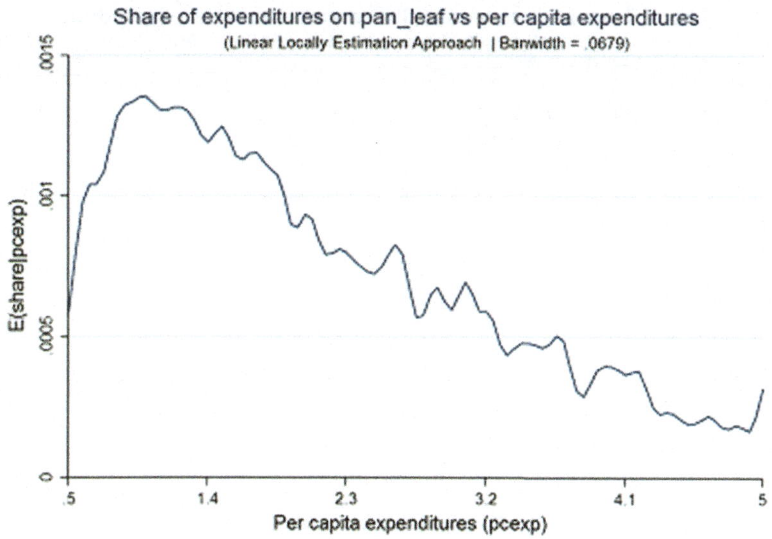


**Fig. 62** Engel curve for leaf pan

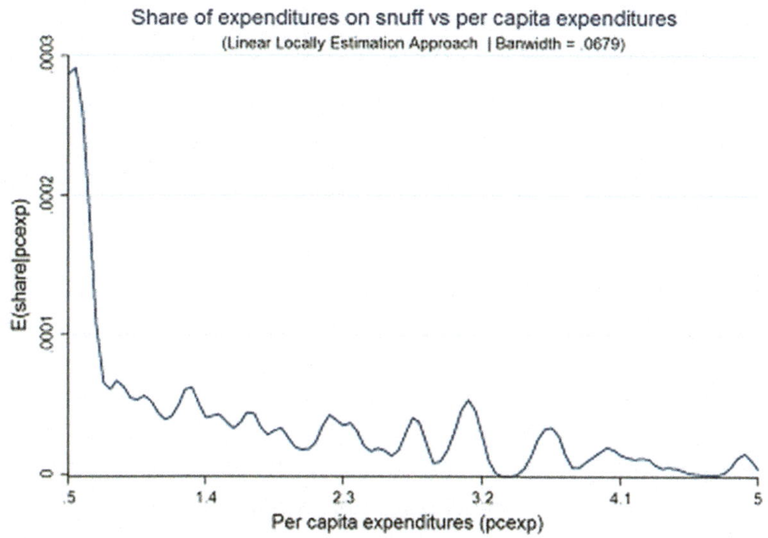


**Fig. 63** Engel curve for snuff

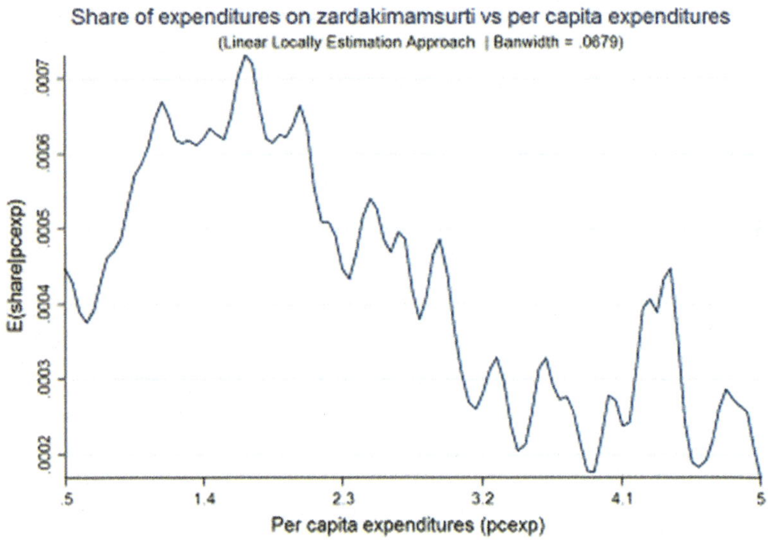


**Fig. 64** Engel curve for zarda

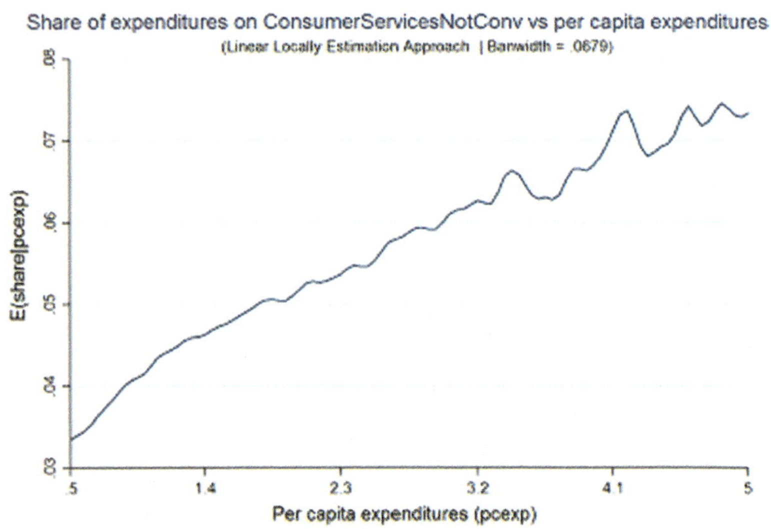


**Fig. 65** Engel curve for consumer services

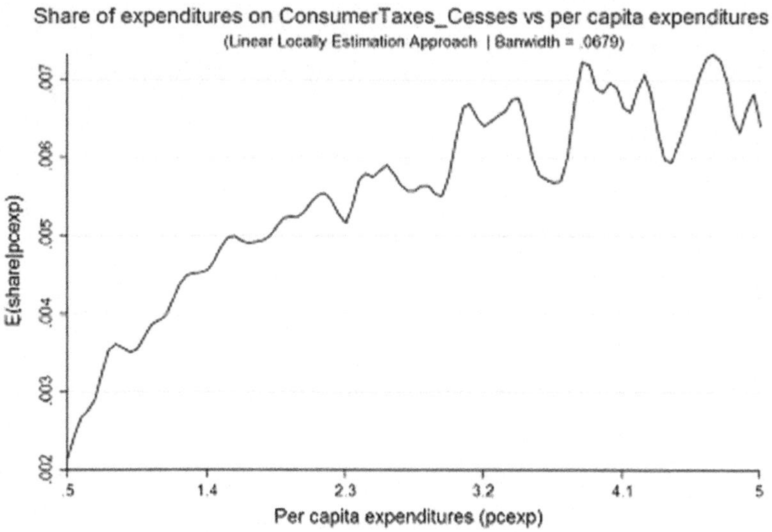


**Fig. 66** Engel curve for consumer taxes and cesses

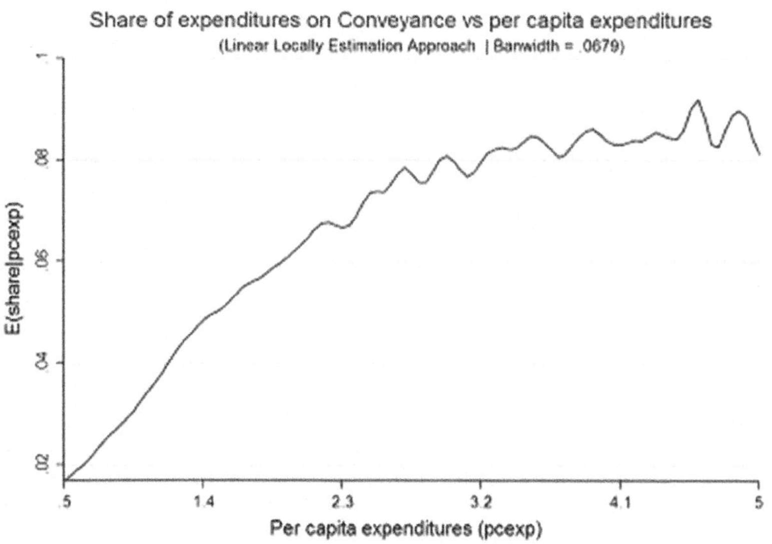


**Fig. 67** Engel curve for conveyance

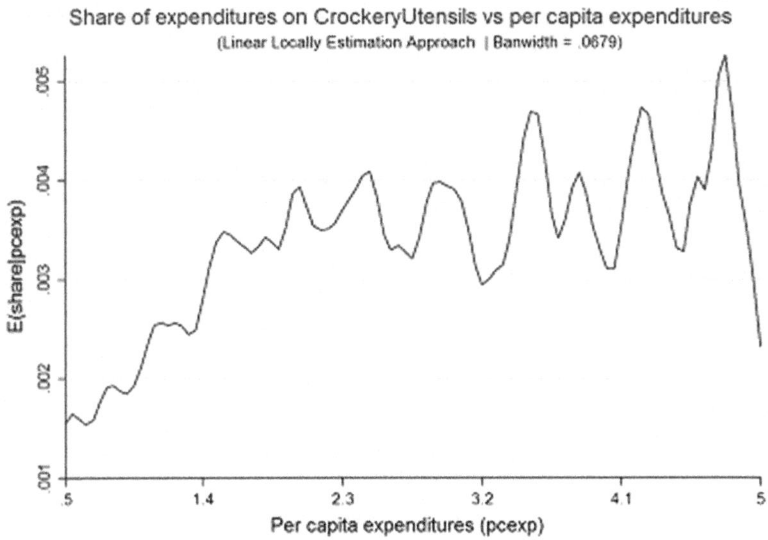


**Fig. 68** Engel curve for crockery utensils

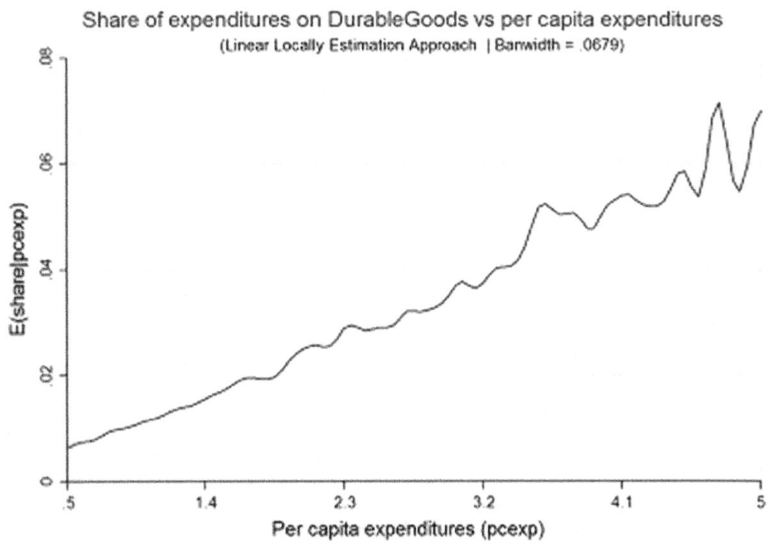


**Fig. 69** Engel curve for durable goods

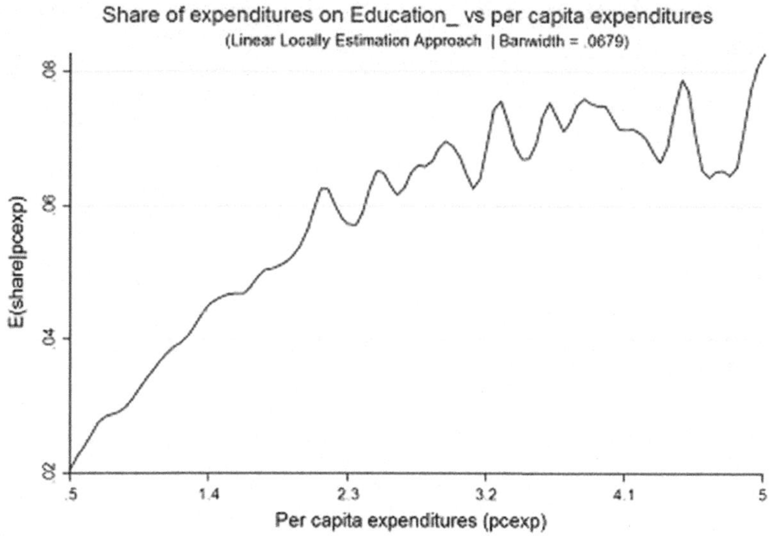


**Fig. 70** Engel curve for education

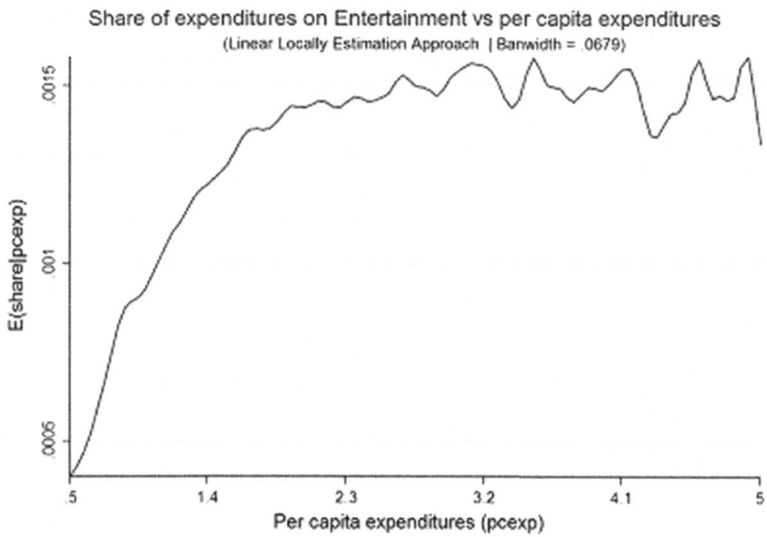


**Fig. 71** Engel curve for entertainment

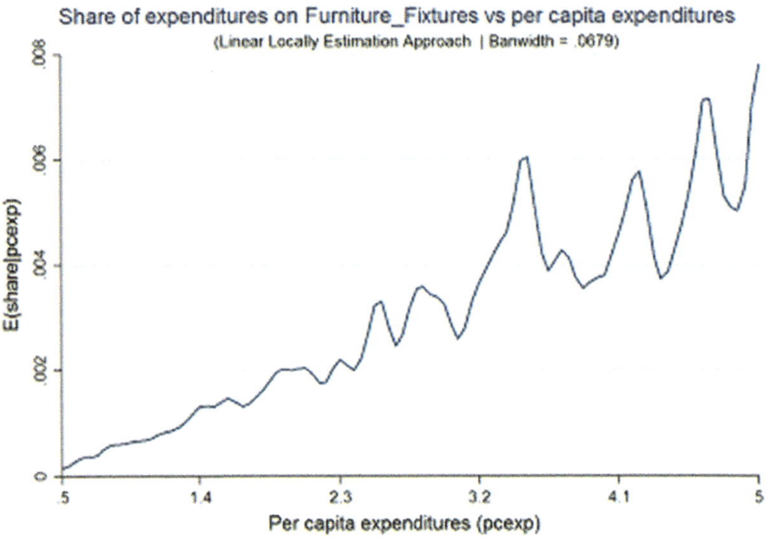


**Fig. 72** Engel curve for furniture

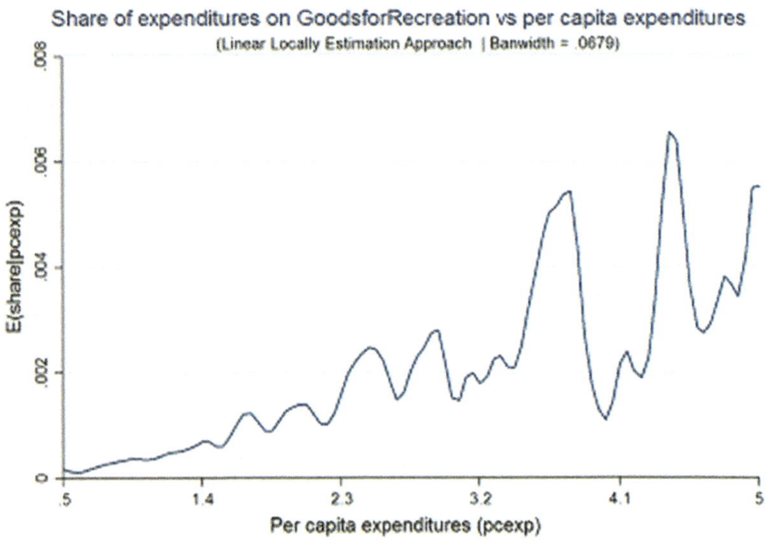


**Fig. 73** Engel curve for goods for recreation

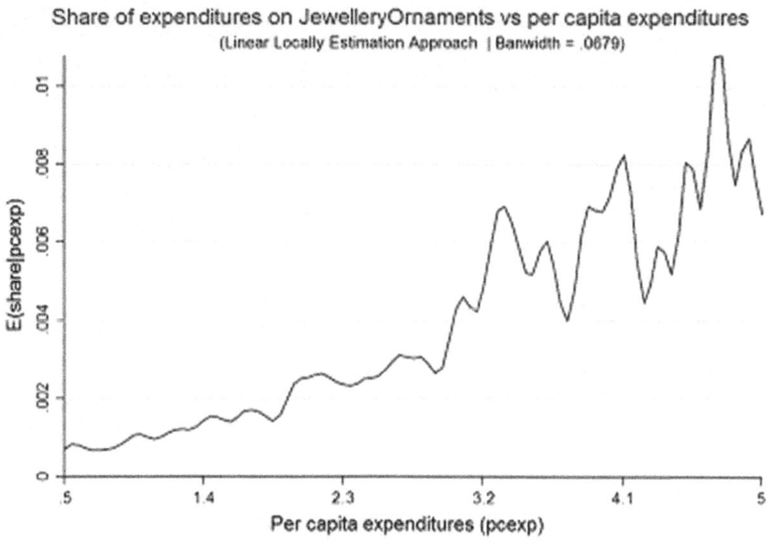


**Fig. 74** Engel curve for jewellery and ornaments

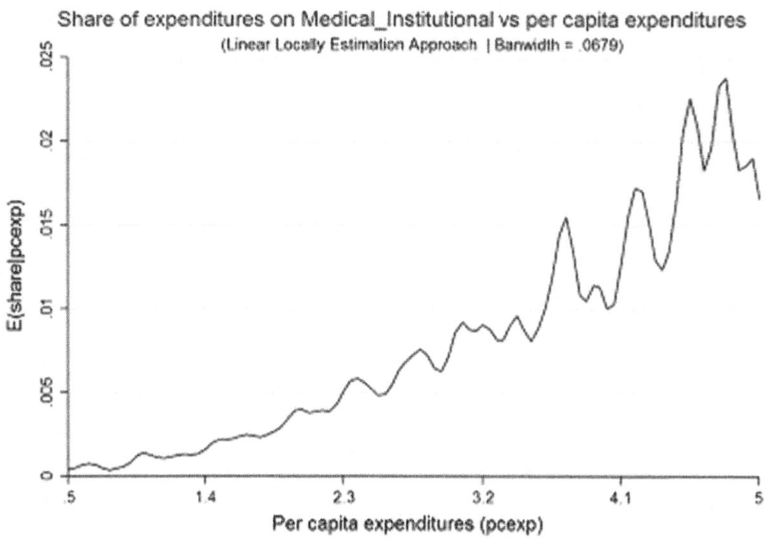


**Fig. 75** Engel curve for medical (institutional)

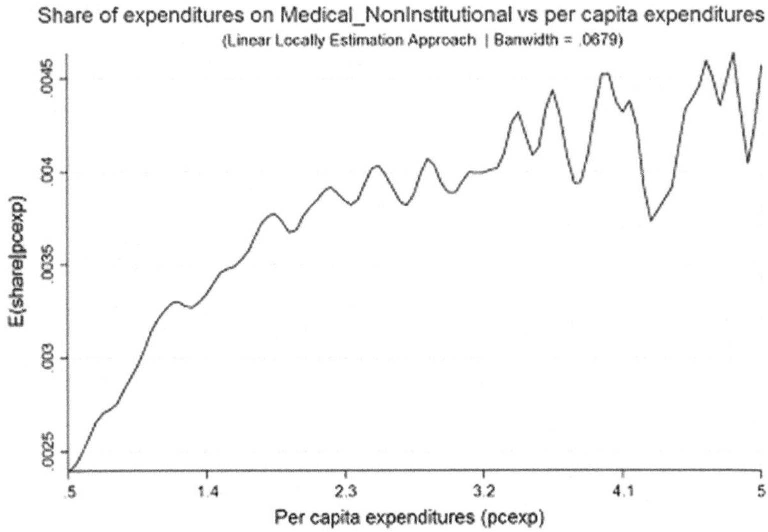


**Fig. 76** Engel curve for medical (non-institutional)

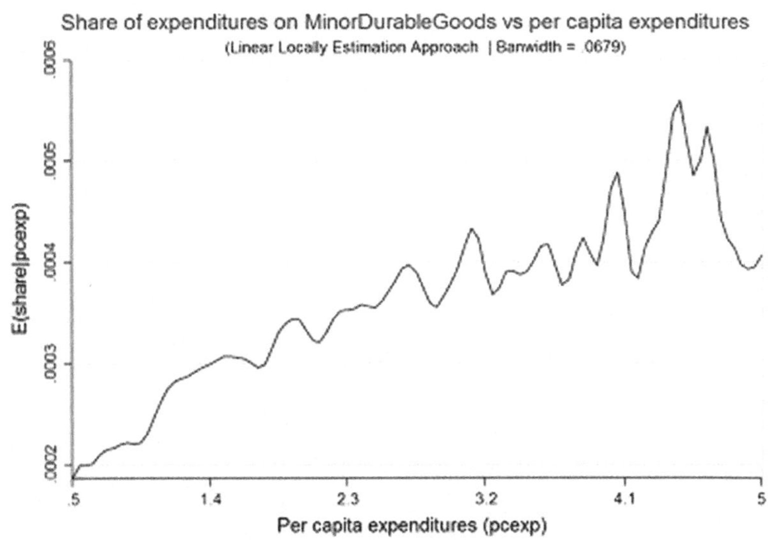


**Fig. 77** Engel curve for minor durable goods

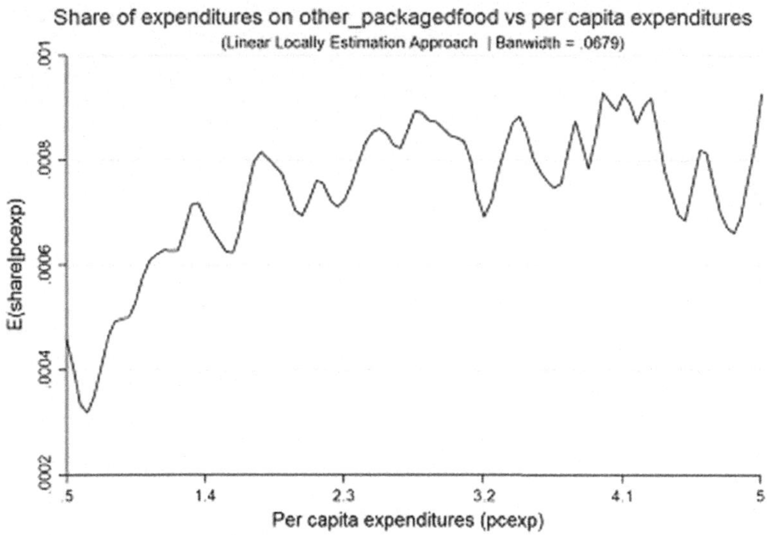


**Fig. 78** Engel curve for packaged food (others)

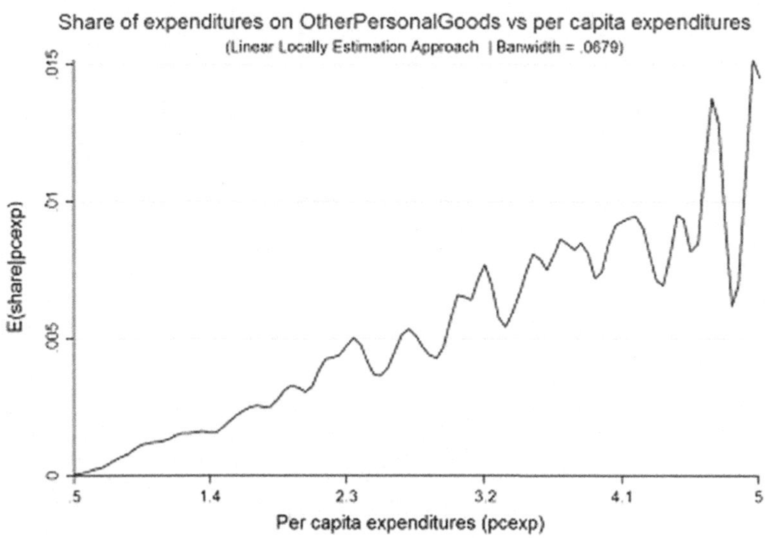


**Fig. 79** Engel curve for other personal goods

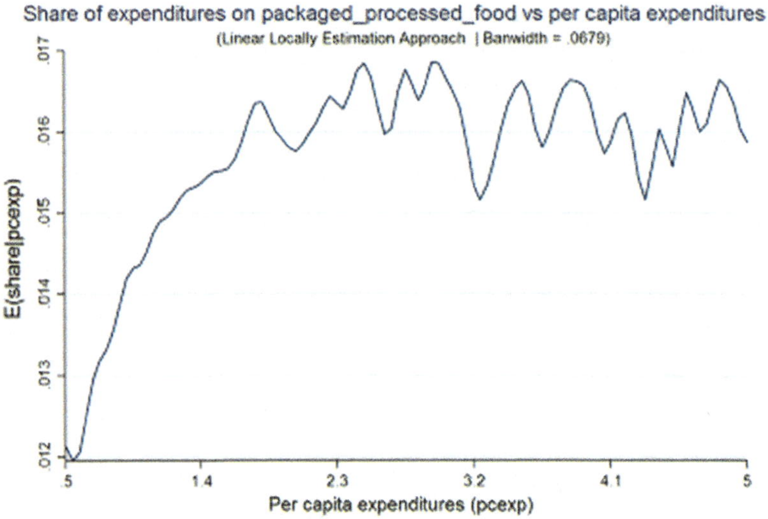


**Fig. 80** Engel curve for packaged processed food

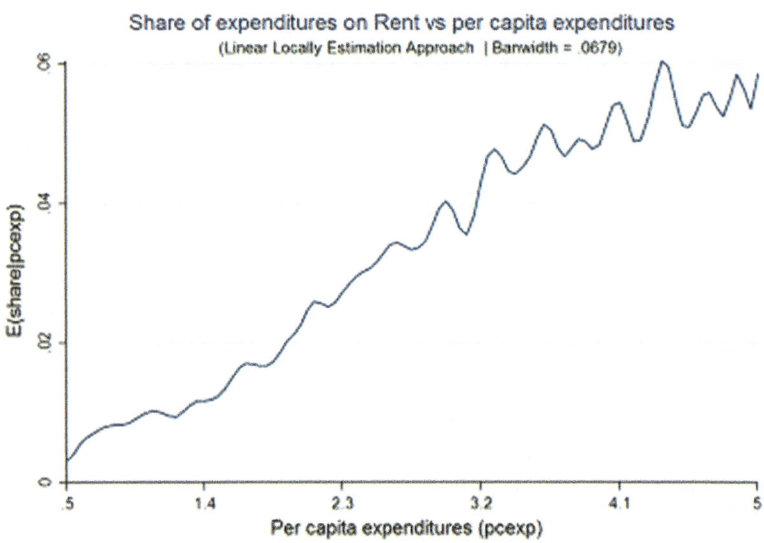


**Fig. 81** Engel curve for rent

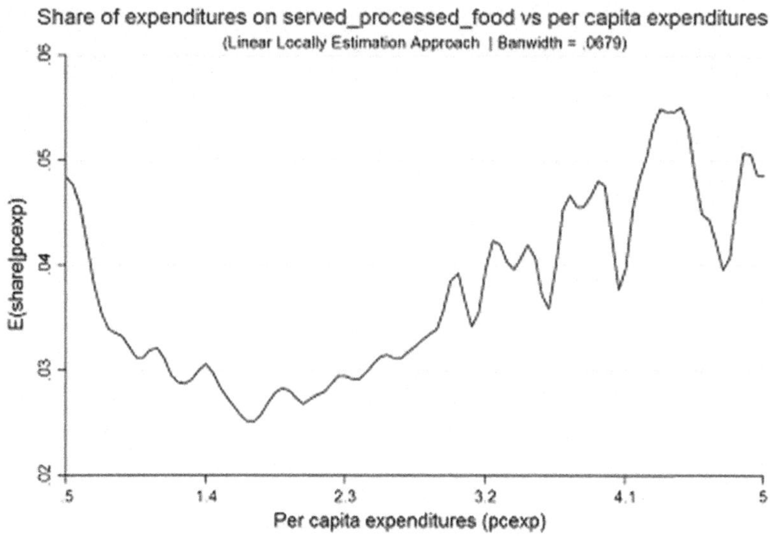


**Fig. 82** Engel curve for served processed food

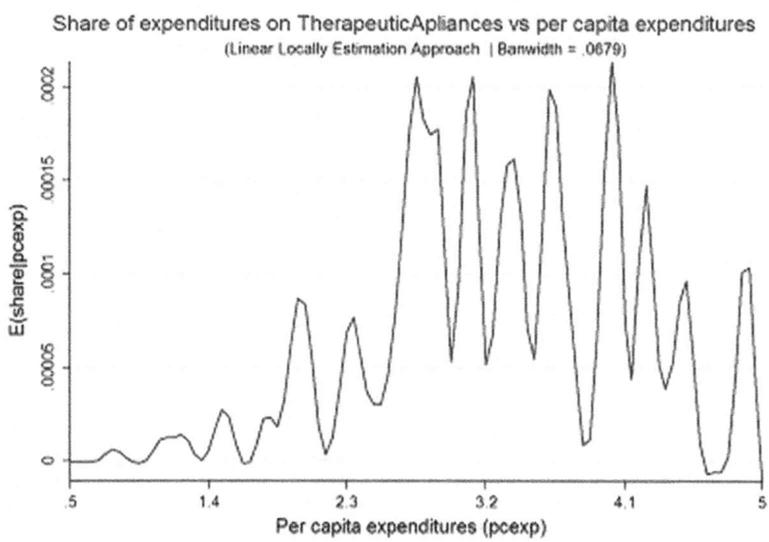


**Fig. 83** Engel curve for therapeutic appliances

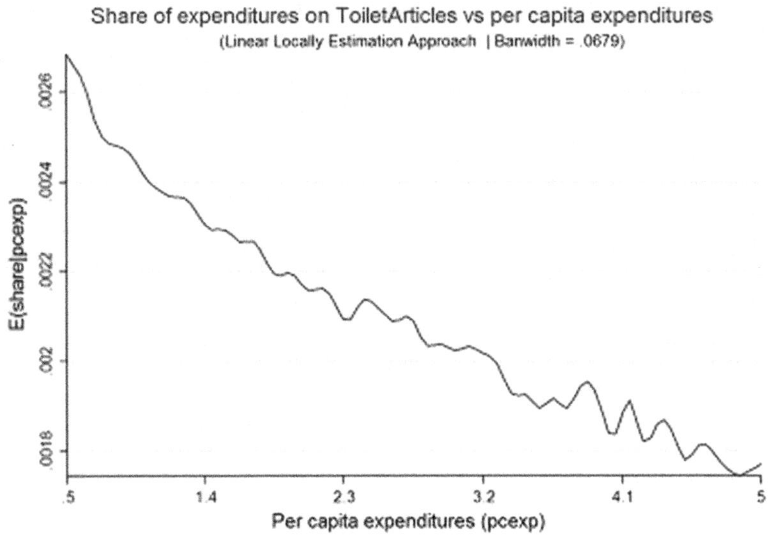


**Fig. 84** Engel curve for toilet articles

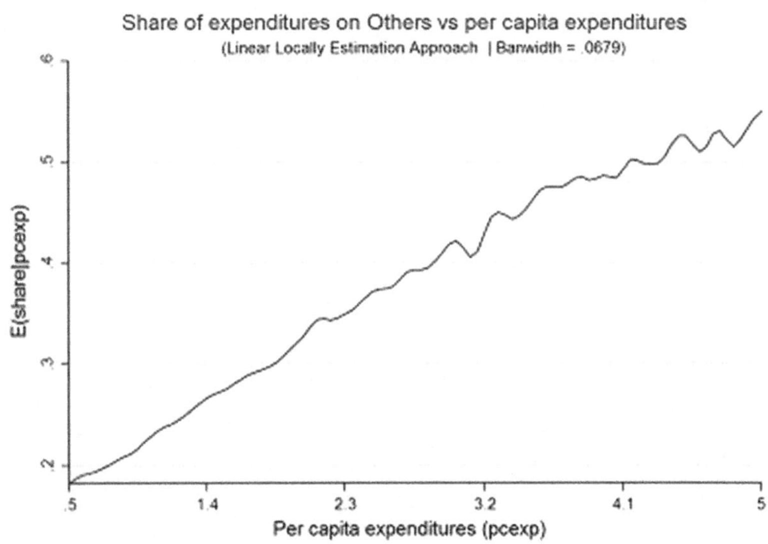


**Fig. 85** Engel curve for others

## References

Central Board of Indirect Taxes and Custom (CBIC). (2019). *Goods and service tax (GST) concepts and status*. Department of Revenue, Ministry of Finance, Government of India.

Deaton, A., Grimard, F., & Mundial, B. (1992). *Demand analysis and tax reform in Pakistan* (No. 85). World Bank.

Gemmell, N., & Morrissey, O. (2002). *The poverty impacts of revenue systems in developing countries: A report to the Department for International Development*. DFID.

Jäntti, M. (2004). *The distribution of the tax burden in Finland 1985–2001*. Mimeo.

Muñoz, M. S., Cho, S. S. W. (2003). *Social impact of tax reform: The case of ethiopia* (No. 3-232). International Monetary Fund.

National Sample Survey Organization (NSSO). (2013). *Household consumer expenditure survey 2011–12 (68th round)*. Ministry of Statistics & Programme Implementation (MOSPI).

Prasada, P. (2005). Incidence of commodity taxation on income distribution in Sri Lanka. In *The PEP meeting in Colombo*. Planning Commission of India. www.planningcommission.nic.in

Roy, P., Raychaudhuri, A., & Sinha, S. K. (2010). Is value added tax (VAT) reform in India poverty improving? An analysis of data from five major States. *Indian Economic Review*,131–158.

Sahn, M. D. E., & Younger, M. S. D. (1999). *Dominance testing of social sector expenditures and taxes in Africa* (No. 99-172). International Monetary Fund.

Yitzhaki, S., & Lewis, J. D. (1996). Guidelines on searching for Dalton-improving tax reform: An illustration with data from Indonesia. *The World Bank Economic Review, 10*(3), 541–562.

Yitzhaki, S. (1994). On the progressivity of commodity taxation. In *Models and measurement of welfare and inequality* (pp. 448–466). Springer.

Younger, S. D., Sahn, D. E., Haggblade, S., & Dorosh, P. A. (1999). Tax incidence in Madagascar: An analysis using household data. *The World Bank Economic Review, 13*(2), 303–331.

# Public Expenditure Quality of States for Education and Health, Does Rationalisation of Grants Matter?

**Vikas Dixit**

## 1 Introduction

There is a general belief that, pursuant to the recommendations of the Fourteenth Finance Commission (FC-XIV), the increase in general purpose transfers through enhanced tax devolution and reduction in specific purpose or conditional grants[1] might have provided greater fiscal autonomy to States. In fact, State Government finances, in general have witnessed a deterioration since 2011–2012, and in particular, the period from 2015 to 2016 has been quite challenging for State Governments so far as the management of their finances are concerned (Government of India, 2020a: p. 43). A recent editorial in Economic and Political Weekly, 21 November 2020[2] notes that despite substantial increase in tax devolution to States from 32 to 42% recommended by FC-XIV, the effective share of States in Central taxes remains almost at its previous level of 32%. This has been mainly on account of Centre having mobilised its additional resources through non-shareable cesses and surcharges, and also, due to cut in corporate tax rates and GST rate cuts as prompted by the Centre. Thus, in actual sense, States have hardly benefited from the changed scheme of intergovernmental fiscal transfers, rather they end up having large debt burdens at the terminal year of the FC-XIV, largely on account of the Ujjwal DISCOM Assurance Yojana (UDAY) scheme for the financial and operational improvement and revival of power distribution companies.

Though States have increasingly relied upon market borrowings to finance their fiscal deficits and they also recourse to off-budget liabilities even to finance their

[1] These grants are mostly in the form of Centrally Sponsored Schemes (CSSs)—an aggressive intervention of the Union in State subjects with a view to ensuring minimum standard of public services to the people and thus promote national development agenda.

[2] Available at https://www.epw.in/journal/2020/46/editorials/state-state-finances.html.

V. Dixit (✉)
Department of Economics, Jadavpur University, Kolkata, West Bengal 700032, India
e-mail: vikalp7983@gmail.com



A. Raychaudhuri and A. Ghose (eds.), *Managing Pandemic and Correcting Development Fundamentals*, India Studies in Business and Economics,
https://doi.org/10.1007/978-981-19-8680-2_11

social services, a pertinent question is whether the most important social services, namely, education and health receive adequate attention from the State Governments. More precisely, whether State Governments spend adequately, effectively and efficiently on these two areas so as to address the ongoing concerns in these areas (Government of India, 2020a: pp. 268–272, 300) and realise final outcomes, which is in the interest of the nation as a whole. In order to answer these questions, an attempt is made in this paper to assess the quality of public expenditures by States on elementary education and rural healthcare through the lens of adequacy, effectiveness and efficiency of expenditure. Here one may argue that private sector has actively shared many basic functions and responsibilities of the Government, including those of providing social services like health and education to the people. It should, however, be noted that despite active and growing private participation in the delivery of various types of public utility services, a large part of the population still depends on Government for availing these services. This is partly due to the fact that basic social services such as health and education, which are meant for all, are quite expensive in the private sector, thus making these services unaffordable for economically weaker sections, especially in the rural areas. Another argument, that is equally valid, and which preserves the crucial role of the government in the provision of basic social services is the strong belief that public sector has well-defined regulatory frameworks in place for different types of services which safeguard the public interest at large. It is because of these reasons that two big-ticket Centrally Sponsored Schemes, Viz., Sarva Shiksha Abhiyan (SSA) and National Rural Health Mission (NRHM) were launched in 2001–2002 and 2005–2006, respectively, with a view of providing universal elementary education and universal rural healthcare services. The present paper, therefore, considers only expenditures by State Governments on elementary education and rural healthcare for assessment as these areas continue to be an important responsibility of State Governments. The rest of the paper is divided into five sections. Section 2 is concerned with the assessment of expenditure adequacy for education and health. It first outlines the methodology to compute the expenditure adequacy index and then presents state-wise results in terms of this index. Likewise, Sects. 3 and 4 will focus on effectiveness and efficiency, respectively, of elementary education and rural health expenditures. In Sect. 5, a simple econometric exercise is conducted to examine the impact of restructuring and rationalisation of grants and schemes on the adequacy, effectiveness and efficiency of States' expenditures on elementary education and rural health. Finally, concluding observations and some policy suggestions are given in Sect. 6.

## 2 Adequacy of Public Expenditure by States on Elementary Education and Rural Healthcare

In order to assess the adequacy of States' public expenditure on elementary education and rural healthcare, one should know the precise shortfalls in expenditures by States on these services. However, the lack of estimates on resource requirements for various public services on a regular basis (taking into account cost disabilities of different States) makes it difficult to directly assess the adequacy of expenditures on these public services. The absence of easy-to-use data on unit cost structures for providing various public services by States makes it further difficult to make such assessments by individual researchers in minor studies such as the present one.

Although the precise estimates on the shortfall in expenditures towards education and health by States are not available, different sources seem to indicate the resource inadequacy for these two services. For example, the National Education Policy, 2020 envisages that the Centre and States have to work together to increase public investment in education sector to reach at 6% of GDP at the earliest.[3] As per the World Talent Ranking released in November, 2020, India stands at thirty-fifth position amongst sixty-three economies of middle and high per capita income in terms of total public expenditure on education to GDP ratio which is 4.4%. India's ranking is 62 when judged in terms of total public expenditure per student enrolled at all levels (USD332) as well as in terms of pupil-teacher ratios at primary and secondary levels, which are 36.66 and 28.52, respectively (Institute for Management Development [IMD], 2020). The current scenario in India's health sector is even worse, and COVID-19 pandemic crisis has exposed it further. According to the National Health Accounts Estimates for India (2015–2016) released in November, 2018, Government health expenditure accounted for 1.18% of GDP[4] (30.6% of total health expenditure), whilst households out of pocket expenditure constituted 60.6% of total health expenditure and 2.3% of GDP with wide interstate variations (National Health Systems Resource Centre, 2018). The National Health Policy, announced in 2017, aims at doubling public health spending to 2.5% of GDP by 2025 (Government of India, 2017). India's aggregate public health expenditure is much less than that of other countries (Government of India, 2020a: pp. 269–270), especially when India's public investment in healthcare is compared with some other peer member economies.[5]

In the light of the observations from various sources discussed above, and in view of the fact that the estimates of resource requirements for services like education and health are not attempted and provided on a regular basis by any Government and non-Government organisation, the present analysis of adequacy and effectiveness of public expenditure by States on elementary education and rural healthcare has no other option but to assess the relative performance of States in these contexts as the next good approximation. To be more specific, the adequacy of a particular State is thus assessed vis-à-vis the best performing State. In other words, how adequate a State's Government expenditure is relative to the best performing State. This implies that we are interested in expenditure adequacy of a State which increases being closer

[3] Available at https://pib.gov.in/PressReleaseIframePage.aspx?PRID=1654058.

[4] This ratio of general Government (Centre and States combined) health expenditure to GDP comes out to be less than 1% during 2018–2019 (Government of India, 2020a: p. 268).

[5] See https://www.livemint.com/news/india/india-s-economy-needs-big-dose-of-health-spending-11586365603651.html.

to the best performing State. The similar type of concept is applied whilst assessing the effectiveness in terms of output/outcome oriented performance.

For the above purpose, this analysis assumes that a State with the highest per capita spending will be the best performer in terms of adequacy of public spending and vice versa. Similarly, a State having the highest achievement scores in terms of output/outcome indicators will be considered as the best performer in terms of public expenditure effectiveness (assuming that there exists a direct and strong relationship between public expenditure and output/outcome, assuming further that other factors affecting this relationship remain unchanged). In this sense, the methodology being considered in this study for computing the adequacy of public expenditure is dynamic in nature, as it takes into account changes in population and prices which are two most important factors affecting this relation. Had there been precise estimates of expenditure shortfall available from some authentic source for elementary education and rural healthcare for the desired sample period, those estimates would have been used as yardstick measures for comparing the performances of all States. In order to examine the adequacy of public expenditures of States on elementary education and rural healthcare, the methodology of Lalvani et al. (2009) is followed. Various steps involved in the computation of adequacy indices from these two types of expenditures for different States are explained below.

Step 1. Conversion of expenditure categories.

The Government expenditure categories on elementary education and rural healthcare are considered for the period from 2010–2011 to 2017–2018 (all actual figures) for each of the twenty-nine States (including the erstwhile State of Jammu and Kashmir). These expenditure categories are converted at constant prices using State-wise data on consumer price index (CPI) with base 2012 = 100. The two expenditure categories for each State are further converted perhead of relevant population of respective State. In other words, whereas the expenditure on elementary education (at constant prices) of a State is converted in terms of per student expenditure (for all students enrolled in Government and private-aided schools at elementary level in that particular State), the expenditure on rural healthcare (at constant prices) is converted perhead of rural population of that State. The State-wise enrolment data of students at elementary level is obtained from publications of Unified-District Information System for Education (U-DISE) and the State-wise rural population is obtained by subtracting urban projected population from total projected population of every State made available by the report of the Technical Group on Population Projections for India and States 2011–2036 (Government of India, 2020b). State-wise CPI data have been collected from the website of the Ministry of Statistics and Programme Implementation, Government of India, whilst the data on the two expenditure categories are obtained from Finance Accounts of various years of respective States.

Step 2. Transformation of expenditure series.

Each of the two converted expenditure categories from Step 1 is averaged over four years' period from 2010–2011 to 2013–2014 (called pre-rationalisation period) and from 2014–2015 to 2017–2018 (called post-rationalisation period).[6] This is partly guided by the purpose of the present analysis and partly to avoid any outlier in the data. Each averaged expenditure category for both pre and post-rationalisation periods of a particular State is then transformed separately by multiplying it with the inverse of the distance from the best performing State. The rationale behind computing the inverse of this distance is that the closer a State is to the best performing State (i.e. the smaller the distance in the denominator), the higher would be the newly transformed expenditure category. This is explained mathematically in the following manner:

$$ET_{ij} = E_{ij} \div \left(E_{im} - E_{ij}\right) \tag{1}$$

In the above equation, $ET_{ij}$ is the transformed expenditure category corresponding to the expenditure category $E_{ij}$, where subscripts $_i$ and $_j$ denote category (elementary education or rural healthcare) and State, respectively. The denominator $(E_{im} - E_{ij})$ represents the distance of $\text{State}_j$ from $\text{State}_m$ ($\text{State}_m$ being the best performing State) in terms of real perhead expenditure $E$ of category $_i$. Thus, lower the distance of a State from the best performing State, higher is its transformed expenditure and vice versa. Since the denominator of the best performing State would be zero, therefore, the expenditure category of the best performing State would be transformed as under:

$$ET_{im} = ET_{ik} + ET_i^{-} \tag{2}$$

where, the transformed expenditure category of the best performing State, $ET_{im}$ is the sum of transformed expenditure category of the next best performing State, $ET_{ik}$ and the average of all other States' transformed expenditures, $ET_i^{-}$.

Step 3. Computing the expenditure adequacy index.

The adequacy index, denoted by $Q$ of expenditure, $E$ corresponding to the category, $_i$ (elementary education or rural healthcare) for a State, $_j$ is computed as:

$$QE_{ij} = \left(ET_{ij} \div ET_i^{-}\right) \times 100 \tag{3}$$

To put Eq. (3) in simple words, each transformed expenditure category is normalised by dividing it by the average of all States and multiplying the quotient by 100 to get the expenditure adequacy index for a State corresponding to a particular category. Thus, States performing above average will have expenditure adequacy index greater than 100 and those performing less than average will be having less than 100 as their expenditure adequacy index.

[6] Here rationalisation means rationalisation of tied grants. The signs of grant rationalisation attempts were visible since 2014–2015 when budget provisions were made for 66 CSSs as against 137 CSSs and 5 scheme-based Additional Central Assistance (ACA) earlier. This number was further brought down to 30 along with some other guidelines providing greater flexibility to States in CSS. Also, all Central Assistance started flowing through State budgets since 2014–2015 against the earlier practice of directly transferring it to the implementing agencies.

Tables 1A and 1B contain the expenditure adequacy indices with respect to elementary education and rural healthcare for eighteen general States and eleven North-East and Himalayan (NE-H) States, respectively, during pre and post-rationalisation periods. Table 1A shows that Goa, Haryana and Kerala have performed above average in terms of their expenditure adequacy indices for both elementary education as well as for rural healthcare services during both pre-rationalisation and post-rationalisation periods. Whilst Chhattisgarh has performed above average in respect of its expenditure adequacy index for rural healthcare services during both periods under analysis, Maharashtra's above average performance is noticed for elementary education during both periods. All the States, which are found to perform below average in terms of their expenditure adequacy index for elementary education have shown an increase in their index values from pre-rationalisation period to post-rationalisation period. On the other hand, with regard to expenditure adequacy index for rural healthcare services, the below average performers in both periods have shown mixed trends. Whilst Bihar, Karnataka, Maharashtra and West Bengal amongst these States exhibited an increase in their index values, Madhya Pradesh, Rajasthan, Tamil Nadu and Uttar Pradesh depicted a decline in their corresponding index values from pre-rationalisation period to post-rationalisation period. It may also be noted that the variation amongst States [as measured by the coefficient of variation (CV)] is observed to be larger for expenditure adequacy index of elementary education as compared to that of rural healthcare services during both pre and post-rationalisation periods. However, when comparing the two periods under analysis, CV of expenditure adequacy index for elementary education has fallen, whilst that of rural healthcare services rose from pre-rationalisation period to post-rationalisation period.

A glance at the relative positions of different States in terms of expenditure adequacy indices for elementary education and rural healthcare services (given in Table 1A) seems to reveal varying expenditure priorities of these States for the two services under consideration. Only Goa has occupied and retained the first position during both periods under analysis and for both categories of services being considered. Kerala, which occupied the second position in respect of expenditure adequacy index for elementary education during both pre and post-rationalisation periods, stood at the third and fourth positions in terms of rural healthcare services during pre and post-rationalisation periods, respectively. On the other hand, Chhattisgarh, which was at the eleventh position in respect of elementary education, stood at the second position with regard to the rural healthcare services. Maharashtra is yet another distinguishing State, which performed fairly well in terms of expenditure adequacy index for elementary education, but it reached the bottom in terms of its index for rural healthcare services.

The eight North-East States and three Himalayan States (referred to as NE-H States taken together) exhibit many common trends like those for eighteen other States. It may be seen from Table 1B that generally, the below average performer NE-H States have tended to show a sharp increase in their expenditure adequacy indices for both categories of services from pre-rationalisation period to post-rationalisation period. Many States have actually risen from an extremely low value of expenditure

**Table 1A** Public expenditure adequacy index—eighteen states

| | Expenditure adequacy index | | | |
|---|---|---|---|---|
| | Elementary education | | Rural healthcare | |
| | Pre-rationalisation period | Post-rationalisation period | Pre-rationalisation period | Post-rationalisation period |
| Andhra Pradesh | 49.96 [8] | 110.93 [5] | 103.3 [8] | 52.39 [13] |
| Bihar | 13.85 [17] | 17.74 [18] | 40.27 [15] | 45.26 [16] |
| Chhattisgarh | 40.29 [11] | 67.31 [11] | 170 [2] | 250.64 [2] |
| Goa | 500 [1] | 346.82 [1] | 260 [1] | 336.71 [1] |
| Gujarat | 63.94 [7] | 79.76 [9] | 114.69 [6] | 90.92 [7] |
| Haryana | 111.56 [4] | 228.25 [3] | 120.21 [5] | 160.24 [3] |
| Jharkhand | 21.71 [15] | 31.64 [16] | 107.14 [7] | 52.54 [12] |
| Karnataka | 71.46 [6] | 81.17 [8] | 26.64 [16] | 65.96 [10] |
| Kerala | 425 [2] | 261.34 [2] | 146.44 [3] | 142.06 [4] |
| Madhya Pradesh | 27.33 [13] | 53.22 [13] | 57.16 [14] | 38.5 [17] |
| Maharashtra | 126 [3] | 115.1 [4] | 8.97 [17] | 10.06 [18] |
| Odisha | 29.33 [12] | 39.38 [15] | 80.24 [11] | 133.61 [5] |
| Punjab | 24.86 [14] | 42.05 [14] | 142.07 [4] | 79.52 [9] |
| Rajasthan | 48.64 [9] | 63.81 [12] | 95.36 [9] | 83.36 [8] |
| Tamil Nadu | 85.82 [5] | 86.9 [6] | 78.95 [12] | 63.63 [11] |
| Telangana | NA | 69.52 [10] | NA | 51.18 [14] |
| Uttar Pradesh | 41.07 [10] | 81.57 [7] | 64.49 [13] | 46.82 [15] |
| West Bengal | 19.17 [16] | 23.49 [17] | 84.07 [10] | 96.58 [6] |
| CV (in per cent) | 140.74 | 89.06 | 59.45 | 81.57 |

*Note* Figures within brackets indicate State's relative position (rank) in terms of the index. The coefficient of variation (CV) gives the percentage of variability amongst States in terms of their index values
*Source* Author's computation using data from Finance Accounts of respective States

adequacy index for elementary education during pre-rationalisation period to post-rationalisation period. Only Himachal Pradesh and Sikkim have performed above average in respect of elementary education during both pre and post-rationalisation periods, Mizoram was the above average performer during post-rationalisation period alone. On the other hand, Arunachal Pradesh and Mizoram are the above average performers in respect of rural healthcare services. Here it should be noted that almost like the group of eighteen States, the above average performers amongst eleven NE-H States during both periods have shown a tendency of decline from pre-rationalisation period to post-rationalisation period. The variation in the values of

**Table 1B** Public expenditure adequacy index—eleven NE-H states

| | Expenditure adequacy index | | | |
|---|---|---|---|---|
| | Elementary education | | Rural healthcare | |
| | Pre-rationalisation period | Post-rationalisation period | Pre-rationalisation period | Post-rationalisation period |
| Arunachal Pradesh | 0.1 [8] | 77.76 [5] | 502.87 [1] | 350.77 [1] |
| Assam | 0.05 [10] | 11.92 [11] | 6.88 [11] | 33.8 [10] |
| Himachal Pradesh | 523.17 [2] | 129.68 [3] | 22.91 [5] | 52.78 [6] |
| Jammu and Kashmir | 0.09 [9] | 43.31 [7] | 10.45 [10] | 45.68 [8] |
| Manipur | 0.11 [6] | 36.2 [8] | 25.43 [4] | 102.1 [3] |
| Meghalaya | 0.11 [7] | 18.58 [9] | 20.92 [6] | 40.66 [9] |
| Mizoram | 0.23 [4] | 350.03 [1] | 443.15 [2] | 275.84 [2] |
| Nagaland | 0.3 [3] | 88.71 [4] | 15.56 [7] | 50.16 [7] |
| Sikkim | 575.61 [1] | 275.04 [2] | 27.96 [3] | 61.31 [5] |
| Tripura | 0.03 [11] | 12.62 [10] | 10.47 [9] | 22.07 [11] |
| Uttarakhand | 0.21 [5] | 56.17 [6] | 13.4 [8] | 64.83 [4] |
| CV (in per cent) | 222.49 | 112.2 | 185.02 | 108.71 |

*Notes* Same as for Table 1A
*Source* Same as for Table 1A

expenditure adequacy index amongst eleven NE-H States has generally been higher as compared to that for the group of eighteen States for both categories of services and for both periods under analysis. The coefficient of variation, however, declined for eleven NE-H States for both categories of services from pre-rationalisation period to post-rationalisation period.

Before this section is concluded, a corollary is worth noting. The decline in own tax and non-tax revenues of States was one of the various factors that contributed to the steady worsening of aggregate fiscal indicators of the States from 2011 to 2012 onwards (Government of India, 2020a: p. 78). The bulk of the increase in aggregate revenue receipts of the States as a percentage of GDP between 2011–2012 and 2018–2019 was mainly on account of increased devolution and grants-in-aid from the Union. The increased tax devolution was mainly due to the implementation of the recommendations of FC-XIV. In respect of the increased grants to States from the Union, it may be noted that compensation to States on account of GST is booked as grants-in-aid to States. Moreover, a part of the increase in grants-in-aid from the Union to the States was due to the fact that from 2014 to 2015, all Union plan grants began to be routed through the State budgets owing to the change in methodology of disbursing the grants under various CSSs. However, since 2015–2016 a reduction in these grants was witnessed mainly due to the discontinuation of the financial assistance provided to States in the form of Normal Central Assistance (NCA), Special Central Assistance (SCA) and Special Plan Assistance (SPA) given by the erstwhile Planning Commission (Government of India, 2020a: p. 80).

All the trends presented and discussed above with respect to expenditure adequacy index as well as the corollary of the preceding paragraph seem to support the case for increase in the relative share of general purpose transfers to States. This also seems true for eleven NE-H States, for which the reduction in specific purpose grants (more especially, Special Central Assistance) used to matter a lot as compared to the group of eighteen other States.

## 3 Effectiveness of Public Expenditure by States on Elementary Education and Rural Healthcare

The measurement of effectiveness as well as the efficiency of public expenditure is even more challenging than estimating expenditure adequacy, and this challenge is mainly due to the conceptual issues in these two terms. Whilst the efficiency relates inputs with outputs (achieving higher outputs with same level of inputs, or achieving the same level of outputs with lower inputs), the effectiveness establishes the relationship between inputs, outputs and outcome (the ultimate goal to be realised). Thus, when a Government spends on healthcare services, the funds are used on building up of health infrastructure, appointment of doctors, availability of medicines and vaccines, etc.; all this is done to see a healthy society in terms of improved life expectancy, reduced mortality, etc. Similarly, Government expenditure on education is used to increase educational attainments, improve pupil-teacher ratio, strengthening school/college infrastructure, etc.; but the final goal is to see an educated society through improved learning outcomes, increased literacy, improved qualifications of different age group population, etc. However, these relationships between inputs (especially public expenditure, which has to meet multiple objectives), outputs and outcomes are not that simple to work with, as many exogenous factors affect this relationship. Furthermore, the application of improved techniques to measure efficiency and effectiveness is often hampered by the lack of suitable data.[7]

Improving the effectiveness and efficiency of public expenditure is the goal of every Government (national or subnational), as it helps maintain fiscal discipline imposed by fiscal legislations and also makes it possible to realise increased value for money. Thus, improving effectiveness and efficiency of public expenditure is very crucial for Indian States, which are generally fiscally weak and heavily rely on Central transfers and even on off-budget borrowings to finance various public services. They formulate and implement their fiscal policies under a self-imposed fiscal discipline. It is in this context that this part of the present paper attempts to measure effectiveness, whilst the next part will be devoted to measure the efficiency

[7] See, for example, Mandl et al. (2008) for a discussion on issues in the measurement of effectiveness and efficiency of public spending.

of public expenditure of States on elementary education and rural healthcare. Various steps involved in the measurement of effectiveness index are given below.

Step 1. Choice of outcome indicators.

In order to measure the effectiveness of public expenditures on elementary education and rural healthcare of States, it is necessary that these two categories of expenditures be linked with their respective outcomes (the ultimate goals to be achieved by States), which are, generally speaking, universalising elementary education through SSA and Right to Education Act of 2009 and universal rural healthcare through NRHM. These two outcomes of universalising elementary education and rural healthcare have been proxied by a set of limited output indicators in this study. The two most important and easily monitorable and measureable goals to achieve universal elementary education are: increasing the gross enrolment ratio (GER) and reducing pupil-teacher ratio (PTR) at primary and upper primary levels. Moreover, improvement in learning outcomes is also captured through different measures, such as examination pass-out rate, basic literacy in reading and arithmetic. In order to achieve the objective of universal healthcare in rural areas, it is necessary that rural healthcare infrastructure be strengthened and trained and skilled health workers as well as qualified specialists be appointed so as to cater to the demand for rural healthcare services by rural population. Thus, for measuring the effectiveness of elementary education expenditure, five outcome proxies have been chosen, namely, GER in elementary schools, PTR at primary level, PTR at upper primary level, percentage of students in class V who can read at least class II text and percentage of students in class V who can perform division. Whilst the data pertaining to GER and PTR have been taken from Elementary Flash Statistics of the Unified-District Information System for Education (U-DISE), the data on basic literacy on reading and arithmetic have been taken from Annual Status of Education Report (ASER).

For rural healthcare, the following twenty outcome proxies (nineteen focussing on supply-side and one on demand-side) are considered:

Per cent shortfall in Sub Centres (SCs), per cent shortfall in Primary Health Centres (PHCs), per cent shortfall in Community Health Centres (CHCs), per cent SCs without regular water supply, per cent SCs without electric supply, per cent SCs without all-weather motorable approach road, per cent PHCs without regular water supply, without electric supply, without all-weather motorable approach road, per cent shortfall in doctors at PHCs, per cent shortfall in total specialists at CHCs, per cent shortfall in health workers (HW) (f)/Auxiliary Nursing Midwives (ANM) at SCs, per cent shortfall in HW (m) at SCs, per cent shortfall in Health Assistants (HA) (f)/Lady Health Visitor (LHV) at PHCs, per cent shortfall in HA (m) at PHCs, per cent shortfall in Radiographers at CHCs, per cent shortfall in Pharmacists at PHCs and CHCs, per cent shortfall in Laboratory Technicians at PHCs and CHCs, per cent shortfall in Nursing Staff at PHCs and CHCs and per cent distribution of hospitalisation cases during last 365 days in public hospitals (rural).

All the first nineteen outcome proxies relating to per cent shortfall are compiled from various issues of Rural Health Statistics, an annual publication of the Ministry of Health and Family Welfare, Government of India. Data on per thousand distribution of hospitalisation cases in public hospitals in rural areas (converted in percentage terms for our purpose) are taken from 71st and 75th Rounds of National Sample Survey Organisation on Social Consumption: Health. Except the last one demand-side health outcome proxy, all other proxy indicators are available on a consistent and annual basis for all States for elementary education as well as for rural healthcare. This enables regular monitoring of States' performance on these two services of considerable importance.

Step 2. Measuring the effectiveness index.

After choosing the output indicators as proxies of outcomes on elementary education and rural healthcare, the next step is to use them into suitable index. Here, steps 2 and 3 of expenditure adequacy index will be used. What is important to note here is the one year lag between expenditure and outcome that is considered in this analysis. Whilst the expenditure categories are taken over the period from 2010–2011 to 2017–2018, the outcome proxies are considered over the period from 2011–2012 to 2018–2019. This simply implies that the realised outcome is the result of lagged public expenditure (at least by one year). It is further assumed that other factors affecting outcome indicators remain constant across States and over the sample period under analysis, and so, public expenditure bears a direct and strongly significant impact on the achievement of final outcome across all States. All the outcome indicators are, therefore, averaged over two subperiods (each consisting of four years), Viz., 2011–2012 to 2014–2015 (pre-rationalisation period) and 2015–2016 to 2018–2019 (post-rationalisation period). There are two types of outcome proxies—those whose higher values imply better achievements (namely, GER, basic reading and arithmetic literacy and per cent distribution of hospitalisation cases during last 365 days in public hospitals (rural). The transformation of these two indicators will be done using Eqs. (1) and (2) as set out in case of expenditure adequacy. In case of other indicators, lower values imply better achievements (these include PTR in primary and upper primary schools and all rural health outcome indicators relating to per cent shortfall). Their transformation would be done using the following equation:

$$GT_{ij} = G_{ij} \div \left(G_{ij} - G_{in}\right) \tag{4}$$

In this equation, $GT_{ij}$ is the transformed $_{i\text{th}}$ indicator for State $_j$ and $G_{in}$ is the $_{i\text{th}}$ indicator of the best performing State $_n$ (having the least value). The indicator of the best performing State will be transformed using Eq. (2) of the expenditure adequacy.

Step 3. Computing the expenditure effectiveness index.

The aggregate performance indicator of each State and for each category (elementary education and rural healthcare) is computed by taking the simple average of all transformed outcome proxies of that State corresponding to the respective category. The expenditure effectiveness index, denoted by $F$ for category $_i$ and State $_j$ is computed from the aggregate performance indicator $P$ corresponding to that category and State in the same manner as the expenditure adequacy index using Eq. (3).

The effectiveness indices, computed in the manner described above, for both categories of expenditures under analysis are reported in Tables 2A and 2B for two groups of eighteen general and eleven NE-H States, respectively. It is seen from Table 2A that a decline is observed in the effectiveness index value for elementary education from pre-rationalisation period to post-rationalisation period for as many as eleven States. Contrary to this, thirteen States have witnessed an increase in their effectiveness index value for rural healthcare services over these two periods under analysis. Nine States, namely, Andhra Pradesh, Bihar, Chhattisgarh, Goa, Gujarat, Jharkhand, Madhya Pradesh, Tamil Nadu and Uttar Pradesh are found to commonly share these two trends. Goa, Kerala, Madhya Pradesh and Punjab have performed above average in terms of effectiveness index for elementary education during pre-rationalisation period, but (except Punjab) their index values fell sharply to reach below average during post-rationalisation period. Haryana and Punjab are the only two States which showed above average performance during post-rationalisation period in terms of effectiveness index for elementary education. With regard to the effectiveness index for rural healthcare services, five States, Viz., Gujarat, Karnataka, Odisha, Tamil Nadu and West Bengal have exhibited above average performance during both pre as well as post-rationalisation periods. Kerala performed above average only during pre-rationalisation period, whereas Andhra Pradesh, Goa, Rajasthan and Telangana are the above average performers during post-rationalisation period only.

A comparison of trends presented in Table 2A with those given in Table 1A seem to provide hardly any relation between States' performance in terms of expenditure adequacy index and in terms of effectiveness index. For example, Goa, Haryana and Kerala, which performed above average in terms of expenditure adequacy index for both categories of services during both pre and post-rationalisation periods did not perform consistently above average in terms of effectiveness index. Moreover, Chhattisgarh and Maharashtra, which performed above average in terms of their expenditure adequacy indices for rural healthcare services and elementary education, respectively, during both pre and post-rationalisation periods, are found to perform below average in their respective categories of services with respect to effectiveness index over the two periods. On the other hand, the above average performance of Punjab is more pronounced in terms of its effectiveness index as compared to that in terms of expenditure adequacy index. Furthermore, Karnataka, Tamil Nadu and West Bengal, which performed above average in terms of their effectiveness indices for rural healthcare services during both pre and post-rationalisation periods were below average performers in terms of their expenditure adequacy indices for both categories and over both periods.

In case of eleven NE-H States too, trends given in Table 2B seem to portray a mixed picture. States like Himachal Pradesh, Jammu and Kashmir, Nagaland, Tripura and Uttarakhand have registered an increase in their effectiveness index values for both elementary education as well as for rural healthcare services from pre-rationalisation period to post-rationalisation period. On the other hand, Assam and Manipur show an increase in their effectiveness index value for elementary education, while a fall for rural healthcare services over the two periods. Just contrary trends are visible in case of Arunachal Pradesh, Meghalaya and Mizoram. Sikkim depicts a sharp decline

**Table 2A** Public expenditure effectiveness index—eighteen states

| | Effectiveness index | | | |
|---|---|---|---|---|
| | Elementary education | | Rural healthcare | |
| | Pre-rationalisation period | Post-rationalisation period | Pre-rationalisation period | Post-rationalisation period |
| Andhra Pradesh | 65.37 [8] | 37.74 [13] | 76.82 [10] | 113.5 [4] |
| Bihar | 26.64 [16] | 23.64 [18] | 57.97 [16] | 97.9 [10] |
| Chhattisgarh | 84.66 [6] | 61.79 [7] | 71.29 [12] | 95.4 [12] |
| Goa | 230.19 [3] | 62.32 [6] | 92.61 [7] | 146.82 [1] |
| Gujarat | 37.05 [15] | 29.5 [15] | 108.33 [4] | 110.3 [5] |
| Haryana | 92.41 [5] | 482.5 [2] | 68.84 [13] | 77.1 [16] |
| Jharkhand | 46.67 [13] | 25.15 [16] | 57.17 [17] | 76.43 [17] |
| Karnataka | 45.98 [14] | 46.32 [11] | 220.95 [2] | 101.35 [8] |
| Kerala | 279.08 [2] | 97.32 [3] | 234.2 [1] | 88.49 [14] |
| Madhya Pradesh | 229.5 [4] | 30.16 [14] | 75.56 [11] | 81.91 [15] |
| Maharashtra | 47.28 [12] | 55.12 [10] | 85.31 [9] | 96.61 [11] |
| Odisha | 51.33 [11] | 56.36 [8] | 132.92 [3] | 123.2 [2] |
| Punjab | 308.97 [1] | 513.08 [1] | 87.71 [8] | 102.63 [7] |
| Rajasthan | 53.56 [10] | 78.4 [5] | 68.28 [14] | 91.59 [13] |
| Tamil Nadu | 72.59 [7] | 55.88 [9] | 105.22 [6] | 108.07 [6] |
| Telangana | NA | 82.83 [4] | NA | 114.21 [3] |
| Uttar Pradesh | 26.52 [17] | 24.06 [17] | 66.25 [15] | 73.72 [18] |
| West Bengal | 56 [9] | 37.82 [12] | 108.27 [5] | 100.76 [9] |
| CV (in per cent) | 91.09 | 146.35 | 51.29 | 18.2 |

*Notes* Same as for Table 1A

*Source* Author's computation using data from Elementary Flash Statistics (various years), Unified-District Information System for Education (U-DISE); Annual Status of Education Report (ASER), Lokniti; Rural Health Statistics (various years), Ministry of Health and Family Welfare, Government of India; and National Sample Survey Organisation 71st and 75th Rounds on Social Consumption: Healthcare

in the values of its effectiveness index for both categories of services over the two periods. Like the group of eighteen other States, no systematic relationship could be observed between the expenditure adequacy index and effectiveness index for eleven NE-H States (Tables 1B and 2B, respectively). For instance, Arunachal Pradesh, which performed above average in terms of expenditure adequacy index for rural healthcare services during both pre and post-rationalisation periods, achieved below average scores in terms of effectiveness index for the same category of service during both periods. Contrary to this, Himachal Pradesh performed above average in terms of both expenditure adequacy index as well as effectiveness index for elementary education during both periods under analysis. However, Jammu and Kashmir and Tripura, which had below average scores in terms of expenditure adequacy index for both types of services being considered, achieved above average scores in terms of expenditure effectiveness index with respect to rural healthcare during both pre and post-rationalisation periods. Manipur and Meghalaya also performed relatively better in terms of their effectiveness index as compared to expenditure adequacy index. Assam, Nagaland and Uttarakhand are found to be below average performers in terms of both indices for both types of services and during both periods under analysis. Mizoram and Sikkim revealed no systematic pattern.

As a final remark, it is to be noted that the coefficient of variation pertaining to effectiveness index of elementary education increased for eighteen general States, whereas it fell for eleven NE-H States from pre-rationalisation period to post-rationalisation period (Tables 2A and 2B respectively). However, the group of eleven NE-H States witnessed higher variability in their effectiveness index for elementary education as compared to the group of eighteen general States during pre-rationalisation period, but this trend got reversed during post-rationalisation period. In case of rural healthcare, the CV of eighteen general States as well as that of eleven NE-H States fell from pre to post-rationalisation periods, and during both periods,

**Table 2B** Public expenditure effectiveness index—eleven NE-H states

| | Effectiveness index | | | |
|---|---|---|---|---|
| | Elementary education | | Rural healthcare | |
| | Pre-rationalisation period | Post-rationalisation period | Pre-rationalisation period | Post-rationalisation period |
| Arunachal Pradesh | 64.29 [6] | 50.3 [8] | 27.17 [8] | 34.56 [9] |
| Assam | 12.01 [11] | 40.95 [11] | 53.82 [5] | 31.15 [10] |
| Himachal Pradesh | 100.48 [4] | 278.49 [1] | 23.57 [9] | 53.36 [7] |
| Jammu and Kashmir | 18.12 [8] | 49.66 [9] | 160.88 [3] | 244.57 [1] |
| Manipur | 73.95 [5] | 248.09 [2] | 285.81 [2] | 126.45 [4] |
| Meghalaya | 106.92 [3] | 87.31 [4] | 48.93 [6] | 166.57 [3] |
| Mizoram | 341.55 [1] | 107.77 [3] | 32.39 [7] | 40.03 [8] |
| Nagaland | 16.83 [10] | 51.53 [7] | 17.61 [10] | 22.83 [11] |
| Sikkim | 326.75 [2] | 60.36 [6] | 306.12 [1] | 91.68 [5] |
| Tripura | 21.44 [7] | 49.53 [10] | 127.17 [4] | 222.41 [2] |
| Uttarakhand | 17.66 [9] | 76.02 [5] | 16.54 [11] | 66.39 [6] |
| CV (in per cent) | 120.86 | 83.39 | 107.55 | 79.35 |

*Notes* Same as for Table 1A
*Source* Same as for Table 2A

the variability for eleven NE-H States is observed to be higher as compared to that of eighteen general States.

## 4 Efficiency of Public Expenditure of States on Elementary Education and Rural Healthcare

Step 1. Choice of input and output indicators.

While public expenditure (corresponding to each of the two categories on elementary education and rural healthcare) of a State (as a percentage of its GSDP) will serve as the only input, it will be linked with a set of outputs. Thus, for public expenditure on elementary education as an input, there will be five output indicators, namely, GER at elementary level, inverse of PTRs at primary and upper primary levels, percentage of students enrolled in Government schools in class V who can read at least class II level text and percentage of students in class V who can perform division. In case of rural healthcare expenditure as an input, two output indices have been constructed from twenty output indicators mentioned above in case of effectiveness index. These two output indices are: Access to Rural Healthcare Index (ARHI) and Availability of Rural Healthcare (VRHI). The first output index, ARHI is constructed from the simple average of four outcome indicators (all transformed on a common scale), namely, per cent shortfall in SCs, per cent shortfall in PHCs, per cent shortfall in CHCs and per cent distribution of hospitalisation cases during last 365 days in public hospitals (rural). The second output index, VRHI is constructed from the simple average of remaining sixteen outcome indicators (all transformed on a common scale). In order to transform various output indicators on a common scale so as to construct the above mentioned indices, the minimum and maximum values for each of the twenty indicators for each year of the sample period (2011–2012 to 2018–2019) have been chosen across States. After choosing these maxima and minima, following equations are applied to transform the indicators.

$$I1 = [(\text{Maximum} - \text{Actual}) \div (\text{Maximum} - \text{Minimum})] \times 100 \tag{5}$$

$$I2 = [(\text{Actual} - \text{Minimum}) \div (\text{Maximum} - \text{Minimum})] \times 100 \tag{6}$$

Equation (6) is applied to transform only one indicator, i.e. per cent distribution of hospitalisation cases during last 365 days in public hospitals (rural). All other nineteen indicators are transformed using Eq. (5). All these transformed indicators are averaged to form the two output indices (as stated above) for pre and post-rationalisation periods.

Step 2. Measuring efficiency of expenditure.

Being quite aware of the merits and demerits of both parametric and non-parametric techniques available in the literature, the non-parametric technique of Data Envelopment Analysis (DEA) has been applied in the present study to measure the efficiency of public expenditures on elementary education and rural healthcare. Given the low levels of public spending on these two important social services and also the fiscal constraints of States, the ultimate goal should be to maximise the output out of the given level of expenditure. DEA is, therefore, applied in an output-oriented setting with variable returns to scale. Appendix of this paper summarises the essentials of DEA and explains the meaning of efficiency scores. Figure 1a, b give the plots of the efficiency scores of public expenditures on elementary education and rural healthcare services respectively for eighteen general States, while the corresponding public expenditure efficiency scores with respect to elementary education and rural healthcare services for eleven NE-H States are displayed in Fig. 2a, b, respectively.

Figure 1a shows that four States, namely, Goa, Kerala, Madhya Pradesh and Punjab during pre-rationalisation period and nine States, Viz., Chhattisgarh, Goa, Haryana, Kerala, Odisha, Punjab, Rajasthan, Tamil Nadu and Telangana during post-rationalisation period operated at efficiency frontier so far as expenditure on elementary education was concerned. In other words, with given level of public spending on elementary education and given technology, these States have been able to achieve the maximum possible output. Bihar and Uttar Pradesh emerged as the least efficient States in this respect during both periods. Most of the States have depicted an increase in their efficiency of elementary education expenditure from pre-rationalisation period to post-rationalisation period. In respect of public expenditure efficiency for rural healthcare, Fig. 1b depicts that Goa, Karnataka, Maharashtra, Odisha, Punjab and Tamil Nadu are observed to be operating on the efficiency frontier during pre-rationalisation period, while Gujarat joined Goa, Maharashtra and Punjab on the efficiency frontier during post-rationalisation period. What is alarming to observe is a sharp decline in the efficiency of public expenditure on rural healthcare for many States from pre-rationalisation period to post-rationalisation period. In this respect, States like, Bihar, Jharkhand, more surprisingly Kerala, Odisha, Rajasthan, Tamil Nadu, Uttar Pradesh and West Bengal deserve special attention.

In case of eleven NE-H States, it is revealed from Fig. 2a that most of the States are operating with full efficiency with regard to their public expenditure on elementary education during both pre and post-rationalisation periods. However, when it comes to the efficiency of public expenditure on rural healthcare services, Fig. 2b shows that six States during pre-rationalisation period and only three during post-rationalisation period are operating on the efficiency frontier. This shows the extent of decline in the efficiency scores of NE-H States over the two periods. All these trends in efficiency scores should, however, be interpreted with care, as they are sensitive to choice of variables (inclusion and exclusion of input and output indicators) as well as the sample size.

For comparative purpose, the expenditure efficiency indices (computed using the efficiency scores in line with expenditure adequacy index) are also reported in Tables 3A and 3B for the group of eighteen general States and eleven NE-H States, respectively, for elementary education and rural healthcare services. These efficiency

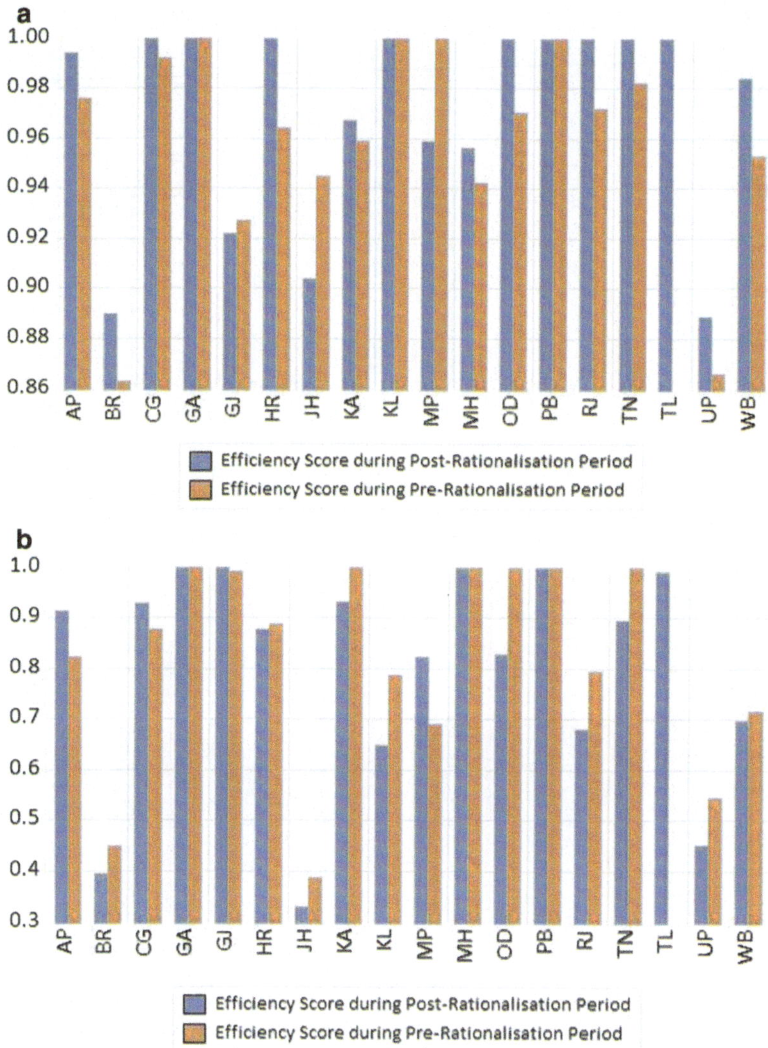


**Fig. 1** **a** Public expenditure efficiency scores for elementary education—eighteen states. **b** Public expenditure efficiency scores for rural healthcare—eighteen states. *Source* Obtained based on efficiency scores computed using DEAP Ver2.1

indices for the two groups of States and also for both categories of services being considered have been compared with expenditure adequacy indices and effectiveness indices in Table 4 in terms of performance grades. It may be noticed from Table 4 that majority of States in both groups are found to perform below average, and this below average performance is most pronounced in terms of expenditure adequacy index, a little less in terms of effectiveness index and least in terms of efficiency index (barring rural healthcare which has more below average performers as compared to

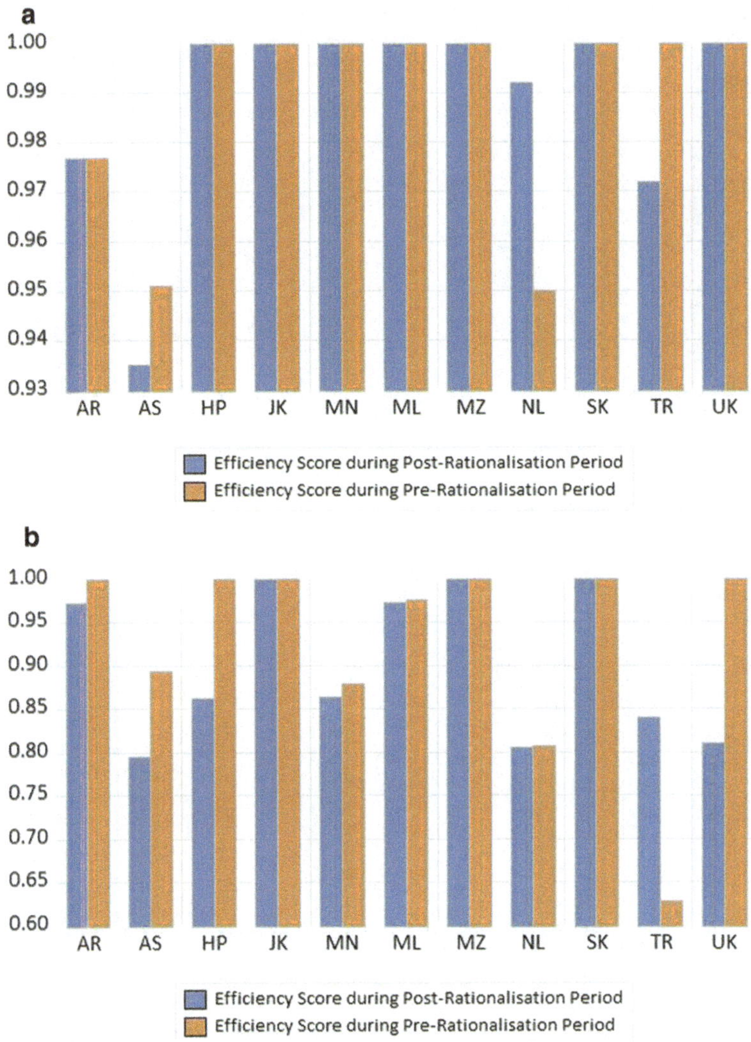


**Fig. 2** **a** Public expenditure efficiency scores for elementary education—eleven NE-H states. **b** Public expenditure efficiency scores for rural healthcare—eleven NE-H states. *Source* Obtained based on efficiency scores computed using DEAP Ver2.1

elementary education in terms of efficiency index). Thirteen out of seventeen States (except non-existent Telangana) during pre-rationalisation period and thirteen out of eighteen States during post-rationalisation period performed below average in terms of their expenditure adequacy indices for elementary education; and interestingly, these below average performing States showed an increase in their index values from pre-rationalisation period to post-rationalisation period. The other four States, namely, Goa, Haryana, Kerala and Maharashtra revealed above average performance in this respect during both periods, but except Haryana, other three States witnessed a decline in their index values from pre to post-rationalisation periods. In case of eleven NE-H States too, majority of States indicate below average performance with increasing tendency in their expenditure adequacy indices for elementary education from pre to post-rationalisation periods. Only Himachal Pradesh and Sikkim show above average performance in both periods but with declining tendency in their index values, while Mizoram performed above average only during post-rationalisation period. Interestingly, in terms of expenditure adequacy index for rural healthcare services, it may be noticed from Table 4 that nine out of eighteen other category States have performed above average at least during one of the two periods under study. Majority of general States, which have performed below average during both periods had a tendency to decline. However, for the group of eleven NE-H States, majority of States showed below average performance though with increasing tendency in their index values from pre to post-rationalisation periods.

In terms of effectiveness index for elementary education, it is seen from Table 4 that thirteen out of seventeen States during pre-rationalisation period and sixteen out of eighteen States during post-rationalisation period depict below average performance, and eight of these States show a fall in their index values. Majority of eleven NE-H States also indicate a below average performance. With regard to effectiveness index for rural healthcare services, majority of eighteen States show above average performance during at least one of the two periods. However, in the group of eleven NE-H States, as many as six States show below average performance.

In terms of public expenditure efficiency index for elementary education, it may be noticed from Table 4 that majority of eighteen States show above average performance during at least one of the two periods. Similar trends are visible for eleven NE-H States. In case of expenditure efficiency index with respect to rural healthcare services, ten out of eighteen States and four out of eleven NE-H States show below average performance in terms of their efficiency indices.

All these trends, as discussed above, seem in sharp contrast to the general belief that States generally spend adequately, but large outlays do not necessarily get translated into better outputs and outcomes (Lalvani et al., 2009). Then what do the trends presented above indicate? Actually, the below average performance by most of the States in both groups in terms of expenditure adequacy index may be attributed to a number of factors apart from varying spending priorities amongst States on different services and varying absorptive capacities, institutions, etc. At the first place, it should be noted that while the increase in the general purpose transfers to States through enhanced tax devolution seems to have augmented their spending towards such basic services as education and health, the increased share of general purpose transfers might not have been that effective enough so as to have a significant impact on their expenditures for elementary education and rural healthcare (the introductory paragraph of Sect. 1 of this paper is worth noting in this connection). Secondly, the commensurate reduction in specific purpose grants through changed funding pattern for many CSSs (including National Health Mission and elementary education) as a result of rationalisation and restructuring of grants might have put additional burden on State Government finances and would have restricted their

**Table 3A** Public expenditure efficiency index—eighteen states

| | Expenditure efficiency index | | | |
|---|---|---|---|---|
| | Elementary education | | Rural healthcare | |
| | Pre-rationalisation period | Post-rationalisation period | Pre-rationalisation period | Post-rationalisation period |
| Andhra Pradesh | 66.51 [7] | 137.49 [10] | 9.88 [10] | 25.63 [8] |
| Bihar | 10.3 [17] | 6.71 [17] | 1.74 [16] | 1.57 [17] |
| Chhattisgarh | 202.79 [5] | 168.75 [1] | 15.01 [9] | 31.56 [7] |
| Goa | 255.08 [1] | 168.75 [1] | 236.08 [1] | 332.59 [1] |
| Gujarat | 20.77 [15] | 9.81 [15] | 210.3 [7] | 332.59 [1] |
| Haryana | 43.79 [10] | 168.75 [1] | 16.67 [8] | 17.36 [10] |
| Jharkhand | 28.1 [13] | 7.82 [16] | 1.35 [17] | 1.18 [18] |
| Karnataka | 38.25 [11] | 24.32 [12] | 236.08 [1] | 33.05 [6] |
| Kerala | 255.08 [1] | 168.75 [1] | 7.76 [12] | 4.46 [15] |
| Madhya Pradesh | 255.08 [1] | 19.41 [13] | 4.75 [14] | 11.14 [12] |
| Maharashtra | 26.56 [14] | 18.03 [14] | 236.08 [1] | 332.59 [1] |
| Odisha | 52.88 [9] | 168.75 [1] | 236.08 [1] | 11.61 [11] |
| Punjab | 255.08 [1] | 168.75 [1] | 236.08 [1] | 332.59 [1] |
| Rajasthan | 56.77 [8] | 168.75 [1] | 8.19 [11] | 5.15 [14] |
| Tamil Nadu | 89.22 [6] | 168.75 [1] | 236.08 [1] | 20.34 [9] |
| Telangana | NA | 168.75 [1] | NA | 299.05 [5] |
| Uttar Pradesh | 10.57 [16] | 6.65 [18] | 2.53 [15] | 1.98 [16] |
| West Bengal | 33.16 [12] | 51.04 [11] | 5.36 [13] | 5.55 [13] |
| CV (in per cent) | 98.87 | 76.44 | 114.4 | 144.65 |

*Notes* Due to many States being on the efficiency frontier, they occupy the similar top position, and it is not fare to rank a State lower than any other by any means which has shared the efficiency frontier and hence the same index. Figures within brackets indicate ranks.
*Source* Same as for Table 2A

spending to social services, such as education and health which always suffer at the cost of increase in committed liabilities, like interest burden on account of UDAY, pay revision, and above, all, because of politico-fiscal aspect, such as loan waiver for farmers. To add to these is the variable nature of Central Government transfers to States which is also reflected in States' revenue projections and expenditure planning/management (Chakraborty et al., 2019; Reserve Bank of India, 2019). The issues associated with the design and implementation of Centrally Sponsored Schemes (Choudhury and Mohanty, 2018; Kapur, 2019; Rao, 2017) make it further difficult for Central releases to pass through various stages and serve the intended

**Table 3B** Public expenditure efficiency index—eleven NE-H states

| | Expenditure efficiency index | | | |
|---|---|---|---|---|
| | Elementary education | | Rural healthcare | |
| | Pre-rationalisation period | Post-rationalisation period | Pre-rationalisation period | Post-rationalisation period |
| Arunachal Pradesh | 73.42 [2] | 31.99 [3] | 153.12 [1] | 158.47 [2] |
| Assam | 33.55 [3] | 10.83 [5] | 25.27 [3] | 17.7 [8] |
| Himachal Pradesh | 120.02 [1] | 133.95 [1] | 153.12 [1] | 28.51 [4] |
| Jammu and Kashmir | 120.02 [1] | 133.95 [1] | 153.12 [1] | 215.25 [1] |
| Manipur | 120.02 [1] | 133.95 [1] | 21.57 [4] | 29 [3] |
| Meghalaya | 120.02 [1] | 133.95 [1] | 116.87 [2] | 158.47 [2] |
| Mizoram | 120.02 [1] | 133.95 [1] | 153.12 [1] | 215.25 [1] |
| Nagaland | 32.84 [4] | 93.37 [2] | 12.53 [5] | 18.85 [7] |
| Sikkim | 120.02 [1] | 133.95 [1] | 153.12 [1] | 215.25 [1] |
| Tripura | 120.02 [1] | 26.14 [4] | 5.04 [6] | 23.79 [5] |
| Uttarakhand | 120.02 [1] | 133.95 [1] | 153.12 [1] | 19.46 [6] |
| CV (in per cent) | 35.83 | 51.13 | 67.54 | 90.82 |

*Note* Same as for Table 3A
*Source* Same as for Table 2A

purpose. This, along with State-specific administrative difficulties, weak institutions, etc., gives rise to poor financial management and defective budgetary control in States that in turn, leads to the wastage of a substantial amount of resources. Financial irregularities have become an inherent feature of both Union and State budgets. Though the effectiveness and efficiency of public expenditures of States largely depend on their institutions, governance and their absorptive capacities, it may be correct (to some extent) to assume that States, irrespective of their level of development, fiscal ability, etc., when adequately empowered with fiscal resources try to spend them in an effective and efficient manner for basic services under their list. This issue is, however, a matter of indepth research and debate, and is beyond the scope of this paper. However, in what follows, a simple econometric exercise is conducted to examine this issue in brief.

**Table 4** A comparative summary of states on public expenditure adequacy, effectiveness and efficiency indices

| | Expenditure adequacy index | | Effectiveness index | | Expenditure efficiency index | |
|---|---|---|---|---|---|---|
| | Elementary education | Rural healthcare | Elementary education | Rural healthcare | Elementary education | Rural healthcare |
| | Performance grade | Performance grade | Performance grade | Performance grade | Performance grade | Performance grade |
| *Group of eighteen states* | | | | | | |
| Andhra Pradesh | $A_2$ | $A_1$ | B − | $A_2$ | $A_2$ | B + |
| Bihar | B + | B + | B − | B + | B − | B − |
| Chhattisgarh | B + | $A_3$ + | B − | B + | $A_3$ − | B + |
| Goa | $A_3$ − | $A_3$ + | $A_1$ | $A_2$ | $A_3$ − | $A_3$ + |
| Gujarat | B + | $A_1$ | B − | $A_3$ + | B − | $A_3$ + |
| Haryana | $A_3$ + | $A_3$ + | $A_2$ | B + | $A_2$ | B + |
| Jharkhand | B + | $A_1$ | B − | B + | B − | B − |
| Karnataka | B + | B + | B + | $A_3$ − | B − | $A_1$ |
| Kerala | $A_3$ − | $A_3$ − | $A_1$ | $A_1$ | $A_3$ − | B − |
| Madhya Pradesh | B + | B − | $A_1$ | B + | $A_1$ | B + |
| Maharashtra | $A_3$ − | B + | B + | B + | B − | $A_3$ + |
| Odisha | B + | $A_2$ | B + | $A_3$ − | $A_2$ | $A_1$ |
| Punjab | B + | $A_1$ | $A_3$ + | $A_2$ | $A_3$ − | $A_3$ + |
| Rajasthan | B + | B − | B + | B + | $A_2$ | B − |
| Tamil Nadu | B − | B − | B − | $A_3$ + | $A_2$ | $A_1$ |
| Telangana | B | B | B | A | A | A |
| Uttar Pradesh | B + | B − | B − | B + | B − | B − |
| West Bengal | B + | B + | B − | $A_3$ − | B + | B + |
| *Group of eleven NE-H states* | | | | | | |
| Arunachal Pradesh | B + | $A_3$ − | B − | B + | B − | $A_3$ + |
| Assam | B + | B + | B + | B − | B − | B - |
| Himachal Pradesh | $A_3$ − | B + | $A_3$ + | B + | $A_3$ + | $A_1$ |
| Jammu and Kashmir | B + | B + | B + | $A_3$ + | $A_3$ + | $A_3$ + |
| Manipur | B + | $A_2$ | $A_2$ | $A_3$ − | $A_3$ + | B + |
| Meghalaya | B + | B + | $A_1$ | $A_2$ | $A_3$ + | $A_3$ + |
| Mizoram | $A_2$ | $A_3$ − | $A_3$ − | B + | $A_3$ + | $A_3$ + |

(continued)

**Table 4** (continued)

| | Expenditure adequacy index | | Effectiveness index | | Expenditure efficiency index | |
|---|---|---|---|---|---|---|
| | Elementary education | Rural healthcare | Elementary education | Rural healthcare | Elementary education | Rural healthcare |
| | Performance grade | Performance grade | Performance grade | Performance grade | Performance grade | Performance grade |
| Nagaland | B + | B + | B + | B + | B + | B + |
| Sikkim | $A_3$ − | B + | $A_1$ | $A_1$ | $A_3$ + | $A_3$ + |
| Tripura | B + | B + | B + | $A_3$ + | $A_1$ | B + |
| Uttarakhand | B + | B + | B + | B + | $A_3$ + | $A_1$ |

*Notes* A indicates above average performance and B denotes below average performance. Subscripted numbers 1, 2 and 3 after the letter A signify the above average performance is only during pre-rationalisation period, only during post-rationalisation period and during both pre and post-rationalisation periods, respectively. Thus, if a State shows below average performance on a particular index in a particular category during both periods, its corresponding grade is B. In cases of above average performance and below average performance during both pre as well as post-rationalisation periods, the plus (+) and minus (−) signs after the performance grades are used to indicate if the index value has increased or decreased respectively from pre-rationalisation period to post-rationalisation period
*Source* Tables 1A, 2A and 3A for the group of eighteen States and Tables 1B, 2B and 3B for eleven NE-H States

# 5 Impact Assessment of CSS Rationalisation on Public Expenditure by States on Elementary Education and Rural Healthcare

This section of the present paper attempts to empirically investigate the impact of restructuring/rationalisation of grants under State Plan Schemes and Centrally Sponsored Schemes (earlier categorised as plan grants) on the quality of public expenditure for elementary education and rural healthcare. The rationalisation and restructuring of conditional grants has two components, namely, (a) reduction in Central spending on schemes through changed sharing pattern; and (b) reduction in the total number of schemes by discontinuing some schemes, whilst merging some other schemes with smaller outlays into suitable groups. It should, however, be noted that for promoting the idea of cooperative and competitive federalism, any attempt to rationalise the conditional grants through reduced Central support should be complemented by providing adequate fiscal resources to States through increased relative share of general purpose grants (as was recommended by FC-XIV). In the light of this and also keeping in view the discussion of the last paragraph of the preceding section, it is hypothesised that the rationalisation and restructuring of CSSs (through a compositional shift in favour of untied transfers) complemented by good governance of a particular State improves its quality of public expenditure. Since the quality of public expenditure (for the purpose of this paper) is defined in terms of expenditure adequacy, effectiveness and efficiency, the specific hypotheses to be tested are as under:

I. The restructuring/rationalisation of specific purpose grants through compositional shift in favour of untied grants improves the adequacy of public expenditures of States for elementary education and rural healthcare; and
II. The grant-rationalisation induced adequacy of public expenditure, when complemented by good governance of a particular State leads to more effective and efficient utilisation of its public funds for elementary education and rural healthcare.

In order to test the above stated two hypotheses, the regression equations are specified accordingly. A set of twelve cross sectional regressions (six regressions for each of the two periods—pre and post-rationalisation periods) have been estimated. The three regressions corresponding to each period and each category of service (i.e. elementary education and rural healthcare) consider expenditure adequacy index, effectiveness index and inefficiency scores as the dependent variables, respectively. In the regression with public expenditure adequacy index as the dependent variable, three independent variables, namely, the grant-rationalisation measure (GR), the State dummy (DS) (defined as 1 for State belonging to the group of eighteen States, 0 otherwise) and an interaction term of these two variables (DSGR) have been considered. In this paper, a simple measure—the ratio of grants under State Plan Schemes and Centrally Sponsored Schemes (representing specific purpose transfers) to tax devolution (representing general purpose transfers) is used as a measure of grant-rationalisation (GR). Lower the ratio, better is the restructuring of grants in favour of general purpose grants towards providing greater fiscal autonomy to States. Thus, the sign of the estimated coefficient of this variable with expenditure adequacy variable should be negative to indicate a positive impact. The coefficient of the interaction term (DSGR) estimated from regression with expenditure adequacy as the dependent variable is multiplied with the logarithm of the public expenditure adequacy index so as to obtain a new variable, called grant-rationalisation induced adequacy of public expenditure (GRDQ). This newly obtained variable, GRDQ is put to serve as an explanatory variable in regressions with either of effectiveness index or inefficiency scores as the dependent variable. This new explanatory variable is combined with governance indicator (GOV) (proxied by the Public Affairs Index),[8] State dummy (DS) (as defined above) and an interaction term of the three, GRDQ, GOV and DS and is denoted by GSGRDQ.

Whilst the regressions with expenditure adequacy and effectiveness indices as the dependent variables have been estimated using Least Squares method, the regression with inefficiency scores has been estimated using TOBIT type procedure following Mohanty and Bhanumurthy (2018). The choice of TOBIT method over Ordinary Least Squares technique is guided by the fact that the inefficiency scores are truncated and lie between 0 and 1. The efficiency scores, obtained using DEA and displayed in Figs. 1a, b and 2a, b reveal that States on the efficiency frontier (or fully efficient States) have an efficiency score equal to 1, whilst less efficient States achieve an

[8] In this paper, PAI2016 and PAI2019 have been considered as governance measures for regressions corresponding to pre and post-rationalisation periods; though the author is aware of the non-comparability of these indices.

efficiency score less than 1. The TOBIT analysis is conducted on inefficiency scores ($I$) as the dependent variable, where $I$ = 1-efficiency score. Given the interest of this paper to find the explanation for the variation in observed inefficiencies, the left censor is used for States having $I \leq 0.1$ (i.e. fully efficient States) as zeros. By doing so, a group of efficient States is formed whose efficiency score is at least 0.9 and limit the remaining observable cases only to inefficient States. Thus, the TOBIT regression used in this paper is of the following type:

$$\begin{aligned} I_i^* &= X_i\beta + \varepsilon_i \\ I_i &= I_i^*, \quad \text{if } I_i* > 0.1, \\ Ii &= 0, \quad \text{otherwise.} \end{aligned} \tag{7}$$

where $I_i$ is a latent variable, which is unobservable; $X_i$ is a vector of explanatory variables, (i.e. GRDQ, GOV, DS and GSGRDQ, as defined in the preceding paragraph); $\beta$ is a vector of parameters to be estimated; $\varepsilon_i$ represent error terms following a normal distribution; the subscripted $i$ represents the $i_{\text{th}}$ State.

The estimation results of these different types of regressions are summarised in Table 5.

The estimation results given in Table 5 seem to provide general evidence in support of increasing the relative share of untied grants in total Central Government fiscal transfers to States under the process of rationalisation; this tends to increase the adequacy of public expenditures of States for elementary education and rural healthcare services. For example, the negative sign of the estimated coefficients of the interaction term of grant-rationalisation measure with State dummy (for both elementary education and rural healthcare) during both pre as well as post-rationalisation periods support this finding. The negative coefficients of DSGR in case of both elementary education and rural healthcare services are far greater in magnitude and are also statistically significant when estimated for post-rationalisation period. Another variable of our direct interest is the grant-rationalisation induced adequacy of public expenditure complemented by good governance (GSGRDQ) which is found to be statistically significant with coefficients having expected signs (though not strong enough in case of regressions with inefficiency scores as the dependent variable). The governance indicator (GOV) occurred with positive and negative signs in case of public expenditure effectiveness index and inefficiency scores as dependent variables respectively thereby indicating the positive impact of governance on the quality of public expenditure.

## 6 Concluding Observations and Some Policy Suggestions

The analysis of the present paper aimed at assessing the quality of public expenditures of States for elementary education and rural healthcare through the lens of public expenditure adequacy, effectiveness and efficiency indices. Whilst doing so,

**Table 5** Regression estimation results

| Explanatory variables | Dependent variables | | | | | |
|---|---|---|---|---|---|---|
| | Public expenditure adequacy index | | Public expenditure effectiveness index | | Public expenditure inefficiency scores | |
| | Elementary education | Rural healthcare | Elementary education | Rural healthcare | Elementary education | Rural healthcare |
| *Pre-rationalisation period estimation results* | | | | | | |
| C | 117.85 | −264.08 | −1297.93* | 398.63*** | 0.45** | 1.66* |
| GR | −2.35 | 176.72** | NA | NA | NA | NA |
| DS | 42.48 | 299.76 | 521.05** | −259.17** | 0.08 | 0.04 |
| DSGR | −74.56 | −191.52 | NA | NA | NA | NA |
| GRDQ | NA | NA | −4.01** | 0.44 | 0.0005 | 0.0001 |
| GOV | NA | NA | 1847.23* | −164.73 | −0.76** | −3.17* |
| GSGRDQ | NA | NA | 9.35* | −0.93 | 0.0003 | −0.00008 |
| *R*-squared | 0.14 | 0.27 | 0.55 | 0.29 | NA | NA |
| Adj. *R*-squared | 0.03 | 0.18 | 0.47 | 0.16 | NA | NA |
| *F*-statistic | 0.25 | 3** | 6.98* | 2.32*** | NA | NA |
| Method of estimation | LS | LS | LS | LS | TOBID | TOBID |
| Sample observations | 28 | 28 | 28 | 28 | 28 | 28 |
| *Post-rationalisation period estimation results* | | | | | | |
| C | 0.08 | −437.53*** | 21.44 | 344.02** | 0.09 | 0.2 |
| GR | 122.56 | 527.02** | NA | NA | NA | NA |
| DS | 297.47 | 780.46* | 1.61 | −197.73* | 0.05** | −0.007 |
| DSGR | −584.4** | −1116.84* | NA | NA | NA | NA |
| GRDQ | NA | NA | −0.07 | 0.07 | 0.08*** | 0.002 |
| GOV | NA | NA | 118.37** | −128.48*** | −0.78** | −0.43** |
| GSGRDQ | NA | NA | 0.85** | −0.09*** | −0.63*** | −0.34*** |
| *R*-squared | 0.25 | 0.39 | 0.3 | 0.28 | NA | NA |
| Adj. *R*-squared | 0.15 | 0.32 | 0.18 | 0.16 | NA | NA |
| *F*-statistic | 2.71*** | 5.39* | 2.52*** | 2.37*** | NA | NA |
| Estimation method | LS | LS | LS | LS | TOBID | TOBID |
| Sample observations | 29 | 29 | 29 | 29 | 29 | 29 |

*Notes NA*: not applicable; *, ** and *** indicate whether the estimated regression coefficient is statistically significant at $p \leq 0.01$, $0.01 < p \leq 0.05$ and $0.05 < p \leq 0.10$, respectively.
*Source* Author's estimation using EViews11

the attempt is made to examine if the process of restructuring and rationalisation of Central Government fiscal transfers to States has had any significant impact on public expenditure quality. It is found from the analysis of this paper (Sects. 2, 3 and 4) that though there are some signs of improvement in the quality of public expenditure, especially in terms of expenditure adequacy index after the rationalisation of grants happened, most of the States are, however, observed to be below average performers; and this below average performance is most pronounced in case of expenditure adequacy index, a little less in case of expenditure effectiveness index and least in case of expenditure efficiency index (barring rural healthcare in which case, more below average performers are observed in terms of efficiency index). All these trends call for an effective Central fiscal transfers to States in the form of greater untied grants through tax devolution which States can use freely to suit their priorities and local preferences. In this connection, it is suggested that the effective share of tax devolution (excluding other transfers) to States out of the divisible pool should not be less than 50% in any case and in any year.[9] The Fifteenth Finance Commission (FC-XV) observes that the Union Government has, in practice, been transferring about 50% of its gross revenue receipts (gross tax revenue + gross non-tax revenue) to States (with about 2% variation on each side) (Government of India, 2020a: p. 154). It should, however, be noted (as is also mentioned by FC-XV) that Constitutionally Union is not obligated to share its non-tax revenues with the States. The simple implication of this is that the transfers provided from the Centre to the States from its non-tax revenues are discretionary in nature and may be a significant source of uncertainty and torture (in terms of rigid conditions, etc.) for States at any point of time. The robust policy design should not be based on past experiences, rather it should have a logical and legal backing so as to avoid any conflict and instability between Centre and States in future. Thus, in order to bring greater stability and predictability in Central transfers to States, it is necessary that these transfers should largely comprise of devolution of Central taxes which are considered conducive to States' fiscal autonomy.

The results of empirical exercise of this paper seem to suggest the joint responsibility of the Central as well as State Governments in making any attempt to rationalise grants successful towards effective delivery of public services. Whilst the share of untied transfers has to be increased by the Centre to provide greater fiscal autonomy to States, the States, in turn, need to improve their system of governance (of course with active and greater participation of local governments) for achieving an effective and efficient utilisation of public funds. Towards this end, States need to prevent leakages in their fund flows to the implementing agencies by improving financial management and budgetary control.

[9] This is author's own observation based on the assessment of the volume of Central fiscal transfers (both general purpose as well as specific purpose) in relation to States' needs in the past. This 50% recommendation is not backed by any scientific computation as such. The author is of the view that at least 50% of the total Central Government transfers should be given to States so as not to impose any conditionality on them with regard to the utilisation and/or any matching requirement on such transfers.

**Acknowledgements** This paper is an outcome of a recently completed project on grant rationalisation and quality of public expenditure of States for education and health, funded and sponsored by Planning and Development Unit (NITI Aayog), through Jadavpur University. The views expressed in this paper are those of the author.

This paper was presented in NIPFP-IIPF conference held during 29–30 June 2021. The author is thankful to Mr. A. N. Jha (conference session chair), Ms. Sandhya Garg (discussant) and other participants for providing their valuable feedback.

## Appendix: Essentials of Data Envelopment Analysis and Meaning of Efficiency Scores[10]

The Data Envelopment Analysis (DEA), firstly introduced by Farrell (1957) and later extended by Charnes et al. (1978) and Banker et al. (1984), is a non-parametric method to calculate or estimate the shape of the efficiency frontier. The efficiency frontier is a set of points that shows the efficient combination of inputs and outputs which can be obtained in the systems examined. DEA constructs an efficiency frontier using input and output data for the entire sample following a mathematical programming procedure. In other words, DEA is based on a linear combination of inputs and outputs in order to specify the efficiency frontier. Convexity of the set of input–output combinations is assumed since this method constructs an envelope around the observed combinations. By assumption, the frontier determines the best or efficient practices and the distance of a decision making unit (DMU) from the frontier measures its potential efficiency gain. The efficiency score, in the presence of multiple inputs and outputs is defined as:

$$\text{Efficiency} = \text{Weighted Sum of Outputs} \div \text{Weighted Sum of Inputs}.$$

Assuming that there are $n$ DMUs, each with $m$ inputs and $s$ outputs, the relative efficiency score of a test $\text{DMU}_p$ is obtained by solving the following model

$$\text{Max}\left\{\sum\left[v_k y_{kp}\right] \div \sum\left[u_j x_{jp}\right]\right\}, \tag{8a}$$

Subject to

$$\left\{\sum\left[v_k y_{kj}\right] \div \sum\left[u_j x_{ji}\right]\right\}; \tag{8b}$$

st $v_k, u_j \geq 0 \; \forall \, j$ and $k$,

[10] This appendix largely draws upon Fancello et al. (2014), Zuhdia and Prasetyo (2013) and Martín-Gambo and Iribarren (2021).

where: $k = 1$ to $s$; $j = 1$ to $m$; $i = 1$ to $n$; $y_{ki}$ = amount of output k produced by DMU $i$; $x_{ji}$ = amount of output $j$ produced by DMU $i$; $v_k$ = weight given to output $k$; $u_j$ = weight given to output $j$.

Each DMU selects input and output weights that maximise its efficiency score. In general, a DMU is considered to be efficient (or on the efficiency frontier) if it obtains a score of 1, whilst a score of less than 1 implies that it is inefficient.

A wide variety of DEA models have been proposed in the literature. These models are formulated according to a set of technical features. These include: model orientation (model oriented to inputs and/or outputs), model metrics (radial or nonradial), and display of the production possibility set [e.g. constant returns to scale (CRS) or variable returns to scale (VRS)]. Regarding model orientation, three variants are distinguished: input-oriented, output-oriented, and nonoriented. An input-oriented model means that an inefficient entity becomes efficient by reducing its inputs whilst its outputs remain at least at the same level. On the other hand, in an output-oriented model, the conversion of the DMU into efficient entity is achieved with an increase in outputs whilst inputs remain unchanged. A nonoriented (or mixed) model pursues both an increase in outputs and a decrease in inputs. Depending on the model metrics, two variants are differentiated: radial and nonradial models. Radial models are represented by the CCR model developed by Charnes et al. (1978), and they are based on proportional changes in the levels of inputs or outputs. In contrast, nonradial models such as the slacks-based measure of efficiency (SBM) model do not handle proportional changes in inputs or outputs, but specific slacks for each input or output. Finally, the concept of returns to scale has been widely explored within the different DEA frameworks. A DMU operates at CRS if an increase in its input levels leads to a proportional increase in its output levels. If it is suspected that this proportional effect does not occur, an extended version considering VRS (Banker et al., 1984) should be used. The CRS efficiency frontier measures the maximum output-input slope from the original point, whilst VRS efficiency frontier sorts the slopes starting from the DMU having minimum input. In Fig. 3 displayed below, both DMUs C and D are efficient in CRS and VRS methods. DMUs A, B and E are considered efficient under VRS, but not under CRS.

The major advantage of non-parametric approach, in general and more especially, that of DEA method is its transparency and capability to handle multiple inputs and outputs with varying units of measurement from one another. Furthermore, unlike the Stochastic Frontier Analysis (SFA) under parametric approach, the use of DEA does not require the assumptions about the specific functional form of the production function. The main disadvantage of DEA method is that the efficiency of each DMU depends on the efficiency of the other DMUs, and it is impossible to prove that all DMUs under analysis are inefficient. Besides this, the non-parametric approach, in general, suffers from its deterministic nature. Results tend to depend largely on the size and composition of the sample as well as on the selection of input and output variables used. Moreover, non-parametric methods tend to be sensitive to measurement errors, statistical noise and outliers.

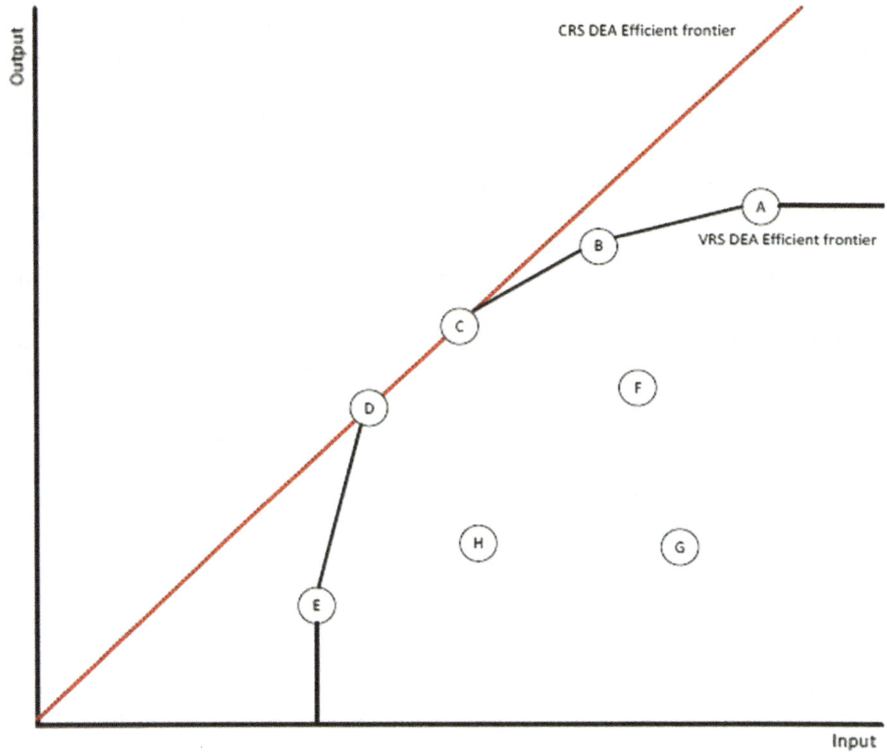


**Fig. 3** Comparison of efficient frontier between CRS and VRS methods. *Source* Prasetyo and Zuhdia (2013)

## References

Banker, R. D., Charnes, A., & Cooper, W. W. (1984). Some models for estimating technical and scale inefficiencies in data envelopment analysis. *Management Science, 30*(9), 1078–1092.

Chakraborty, L., Chakraborty, P., & Shrestha, R. (2019). *Budget credibility of subnational governments: Analysing the fiscal forecasting errors of 28 states in India* (NIPFP Working Paper No. 280). National Institute of Public Finance and Policy. https://www.nipfp.org.in/media/medialibrary/2019/09/WP_2019_280.pdf

Charnes, A., Cooper, W. W., & Rhodes, E. (1978). Measuring the efficiency of decision making units. *European Journal of Operational Research, 2*(6), 429–444.

Choudhury, M., & Mohanty, R. K. (2018). *Utilisation, fund flows and public financial management under the National Health Mission* (NIPFP Working Paper No. 227). National Institute of Public Finance and Policy. https://www.nipfp.org.in/media/medialibrary/2018/05/WP_2018_227.pdf

Fancello, G., Uccheddu, B., & Fadda, P. (2014). Data envelopment analysis (D.E.A.) for urban road system performance assessment. *Procedia—Social and Behavioral Sciences, 111*, 780–789.

Farrel, M. J. (1957). The measurement of productive efficiency. *Journal of Royal Statistics Society, Series A, 120*, 253–281.

Government of India. (2017). *National health policy 2017*. National Health Portal. https://www.nhp.gov.in/nhpfiles/national_health_policy_2017.pdf

Government of India. (2020a). *Report of the fifteenth finance commission for 2021–26*. https://fincomindia.nic.in/ShowContentOne.aspx?id=9&Section=1

Government of India. (2020b). *Population projections for India and States 2011–2036*. Report of the Technical Group on Population Projections. National Commission on Population, Ministry of Health and Family Welfare. https://main.mohfw.gov.in/sites/default/files/Population%20Projection%20Report%202011-2036%20-%20upload_compressed_0.pdf

Institute for Management Development. (2020). *World talent ranking*. https://www.imd.org/wcc/world-competitiveness-center-rankings/world-talent-ranking-2020/

Kapur, A. (2019). *Towards 'cooperative' social policy financing in India. Part of 'policy challenges—2019–2024: The big policy questions for the New Government and possible pathways', Centre for Policy Research*. https://www.cprindia.org/news/towards-%E2%80%98cooperative%E2%80%99-social-policy-financing-india

Lalvani, M., Hajra, K. S., & Pazhayathodi, B. (2009). *Introducing expenditure quality in intergovernmental transfers: A triple-E framework. DRG studies*. Occasional Publication of the Reserve Bank of India. https://rbidocs.rbi.org.in/rdocs/Publications/PDFs/IETATF140809.PDF

Mandl, U., Dierx, A., & Ilzkovitz, F. (2008). *The effectiveness and efficiency of public spending*. Economic Papers, Directorate-General for Economic and Financial Affairs, European Commission. https://ec.europa.eu/economy_finance/publications/pages/publication11902_en.pdf

Martín-Gambo, M., & Iribarren, D. (2021). *Coupled life cycle thinking and data envelopment analysis for quantitative sustainability improvement*. In J. Ren (Ed.), *Methods in sustainability science* (pp. 295–320). Elsevier (Chapter 16). https://doi.org/10.1016/B978-0-12-823987-2.00003-9

Mohanty, R. K., & Bhanumurthy, N. R. (2018). *Assessing public expenditure efficiency at Indian States*. (NIPFP Working Paper No. 225). National Institute of Public Finance and Policy. https://www.nipfp.org.in/media/medialibrary/2018/03/WP_2018_225.pdf

National Health Systems Resource Centre. (2018). *National health accounts estimates for India (2015–16)*. Ministry of Health and Family Welfare, Government of India. https://main.mohfw.gov.in/sites/default/files/NHA_Estimates_Report_2015-16_0.pdf

Prasetyo, A. D., & Zuhdia, U. (2013). The government expenditure efficiency towards the human development. *Procedia Economics and Finance, 5*, 615–622.

Rao, M. G. (2017). *Central transfers to States in India, rewarding performance while ensuring equity*. Final report of a study submitted to NITI Aayog. http://niti.gov.in/writereaddata/files/document_publication/Final%20Report_25Sept_2017.pdf

Reserve Bank of India. (2019). *Fiscal position of State Governments (II). State finances a study of budgets of 2019–20*. Annual Publication. https://rbidocs.rbi.org.in/rdocs/Publications/PDFs/02CH300920199E07E05E3634401CB132FB7541C4B977.PDF

# Measurement and Determinants of Efficiency of Government and Government-Aided Secondary Schools in Kolkata: An Application of Data Envelopment Approach

Arpita Ghose and Sangita Choudhury

## 1 Introduction

Education occupies an important position in every major economy of the world. It helps to accelerate the rate of growth and to equalize the distribution of income. It is widely accepted that education helps to upgrade the general standard of living in a society. Therefore, positive social change is likely to be associated with the production of qualitative citizenry. Education plays a significant role in a rapidly changing work environment due to technological advances. Economists regard education as both consumer and capital good because it offers utility to a consumer and also serves as an input into the production of other goods and services. As a capital good, education can be used to develop the human resources necessary for economic and social transformation. The focus on education as a capital good relates to the concept of human capital, which emphasizes that the development of skills is an important factor in production activities. The economic prosperity and functioning of a nation depend on its physical and human capital stock.

The growing popular interest in education has been paralleled by the development of an immense literature on the role of human capital in economic growth. The importance of education and human capital has been brought out in many studies of endogenous growth literature (Lucas, 1988; Romer, 1990 among others). Lucas (1988) assumed that in addition to the stock of physical capital, there is a metaphysical variable called human capital. A fraction of labor is devoted to production, while the remainder is devoted to accumulation of human capital. The average level of human capital in the economy determines the level of total factor productivity.

A. Ghose (✉)
Department of Economics, Jadavpur University, Kolkata, India
e-mail: arpitaju@gmail.com

S. Choudhury
Department of Applied Economics, Maulana Abul Kalam Azad University of Technology, Kalyani, Haringhata, West Bengal, India

 
A. Raychaudhuri and A. Ghose (eds.), *Managing Pandemic and Correcting Development Fundamentals*, India Studies in Business and Economics,
https://doi.org/10.1007/978-981-19-8680-2_12

Initially, there is a constant returns to scale; however because of the growth of human capital, the economy can take benefit of overall increasing returns to scale, and output increases more than in proportion to increase in the supplies of factors of production (Romer, 1986). Romer (1990) assumes that the growth of productivity depends on the existing stock of ideas and the number of people devoting their time to the accumulation of new ideas. According to the approach chosen by Romer (1990), it is the level of human capital, not its rate of accumulation, which influences the rate of productivity growth. This result is due to the fact that in these models, human capital is an input in the production of new ideas, and therefore an important determinant of the pace of innovations. In particular, its potential contribution to economic prosperity, through innovation and knowledge exchange to the wider society, is regarded as vitally important for economic development and growth. Consequently, economic growth should tend to accelerate as more human capital is employed in research. Countries with a high amount of human capital would be expected to have a higher level of steady-state income. In this case, the prediction delivered by the augmented Solow model would be equivalent to the one made by Romer. Growth should be positively correlated with the initial level of human capital. Mankiw et al. (1992) presented a simple extension to the Solow model by incorporating human capital as a separate input; the production technology of this model comes to be known as the human capital augmented Solow model. The human capital augmented Solow model predicts that, other things being equal, a country should have a higher level of per capita income if it has a higher amount of human capital. It is the education and the creation of human capital that was responsible for both the differences in labor productivity and the differences in overall levels of technology (Barro, 1991).

Having established the importance of human capital in economic development, the role of expansion of education can be justified. Education can be viewed as an investment in human capital. Many of the developing nations have thus realized that the principal mechanism for developing human knowledge is the development of education system.

In the Indian context, sufficient educational achievement has been made with respect to literacy rate. Indian literacy rate according to 2011 census stands at 74% compared to 12% at the end of British rule in 1947. The gross enrollment ratio (GER) has increased from 67.35% in 2012–2013 to 79.35% in 2016–2017. In 2016–2017, at secondary level, GER for boys and girls is 78.51% and 80.29%, respectively. According to the report of Unified District Information System for Education Plus (UDISE+) 2019–2020, for school education in India and at secondary level, GER has increased to 77.9% from 76.9% in 2018–2019. GER has improved by nearly 10% in secondary between 2012–2013 and 2019–2020.

Coming to the school education, among the four levels such as primary, upper primary, secondary, and higher secondary, secondary education is a stepping stone to higher education that equips and empowers students with skills required for entering the job market. The Rashtriya Madhyamik Shiksha Abhiyan (RMSA)—integrated, launched to enhance access and improve quality of education at secondary stage, envisages enhancing the enrollment for classes IX–X by providing a secondary school within a prescribed distance of every habitation, improving quality of education imparted at secondary level by making all secondary schools confirm to prescribed norms, removal of gender, socio-economic, and disability barriers, usual access to secondary level of education.

*Thus, given the fact that there is a significant achievement in GER at the secondary level, it is worthwhile to map GER to the other indicator like efficiency. Basic question is whether the different schools are technically efficient in the sense that whether maximum output given the amount of resources is being generated. In tune with* Hulten (1996) *one may argue, it may be possible that there is some extent of inefficiency, and in that case, India may be forgoing economic growth as it is not possible for India to produce maximum educational output producible because of the existence of such inefficiency. A related question is that what are the major factors influencing technical efficiency of different schools?*

Several literatures exist on measurement of technical efficiency scores (TE). Charnes et al. (1978, 1981) introduced data envelopment analysis (DEA) which is a linear programming method, for efficiency measurement considering several decision-making units (DMU) in multiple inputs and multiple outputs framework. They included non-profit public entities like schools as DMUs which produce measurable output from measurable inputs but with lack of market prices of outputs (and sometimes some inputs also) and constructed a benchmark production function, using linear programming under the assumption of constant returns to scale. Later Banker et al. (1984) extended the Charnes et al. (1978) model to variable returns to scale. The advantage of DEA is that it does not depend on the prior specification of functional form of the criterion function.

Some literatures are available around the globe relating to study on efficiency of the school education (Adkins & Moomaw, 2007; Andrews et al., 2002; Arshad, 2014; Bradley & Taylor, 2002; Bessent & Bessent, 1980; Bonesronning & Rattsq, 1994; Ciro & Torres, 2018; Driscoll et al., 2003; Gavurova et al., 2017; Hanushek, 1996; Haug & Blackburn, 2017; Krueger, 2003; Leithwood & Jantzi, 2009; Levin, 1997; Masci et al., 2018; Newman et al., 2006; Sotiriadis et al., 2018), among others. The perusal of the literatures suggest that following factors were considered for determining TE of school education: (i) teacher education and experience, teacher salary (Adkins & Moomaw, 2007); (ii) school characteristics (Andrews et al., 2002; Bradley & Taylor, 2002; Driscoll et al., 2003; Krueger, 2003; Leithwood and Jantzi, 2009; Newman et al., 2006); (iii) socio-economic background of the child (Ray, 1991); (iv) role of school management (Masci et al., 2018); (v) educational qualification and experience of headmaster/mistress/principal of the school (Masci et al., 2018); (vi) some basic aspects of education: deprivation aspects; social aspects and policy aspects (Sengupta & Pal, 2010, 2012).

In the Indian context, there are some literatures relating to technical efficiency of school education (Ghose, 2017; Kingdon, 1996; Mohapatra, 2015; Purohit, 2015; Sankar, 2007; Sengupta & Pal, 2010, 2012; Singh et al., 2018; Tyagi et al., 2009), Bhanja and Ghose (2022), Choudhury and Ghose (2022) among others. However, most of the Indian school level studies are based on secondary data source, and there is a dearth in the literature relating to technical efficiency at school level in Indian context using primary survey data, and the present study attempts to fill up the literature gap in this direction. Further, for country like India, the efficiency of the school is expected to be influenced by the availability of fund that the schools receive from the government. Relevantly, it may be mentioned that Sengupta and Pal (2010, 2012) considered some basic aspects of education; like deprivation aspects; social aspects, and policy aspects which may affect TE. Using Anand and Sen (1997) formula for human poverty index, Sengupta and Pal (2010) derived grand poverty index comprising of various poverty indicators of education system. The estimated results of TE of primary school education in India for the year 2005–2006 using secondary data indicate that poverty indicators have negative impacts on TE, whereas social and policy indicators are not significantly related to efficiency improvement. Sengupta and Pal (2012) repeated the similar exercise for Burdwan district of West Bengal, India, for the year 2005–2006, where TE is positively affected by social indicators, negatively by school poverty indicators and policy indicators. Thus, the favorable effect of the policy variables on TE has not been obtained in this study. The limitation of Sengupta and Pal is that they have used composite index for determinant analysis. But in order to have a definite policy for improvement of TE, the role of each of the items under the broad indicators like infrastructure, school characteristics, policy variable, etc., on TE needs to be found out. It may be possible that one variable under the broad indicator is significant, while the other is not. This differential effect cannot be captured if we take a composite index comprising of different variables as the composite index cannot distinguish between a variable which is significant and a variable which is not. Further, the government may undertake policy measures for some targeted group, which may influence the efficiency level of the schools, and this issue needs to be addressed.

Given this back drop, *present chapter attempts to contribute to the literature in the following directions.*

*First of all*, this chapter measures TE of different government and government-aided schools for secondary education level in Kolkata based on primary survey data collected through multistage stratified random sampling procedure of 25 sample schools, using non-parametric method of data envelopment analysis (DEA) and then determines the factors influencing such TE. The study actually addresses the question whether different government and government-aided secondary schools in Kolkata are technically efficient in the sense that they are generating maximum school output given the existing resources available at school and considers how the efficiency score can be improved. The reason for the choice of public sector school is that the charges of government schools are very low, and hence, it is necessary to investigate the extent of TE of such low charges schools. *Secondly*, while collecting the data, it has been found that most of the students undertake private tuition. It is likely that the effect of private tuition is felt on the efficiency of the schools, and TE may be inflated because of the students taking private tuition. The relevant question is what is the part of the variation of TE of these schools, which is not explained by the private tuition taken by the students. The present chapter has obtained the extent of such variation, which has been unexplored in the literature dealing with efficiency of school education till date. *Thirdly*, it may be pointed out that to ease out financial constraints of the household in the face of increase in significant cost of education, it is imperative that the government should take appropriate measures to maintain quality of education and impart skill through education, so that the household can continue sending their children, specifically the girl children to schools to complete the desired level of education, which ensure employability and returns to their investment. At present, Government of West Bengal is pursuing a policy of helping economically backward families with cash transfer, to improve the life and status of girls and to support the education of girl child, so that they do not arrange for the marriage of the girls before eighteen years (Kanyashree Prakalpa). *The question is whether such type of intervention also adds to the efficiency of the school?* At the same time, the government and government-aided schools receive funds from the government of West Bengal, and the basic question is whether the availability of these funds add to the efficiency of the schools. *The present chapter attempts to answer these questions.* The perusal of the literatures suggest that there is a dearth in the study containing a detailed analysis of the determinants of TE after taking into account *the impact of the percentage number of students taking private tuition, government policy interventions as mentioned above*, along with the impact of different factors like role of the head of the school (headmaster/mistress/principal) in school management and framing policies, characteristics of head of the school, characteristics of the teachers, school infrastructure, school characteristics and student composition-related variables, student's characteristics and socio-economic background of the students and student's perception about different attributes for secondary level of education; exploring primary survey data. *The present chapter attempts to highlight these unexplored issues in the literature dealing with TE of schools in the Indian context. Fourthly*, another departure from the literature is that while finding out the determinants, the present chapter will not attempt to construct a composite index for infrastructural variables, the variables with school characteristics, policy variables, etc., and find out the effect of this constructed index on TE, as attempted by some of the previous authors as argued above. The reason is that in order to undertake appropriate policy for enhancing TE, it is the effect of the particular variable on TE that matters. Some policy measures are suggested to improve TE of the schools at the secondary level.

Rest of the study unfolds as follows. Section 2 discusses the methodology, determinants of TE and data sources. Estimated results are presented in Sect. 3. Section 4 represents summary and conclusions and recommends some policy suggestions.

## 2 Methodology of Estimation, Determinants of TE and Data Sources

### 2.1 Methodology of Estimation of TE

Like other production system, an educational production function is the relationship between school inputs and a measure of school output, and education system can also be viewed as the production function satisfying the relationship between input and output. Following the literature on the methodology of DEA (see Ray, 2004), an educational production function is defined as follows:

$$Y = Af(Xa, \ldots, Xm)$$

where $Y$ = some measure of school output—for example, a score on a scholastic achievement battery; $Xa$, ..., $Xm$ = variables measuring the school inputs. The variables here would typically include the amount and quality of teaching services.

The term $A$ can be thought of as a shift parameter, being function of (i) $I_1, I_2, \ldots,$ in representing the favorable infrastructure variables, (ii) $\text{PR}_1$, $\text{PR}_2$, ..., PR$q$ representing poor infrastructure variables, (iii) $E_1, E_2, \ldots, E_P$ representing environmental influences of learning outside the school, e.g., the parents' educational attainment and or atmosphere at home, (iv) $\text{PO}_1$, $\text{PO}_2$, ..., $\text{PO}_k$ representing policy variables.

Educational outcome can be viewed as a production process, where inputs of labor, capital, and organization are applied to the relatively 'unfinished' child, and an output-pupil achievement results. The objective is to generate the maximum possible achievement using a given amount of school resources.

There are two components of efficiency: technical efficiency (TE) and allocative efficiency (AE). TE of a decision-making unit (DMU) is measured by either (i) output-oriented (OUTTE) approach showing the maximum output quantities that can be proportionately increased without altering input quantities or (ii) input-oriented (INPTE) approach representing the maximum amount of input quantities, which can be proportionately reduced without changing quantities produced as output. Allocative efficiency reflects the ability of a DMU to use the inputs in optimal proportions, given their respective price. *This chapter considers measurement and the determinants of TE, in particular OUTTE.*

TE measurement is a two-step problem. First, a benchmark production function, known as frontier, has to be constructed which is supposed to be perfectly efficient. Secondly, comparison of the observed performance of DMU with the benchmark is the basic approach of measuring TE. Figure 1 represents OUTTE and INPTE in case of single input and output framework.

In Fig. 1, input $x$ is measured along the horizontal axis, and output $y$ is measured along the vertical axis. Point $A$ $(x_0, y_0)$ represents the actual input–output bundle of a DMU at a point $A$. $y^* = f(x_0)$, where $y^*$ is the maximum output producible from input $x_0$. The *output-oriented* measure of TE of DMU at point $A = \frac{y_0}{y^*}$ which is the comparison of actual output to maximum possible output, given the input. The *input-oriented* measure of TE of DMU at point $A$ is $x^*/x_0$, which is the comparison of minimum input required with the actual input in use, to produce the given level of output (Fig. 2).

Given the actual input–output bundle, output-oriented technical efficiency (OUTTE) is estimated here by constructing the frontier under VRS using non-parametric DEA following Banker et al. (1984), after making a number of fairly general assumptions about the nature of the underlying production technology, namely (i) all actually observed input–output combinations are feasible, (ii) the

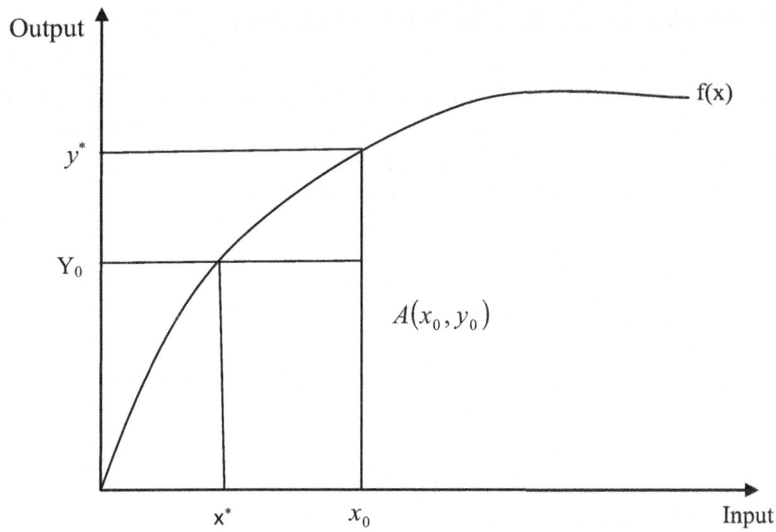


**Fig. 1** Output-oriented and input-oriented technical efficiency. *Source* Bhanja and Ghose (2022)

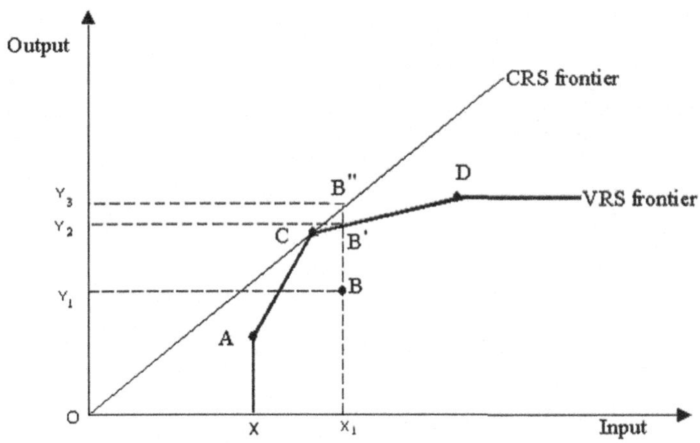


**Fig. 2** Production frontier and returns to scale. *Source* Bhanja and Ghose (2022)

production possibility set is convex, (iii) inputs are freely disposable, and (iv) outputs are freely disposable. The figure shows that given the input utilization $x_1$, the maximum possible output will depend on whether one is following CRS or VRS frontier.

## 2.2 Methodology for Finding Output-Oriented TE

Suppose that there are $N$ DMUs. Each of them is producing '$g$' outputs using '$h$' inputs. The DMU $t$ uses input bundle $x^t = (x_{1t}, x_{2t}, \ldots, x_{ht})$ and produces the output bundle $y^t = \left(y_{1t}, y_{2t}, \ldots, y_{gt}\right)$. This paper assumes VRS.

The specific production possibility set under VRS is given by

$$T^{\mathrm{VRS}} = \left\{ (x, y) : x \geq \sum_{j=1}^{N} \lambda_j x^j;\ y \leq \sum_{j=1}^{N} \lambda_j y^j; \right.$$
$$\left. \sum_{j=1}^{N} \lambda_j = 1;\ \lambda_j \geq 0;\ (j = 1, 2, \ldots, N) \right\} \tag{1}$$

the output-oriented measure of TE of any DMU $t$ under *VRS technology* requires the solution of the following LP problem

$$\max \phi$$
$$\text{Subject to} \sum_{j=1}^{N} \lambda_j y_{rj} \geq \phi y_{rt}; \quad (r = 1, 2, \ldots, g)$$
$$\sum_{j=1}^{N} \lambda_j x_{ij} \leq x_{it}; \quad (i = 1, 2, \ldots, h)$$
$$\phi_{\text{free}}\ \lambda_j \geq 0; \quad (j = 1, 2, \ldots, N)$$
$$\sum_{j=1}^{N} \lambda_j = 1 \tag{2}$$

OUTTE of DMU $t$ can be determined by using Eq. (3).

$$\mathrm{TE}_o^t = \mathrm{TE}_o^t(x^t, y^t) = \frac{1}{\phi^*} \tag{3}$$

where $\phi^*$ is the solution of Eq. (2) showing the maximum value of $\phi$. The maximum output bundle producible from input bundle $x^t$ is $y^*$ and is defined as $y^* = \phi^* y^t$.

An overview of the methodologies for finding technical efficiency of DMU can be found in Ray (2004).

## 2.3 Input and Output Variables for Efficiency Measurement

Relevantly, differences between this educational production function and the standard micro production function are worth mentioning. *First of all,* since the output produced in education is not tangible output; to represent the output, some suitable measures are required.

For efficiency estimation, this study considers multiple output and input variables. The *five output variables* are (i) highest marks obtained in board examination, (ii) percentage of students securing first division, (iii) average marks obtained in Language group, (iv) average marks obtained in Mathematics, and (v) average marks obtained in Science group. *The selected four inputs used are* (i) classroom-student ratio, (ii) teacher–pupil ratio, (iii) percentage of teachers with qualification master degree and above, and (iv) monthly expenditure incurred on per student by the school. The 'percentage of teachers with qualification master degree and above' reflects quality of teacher input.

*Secondly,* computation of the shadow prices of both inputs and outputs is needed, as both the outputs and inputs used do not have market prices.

After obtaining TE scores, second stage regression analysis is resorted to find out the determinants of technical efficiency.

## 2.4 Possible Determinants of Output-Oriented TE

The possible determinants are considered both from school perspective and the student's perspective, i.e., both the school-related determinants and student-related determinants are considered, which can be classified under the following broad heads:

(a) Characteristics of the teachers: Here, the effect of the following variables has been considered: (i) average service experience of full time teachers (in years) (X1), (ii) proportion of part-timers (X2), (iii) average service experience of part-time teachers (X3). The information related to part-time teachers is included as due to lack of sufficient number of full time teachers, schools have to employ part-time teachers, and hence, the basic question is whether these teachers play any significant role in promoting TE?

(b) School infrastructure and administration-related variables: Here, the basic question is can school infrastructure and administration related variables affect efficiency score of the schools significantly? To answer this question, effect of the following variables is considered: (i) proportion of vacant teaching post (X4), (ii) proportion of vacant non-teaching post (X5), (iii) whether the headmaster/mistress (HM) is on duty (X6), (iv) whether there is smart classroom (X7), (v) number of smart classroom (X8), (vi) whether the librarian of the school is on duty (X9), and (vii) whether all laboratory staffs are on duty (X10).

(c) School characteristics and student composition-related variables: Another question is whether more inclusion of backward section in the education system and the school specific characteristics can increase efficiency? Accordingly, effect of the following variables has been considered: (i) proportion of reserve category students (X11), (ii) proportion of physically disabled PD students (X12), (iii) proportion of students taking vocational courses (X13), (iv) percentage of students with English proficiency (X14), (v) class size as represented by the number of sections in the class (X15), (vi) proportion of reserve category teachers (X16), and (vii) ratio of male to female teachers (X17).

(d) Policy-related variables: To answer the question whether government intervention through policy on school education can improve efficiency, the impact of the following variables has been considered: (i) proportion of needy students (who got free studentship) (X18), (ii) amount of government fund received, other than the payment of the salary of teaching and non-teaching staffs (X19), and (iii) proportion of students who got Kanyashree (X20). Here, specifically, the role of the amount of government funds received and the Kanyashree Prakalpa in enhancing the level of efficiency will be investigated. It may be noted that although the variable X11 has been considered as a variable representing composition of the students under the head '*school characteristics and student composition-related variables*', *the variable X11 can also be considered as a policy variable, representing the government policy of social inclusions. In this context, one can ask whether the policy of social inclusion by the government promotes efficiency.*

(e) Headmaster's/mistress (HM) role in school management and framing policies: Another question is whether the role of HM in managing school has any impact in determining TE of the school? To take this into account, the following variables are considered: (i) interaction with teachers and students by the HM while making a decision (X21), (ii) interaction with parents (X22) by the HM while making a decision, (iii) interaction with other school's HM by the HM of the concerned school (X23), and (iv) frequency of interaction with State Education Department by the HM (X24).

(f) Characteristics of headmaster/mistress (HM): Again, the question is—can characteristics of HM of the school influence efficiency of the school? Accordingly, impact of several variables is considered: (i) gender of HM (X25), (ii) age of HM (X26), (iii) experience of HM as head (in years) (X27), (iv) level of education of HM (X28), and (v) salary of HM (gross) (X29).

(g) Socio-economic background of the students and student characteristics: Similarly, one can ask the question, whether student's characteristics and socio-economic background of the students have any role to play in determining TE of the school? For capturing this possible impact, some variables are considered like (i) mother's academic qualification (X30), (ii) father's academic qualification (X31), (iii) monthly parental income (X32), (iv) percentage of student taking private tuition (X33), (v) number of subjects learning from private tutor (X34), (vi) number of hours of study at home (X35), (vii) percentage of students having text book at home (X36), (viii) percentage of students consulting reference book (X37), (ix) travel time (in minutes) to school each way (X38), (x) percentage of students working for earning money (X39), (xi) percentage of younger siblings per student (X40), (xii) percentage of elder siblings per student (X41), and (xiii) percentage of students giving service at home (X42).

(h) Quality of school attributes based on student's perception: The study tries to assess the impact of quality of school attribute in determination of TE. As a means to achieve this goal, student's perceptions on several school attributes are considered for authentic understanding about the quality of school attributes. Specifically, the following aspects are considered: (i) student's perception about regularity of class (X43), (ii) student's perception about quality of teaching (X44), (iii) student's perception about quality of laboratory (X45), (iv) student's perception about quality of drinking water (X46), and (v) student's perception about sanitation facility of the school (X47).

Information on the determinants as specified in the broader categories (a) to (f) is collected from school administration level, whereas information on the variables corresponding to broader categories (g) and (h) is collected from students.

Whole analysis is carried out in two stages. In the *first stage*, the TE of the schools is estimated. In the *second stage*, regression analysis, estimated TE from the first stage, has been considered as dependent variable and the above indicators as explanatory variables. As already been discussed; since the objective is to find out individual impact of explanatory variable, any composite index (representing broader category) has not been constructed to test the effect of the constructed index.

## 2.5 The Method of Data Collection

The study is based on the primary data collected through the questionnaire from 25 different government and government-aided schools located in Kolkata, West Bengal in the year 2019–2020. The collected data consists of two types of survey:

(i) School survey, i.e., information taken from the school administration relating to Secondary level.
(ii) Student survey, i.e., information taken from the students to collect individual information as discussed above and to take into account their perception about the teaching and academic atmosphere of the school, to adjust for the quality of the teaching and also the related variables on their family background.

Procedure of selection of the schools is as follows:

The Department of Education, Government of West Bengal publishes list of schools in Kolkata for 23 Circles. The entire list of the schools for the entire circle has been collected and is treated as population. To select the schools stratified random sampling is followed, taking into account each circle as relevant strata. The proportion of schools in any circle is determined and treated as population proportion. The sample school is selected using random number table, after making the assumption that sample proportion is equal to the population proportion. Let population proportion of the schools of *i*-th strata is $P_i$. Hence, assuming the sample proportion is equal to population proportion, and the targeted number of schools is 25, the number of sample to be selected from $i$-th strata is $25 \times P_{i.}$

While conducting student survey, a random sample of students has been drawn from each school which is selected as follows:

Eight number of students from secondary level (four from the general category and four from reserved category; more specifically, four students from class IX comprising of two from general category and two from reserved category and similarly four students from class X comprising of two from general category and two from reserved category) are selected from each school. The sample consists of both male and female and backward classes.

Data on input and output variables, for secondary level, has been collected from school administration survey. On the other hand, data on possible determinants has been collected by interviewing both school administration as well as students of these schools.

## 2.6 Description and Definition of the Variables

*Regarding the data on school infrastructure and administration-related variables*, it can be said that some of the variables are dummy variables in nature. For example, 'whether the HM is on duty', 'whether there is smart classroom', 'whether the librarian of the school is on duty', and 'whether all laboratory staffs are on duty' are dummy variables; where '1' value represents presence, and '0' value represents absence of respective variables.

*For school characteristics and student composition-related variables*, it is to be pointed out that, while calculating 'proportion of reserve category students', the study has taken into account all the backward social categories, i.e., scheduled caste, scheduled tribe, and other backward class. Since, the study is based on Bengali medium government and government-aided schools; it may be possible that English proficiency of the students can affect TE of the schools positively, and hence, data on 'percentage of students with English proficiency' variable has been noted on the basis of English teacher's perception about student's English proficiency. The 'class size' variable has been represented by number of sections in the specific class.

*Coming to the variables relating to characteristics of the teacher*, it is to be noted that data on 'average service experience of full time teacher' and 'average service experience of part-time teacher' has been collected in terms of years.

*Considering policy-related variables*, it can be mentioned that 'proportion of needy students' is actually measured by the proportion of students (in a specific class) who got free studentship. Further, regarding fund, there are two types of data (i) government fund; 'amount of government fund received' and (ii) funds received from Samagra Shiksha Mission, West Bengal. As per the norm, a part of the funds received from Samagra Shiksha Mission is utilized for student's purposes, and hence, it is used to calculate the input variable-expenditure incurred per student; while estimating TE of the school. Since this chapter is interested in finding out the impact of government fund on TE, the fund received from the government of West Bengal other than the payment of salaries of teaching, and non-teaching staffs is used as an explanatory variable for finding out the determinants of TE.

*For the variables specifying the roles of HM on school management*, it can be mentioned that the 'interaction with teachers and students', 'interaction with parents', and 'interaction with other school's HM' are dummy variables, where '1' value represents 'yes', and '0' value represents 'no'. Since it is desirable that the government schools should maintain sufficient interactions with State Education Department, the frequency of such interaction becomes crucial. 'Frequency of interaction with State Education Department' is a categorical variable in this study, where '1' value represents 'once in six months interaction', '2' represents 'once in a month interaction', and '3' represents 'frequency of interaction once in a week'.

*Coming to the variables relating to characteristics of HM*, it can be said that 'gender of HM' is a dummy variable, where '1' value represents male, and '0' value represents female. The data on 'age of HM' and 'experience of HM as head' variables has been collected in terms of years. Again, 'level of education of HM' is represented by the years of study (only UG = 15, UG + B.ED = 15 + 2 = 17, only PG = 17, PG + B.ED = 17 + 2 = 19, Ph.D. = 17 + 5 = 22, PG + B.ED + M.ED = 17 + 2 + 2 = 21, DOUBLE PG = 17 + 2 = 19, UG + BP.ED = 15 + 3 = 18, PG + BP.ED = 17 + 3 = 20, Ph.D. + B.ED = 22 + 2 = 24, PGBT + DOUBLE PG + Ph.D. 1 + 19 + 5 = 25).The 'salary of HM' is gross salary and measured in terms of rupees.

*Considering the variables relating to* student's *characteristics and socio-economic background*, it can be pointed that 'mother's academic qualification' and 'father's academic qualification' are represented by years of study, where; '0' value represents illiteracy, 4 = literate up to class IV, 8 = literate up to class VIII, 10 = literate up to class X, 12 = literate up to class XII, 15 = literate up to graduation, 17 = literate up to post graduation for both the variables.

*For the parental monthly income variable*, it may be mentioned that income of the family members of the students has been collected by setting some class limits like (i) up to the range of Rs. 10,000 per month, the mean income for this range is taken to be Rs. 5000/–, (ii) between Rs. 10,000–25,000 per month, the mean income for this class limit is taken to be Rs. 12,500/–, (iii) Rs. 25,000–50,000 per month, the mean income for this range is taken to be Rs. 37,500/–.

For the variables, the 'number of subjects learning from private tutor', 'number of hours of study at home', and 'travel time to school each way', the respective variable represents the average value of each of the variables considering respondent students in the class.

*For quality of school attributes based on student's perception related variables*, it can be said that all the student's perception variables, i.e., student's perception about 'regularity of class', 'quality of teaching', 'quality of laboratory', 'quality of drinking water', and 'sanitation facility of the school' are categorical variables. Further, following student's judgment regarding above-mentioned school attributes, '1' value has been assigned for excellent quality, 2 = good, 3 = not bad, 4 = poor quality for each of these perception-related variables.

# 3 Empirical Findings

## 3.1 Descriptive Statistics

Initially, before proceeding for further analysis, developing a brief idea about probable determinants seems crucial. Hence, descriptive statistics of these determinants of technical efficiency (other than dummy and categorical variables) considering secondary levels of education have been shown in Table 1.

## 3.2 Measure of Technical Efficiency

Table 2 represents estimated value of the output-oriented technical efficiency score (TE) under the assumption of VRS for each of the sample schools for secondary level of education along with the mean value of such TE.

Estimated TE results suggest that about 52% of the sample schools are not perfectly efficient; implying that these schools can produce more output with existing resources and the magnitude of TE varies among the schools.

Among these 25 schools and for the secondary level, 18 schools have efficiency above the average level.

## 3.3 Determinants of Output-Oriented TE

Coming to determinants of output-oriented technical efficiency score (TE) after taking into account of different factors as mentioned above, it can be said that while collecting data, it has been observed that most of the students take private tuition, which may in turn inflate the extent of TE of the schools. The relevant question is what is the part of the variation of TE of these schools, which is not explained by the private tuition taken by the students. The present chapter has obtained a measure of the extent of such variation, performing the following steps:

Step I: A regression is obtained taking into account TE of the schools as a dependent variable and the percentage number of students taking private tuition as explanatory variable (X33), after controlling for other determinants of TE, as mentioned above. The variable X33 turns out to be significant in this regression supporting the fact that the extents of TE of the schools are in fact dependent on the fact that the students take private tuition.

Step II: However, the explanatory variable X33 is not exogenous. It in turn gets determined by the other variables within the system. Thus, in the next step, the estimated value of the variable X33 is obtained from the regression where X33 is explained in terms of the other variables.

**Table 1** Descriptive statistics of the determinants of technical efficiency in Secondary Education, Kolkata

| Variables | Mean | Standard deviation | Coefficient of variation |
|---|---|---|---|
| Service experience of full time teacher (in years) | 15.9 | 2.95 | 18.55 |
| Proportion of part-timer teachers | 0.11 | 0.11 | 100.00 |
| Experience of part-time teachers (in years) | 8.6 | 5.52 | 64.19 |
| Proportion of vacant teaching post | 0.18 | 0.15 | 83.33 |
| Proportion of vacant non-teaching post | 0.35 | 0.24 | 68.57 |
| Number of smart classroom | 1 | 0.69 | 69.00 |
| Proportion of reserve category students | 0.20 | 0.14 | 70.00 |
| Proportion of physically disable students | 0.00088 | 0.003 | 340.91 |
| Proportion of students taking vocational courses | 0.09 | 0.24 | 266.67 |
| Percentage of students with English proficiency | 37 | 22.23 | 60.08 |
| Class size | 2 | 0.52 | 26.00 |
| Proportion of reserve category teachers | 0.26 | 0.12 | 46.15 |
| Ratio of male to female teachers | 1.5 | 1.99 | 132.67 |
| Proportion of needy students (who got free studentship) | 0.03 | 0.08 | 266.67 |
| Amount of fund received from (i) Samagra Shiksha Mission and (ii) West Bengal government other than payments of salaries of the teaching and non-teaching staffs in the sample year (in rupees) | 859,694 | 537,696 | 62.55 |
| Proportion of students who got Kanyashree | 0.47 | 0.45 | 95.74 |
| Age of HM | 51.9 | 4.99 | 9.61 |
| Experience of HM as head (in years) | 7.4 | 6.155832 | 83.19 |
| Level of education of HM | 20 | 1.98 | 9.90 |
| Salary of HM (gross) (in rupees) | 76,186 | 9425.58 | 12.37 |
| Mother's academic qualification | 9 | 2.26 | 25.11 |
| Father's academic qualification | 11 | 2.27 | 20.64 |
| Monthly parental income (in rupees) | 12,935 | 7861.17 | 60.77 |

(continued)

**Table 1** (continued)

| Variables | Mean | Standard deviation | Coefficient of variation |
|---|---|---|---|
| Percentage of students taking private tuition | 97.65 | 7.17 | 7.34 |
| Number of subjects learning from private tutor | 6 | 1.51 | 25.17 |
| Number of hours of study at home | 4 | 1.35 | 33.75 |
| Percentage of students having text book at home | 96.39 | 8.55 | 8.87 |
| Percentage of students consulting reference book | 76.17 | 24.40 | 32.03 |
| Travel time (in minutes) to school each way | 19 | 11.14 | 58.63 |
| Percentage of students working for earning money | 8.30 | 17.41 | 209.76 |
| Percentage of younger siblings per student | 50.94 | 32.20 | 63.21 |
| Percentage of elder siblings per student | 49.06 | 32.20 | 65.63 |
| Percentage of students who give their service at home | 54.78 | 26.78 | 48.89 |

*Source* Author's computation with primary survey data for the year 2019–2020

Step III: In the next step, a regression is carried out taking into account TE of the schools as a dependent variable and the estimated value of X33 along with the other explanatory variables. *This is the final representation of the determinants of TE where TE is determined by the fact that the students undertake private tuition.*

Step IV: To obtain that part of the variation of TE of these schools, which is not explained by the percentage number of students taking private tuition, in the next step, a regression is done considering TE of the schools as a dependent variable and only estimated value of X33 (as obtained from Step II) as explanatory variable. The residual of this regression is obtained. This residual shows the extent of TE which is not explained by the percentage number of students taking private tuition and is a measure of TE that we are actually looking for.

Step V: In final step, the residual as obtained in step IV representing the extent of TE which is not explained by the number of students taking private tuition is explained in terms of the other variables to confirm what are the other major determinants of TE, apart from the variable, the percentage number of students taking private tuition.

The results of the regression as described in step I are presented in Table 3.

Since the model is based on cross-section regression, there may be the presence of heteroskedasticity, which is tested by using Breusch–Pagan test. The regression model of Table 3 has the estimated value of the Breusch–Pagan test statistic; Wald chi-square = 0.83, with $p$-value, Prob > chi-square = 0.3621, which is higher than an

**Table 2** Extent of technical efficiency (TE) of different government and government-aided schools in Kolkata at the secondary level

| Serial number | Schools | Extent of TE |
|---|---|---|
| 1 | School 1 | 1.00 |
| 2 | School 2 | 1.00 |
| 3 | School 3 | 0.984 |
| 4 | School 4 | 0.737 |
| 5 | School 5 | 1.00 |
| 6 | School 6 | 0.859 |
| 7 | School 7 | 1.00 |
| 8 | School 8 | 1.00 |
| 9 | School 9 | 1.00 |
| 10 | School 10 | 1.00 |
| 11 | School 11 | 0.784 |
| 12 | School 12 | 1.00 |
| 13 | School 13 | 1.00 |
| 14 | School 14 | 0.996 |
| 15 | School 15 | 0.871 |
| 16 | School 16 | 1.00 |
| 17 | School 17 | 0.972 |
| 18 | School 18 | 1.00 |
| 19 | School 19 | 0.820 |
| 20 | School 20 | 0.776 |
| 21 | School 21 | 0.683 |
| 22 | School 22 | 1.00 |
| 23 | School 23 | 0.956 |
| 24 | School 24 | 0.936 |
| 25 | School 25 | 0.945 |
| *Mean* | | 0.933 |

*Source* Author's computation with primary survey data for the year 2019–2020

appropriate threshold value 0.05 (e.g., $p > 0.05$), the null hypothesis of homoskedasticity is accepted. Thus, OLS has been applied to estimate the parameters of the model.

The figures presented in Table 3 suggest *significant* relationship between TE and the following variables:

(1) Headmaster/mistress/principal's role in school management and framing policies like whether for school management and taking the policy decision headmaster/mistress/principal interacts with student and teacher (X21). In fact apart from the variable X21, the variable Z9 (=X21 * X24) showing

**Table 3** Determinants of output-oriented technical efficiency score (TE) taking into account original value of the percentage of students taking private tuition

| Variables | Coefficient | *t*-value | *p*-value | |
|---|---|---|---|---|
| C | −0.202493 | −0.728327 | 0.4849 | Adjusted $R$-square = 0.832543 |
| X1 | −0.011222 | −3.205113 | 0.0107 | |
| X15 | 0.144856 | 5.067341 | 0.0007 | |
| X21 | 0.099318 | 2.342531 | 0.0438 | |
| X27 | −0.006837 | −3.097046 | 0.0128 | |
| X19 | 7.87E−08 | 3.061691 | 0.0135 | |
| X11 | 0.369413 | 4.219407 | 0.0022 | |
| X20 | 0.002049 | 2.434865 | 0.0377 | |
| Z1 | −1.84E−05 | −2.903391 | 0.0175 | |
| Z9 | 0.054111 | 3.435406 | 0.0074 | |
| X36 | 0.001554 | 1.114552 | 0.2939 | |
| X9 | 0.070530 | 2.831028 | 0.0197 | |
| X33 | 0.005191 | 1.920728 | 0.0870 | |
| X8 | 0.033693 | 1.627196 | 0.1381 | |

*Source* Author's computation with primary survey data for the year 2019–2020

the interaction between the two variables X21 and how frequently headmaster/mistress/principal interacts with State Legislative and State Education Department (X24) turns out to be significant. These variables are positively related to TE implying definite *role of the headmaster/mistress/principal in fostering TE of the school.* The existence of the interaction term X21 * X24 in turn implies that given the value of X21, the level of TE will also depend on the value of X24 and vice versa.

(2) Service experience of headmaster/mistress/principal (X27): This variable negatively affects TE suggesting that the schools with relatively junior headmaster/mistress/principal will have more TE as compared to schools with relatively senior Headmaster/mistress/principal.

(3) Service experience of the full time teacher (X1): This variable negatively affects TE, showing that the school with relatively junior full time teachers will be able to acquire higher level of TE.

(4) School infrastructure like (i) the number of smart classroom in the school (X8); the positive relationship between TE and this variable supports that the school with more number of smart classrooms will be able to acquire higher level of TE, however, the level of significance is low, (ii) whether the librarian of the school is on duty (X9), this variable positively affects TE implying that the school for which the librarian is on duty, the TE will be higher.

(5) The policy variables, namely (i) amount of government fund received other than the salaries of the teaching and non-teaching staffs (X19), the positive relationship of this variable with TE implies that allocation of more government

fund to the school will promote TE and (ii) the proportion of students who got Kanyashree (X20); there is a nonlinear inverted U-shaped relationship of X20 with TE (the coefficient of X20 is positive, while the coefficient of its square term 'Z1' is negative). This result supports that the TE initially increases with the proportion of students who got Kanyashree, but up to a limit; there is a threshold level after which TE falls with increase in X20. However, the marginal effect of TE with respect to Kanyashree variable at its mean value is positive for present sample, implying that an increase in Kanyashree will lead to an increase in TE. It happens because the mean value of Kanyashree is less than that of the threshold value after which its negative effect will be felt.

(6) School characteristics, student composition, and students characteristics like (i) class size, as represented by the prevalence of the number of sections in any particular class (X15); the positive relationship between TE and this variable supports that larger size of the class will promote efficiency, (ii) the proportion of reserved category student (X11) in the class; this variable is positively related to TE depicting that the policy of social inclusion of the government will in fact improve TE, (iii) proportion of students having text book at their home (X36); positive relationship exists between TE and X36; suggesting that the school with relatively greater percentage of students having text book at home will be able to acquire higher level of TE, however, the level of significance is low and (iv) ***percentage of students taking private tuition (X33), this variable is positively related to TE implying that the school with relatively greater percentage of students taking private tuition will be more technically efficient***. The goodness of fit is also reasonably good.

The figures presented in Table 3 establish our hunch that TE of the school is in fact gets determined by the percentage of students taking private tuition. Thus, the percentage number of students taking private tuition may in turn inflate the extent of TE of the schools. The relevant question is what part of the variation of TE of these schools is not explained by the private tuition taken by the students.

To find out such variation of TE of the schools, we have performed the steps II to IV as mentioned above. First of all, note that in the above regression presented in Table 3, the percentage of students who undertake private tuition (X33) is exogenous variable, which may not be true. Rather, this variable X33 may be endogenous, determined within the system, by some other variables.

To test the presence of heteroskedasticity, Breusch–Pagan test is used, the estimated value of this test statistic, i.e., Wald chi-square = 8.19, with $p$-value, Prob > chi-square = 0.0042, which is less than an appropriate threshold value 0.05 (e.g., $p < 0.05$); thus, the alternative hypothesis of heteroskedasticity is accepted. Hence, generalized least square method needs to be applied to estimate the parameters of the model. Here, several alternative regressions are performed to explain the behavior of the percentage of students undertaking private tuition; and the best result is presented in Table 4.

The figures presented in Table 4 suggest significant relationship between percentage number of the students taking private tuition and the following variables:

**Table 4** Determinants of the percentage number of students taking private tuition

| Variables | Coefficient | *z*-value | *p*-value | |
|---|---|---|---|---|
| C | 95.8076 | 20.42 | 0.0000 | Wald chi 2 = 43.07<br>Pr > Chi 2 = 0.000 |
| X38 | 0.3832 | 4.06 | 0.0049 | |
| X39 | −0.2979 | −4.92 | 0.000 | |
| X30 | −1.3813 | −2.66 | 0.008 | |
| X31 | 1.1320 | 2.12 | 0.034 | |
| Z15 | 6.0302 | 1.85 | 0.064 | |
| X41 | -0.0605 | −2.13 | 0.033 | |

*Source* Author's computation with primary survey data for the year 2019–2020

1. Travel time (in minutes) to school each way (X38), this variable is positively related to percentage of students taking private tuition, implying that, if the travel time to school is large, it is more likely that the students will opt for not going to the school and attend private tuition.
2. Mother's academic qualification (X30), this variable is negatively related to percentage of students taking private tuition, which may suggest that if the level of mother's academic qualification is low, it is more likely that the student will get less help from his/her mother for teaching purposes at home, and hence, the mother will send the child for private tuition.
3. Father's academic qualification (X31), this variable is positively related to percentage of students taking private tuition, which may suggest that if the level of father's academic qualification is high, his ambition of achieving high academic qualification of his child will also be high, and hence, it is more likely that the father will send his child for private tuition.
4. The interaction between proportion of vacant teaching post (X4) and students perception about regularity of class (X43); the interaction between proportion of vacant teaching post (X4) and students perception about regularity of class (X43) is represented by the variable Z15, bears positive relation with percentage of students taking private tuition. This result in turn implies that if there is an increase in the number of vacant teaching post and or the decline in the regularity of the classes (as shown by higher sample value of the perception variable), it is more likely that the students will go for private tuition.
5. Percentage of students working for earning money (X39), this variable has negative relation with percentage of students taking private tuition, implying that if the students are more engaged in work and devote time for earning money, it is less likely that they will go for private tuition.
6. Percentage of elder siblings per student (X41); this variable is negatively related to percentage of students taking private tuition implying that if there is more number of elder siblings, then they can help the student for teaching at home, and parents will be reluctant to send their child for private tuition.

The goodness of fit of this regression is good.

**Table 5** Determinants of technical efficiency score (TE) taking into account estimated value of the percentage of students taking private tuition as explanatory variable

| Variables | Coefficient | *t*-value | *p*-value | |
|---|---|---|---|---|
| C | −0.5581762 | 1.38 | 0.196 | Adjusted *R*-square = 0.8330 |
| X1 | −0.117604 | −3.47 | 0.006 | |
| X15 | 0.12554197 | 3.82 | 0.003 | |
| X21 | 0.1264107 | 3.11 | 0.011 | |
| X27 | −0.06687 | −3.24 | 0.009 | |
| X19 | 6.04 E−08 | 2.97 | 0.014 | |
| X11 | 0.3672129 | 4.26 | 0.002 | |
| X20 | 0.008876 | 2.34 | 0.0438 | |
| Z1 | −5.4E−05 | −2.83 | 0.0197 | |
| Z9 | 0.250264 | 1.64 | 0.133 | |
| X36 | 0.0034903 | 2.31 | 0.044 | |
| X9 | 0.0715772 | 2.92 | 0.015 | |
| X8 | 0.034692 | 1.65 | 0.131 | |
| HX33 | 0.0081762 | 2.25 | 0.048 | |

*Source* Author's computation with primary survey data for the year 2019–2020

Based on the estimated values of the parameters of this regression explaining the behavior of private tuition (X33) as performed in step II and reported in Table 4, the estimated values of X33 are obtained, which is then used as an explanatory variable to get the determinants of TE along with the other explanatory variables in step III, the result of which is presented in Table 5. This regression reports the explained behavior of TE of the schools in terms of the included explanatory variables.

For the regression model as presented in Table 5, the estimated value of the Breusch–Pagan test statistic; Wald chi-square = 0.47 has a *p*-value, Prob > chi-square = 0.4941, which is not less than an appropriate threshold value 0.05 (e.g., $p > 0.05$), the null hypothesis of homoskedasticity is accepted. Thus, OLS has been applied to estimate the parameters of the regression model as depicted in Table 5.

The comparison of the Table 5 with that of Table 3 suggests that the determinants of TE, their sign conditions, and the statistical significance other than the estimated value of the percentage number of students taking private tuition (HX33) are same and has already been explained while interpreting the results of Table 3. However, the magnitude of the coefficients of the explanatory variables varies. The impact of HX33 on TE is self-explanatory. Since HX33 is a significant determinant of TE, the variables, which are significantly affecting the percentage numbers of students taking private tuition, will in turn have an indirect effect on TE of the schools. The goodness of fit of the regression presented in Table 5 is also good. In the next step IV, a regression is performed taking into account of TE of the schools as a dependent variable and estimated value of the percentage number of students taking private tuition (HX33) as explanatory variable, and the residual of this regression (RY) is obtained. RY shows that part of the variation of TE of the schools which is not explained by the percentage number students taking private tuition that actually is looked for in this chapter and is represented in Table 6.

The figures presented in Table 6 suggest that a huge amount of variation of TE is explained by the percentage of students taking private tuition and that part of the variation not explained by the percentage of students taking private tuition is small and ranges from 1.5% to 23.8%, with mean value 8.28%.

**Table 6** Extent of total variation of TE which is not explained by the percentage of the students taking private tuition

| Serial number | Schools | Extent of the variation of TE which is not explained by the percentage of the students taking private tuition |
|---|---|---|
| 1 | School 1 | 0.07807 |
| 2 | School 2 | 0.07294 |
| 3 | School 3 | 0.01541 |
| 4 | School 4 | 0.19561 |
| 5 | School 5 | 0.05158 |
| 6 | School 6 | 0.03086 |
| 7 | School 7 | 0.0729 |
| 8 | School 8 | 0.04601 |
| 9 | School 9 | 0.08113 |
| 10 | School 10 | 0.06277 |
| 11 | School 11 | 0.13566 |
| 12 | School 12 | 0.06165 |
| 13 | School 13 | 0.04417 |
| 14 | School 14 | 0.0559 |
| 15 | School 15 | 0.05569 |
| 16 | School 16 | 0.06737 |
| 17 | School 17 | 0.07418 |
| 18 | School 18 | 0.06017 |
| 19 | School 19 | 0.11422 |
| 20 | School 20 | 0.18266 |
| 21 | School 21 | 0.23837 |
| 22 | School 22 | 0.06768 |
| 23 | School 23 | 0.04002 |
| 24 | School 24 | 0.08215 |
| 25 | School 25 | 0.08274 |
| *Mean* | | 0.08280 |

*Source* Author's computation with primary survey data for the year 2019–2020

**Table 7** Determinants of that part of the variation of technical efficiency which is not explained by the percentage of students taking private tuition

| Variables | Coefficient | *t*-value | *p*-value | |
|---|---|---|---|---|
| C | −0.692787 | −4.938104 | 0.0006 | Adjusted *R*-square =0.852814 |
| X1 | −0.011954 | −3.838688 | 0.0033 | |
| X15 | 0.150758 | 5.854412 | 0.0002 | |
| X21 | 0.111050 | 2.857086 | 0.0170 | |
| X27 | −0.007744 | −3.926376 | 0.0028 | |
| X19 | 4.84E−08 | 2.954758 | 0.0144 | |
| X11 | 0.334073 | 4.142709 | 0.0020 | |
| X20 | 0.001825 | 2.364252 | 0.0397 | |
| Z1 | −1.54E−05 | −2.723513 | 0.0214 | |
| Z9 | 0.039062 | 2.803166 | 0.0187 | |
| X36 | 0.002908 | 2.288500 | 0.0451 | |
| X9 | 0.075806 | 3.606313 | 0.0048 | |
| X8 | 0.020187 | 1.058517 | 0.3147 | |

*Source* Author's computation with primary survey data for the year 2019–2020

This in turn implies, the level of TE of the schools will be low if the students do not undertake private tuition.

Accordingly, it will be also interesting to find out the factors explaining the extent of TE which is not explained by the percentage of students taking private tuition (RY). The results of the regression explaining such factors are presented in Table 7.

The figures presented in Table 7 suggest that the determinants of TE apart from the variable the percentage number of students taking private tuition are same as the case explained in Tables 3 and 5, respectively. The goodness of fit is also reasonably good. This in turn also justifies the creditability of the regression presented in Table 7.

## 4 Summary and Policy Suggestions

This chapter adds to the existing literature by measuring technical efficiency scores (TE) of 25 government and government-aided schools for secondary education in Kolkata, using primary survey data collected through stratified random sampling procedure, employing data envelopment analysis, and also finding out the determinants of such efficiency. It is found that about 52% of the sample schools are not fully technically efficient, implying that these schools can produce more output with existing resources, and also the magnitude of TE varies among the schools.

*The data suggests that most of the students of the sample schools undertake private tuition, which may inflate the level of TE. Thus, natural question is what will be the*

*situation of efficiency if the students did not undertake private tuition? Or,* what is the part of the variation of TE, not explained by the percentage number of students taking private tuition?

*To answer this question, first, TE is explained in terms of the percentage number of students taking private tuition along with the other determinants. However, the percentage number of students taking private tuition may be dependent on the other variables of the system. Thus, the determinants of the percentage number of students taking private tuition and hence the estimated value of the percentage number of students taking private tuition (HX33) is obtained. Then, TE is regressed on HX33, and the residual of this equation (RY) is obtained. RY shows that part of the variation of TE which is not explained by the percentage number of students taking private tuition.*

The results suggest that a huge amount of variation in TE is explained by the percentage of students taking private tuition; that part of the variation, not explained by the percentage of students taking private tuition is in fact very low, and it will range from 1.5%. to 23.8% with a mean value 8.28%. This in turn implies, the level of TE of the schools will be low if the students do not undertake private tuition. It raises a serious concern and warns us to think about how to improve the situation.

The other variables which influence TE are:

(1) The role of headmaster/mistress (HM) in school management: While taking policy decision, whether HM interacts with students and teachers, and also the interaction between this variables with the variable specifying the frequency of interaction of HM with State Education Department is positively significantly related to TE, highlighting positive role of HM in fostering TE. The existence of interaction term implies, given the value of one variable, the level of TE will in turn depend on the value of the other and vice versa, showing the importance of both of these variables in determining TE.
(2) Characteristics of HM: Service experience of HM negatively and significantly affects TE, suggesting that schools with relatively junior HM will be more technically efficient as compared to the schools with senior HM.
(3) Characteristics of the teachers: Service experience of full time teachers is negatively and significantly influencing TE meaning that TE of schools with relatively junior full time teachers will be higher as compared to the schools with relatively senior teachers.
(4) School infrastructure and administration-related variables: The variable 'whether the librarian of the school is on duty' is positively and significantly related to TE implying that TE of schools in which librarian is on duty is higher as compared to the schools where librarian is not on duty. Again, number of smart classroom in the school is another positively determining factor of TE, meaning that the TE of schools with more number of smart classrooms will be higher. However, the level of significance of this variable is low.
(5) Policy variables: 'Proportion of students got Kanyashree', a supporting scheme for the girl students by the government of West Bengal, bears a nonlinear inverted U-shaped relationship with TE, meaning that TE initially increases with

Kanyashree, but up to a level, after which the level of TE falls with increase in Kanyashree. Thus, TE of the schools cannot be increased indefinitely by increasing the number of Kanyashree. However, the marginal effect of this variable on TE calculated at its mean value is positive, implying that for the present sample, an increase in number of Kanyashree will increase TE. The reason is that the sample mean value of Kanyashree is below the optimum value of number of Kanyashree up to which the positive effect of Kanyashree on TE is felt. Further, 'amount of government fund received other than the payment of the salaries of teaching and non-teaching staffs' is positively and significantly affecting TE of the schools suggesting that allocation of more government fund to the school will promote TE.

(6) 'School characteristics, student composition', and 'student's characteristics': Class size as represented by the number of sections in the class is positively and significantly determining TE of the schools meaning that schools with larger class size will acquire higher TE. Also, 'proportion of reserved category students' in the class is positively and significantly determining TE implying that the policy of social inclusion of the government for backward section in formal education system actually improves the TE. Again, 'proportion of students having text book at home' is positively and significantly affecting TE, suggesting that TE of the schools with relatively greater percentage of students having text book at home at secondary level will be higher.

Relevantly, it will be of interest to note that following factors are identified as the determinants of the number of students taking private tuition:

(i) *Travel time (in minutes) to school each way*: This variable is positively related to the number of students taking private tuition, implying that, if the travel time of the school is large, it is more likely that the students will opt for not going to the school and attend private tuition. (ii) *Mother's academic qualification*: This variable is negatively related to private tuition, suggesting that if the level of mother's academic qualification is low, it is more likely that the student will get less help from their mother for teachings at home, and hence opt for private tuition. (iii) *Father's academic qualification*: This variable is positively related to private tuition, which may suggest that if the level of father's academic qualification is high, his ambition of achieving high academic qualification of his child will also be high, and hence, it is more likely that the father will send his child for private tuition, (iv) *the interaction between proportion of vacant teaching post and student's perception about regularity of class*: This variable has positive relation with the percentage number of students taking private tuition implying that if there is an increase in the number of vacant teaching post and or the decline in the regularity of the classes in the school, it is more likely that the student will go for private tuition. (v) *Percentage of students working for earning money*: This variable has statistically significant negative relation with the percentage number of students taking private tuition implying that if the students are more engaged in work for earning money, it is less likely that they will go for private tuition, as they can devote less time for private tuition. (vi) *Percentage of elder siblings per student*: This variable is significantly and negatively related to the percentage number of students taking private tuition, implying that if there is more number of elder siblings, then they can help the student for teaching at home, and hence, the students will not go for private tuition, or parents will be reluctant to send their child for private tuition.

*Using the estimated results based on the significant explanatory variables, following policy suggestions can be prescribed from the analysis*: *First of all*, TE will increase with the availability of government fund, and hence, the government should provide more fund to the school for attaining higher level of efficiency. But it is not the sole factor responsible. *Secondly*, since as justified in the empirical findings, for the present sample, the marginal effect of Kanyashree at its sample mean value is positive, an increase in Kanyashree can foster TE. *Thirdly*, while taking the policy decision whether HM interacts with students and teachers, and also the frequency of interaction with State Education Department by HM is positively affecting TE; hence, it is recommended that while taking any policy decision HM should interact with students and teachers and also interact with State Education Department frequently for boosting up TE. *Fourthly*, since service experience of HM and of full time teachers is negatively related to TE of the school, it is recommended that government should initiate new appointments of the HM in the schools and the new teachers for increasing TE (and both of these to be continued). *Fifthly*, since TE of the school for which the librarian is on duty is higher, it is recommended that if in any school the librarian is not on duty, then school must make some arrangements to provide temporary/part-time librarian. *Sixthly*, since 'proportion of reserved category students' in the class is positively and significantly related to TE, it is recommended that government should continue the policy of social inclusion in education. *Seventhly*, since TE is positively related to the percentage of students having text book at home, if any student do not have the text book, the school should arrange for providing it to the students. *Eighthly*, since 'percentage of students taking private tuition' is positively related to TE, suggesting that the students derive lesser academic benefit from their own school, and it is also evident that the private tuition is the major driver of the variation of TE. The amount of variation of TE which is not explained by the number of students taking private tuition is very low; it is recommended that school should make some arrangements to increase teachers–students interaction to discuss about the problems that the students are facing in the school and how to solve these problems, so that the students can ultimately do away with the private tuition.

One of the interesting findings of this chapter is that (i) *the interaction between proportion of vacant teaching post and student's perception about regularity of class and* (ii) *the mother education level is significant determinants of* the percentage number of students taking private tuition and hence of TE of the schools. An increase in the number of vacant teachers or irregularities of the classes (as revealed by the student's perception variable) will increase the percentage number of the students taking private tuition. Thus, the school should pay attention to improve the regularities of holding classes and fill up the vacant teaching staffs. It is suggested that the school should take initiative to arrange for taking *student's feedback about regularity of class from time to time for monitoring and improving the situations. Similarly, since an increase in the education level of the mother will reduce the percentage number of students taking private tuition; the government should pay more attention to improve the situation regarding female education.*

**Acknowledgements** This chapter is a part of the project funded by Planning and Development Unit (NITI Aayog), Jadavpur University, Kolkata. The fund provided by the Planning and Development Unit is gratefully acknowledged. The authors are extremely grateful to Samagra Shiksha Mission for giving the necessary permission and making arrangements for collecting the data. The authors are indebted to the comments made by Professor Indrani Chakraborty, Institute of Development Studies Kolkata, and Professor Achin Chakraborty, The Director, Institute of Development Studies Kolkata, for their comments on the earlier draft. The authors sincerely acknowledge the help made by Ms. Sampita Neogi, for collection and compilation of the data. The authors are also grateful to the participants of the online seminar on presentations of ongoing projects of the Planning and Development Unit, Jadavpur University, held on October 2, 2020 for their valuable comments. However, usual disclaimer applies.

## References

Adkins, L. C. & Moomaw, R. L. (2007). Analyzing the technical efficiency of School Districts in Oklahoma. *Journal of Economic Insight, Missouri Valley Economic Association, 33*(2), 41–61.

Anand, S, & Sen, A. (1997). *Concepts of human development and poverty: A multidimensional perspective, in poverty and human development process* (pp. 1–20). United Nations Development Programme.

Andrews, M., Duncombe, W., & Yinger, J. (2002). Revisiting economies of size in American education: Are we any closer to a consensus? *Economics of Education Review, 21*, 245–262.

Arshad, M. N. M. (2014). Efficiency of secondary education in selected OIC countries. *Global Education Review, 1*(4), 53–75.

Banker, R. D., Charnes, A., & Cooper, W. W. (1984). Some models for estimating technical and scale inefficiencies in data envelopment analysis. *Management Science, 30*(9), 1078–1092.

Barro, R. J. (1991). Economic growth in a cross section of countries. *The Quarterly Journal of Economics, 106*(2), 407–443.

Bessent, A. M., & Bessent, E. W. (1980). Determining the comparative efficiency of schools through data envelopment analysis. *Educational Administration Quarterly, 16*, 57–75.

Bhanja, A., Ghose, A. (2022). Input-oriented technical efficiency and its determinants of primary education in West Bengal: A district-level analysis. In S. Bagli, G. Chakrabarti, & P. Guha (Eds.), *Persistent and the emerging challenges to development: Insights for policy-Gmaking in India* (pp. 253–275). Springer Nature.

Bonesronning, H., & Rattsq, J. (1994). Efficiency variation among Norwegian high schools: Consequences of equalization policy. *Economics of Education Review, 3*(4), 289–304.

Bradley, S., & Taylor, J. (2002). The effect of the Quasi–market on the efficiency–equity trade–off in the secondary school sector. *Bulletin of Economic Research, 54*(3), 295–314.

Charnes, A., Cooper, W. W., & Rhodes, E. (1978). Measuring the efficiency of decision making units. *European Journal of Operational Research, 2*(6), 429–444.

Charnes, A., Cooper, W. W., & Rhodes, E. (1981). Evaluating program and managerial efficiency: An application of data envelopment analysis to program follow through. *Management Science, 27*(6), 668–669.

Choudhury, S., & Ghose, A. (2022). Does an increase in enrollment of girls relative to boys stimulate technical efficiency of secondary education? Empirical evidence using non-parametric data envelopment analysis with Indian State level data. In C. Chakraborty & P. Pal (Eds.), *Environmental sustainability, growth trajectory and gender: Contemporary issues of developing economies* (pp. 181–194). Emerald Publishing Limited.

Ciro, A. J., & Torres, G. A. (2018). Economic efficiency of public secondary education expenditure: How different are developed and developing countries? *Desarrollo y Sociedad, 80*, 119–154.

Driscoll, D., Halcoussis, D., & Svorny, S. (2003). School district size and student performance. *Economics of Education Review, 22*, 193–201.

Gavurova, B., Kocisova, K., Belas, L., & Krajcik, V. (2017). Relative efficiency of government expenditure on secondary education. *Journal of International Studies, 10*(2), 329–343.

Ghose, A. (2017). *Efficiency of elementary education in India, empirical evidence using a nonparametric data envelopment approach*. Springer.

Hanushek, E. A. (1996). School resources and student performance. In G. Burtless (Ed.), *Does money matter? The effect of school resources on student achievement and adult success* (pp. 43–73). The Brookings Institution.

Haug, A. A., & Blackburn, V. C. (2017). Government secondary school finances in New South Wales: Accounting for students' prior achievements in a two-stage DEA at the school level. *Journal of Productivity Analysis, 48*(1), 69–83.

Hulten, C. R. (1996). *Infrastructure capital and economic growth: How well you use it may be more important than how much you have* (NBER Working Paper, 5847).

Kingdon, G. (1996). The quality and efficiency of private and public education: A case study of urban India. *Oxford Bulletin of Economics and Statistics, 58*(1), 57–82.

Krueger, A. B. (2003). Economic considerations and class Size. *The Economic Journal, 113*(February), F34–F63.

Leithwood, K., Jantzi, D. (2009). A review of empirical evidence about school size effects: A policy perspective. *Review of Educational Research, 79*(1), 464–490.

Levin, H. M. (1997). Raising school productivity: An x-efficiency approach. *Economics of Education Review, 16*(3), 303–311.

Lucas, R. E., Jr. (1988). On the mechanics of economic development. *Journal of Monetary Economics, 22*(1), 3–42.

Mankiw, N. G., Romer, D., & Weil, D. N. (1992). A contribution to the empirics of economic growth. *The Quarterly Journal of Economics, 107*(2), 407–437.

Masci, C., De Witte, K., & Agasisti, T. (2018). The influence of school size, principal characteristics and school management practices on educational performance: An efficiency analysis of Italian students attending middle schools. *Socio-Economic Planning Sciences, 61*, 52–69.

Mohapatra, R. (2015). Ranking of efficient states of India on the basis of performances in secondary education: An application of super efficiency models. *Asian Journal of Research in Social Sciences and Humanities, 5*(12), 1–15.

Newman, M., Garrett, Z., Elbourne, D., Bradley, S., Noden, P., Taylor, J., & West, A. (2006). Does secondary school size make a difference? A systematic review. *Educational Research Review, 1*, 41–60.

Purohit, B. C. (2015). *Efficiency of education sector: The case of Rajasthan state (India)*. Madras School of Economics Working paper, 121/2015.

Ray, S. C. (1991). Resource-use efficiency in public schools: A study of Connecticut data. *Management Science, 37*(12), 1620–1628.

Ray, S. C. (2004). *Data envelopment analysis: Theory and techniques for economics and operations research*. Cambridge University Press.

Romer, P. M. (1986). Increasing returns and long-run growth. *Journal of Political Economy, 94*(5), 1002–1037.

Romer, P. M. (1990). Endogenous technological change. *Journal of Political Economy, 98*(5), S71–S102.

Sankar, D. (2007). *Education system performance among Indian states: A public expenditure efficiency analysis using Linear Programming Methods.* South Asia Human Development Unit (SASHD) of the World Bank.

Singh, N., Pant, M., & Goel, A. (2018). ANN embedded data envelopment analysis approach for measuring the efficiency of state boards in India. *International Journal of System Assurance Engineering and Management, 9*(5), 1092–1106. Springer, The Society for Reliability, Engineering Quality and Operations Management (SREQOM), India, and Division of Operation and Maintenance, Lulea University of Technology, Sweden.

Sotiriadis, D., Menexes, G., & Tsamadias, C. (2018). Investigating the efficiency of senior secondary schools: Evidence from schools in the Greek region of Central Macedonia. *International Journal of Business and Economic Sciences Applied Research (IJBESAR), 11*(2), 36–43.

Sengupta, A., & Pal, N. P. (2010). Primary education in India: Delivery and outcome—A district level analysis based on DISE data. *Journal of Educational Planning and Administration, 24*(1), 5–21.

Sengupta, A., & Pal, N. P. (2012). Assessing the primary schools—A multi-dimensional approach: A school level analysis based on Indian data. *International Journal of Educational Development, 32*(2), 264–272.

Tyagi, P., Yadav, S. P., & Singh, S. P. (2009). *Efficiency analysis of schools using DEA: A case study of Uttar Pradesh state in India.* https://www.researchgate.net/.../254871435

# Unequal Inequalities in India: Income and Non-income Dimensions

**Achin Chakraborty**

## 1 Post-COVID Economic Inequality

It is now widely known that COVID-19 pandemic has sharply increased economic inequality in India, even though no precise and robust estimate of the depth of its impact is available. Various accounts of economic inequality all converge to the point that the depth of inequality has perhaps reached a rather unprecedented level in India; never before in the seventy five years' history of independent India had there been such a surge in economic inequality. It is unprecedented because, according to some estimate, while 84% of the households saw a decline in their income in 2020, the wealth of a small section of the super-rich increased dramatically. The Forbes billionaires report in October 2021 noted that more than 80% of India's 100 richest persons saw an increase in their wealth as compared to 2020 (Oxfam, 2022). Analyzing data from the Consumer Pyramids Households Survey (CPHS) conducted by the Center for Monitoring Indian Economy (CMIE), Jha and Lahoti (2021) show that inequality has sharply increased during the pandemic, with lower income households having experienced a larger decline in their earnings. They further note that incomes were already on a downward trend prior to COVID-19.

Questions have been raised on the representativeness of CMIE-CPHS data. It has been argued that the survey under-represents the poorest households and is biased toward better-off households because of the manner in which it is conducted. Moreover, the bias toward better-off households has increased over time (Drèze & Somanchi, 2021). In the absence of national data sources for the most recent period, CMIE-CPHS has turned out to be the only source of data that allows us to track changes in household consumption expenditure within a short period of time. CPHS is a periodic panel survey that is being conducted three times a year in successive

A. Chakraborty (✉)
Institute of Development Studies Kolkata, Kolkata, India
e-mail: achinchak@gmail.com

 
A. Raychaudhuri and A. Ghose (eds.), *Managing Pandemic and Correcting Development Fundamentals*, India Studies in Business and Economics,
https://doi.org/10.1007/978-981-19-8680-2_13

four-month 'waves' since January 2014. According to CMIE's Website, the survey is based on an all-India representative sample of over 170,000 households.

People's Research on India's Consumer Economy (PRICE), a Mumbai-based think-tank, also surveyed 200,000 households in the first round and 42,000 households in the second round between April and October 2021, according to their Website. The survey, which is known as ICE360, was spread over 120 towns and 800 villages across 100 districts. The results of the survey show that the annual income of the poorest 20% of Indian households declined by 53% during the first pandemic year, i.e., 2021–2022 from its level in 2015–16. During the same five-year period, the annual income of the richest 20% increased by 39%. We have not come across any critical discussion on this non-government source of data.

The two briefs from the non-government organization Oxfam–*The Inequality Virus* (2021) and *Inequality Kills* (2022) have provided a comprehensive overview of multiple dimensions of inequality during the COVID pandemic, drawing on various sources of information. These two reports provoke us to think further about the connection between rising economic inequality and other aspects of the economy and society. There have been numerous reports in the media highlighting the dramatic contrasts between the overwhelmingly large number of households that experienced income loss and the meteoric rise in the income and wealth of the billionaires during the COVID pandemic. What needs further scrutiny is how it impacts other aspects of human development. The Oxfam briefs highlight the overlapping or intersecting inequalities in which deprivation in elementary education and health are likely to result from the same process that heightens inequality in income and wealth.

The most recent *World Inequality Report 2022* finds that in India while the top 10% and top 1% hold, respectively, 57% and 22% of total national income, the share of bottom 50% has gone down to 13%. However, the report adds that 'over the past three years, the quality of inequality data released by the government has seriously deteriorated making it particularly difficult to assess recent inequality changes' (Chancel et al., 2022, p. 197).

From the brief review of the findings on economic inequality post-COVID presented here, it is apparent that when the dust somewhat settles a good number of conceptual and methodological challenges to reckoning inequality would resurface in the ever growing literature on inequality measurement. In this paper, we take the view that COVID-19 hits India when the country was already known to be a very unequal one with the coexistence of a disproportionately (i.e., relative to the country's median income) large very affluent class on the one hand and a large number of households who are deprived on some of the basic capabilities (Dreze & Sen, 2013). In what follows, we review the continuing challenges to reckoning income inequality in India, and what the evidence shows in this regard; in particular, we look at the evidence on inequality between social groups, besides tracking changes in interpersonal inequality (Sect. 2). In the process, we discuss the methodological underpinnings of the conventional practices. We then move on to the non-income space and reexamine the issues in reckoning inequality in different specific non-income spaces; in particular, we focus on inequality in child undernutrition and what its ethical importance is (Sect. 3). We briefly discuss the importance of the concept of equity in our continuing emphasis on inequality in non-income dimensions. We conclude in Sect. 4.

## 2 Aspects of Income Inequality in India

Reckoning economic inequality in India has always been fraught with challenges because of non-availability of personal income data. In lieu of income data, survey data on reported consumption expenditure at the household level, periodically collected by India's National Sample Survey Office (NSSO), have been used to reckon economic inequality in India for long. As a result, researchers who look for inequality in NSS consumption expenditure data have been quite accustomed to obtaining the Indian Gini in the range of 0.3–0.37 or so. While writing about income inequality in India, Dreze and Sen (2013) noted:

> The conventional economic reading in this respect has been that India is *not* particularly unequal, compared with other countries. This common impression is largely based on comparing the Gini coefficient of per capita *expenditure* in India with that of per capita *income* in other countries (because of the absence of reliable data for India). This is a biased comparison, because the distribution of per capita expenditure, across the world, tends to be less unequal than that of per capita income. (p. 216)

Suggestions were made by scholars involved in international databases on income inequality to adjust the consumption Gini upward so as to make it comparable to income Gini. Deininger and Squire (1996), for example, suggested adding 6.6% points to expenditure-based Ginis to provide better comparability with income-based Gini measures. These suggestions, however, were seen as ad-hoc and rather imperfect alternatives to direct measures of income inequality.

Recently, for more than a decade now, there has been a significant change in the practice of using consumption expenditure data. Important contributions have recently been made to reckon income inequality in India. This change has been possible apparently for two reasons. First, the commendable attempts by the National Council of Applied Economic Research (NCAER) in collaboration with the University of Maryland to collect income data from households through two rounds of nationally representative India Human Development Surveys (IHDS), conducted in 2004–2005 and 2011–2012, which have culminated in a series of research papers on various aspects of human development in India, including the issue of economic inequality. Second, Thomas Piketty and Lucas Chancel of World Inequality Lab in Paris have remarkably combined household surveys and national accounts, as well as the tax data in a systematic way to track the dynamics of Indian income inequality since 1922 (Chancel and Piketty, 2019). The shift in focus from the distribution of consumption expenditure to that of income has dramatically changed our perception about economic inequality in India. The stark reality is that in quantitative terms, such inequality is much deeper than what we knew from the NSS consumption expenditure data.

However, while appreciating as we do the attempts made by Chancel and Piketty to innovatively combine income tax data with NSS consumption expenditure and national accounts data, it is worth recalling that similar attempts were also made by a couple of very fine Indian statisticians in the sixties and seventies of the past century to estimate size distributions of personal income in India. Ahmed and Bhattacharya (1972) are an authoritative in-depth exploration of the technique similar to what Chancel and Piketty have applied and concluded that there was a clear decline in inequality in the estimated per capita income between 1956–1957 and 1963–1964, as indicated by the change in the Lorenz ratio from 0.418 to 0.372. After the pioneering work by Ahmed and Bhattacharya, one would expect to see more of such kind of research, but unfortunately for reasons unknown to us this line of work was not carried further forward. The inequality numbers they arrived at were somewhat lower than what has later been found from calculations based on IHDS data. Since there is no way to ascertain comparability of the different data sets used and methods followed by Ahmed and Bhattacharya (1972) and later researchers who used IHDS data, we are not in a position to conclude whether income inequality has significantly increased in India since 1963–1964. However, Chancel and Piketty (2019) have filled this gap by constructing a long series of inequality measures by combining and harmonizing different sources of data.

From IHDS income data, the Gini index of income inequality is estimated to be as high as 0.52, which places India in the same league as that in Brazil and South Africa (Vanneman & Dubey, 2014; World Bank, 2011). It now at least partially explains why in spite of high growth in India during the first decade of the present century, poverty reduction was not as rapid as one would expect. Had the income inequality been lower, more people could gain from the rapid economic growth than they have (Datt & Ravallion, 2010). Interestingly, not only that income inequality was found to be high in 2004–2005, it also increased in a short period of 5–6 years between the two rounds of IHDS. Studies based on NSS data have also shown that inequality in consumption expenditure has increased in the post-reform period, but the increase has been more in urban than in rural areas.

However, between 2011–2012 and 2017–2018, an altogether different phenomenon happened. Measured inequality in consumption expenditure declined, but it seems to have happened with an unprecedented 'leveling down' process. Based on the draft 2017–2018 National Statistical Office (NSO) Report (75th Round of the National Sample Survey: *Key Indicators: Household Consumer Expenditure in India*), the data for which the Government of India decided not to release, apparently on grounds of the questionable quality of the data presented in it, Subramanian (2020) presents changes in consumption expenditure between 2011–2012 and 2017–2018. Arranging the levels of average consumption expenditure in each of the deciles from the lowest to the highest, for each of the years 2011–2012 and 2017–2018, he observes that '*every* single decile has lost out in the transition from 2011–2012 to 2017–2018' (Subramanian, 2000). He makes the following important observation:

> What we have on evidence is….. a particularly harsh form of 'leveling' down: It is not just that the better-off have been leveled down to the status of the worse-off; it is that *both* the better-off and the worse-off have been brought down, with the relatively advantaged population's

> average incomes declining even more sharply than those of the relatively disadvantaged population. This is not ordinary leveling down, and it is leveling down with a vengeance! (Subramanian, 2000)

## 2.1 Inequality Between Social Groups

The complex social stratification along the lines of caste, tribe, religion, and gender has been a persistent feature of the Indian society for very long time. In the heyday of positivist thinking in social sciences, it was generally presumed that inequalities due to race, gender, and even class background were all forms of ascription that would go away with the development of impersonal market forces. The protagonists of this view shared the same belief in the rationalizing logic of modernity as propounded by the development economists of the earlier generation, even though they differed significantly on whether the market or the central planner would be the agent of modernity. In recent decades, multidimensional accounts of identities that include ethnic, caste, religion, and gender categories, and thus, social identities seem to have come to the center-stage. In India, popular discourses show an overwhelming presence of issues around identities. However, on the changing salience of caste-based differences in the Indian context, there is a counter-position as well. Beteille (2012), for example, criticizes the 'preoccupation' with caste that he observes among the experts who express opinions in the media on Indian affairs. He has argued that 'rapid economic growth and the expansion of middle class are accompanied by new opportunities for individual mobility which further loosens the association between caste and occupation'. In other words, Beteille questions the material basis of the presumed persistence of caste-based differences in a rapidly changing Indian economy. Some of the recent studies have documented how the role of caste has been weaker than before in shaping economic well-being. Migration, expansion of lower and middle castes in non-traditional occupations, changes in agriculture, and most importantly affirmative action—all have led to improvement in the relative position of the Scheduled Castes in India. Yet, the political salience of the caste issue has hardly weakened.

In a recent study focusing on the changes in inter-group inequality in India during the period of rapid growth, Chakraborty and Mukhopadhyay (2020) note that while overall inequality in the interpersonal distribution of income increased the contribution of between-group inequality to total inequality declined between 2004–2005 and 2011–2012.

We applied three alternative measures of inequality to the data collected from two rounds of IHDS—log of mean deviation, Theil's entropy measure, and the generalized entropy measure with the parameter value 2—and have presented in Table 1. As we indicated earlier, this NCAER-Maryland survey data cover almost all the states and union territories of India (except Andaman and Nicobar Islands and Lakshadweep). Using stratified random sampling technique, 27,010 rural households from 1503 villages and 13,126 urban households from over 971 urban blocks were

**Table 1** Changes in income inequality in India by different measures

| IHDS round | Log MD | Theil | GE(2) |
|---|---|---|---|
| Round 1 (2004–05) | 0.51535 | 0.55455 | 1.36538 |
| Round 2 (2011–12) | 0.53376 | 0.57783 | 1.50460 |

*Source* Chakraborty and Mukhopadhyay (2020) calculated from IHDS data

surveyed in 2004–2005. In the second round, conducted in 2011–2012, around 83% of the households were re-interviewed, which also include split households located within the same village or town. Altogether 42,152 households were surveyed in the second round.

There is an important methodological issue in reckoning inequality between-groups. The conventional approach to decompose overall inequality into the between-group and within-group components tends to show very small contribution of between-group inequality. However, even though the decomposition methods give the quantitative contribution of between-group inequality in an overall sense, which according to our calculation had declined, it does not allow us to say anything about the relative attainments of different groups in terms of each group's average income growth. Therefore, in order to examine this further, we look at the respective income shares and population shares of four mutually exclusive and exhaustive social groups, viz., SC, ST, Muslims, and Hindu 'others'. This is one of the simplest approaches toward assessing inequality between-groups—called 'representational inequality' by Reddy and Jayadev (2011)—which substantially differs from the commonly used approach that views inter-group inequality as a constituent part of overall interpersonal inequality. Table 2 allows us to compare the changes in the respective shares, which shows that among the four groups, only the SC households as a group have been able to improve its income share vis-à-vis their population share, which is reflected in a higher ratio of the two shares in IHDS Round 2. This is at the expense of the declining ratios for other three groups.

**Table 2** Income shares and population shares of four social groups in the two rounds of IHDS

| | Round 1 | | | Round 2 | | |
|---|---|---|---|---|---|---|
| | Income share | Population share | Income share/pop share | Income share | Population share | Income share/pop share |
| Muslim | 0.100 | 0.122 | 0.818 | 0.096 | 0.123 | 0.784 |
| SC | 0.153 | 0.218 | 0.701 | 0.173 | 0.220 | 0.787 |
| ST | 0.042 | 0.065 | 0.652 | 0.040 | 0.068 | 0.595 |
| Hindu others | 0.705 | 0.595 | 1.185 | 0.691 | 0.591 | 1.170 |

*Source* Chakraborty and Mukhopadhyay (2020), calculated from India Human Development Survey (IHDS) data

The category Hindu others in Table 2 includes a wide range of sub-categories with significant differences. We therefore further split this category into Brahmins, high castes, and other backward castes (OBC) in order to see if significant differences exist. Now with six mutually exclusive categories, we find that SCs and OBCs have experienced improvement in their respective income shares vis-à-vis population shares, but the ratio of the income share to the population share for each of the other four categories, viz., STs, Muslims, Bahmins, and other high castes, has declined (Table 3).

This can be supported by an alternative way of looking at the data as well. If we look at the average per capita incomes of the households belonging to different categories, our finding on STs is further strengthened. Among the six groups, STs have experienced the smallest growth (in percentage terms) in their average per capita income during the period between 2004–2005 and 2011–2012 (Table 4).

The unfair disadvantage that certain castes and tribes experience in terms of opportunities in education and labor market can be viewed as the culmination of

**Table 3** Income shares and population shares of six social groups in the two rounds of IHDS

| | Round 1 | | | Round 2 | | |
|---|---|---|---|---|---|---|
| | Income share | Population share | Income share/pop share | Income share | Population share | Income share/pop share |
| Brahmin | 0.099 | 0.055 | 1.808 | 0.085 | 0.052 | 1.633 |
| High caste | 0.263 | 0.164 | 1.601 | 0.251 | 0.163 | 1.538 |
| OBC | 0.343 | 0.376 | 0.913 | 0.356 | 0.376 | 0.946 |
| SC | 0.154 | 0.220 | 0.701 | 0.174 | 0.221 | 0.786 |
| ST | 0.043 | 0.065 | 0.651 | 0.040 | 0.067 | 0.597 |
| Muslim | 0.099 | 0.120 | 0.821 | 0.095 | 0.121 | 0.785 |

*Sourcc* Chakraborty and Mukhopadhyay (2020), calculated from India Human Development Survey (IHDS) data

**Table 4** Growth in per capita household incomes of six different groups

| | Round 1 | Round 2 | Growth (%) |
|---|---|---|---|
| | Per capita income | Per capita income | |
| Brahmin | 23,065 | 34,954 | 52 |
| High caste | 24,117 | 36,297 | 51 |
| OBC | 13,953 | 22,183 | 59 |
| SC | 11,724 | 19,255 | 64 |
| ST | 11,103 | 16,575 | 42 |
| Muslim | 12,915 | 19,081 | 48 |

*Source* Chakraborty and Mukhopadhyay (2020), calculated from India Human Development Survey (IHDS) data

the discriminatory social practices that prevailed in the past. The Constitution of India mandated punitive action against all forms of discrimination, and at the same time, adopted the policy of reservation in public employment and publicly funded educational institutions. Even though questions can be raised about the efficacy of the kind of affirmative action policy that has been in place in India for long, it is generally acknowledged that without such policy, the erstwhile disadvantaged groups could hardly move up to the level they have succeeded to reach so far. However, the larger question of whether the reservation policy with respect to public sector jobs and admission to higher education has succeeded in reducing the gaps between the most marginalized group in the Indian society (i.e., the STs), and others still remain. Similar findings on the relative attainments of SCs and STs and OBCs in the context of poverty have also been noted by others. Poverty declined much faster for all the social groups during the period 2004–2005 to 2011–2012 as compared to the period 1993–1994 to 2004–2005. However, the rate of decline in poverty is the highest for SCs and lower than national average for the STs, even though STs show a much higher level of poverty (Panagariya and More, 2013).

## 3 Inequality in Non-income Space

Even when income inequality increases within a country, inequalities measured in terms of certain indicators of human development, such as life expectancy or gross enrollment ratio across population sub-groups may decrease for the obvious reason that the commonly used indicators of health or education are fundamentally different from income in one very important respect. As the average value of an indicator, such as literacy rate, mean years of schooling, or 'average life span' for the whole population, increases with overall prosperity, inequality across sub-groups of population is most likely to decline. This is due to the fact that unlike income almost all these indicators have natural upper limits. Does it therefore mean that instead of worrying about disparity in non-income dimensions of well-being, we should focus exclusively on income inequality? One can reasonably argue that a variety of specific aspects can be thought of which are ethically relevant in the context of non-income dimensions of well-being; and these ethically relevant aspects are not deducible in a straightforward way from the moral arguments against income inequality that we are familiar with. This has important implications for the ways we measure inequality in non-income dimensions in general, and in particular, how we make sense of equity.

The importance of the choice of space in which to reckon inequality has now been well recognized in the literature on economic inequality. Ever since Amartya Sen delivered his Tanner Lecture on Human Values entitled 'Equality of What' in 1979, many scholars have tried to provide foundational arguments in favor of their respective favored spaces which range from resources to functionings. This is one of the most fertile areas in welfare economics in which a growing number of scholars have been contributing toward resolving many conceptual and measurement issues.

While concerns for inequality in the specific dimensions of human functioning, such as health and education are now common, attempts to measure such inequalities have not been matched by thorough discussions of the ethical underpinnings of such measures. In much of the literature since the 1990s on health inequality or equity, it is the concept of 'socio-economic inequality' in health rather than 'pure inequality' that has been more popular. The index widely perceived as the best available one to measure socio-economic inequality of health is the 'concentration index'. A host of studies has used the concentration index in the context of different countries, a review of some of which is found in O'Donnell et al. (2008). The index is based on the moral philosophical premise that a match between cumulative proportions of a health outcome and cumulative proportions of population characterizes a situation of health equity. The point estimate of the concentration index can be calculated from grouped data using the formula:

$$\mathrm{CI} = 2\mathrm{cov}(y_i, R_i)/\mu,$$

where $y$ is the health variable whose inequality is measured, $\mu$ is its mean and $R_i$ is the $i$-th individual's rank in the socio-economic distribution.

However, the ethical implication of comparing entities in terms of the concentration index remains ambiguous if we keep in mind the following important observation of Sen:

> It may be possible to argue that while distribution $x$ is more unequal than $y$ according to some mean independent measure, since y involves a lower mean income than $x$, maybe $y$ represents more 'real' inequality. (Sen, [1973] 1997)

It seems that what Sen calls 'real' inequality is unlikely to be captured exclusively by applying a standard mean independent measure of inequality. It may be recalled that the most popular measures of indices of inequality, such as the Gini coefficient or the coefficient of variation, are mean independent.

Even though Sen made this remark in the context of income, it seems to be more appropriate in the context of non-income dimensions such as health and education and raises questions about the ethical importance of comparing entities in terms of concentration index. Based on his ethical position, Sen introduces what he calls the 'weak equity axiom'. Evaluative inquiries that assess inequalities typically do not explicitly address the question of equity. We explore later the implications—for applied research—of accepting the weak equity axiom in evaluative judgements involving non-income dimensions.

Since we argue that inter-group inequality is the more appropriate concept than interpersonal inequality in the case of non-income dimensions, using data from India Human Development Survey (IHDS) for income in the last section and NFHS for such non-income dimensions as nutrition, we make a comparison between inter-group inequalities in income and various non-income dimensions to show that interesting observations can be made on 'unequal inequalities' in India.

An overall decline in the average level often hides the fact that persons in all socio-economic groups do not experience the same. In the context of such non-income dimension as the nutritional status of children, group inequality deserves greater attention compared to interpersonal inequality. Interpersonal inequality (or what is often called 'pure' inequality) in indicators with a natural upper limit, such as anthropometric scores, is expected to fall with an improvement in the average level. However, a low average level of undernutrition may be consistent with a high between-group inequality if the few remaining undernourished children mostly belong to the lowest socio-economic strata. Much of the work on group inequalities in child nutrition has focused on the axis of economic status, proxied by household wealth, as available in the demographic and health surveys. Child undernutrition has been shown to be associated significantly with household wealth, and wealth-related inequality in child nutrition varies considerably across the Indian states (Mukhopadhyay and Chakraborty, 2019). The NFHS-4 Report for India states that '[t]he prevalence of stunting decreases steadily with an increase in wealth quintiles, from 51 percent of children in households in the lowest wealth quintile to 22 percent of children in households in the highest wealth quintile' (IIPS and ORC Macro 2017).

In Mukhopadhyay and Chakraborty (2019), using NFHS-3 and NFHS-4 data, we made an attempt to assess if the progress in reducing child undernutrition in the major states of India has been pro-poor. Most importantly, we found that a decline in average rates of child stunting was not necessarily accompanied by a commensurate decline in child stunting in the bottom quintile of household wealth (Table 1 in Appendix). We also used different criteria to define a change as pro-poor, drawing on the literature on inequality in the non-income space. We first examined the change in the odds ratio of child stunting in the bottom quintile of households in each of the major states. For this, we ran logistic regression of stunting status of the child (coded as a binary variable, with two categories, stunted and not so) on poverty status of the household (if the household belongs to the bottom wealth quintile or not), controlling for relevant covariates. We included child specific factors (sex, age, birth order), parental characteristics (mother's nutritional status, age at child birth, education, and employment status and father's education) household-level factors (region of residence: state and rural/urban, social group affiliation, sex of household head), and environmental factors (access to sanitation and drinking water facilities) as control variables. We then considered the change in the odds ratio of child stunting in the poorest quintile (vis-à-vis the richer quintiles taken together) in each of the major states, using the 'strong absolute definition' (SAD) of pro-poor change. The other two measures we used were the concentration index (CI) and the 'extended concentration index' (ECI).[1] The results are summarized in Table 5.

[1] See Mukhopadhyay and Chakraborty (2019) for details.

**Table 5** Classification of states according to SAD, CI, and ECI

| Nature of change in child stunting | States |
|---|---|
| Pro-poor by all measures | Kerala, Punjab, Uttarakhand, Maharashtra, West Bengal |
| Non-pro-poor by all measures | Bihar, Jharkhand, Chhattisgarh, Assam |
| Non-pro-poor by SAD, pro-poor by CI and ECI | Karnataka, Odisha |
| Pro-poor by SAD, non-pro-poor by CI and ECI | APT, Gujarat, Uttar Pradesh, Rajasthan, Madhya Pradesh |
| Pro-poor by SAD and CI, non-pro-poor by ECI | Haryana, Tamil Nadu |

*Source* Mukhopadhyay and Chakraborty (2019) calculated from NFHS-3 and NFHS-4 unit level data

Thus, the substantive conclusions regarding the nature of improvement in children's nutritional status in the states often vary, depending on the chosen evaluative criterion. We argue that the differences in substantive conclusions result from the divergence in the ways in which the criteria are defined. However, what emerges from this use of multiple criteria is that there are states like Bihar, Jharkhand, Chhattisgarh, and Assam, where the decline in child stunting was not pro-poor by any of the three criteria, whereas there are five states where the decline was pro-poor by all criteria.

## 4 Conclusion

In this paper, we have touched upon a wide range of issues that have surfaced in discussions on the growing economic inequality in India. First, we made an attempt to present a brief account of the changing nature of income inequality during and after the COVID pandemic drawing on various sources. What distinguishes the post-COVID period from the earlier period is that during COVID-19, the rising inequality has been associated with an absolute decline in the economic conditions of a large number of people, unlike in the period since the 1980s when most people experienced some gain but the poorer classes gained very little. This $K$-type movement indicates sharp polarization between the top few and the huge mass of people at the bottom. The central argument in the paper is that economic inequality had been high in India for quite some time now, and COVID pandemic has exacerbated it in the most recent period. We then took a closer look at the changing income inequality in India roughly during the period of rapid growth and its aftermath. Using two rounds of IHDS and applying the technique of decomposition, we find that overall inequality increased but the contribution of inequality between social groups to the overall inequality declined. We then presented an alternative procedure which would allow us find out how each of the groups had done vis-à-vis others. While the SCs and OBCs share in income improved while that of STs and Muslims deteriorated. Finally, we looked at changes in child stunting between NFHS-3 and NFHS-4 across different states, as an instance of inequality in non-income dimensions. We found that in five states, the declines in the bottom quintile of households were more than the average decline, whereas in four states, declines were less than average. The overall purpose of this paper was to demonstrate that if we want make a substantive statement on changes in economic inequality in India, we need to use multiple sources of data and carefully consider multiple methods in order to check robustness of the statement.

**Acknowledgements** Parts of the paper draw on my earlier work in collaboration with Simantini Mukhopadhyay. I am grateful to her for allowing me to use some of the material.

# Appendix

See Table 6 and Fig. 1.

**Table 6** Quintile-specific stunting rates in the Indian states in 2005–2006 and 2015–2016

| State | NFHS-3 | | | | | NFHS-4 | | | | |
|---|---|---|---|---|---|---|---|---|---|---|
| | Q1 | Q2 | Q3 | Q4 | Q5 | Q1 | Q2 | Q3 | Q4 | Q5 |
| Andhra Pradesh Region | 56.2 | 41.6 | 40.3 | 33.2 | 22.4 | 41.7 | 34.2 | 27.5 | 24.8 | 16.5 |
| Assam | 56.8 | 50.4 | 47.8 | 40.1 | 20.3 | 48.5 | 41.4 | 36.6 | 28.5 | 17.9 |
| Bihar | 66.6 | 58.9 | 57.6 | 56.7 | 33.4 | 57.6 | 54.2 | 49.3 | 43.8 | 29.7 |
| Chhattisgarh | 53.1 | 62.3 | 58.1 | 54.8 | 39.1 | 43.2 | 41.2 | 40.9 | 35.7 | 25.1 |
| Gujarat | 65.8 | 53.2 | 52.4 | 45.9 | 29.6 | 50.9 | 45.4 | 38.3 | 26.5 | 21.1 |
| Haryana | 61.1 | 49.7 | 48.7 | 40.7 | 23.3 | 46.0 | 35.6 | 33.6 | 27.1 | 23.3 |
| Jharkhand | 55.1 | 56.1 | 53.0 | 48.5 | 28.2 | 54.2 | 51.3 | 48.1 | 41.8 | 25.7 |
| Karnataka | 54.1 | 54.1 | 41.7 | 39.5 | 24.9 | 46.8 | 41.5 | 35.7 | 30.9 | 23.5 |
| Kerala | 43.4 | 23.9 | 23.6 | 15.7 | 20.4 | 27.0 | 22.5 | 20.3 | 14.6 | 14.9 |
| Madhya Pradesh | 54.4 | 56.3 | 49.7 | 48.5 | 35.6 | 49.6 | 46.5 | 43.1 | 38.4 | 28.3 |
| Maharashtra | 63.6 | 52.9 | 44.6 | 39.6 | 24.1 | 45.0 | 38.2 | 33.5 | 27.1 | 22.6 |
| Odisha | 63.0 | 58.2 | 43.7 | 38.1 | 18.5 | 47.7 | 39.6 | 34.6 | 26.4 | 19.1 |
| Punjab | 52.7 | 47.0 | 39.9 | 21.4 | 17.0 | 34.8 | 29.0 | 24.1 | 19.6 | 18.3 |
| Rajasthan | 53.0 | 48.6 | 45.9 | 41.5 | 24.8 | 49.5 | 43.4 | 39.0 | 31.5 | 27.0 |
| Tamil Nadu | 67.4 | 60.2 | 59.8 | 53.2 | 39.0 | 35.4 | 31.3 | 23.5 | 25.0 | 19.2 |
| Uttar Pradesh | 67.4 | 60.2 | 59.8 | 53.2 | 39.0 | 58.5 | 52.8 | 47.9 | 39.2 | 27.0 |
| Uttarakhand | 63.9 | 52.5 | 52.0 | 37.7 | 11.8 | 42.4 | 40.6 | 35.3 | 24.2 | 23.2 |
| West Bengal | 57.6 | 53.5 | 42.6 | 33.4 | 13.6 | 41.3 | 37.6 | 32.0 | 27.8 | 18.2 |

*Source* Mukhopadhyay and Chakraborty (2019) calculated from NFHS-3 and NFH- 4 unit level data

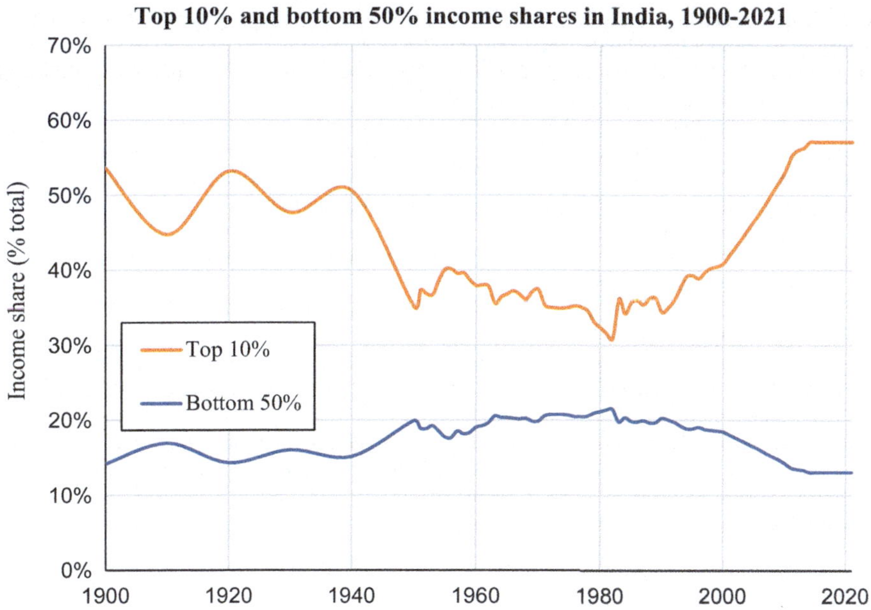


*Interpretation:* The Top 10% income share is equal to 57% in 2021. Income is measured after the operation of pensions and unemployment insurance systems and before income tax.
*Sources and series:* see wir2022.wid.world/methodology, and Chancel and Piketty (2021).

**Fig. 1** Top 10% and bottom 50% income share in India, 1900–2021

## References


Ahmed, M., & Bhattacharya, N. (1972). *Size distribution of per capita personal income in India: 1955–56, 1960–61 and 1963–64*. Economic and Political Weekly, Special Number. Reprinted in Krishnaswami, K. S. (Ed.). (1990). *Poverty and income distribution*. Oxford University Press for Sameeksha Trust.

Beteille, A. (2012). India's destiny not caste in stone, *The Hindu*, February 21, 2012. Available at: http://www.thehindu.com/opinion/lead/indias-destiny-not-caste-in-stone/article2913662.ece

Chakraborty, A., & Mukhopadhyay, S. (2020). Inter-group disparities in growing economies: India among the BRICS'. In B. P. Abraham, P. Ray, & S. Y. Kim (Eds.), BRICS: The quest for inclusive growth. The political economy of the BRICS countries (Vol. 1). World Scientific.

Chancel, L., & Piketty, T. (2019). Indian income inequality, 1922–2015: From British Raj to Billionaire Raj?' *The Review of Income and Wealth, 65*(S1), S33–S62.

Chancel, L., Piketty, T., Saez, E., & Zucman, G., et al. (2022). *World inequality report 2022*. World Inequality Lab.

Datt, G., & Ravallion, M. (2010). Shining for the poor too? *Economic and Political Weekly, 13* February.

Deininger, K., & Squire, L. (1996). A new data set measuring income inequality. *The World Bank Economic Review, 10*(3), 565–591.

Dreze, J., & Sen, A. (2013). *An uncertain glory: India and its contradictions*. Allen Lane.

Drèze, J., & Somanchi, A. (2021). View: New barometer of India's economy fails to reflect deprivations of poor households. *The Economic Times*, June 21, 2021.
Mukhopadhya, S., & Chakraborty, A. (2019). Changing wealth inequalities in child nutrition in Indian states. *Economic and Political Weekly, 55*(10).
O'Donnell, O., van Doorslaer, E., Wagstaff, A., & Lindelow, M. (2008). *Analyzing health equity using household survey data: A guide to techniques and their implementation*. The World Bank.
Oxfam India. (2021). *The inequality virus: Davos India supplement*. Oxfam India.
Oxfam India. (2022). *India kills: India supplement 2022*. Oxfam India.
Panagariya, A., & More, V. (2013). Poverty by social, religious and economic groups in India and its large states: 1993–94 to 2011–12, Working Paper No. 2013–02, Columbia University, Program on Indian Economic Policies, USA.
Reddy, S. G., & Jayadev, A. (2011). Inequalities between groups: Theory and empirics, *World Development, 39*(2), 159–173.
Sen, A. ([1973] 1997) *On economic inequality* (expanded edition). Oxford University Press.
Subramanian, S. (2000). What is happening to rural welfare, poverty, and inequality in India? *Ideas for India*, January 10, 2000.
Vanneman, R., & Dubey, A. (2014). Horizontal and vertical inequalities in India. In J. C. Gornick & M. Jantti (Eds.), *Income inequality: Economic disparities and the middle class in affluent countries*. Stanford University Press (Chapter 16).
World Bank. (2011). *Perspectives on poverty in India: Stylised facts from survey data*. World Bank.

The manufacturer's authorised representative in the EU is Springer Nature Customer Service Centre GmbH, Europaplatz 3, 69115 Heidelberg, Germany. If you have any concerns regarding our products, please contact ProductSafety@springernature.com

Printed and bound by CPI Group (UK) Ltd, Croydon, CR0 4YY
30/09/2026
02225314-0008